Bertha von Suttner

Syracuse Studies on Peace and Conflict Resolution

Harriet Hyman Alonso, Charles Chatfield, and Louis Kriesberg
Series Editors

Bertha
von Suttner

A Life for Peace

Brigitte Hamann

Translated by Ann Dubsky
With an Introduction by Irwin Abrams

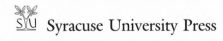 Syracuse University Press

Copyright © 1996 by Syracuse University Press
Syracuse, New York 13244-5160

All Rights Reserved

First Edition 1996

96 97 98 99 00 01 02   6 5 4 3 2 1

The translation was underwritten by the Austrian National Bank, the Austrian Ministry of Science, Research, and Art, and the American Austrian Foundation by a generous grant from the Creditanstalt-Banverein, New York.

Library of Congress Cataloging-in-Publication Data

Hamann, Brigitte.
   [Bertha von Suttner. English]
   Bertha von Suttner : a life for peace / Brigitte Hamann ;
translated by Ann Dubsky ; with an introd. by Irwin Abrams.
     p.   cm. — (Syracuse studies on peace and conflict resolution)
   Translation of: Bertha von Suttner : ein Leben für den Frieden.
   Includes bibliographical references and index.
   ISBN 0-8156-0387-8 (cloth : alk. paper). — ISBN 0-8156-0376-2
(pbk. : alk. paper)
    1. Suttner, Bertha von, 1843–1914. 2. Pacifists—Austria—Biography.
3. Peace movements—Europe—History. I. Title. II. Series.
   JX1962.S8H3613   1996
   327.1′72′092—dc20
   [B]   96-1027

Manufactured in the United States of America

Contents

PEC/ DJY

8/4/ 2000

Brigitte Hamann holds a doctorate in history from the University of Vienna and has an active career as a free-lance historian. She has published widely on eighteenth- and nineteenth-century Austrian and German history, including biographies of Crown Prince Rudolf of Austria (1978) and the Empress Elisabeth (1982; U.S. edition: *The Reluctant Empress* [1986]). She has also compiled the biographical lexicon, *The Hapsburgs* (1988) and has written frequently about historical sources and science, created historical documentaries for television, and is the author of historical children's books.

Ann Dubsky works for the Austrian Broadcast Corporation and is known for her incisive features covering international cultural and political issues. She has translated numerous books in the fine and applied arts, and her translations of the television documentaries include the six-part "Hapsburgs," "Austria II," "Adolf Lanz," and "Mr. Hitler's Religion."

Illustrations

Preface

This is the story of a nineteenth-century woman whom most contemporaries thought of as a utopian, or worse, a fool; and in the end, her cause went unheeded. Her famous call, "Lay Down Your Arms!" which sounded more and more desperate with time, echoed in vain throughout a Europe that was feverish with nationalism and wanted war, a Europe that derided the warnings of "Peace Bertha" as the words of a hysteric female busybody.

The calls for peace that came in the late nineteenth century, however, were not just the demands of individual moralists ignorant of the ways of the world. They were instead a thoroughly realistic answer to the menacing development of modern weapon technology. Nobel's explosives, the new military gases, submarines, and an air force that was successfully deployed for the first time in the 1911 Tripoli War meant that war's capacity for destruction had grown to inconceivable proportions within a few years. "Everything has to be multiplied by a hundred, a thousand: the speed, the light, the power to create and to destroy," wrote Bertha von Suttner in her magazine, *Lay Down Your Arms*. "The equivalent value of ten thousand hours of manual and intellectual labor can be pressed into a performance that lasts one second, and thousands of mortal agonies—into a bomb."[1]

She warned that no side could win a modern war deploying such weapons: "There is no such thing as an end, a settlement in the war of the future: exhaustion, annihilation on both sides!"[2] This realization led to Suttner's demand for a radical change of thought and for dropping the

1. BvS, "Ein Testament," *DWN* 2:3.
2. Ibid.

use of war as a political tool—for no political goal justified the annihilation of mankind. "The self-sacrifice of a few for many may well appear to be virtuous and desirable, but the sacrifice of all for none? That would be the height of madness."[3]

In the face of such visions, all possible human energy ought to be concentrated upon creating the conditions for peace. For Bertha von Suttner that meant a relentless battle not only against Wilhelm II's naval plans and the formation of an air force, but even more, against national and religious fanaticism, against social injustice and human rights violations of all kinds, including discrimination against women. She demanded a drastic change of view from the mighty and from each and every individual: the age-old ideal of the "war hero" must finally give way to that of the "peace hero."

Despite all her disappointments, Bertha von Suttner's somewhat naive belief that humankind would constantly improve itself morally, an idea loosely based on Darwin's thought, gave her the certainty that freedom was possible. Her death in June of 1914 saved her from witnessing the bitter experience of the First World War, the very "war of the future" she had warned of twenty years before.

Four months later, the young Stefan Zweig remorsefully wrote his friend, Romain Rolland, "I, like you, also believed this war could be prevented and that is the *only* reason why we did not fight against it hard enough when there was still time. Sometimes I see good Bertha von Suttner in front of me, saying as she did, 'I know all of you think I am a ridiculous fool. I pray to God you are right.'"[4]

In 1918, after this war had cost the lives of ten million people, Zweig admitted in public:

> But it was this very woman everybody thought had nothing to say to the world except for her four words, who grabbed the root of the most profound thought of the present time with a strong hand. . . . She did not hesitate to demand the seemingly impossible. She herself knew better than anyone else what the great tragedy was in the idea she espoused, about the almost devastating tragedy of pacifism because it never appears to apply to the present, superfluous in peacetime and inane in time of war. Nevertheless, she took it upon herself to be a Don Quixote who fought against windmills. But today we know chillingly what she always knew, that these windmills do not grind the wind, they grind the bones of Europe's youth.[5]

3. *MZA*, 309.
4. Stefan Zweig, *Briefe an Freunde* (Hamburg: Richard Friedenthal, 1984), 32.
5. *NFP*, June 21, 1918.

Of course, Bertha von Suttner's biography brings up many other aspects of her life besides her work for peace, including a strong inclination toward adventure. Her journey—from her youth as a frivolous aristocrat, through her years as a governess, through the bitter poverty in Russia, to the first literary successes, until she finally found her life's calling—also reflects social and cultural reality at the turn of the century and the dying Austrian monarchy. It was this wide spectrum of subjects—liberalism, Austrian aristocracy, and international patronage—that made it so enticing for me to shed light on the life and time of Bertha von Suttner.

My plans were encouraged by the extraordinarily good situation in respect to sources: Bertha von Suttner's opulent literary legacy and that of her closest associate, Alfred Hermann Fried, have been lying practically untouched in the library of the United Nations in Geneva. My very special gratitude goes to the librarian of the collection, Dr. Werner Simon, for his untiring and patient assistance. He and Dr. Anna Benna, director of the Haus-, Hof- und Staatsarchiv in Vienna, made it possible to have some of the important documents brought to Vienna for my use, a situation that cut down immensely on my traveling.

My thanks also go to the associates in the rest of the archives and collections mentioned in the endnotes. I would like to mention one very special thing: the Austrian and the Soviet Academies of Sciences made it possible for me to take a research trip to Georgia. I thank the director of the Shota-Rustaveli Institute in Tbilisi, Dr. G. Zizishvili and his associates, Dr. Guram Tchocholenidse and Tamuna Mamissashvili for their warm hospitality and friendly assistance.

Brigitte Hamann

Vienna
Summer 1995

Introduction

Irwin Abrams

Brigitte Hamann has written an outstanding book about a remarkable woman. As the German writer Martin Gregor-Dellin declared, "Bertha von Suttner belongs without doubt along with George Sand, Cosima Wagner, Marie Curie, Florence Nightingale and the Duse, to the great women of a century which still made it difficult for women to be great."[1] In a public opinion survey done to determine the five most famous women of the age, published in a Berlin newspaper in 1903, Baroness von Suttner was given first place over the queen of Rumania; the actresses, Sarah Bernhardt of France and Eleonore Duse of Italy; and the Austrian writer, Marie von Ebner-Eschenbach.[2] Like George Sand, the queen, and Ebner-Eschenbach, the baroness was a writer, but her best-known work, the novel *Lay Down Your Arms*, was no literary gem, but rather a book which, as the New York *Nation* said after her death, opened the eyes of millions to the horrors of war: "[N]o other brief for peace has won so many converts or exercised so great an influence on all quarters of the globe."[3] Tolstoy compared the book to *Uncle Tom's Cabin* and hoped it would do for war what Harriet Beecher Stowe's novel had done for slavery.[4]

1. Martin Gregor-Dellin, "Bertha von Suttner," in *Der Friedens-Nobelpreis von 1901 bis heute,* 12+ vols. (Munich: Edition Pacis, 1987–), 2:30–93.
2. *Berliner Tageblatt,* May 7, 1903; Hamann, chap. 9, n. 122.
3. *Nation* 98 (June 25, 1914): 745–46.
4. Letter, Leo Tolstoy to Bertha von Suttner, Oct. 10, 1891. *Memoirs of Bertha von Suttner: The Records of an Eventful Life,* authorized English edition, 2 vols. (Boston: Ginn, 1910); repr., with a preface by Irwin Abrams (New York: Garland, 1972), 1:343. See Regina Braker, "Bertha von Suttner as Author: The Harriet Beecher Stowe of the Peace Movement," *Peace and Change* 16, no. 1 (Jan. 1991): 74–96.

It was not only through her writing that Baroness von Suttner worked against war. It was her novel, in fact, that drew her into the movement for peace, which organized internationally in the last decade of the nineteenth century, and of which the Baroness came to be recognized as the "commander-in-chief."

Of those great women named above, Bertha von Suttner was the only one embarked upon a mission to change the world and make it a better place. She worked ceaselessly, writing, lecturing, organizing peace societies, taking a leading role at their international congresses, lobbying with individual rulers and statesmen and with the diplomats at the Hague Peace Conferences. She influenced her friend Alfred Nobel to include peace among his prizes and was granted the Nobel Peace Prize herself.

Despite all the obstacles her movement encountered in the armed peace of the Europe of her day and the rude and cruel personal attacks she had to face in both her own country of Austria-Hungary and the neighboring German Empire, the baroness kept on with the struggle. As her fellow Nobel peace laureate, Alva Myrdal, the great Swedish woman, later phrased such a feeling of determination, "It is not worthy of a human being to give up."[5]

In 1912 at the age of sixty-nine, only two years before she died, when she was not in the best of health and even had to be assisted to the podiums from which she spoke, von Suttner set out for a seven-month lecture tour in the United States, invited by women's groups. To the dismay of her friends, she insisted on booking a freighter, declaring, "I'm not on a joy ride; I'm making a last crusade for the cause." Fortunately, a strike forced her to take a passenger ship.

It was a triumphal tour. Hamann tells how the baroness spoke in schools, in churches, and in lecture halls, always to packed audiences. Her experiences included a conversation with President William H. Taft, who agreed with her about peace; visits with J. P. Morgan, William Jennings Bryan, and the mother of newspaper magnate William Randolph Hearst; a speech to the meeting of the National Education Association in Chicago; and her first football game, where she sat in a box draped with a white flag of peace and watched Columbia trounce Missouri. It was estimated that she traveled some twenty-five thousand miles and spoke to more than four hundred thousand people of all classes.

She spoke before many women's clubs and to a suffragist congress in

5. Irwin Abrams, *The Nobel Peace Prize and the Laureates* (Boston: G. K. Hall, 1988), 236.

Philadelphia. The campaign for women's suffrage in many states was in full swing. When the baroness spoke in San Francisco shortly after women had gained the right to vote in California the year before, she began her address, "Ladies and Gentlemen, Voters of California." She quoted approvingly the words of President Taft: "If the United States have a mission, it is to develop the Principle of the Brotherhood of Man into a living palpable force," adding, doubtless to the delight of her audience, "The one half of humanity that has never borne arms is today ready to blaze into this living palpable force. Perhaps the universal Sisterhood is necessary before the Universal Brotherhood is possible."[6]

She concluded her talk by telling how she had been received by President Theodore Roosevelt when in the country for the 1904 peace congress and how he had promised to try to do his best for the cause of peace. He had indeed helped end the Russo-Japanese War, for which he received the 1906 Nobel Peace Prize, and he had worked for arbitration. Later the baroness learned that in the presidential campaign then under way, Roosevelt was attacking the peace policies of Taft, and when she read other belligerent comments by her fellow Nobel laureate, she allowed herself to criticize him publicly.[7] She was glad that the election was won by Woodrow Wilson, known to be a friend of peace.

At the end of her tour, she spent a week in New York City, lecturing at Columbia University and elsewhere, and being honored at a banquet presided over by Andrew Carnegie. He later promised her a pension for the rest of her life. At the banquet she spoke of America as "the cradle of peace."[8] As she had said in San Francisco, "America is the Future embodied so far as my generation shall see it realized!"

She returned to Vienna just before Christmas to find her associate, Alfred Hermann Fried, busily preparing for the world peace congress that was to be held there in 1914 in her honor. A fellow Austrian, Fried had joined the peace movement after reading *Lay Down Your Arms* and had become its leading publicist and theoretician, for which achievements he had been granted the Nobel Peace Prize in 1911.

6. The original typescript in English of "The Speech in San Francisco in June 1912" is in the Suttner-Fried Collection at the United Nations Library, Geneva, and is printed in Beatrix Kempf, *Woman for Peace: The Life of Bertha von Suttner,* tr. from the German (Park Ridge, N.J.: Noyes, 1973), 179–85.

7. In an article excerpted from *Christian Work and Evangelist,* Rev. Frederick Lynch reported that the baroness had told him when they were together in New York in 1912 that Roosevelt was to be compared with Nero and Napoleon: "[A]ll three seemed to love slaughter." *Literary Digest* 49 (Aug. 1, 1914): 197–98.

8. *New York Times,* Dec. 10, 1914.

The baroness was delighted to hear that Fried managed to get members of the Austrian government, including Foreign Minister Count Berchtold, to be honorary patrons of the peace congress. Best of all, a delegation from the congress was to be received by Emperor Franz Josef. The baroness had often been received by royalty and statesmen of other lands, but never by her own sovereign.

Another honor was to be granted her. A film of *Lay Down Your Arms,* to be made by a Danish company, was to premier at the congress. The baroness doubted if it would get past the Austrian censors. In April 1914 the cameramen came to her apartment to shoot a scene of the author at her desk, with which the movie would begin, and we do have those few seconds of Bertha von Suttner on film.

The baroness was becoming increasingly fatigued, and at the end of May she was unable to participate in the important women's congress as she had planned. Unable to keep on with her writing, she wondered whether she was getting lazy or whether it was an illness; then she was diagnosed as having cancer of the stomach. The baroness refused further treatments, saying she had lived long enough, achieved something in her life, and if her time was up, so be it. In her final delirium, she murmured, "Lay Down Your Arms. Tell everybody!" On June 21, 1914, she died, having peacefully gone to sleep "like a tired person in the evening."

Seven days later Archduke Franz Ferdinand, Austria's heir apparent, was assassinated in Sarajevo by a young Serb nationalist, and Count Berchtold and the other policymakers of Europe stumbled into the war that Baroness von Suttner and her colleagues had tried so hard to prevent. The peace congress was naturally called off, but the film was completed, to be shown in the United States during the effort to keep that country out of war, which also failed.[9]

Despite Bertha von Suttner's fame, many regarded her as utopian, and "her cause went unheeded," as Hamann says in her foreword to this book. The war swept away the little peace army of which she had been commander-in-chief, and even the socialists, in whom she had expressed some hope, marched against one another behind the flags of their respective countries. Her great propaganda novel was now completely out of date, as the horrors of the First World War, which she had herself predicted, made her graphic scenes of the conflicts of the mid-nineteenth century seem almost like civilized warfare. There were some people in the

9. Andrew Kelly, "Film as Antiwar Propaganda: *Lay Down Your Arms* (1914)," *Peace and Change* 16, no. 1 (Jan. 1991): 97–112. The film premiered in Denmark in 1915 and was not shown in Germany until after the war. In 1951 a new film of the novel was made in Germany, directed by Harold Braun, which was shown at Cannes and won other prizes.

postwar period, however, who recalled how her novel had moved them during their youth. Willy Brandt, who won the Nobel Peace Prize as chancellor of the Federal Republic of Germany, was one of them.[10]

What mainly kept interest in the baroness alive, however, was her autobiography, which appeared in Germany in 1909 and, in English, in Boston and London the following year. Here she gave a fascinating account of her early years growing up as Countess Kinsky of the Austrian aristocracy. She told of how, as governess of the daughters of a baronial family, she and the son Arthur had fallen in love with one another, leading her to leave, when the mother found out, to take a job in Paris with a Monsieur Alfred Nobel, only to return to Vienna after a week to elope with her beloved Arthur to the Caucasus in what is now Georgia. They returned to Vienna as published writers after a nine-year honeymoon, to be forgiven by his parents and to live happily ever after. Part 2 of her memoirs tells of the writing of *Lay Down Your Arms,* of her rise to leadership in the peace movement, and of her continued friendship with Nobel and its consequences. The book ends with the death of Arthur in 1902, when only the words of his testament that she should go on working for them both keeps her on course.

This could be the scenario for a Viennese operetta, and more than one biographer has put pen to paper to retell the romantic tale, several in an outright fictional format.[11] The story of Nobel and the baroness even reached the pages of the *Readers Digest*. In 1931 Frau Fried sold her husband's papers to the Library of the League of Nations in Geneva. These included the diaries and correspondence of Bertha von Suttner, who had willed them to Fried.

For a long time these materials were not organized to be used for research, and none of the popular biographers of the baroness was aware of them. Even the first biography by a historical scholar, Caroline E. Playne, although still useful because she could supplement information from the memoirs and Fried's peace journal, *Die Friedenswarte,* with her own personal memories of the baroness, somehow missed Fried's publication of von Suttner's diaries for the last months of her life.[12] I was able

10. See Willy Brandt's foreword to the reprint of *Die Waffen nieder!* (Hildensheim: Gerstenberg, 1977).

11. Irwin Abrams, "Bertha von Suttner and the Nobel Peace Prize," *Journal of Central European Affairs* 22, no. 3 (Oct. 1962): 286–307, esp. n. 1; idem, "Bertha von Suttner (1843–1914): Bibliographical Notes," *Peace and Change* 16, no. 1 (Jan. 1991): 64–73. The most recent "biographical novel" was published in Norway in 1991 by Gerd G. Saue.

12. "Aus den Tagebüchern Bertha von Suttners. Die Aufzeichnungen aus den letzten Lebenstagen (Januar bis Juni 1914)," *Die Friedenswarte* 22 (1920): 192–98. In 1949 the journal published diary pages written during the second Hague Peace Conference: ibid. 49 (1949): 24–28. See also Caroline E. Playne, *Bertha von Suttner and the Struggle to Avert the World War* (London: Allen & Unwin, 1936).

to see a few of the documents at the League library in 1936–37, when researching my doctoral dissertation on the history of the European peace movement. In 1956 the whole collection was still not put in order, but I could use Nobel's letters to the baroness to match her letters to him, which I used in Stockholm, together with parts of her diaries. With these materials I wrote an article (see note 11) showing the influence of the baroness on Nobel in establishing his peace prize. At about the same time Ursula Jorvald, the Norwegian peace activist, used these materials for her polemical tract emphasizing the same point.[13]

In 1964 the first scholarly biography of the baroness appeared, written by Beatrix Kempf, of the Austrian Foreign Office, whose attention was drawn "by chance" to the wealth of the Suttner-Fried Collection in Geneva. Her book was well researched and written with insight, providing a positive assessment of the baroness. First published in Vienna, it was reprinted and published twice in Germany, first in 1979 and next in 1987, when interest in the baroness was rising again. Translations were published in London in 1972 and in the United States in 1973.[14] Kempf edited the correspondence between the baroness and Nobel, but this was never published. Copies of her manuscripts have been acquired by the Swarthmore College Peace Collection in Pennsylvania.

Enter Brigitte Hamann, a German journalist who came to Vienna to study history at the university and who was especially interested in seeking out and researching original sources. For her doctoral dissertation on Crown Prince Rudolf she found hitherto unpublished material and produced a biography that is regarded as definitive, *Rudolf, Kronprinz und Rebell* (Rudolf, crown prince and rebel) (1978). Her researches led her to the Swiss archives in Bern, where once more she discovered new material, this time about Empress Elisabeth, and again wrote an authoritative biography: *Elisabeth: Kaiserin wider Willen,* published in Austria and Germany in 1982. This has been her most successful book, translated into a number of languages. The English version, *The Reluctant Empress: A Biography of Empress Elisabeth of Austria* (New York: Knopf, 1986), was published in paperback by Ulstein in Berlin in 1994.

Hamann went on to write and edit a number of books on the Hapsburgs, including books for children about Maria Theresa and Mozart, written when her own children were young. She is considered the leading authority on the Austrian dynasty and on Vienna at the turn of the last century.

13. Ursula Jorfald, *Bertha von Suttner og Nobels Fredspris* (Oslo: Forum, 1963).
14. Abrams, "Bibliographical Notes," 72, n. 18.

It is no surprise that when in Switzerland Hamann heard about the treasure trove of Suttner-Fried papers, still largely unexploited, she was attracted to consider Bertha von Suttner as a likely subject for her next biography. Here was not only an interesting personality and the timely theme of war and peace, but a life that mirrored many aspects of the social and cultural developments of her day, which has been Hamann's special period of study.

Hamann was not satisfied to use just the Geneva materials, which had represented such an opportunity to Kempf. She followed her usual pattern of tracking down new sources. At the Austrian National Library in Vienna, she located a collection of Arthur von Suttner's papers that included a letter from Nobel to the baroness that nobody had seen before. She also found the correspondence between the baroness and Ritter von Bartolomeus Carneri, an Austrian liberal philosopher, writer, and politician; her first letter to him from the Caucasus had led to a deep friendship and a frank and abundant exchange of letters over the years.

The search for documents took Hamann to other lands, to Soviet Georgia, where no previous scholar had looked for traces of the nine years the Suttners had spent there, to the papers in Jerusalem of their good friend Theodor Herzl, to the archives of Nobel in Stockholm, of Albert I in Monaco, and of the Carnegie Endowment of International Peace in Washington, D.C.

Expertly using these new documents and the diaries and correspondence, Hamann follows the baroness through the years in great detail, letting her tell much of the story in her own words. It is a different picture of Bertha von Suttner, however, than the one the baroness has given us in her memoirs, upon which most previous writers have relied heavily. In the autobiography, for example, we read of all the public activities that brought Suttner world renown. In Hamann we learn of her private anxieties, the nagging financial worries that pressured her to turn out writing for pay rather than for art. Nor did the demands of the peace cause permit the leisure in which one can write after consulting the soul: "When I think of the novels I *could* write," she lamented. After a novel she had submitted was rejected, she blamed it on her reputation as a peace activist: "In the eyes of the public the pacifist has slain the authoress." But if she had sacrificed her art for the cause, she felt the cause had the higher priority.

In the memoirs the baroness and her Arthur have a perfect marriage. What she confided to her diary, but to no one else, gives a very different picture. In his last years Arthur's love for her was cooling, and he became infatuated with his young niece. Kempf dismisses the situation as merely an "episode." Hamann takes it more seriously, and the excerpts she quotes from the diary substantiate her interpretation.

Hamann tells this sad story in the chapter titled "Human, All Too Human." The baroness becomes very human in her pages. Hamann writes of her subject sympathetically, but she gives a balanced picture, faults and all. Some of us would think that this makes a great woman really greater, but one hears that the feminists in Vienna may be resentful.

What makes Dr. Hamann's book outstanding is that the qualifications of the author so well match the unusual value of the sources and the significance of the subject. Hamann combines the talents of a polished writer with the skills of a research scholar who is very much at home in the Vienna of the period she portrays. She has told a highly personal story, and she has told it exceptionally well. As such, it is not likely to be surpassed.

The end of Bertha von Suttner's "life for peace" in June 1914 was followed soon by the end of the peace itself, because the First World War began in August. There was no world peace congress in Vienna, and the monument that the peace movement planned to have built in her honor was not built. Was her life, then, a failure? Hardly. She was, as Gregor-Dellin wrote, a great woman in a century "which still made it difficult for women to be great." As the writer of an internationally renowned book, the "commander-in-chief" of a world movement, the first woman to win the Nobel Peace Prize, the idealist who, despite all the obstacles that stood in the way to her goal and all the ridicule and abuse she had to face, refused to give up, Bertha von Suttner was an example in her age of what a member of the "Universal Sisterhood" could do. And she was no saint on some kind of pedestal, but "human, all too human."

Bertha von Suttner was also living in a nationalist age that made it difficult for advocates of peace to advance their cause. The peace activists were well aware of how meager were their resources of personal influence and power, she declared in her Nobel lecture in 1906, "but when they realistically consider themselves and the ideal they serve, they see themselves as the servants of the greatest of all causes."

The monument to Bertha von Suttner which was never built lies rather in her remarkable achievements as a woman at a time when women were largely excluded from public life and as an outstanding pioneer of a cause that would one day be generally recognized as the greatest of all.

A Note on Further Reading

Both the *Memoirs of Bertha von Suttner* and her novel *Lay Down Your Arms* were reprinted in the Garland Library of War and Peace with prefaces by Irwin Abrams (New York: Garland, 1972). The *Memoirs* well repay reading, especially with Hamann in hand. The novel is a historic antiwar document.

The best short scholarly biography of the baroness, with well-chosen excerpts from writings and speeches, is Beatrix Kempf, *Woman for Peace: The Life of Bertha von Suttner* (Park Ridge, N.J.: Noyes, 1973). An example of the more popular genre is Emil Lengyel, *And All Her Paths Were Peace* (Nashville: Nelson, 1975).

Recent scholarly attention is illustrated by Regina Braker, "Bertha von Suttner as Author: The Harriet Beecher Stowe of the Peace Movement," *Peace and Change* 16, no. 1 (Jan. 1991): 74–96; Andrew Kelly, "Film as Antiwar Propaganda: *Lay Down Your Arms* (1914)," *Peace and Change* 16, no. 1 (Jan. 1991): 97–112; and Irwin Abrams, "Bertha von Suttner (1843–1914): Bibliographical Notes," *Peace and Change* 16, no. 1 (Jan. 1991): 64–73. Abrams presents a comprehensive review of the recent literature.

Also see the pages on Bertha von Suttner in the authoritative book by Abrams on *The Nobel Peace Prize and the Laureates* (Boston: G. K. Hall, 1988), 4–8, 19–20, 22–23, 53–56, as well as in his early study of her influence on Alfred Nobel, "Bertha von Suttner and the Nobel Peace Prize," *Journal of Central European Affairs* 22, no. 3 (October 1962): 286–307. This subject is also addressed by Kenne Fant in his well-written book *Alfred Nobel: A Biography,* tr. from the Swedish (New York: Arcade, 1993).

Two able histories of the peace movement contribute to our understanding of the setting within which the baroness championed the cause of peace: the landmark study by Roger Chickering, *Imperial Germany and a World without War: The Peace Movement and German Society, 1892–1914* (Princeton, N.J.: Princeton Univ. Press, 1975) and the innovative comparative approach of Sandi E. Cooper, *Patriotic Pacifism: Waging War on War in Europe, 1815–1914* (New York: Oxford Univ. Press, 1991).

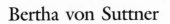

Bertha von Suttner

1

Countess Kinsky

The youthful Bertha was pretty much of a nonentity, after all," the famous pacifist commented in her diary at the age of sixty-four. She was writing her memoirs at the time and thinking about her life. The only thing she counted as an achievement was her relentless work for peace. With this effort on behalf of the peace movement "the real Bertha von Suttner is born, the person in whom the world is interested," she said.[1]

When she started working for the peace movement, Suttner was already forty years old; more than half her life was over. Even though she herself ridiculed her youth as an innocuous Austrian aristocrat, these years were undeniably important to the special way she had of going about her work.

On June 9, 1843, Bertha Sophia Felicita Countess Kinsky von Chinic und Tettau was born in Palais Kinsky on the Altstädter Ring in Prague, one of the most beautiful rococo houses in the Bohemian capital. The princes and counts Kinsky were and still are one of the noblest families of Bohemia. Their history is filled with revolt against imperial power, conspiracies, and violent death, and it bears witness to an unbendable aristocratic self-assurance.

The family's most turbulent period was the early seventeenth century. Ulrich Kinsky was one of the Protestant nobles who rebelled against the emperor in 1618 and threw the imperial officials out of a window of Prague Castle. The "Defenestration of Prague" made history and ushered in the Thirty Years' War. In this war Wilhelm Kinsky was one of General Wallenstein's closest friends and his confidant in dealings with Cardinal Richelieu in Paris. He was murdered together with Wallenstein in Eger in 1634. The details can be read in Friedrich von Schiller's drama written in 1799, "Wallenstein."

1

In the century that followed, the Kinskys were somewhat more restrained. They were ambassadors, court chancellors, and ministers in the service of the emperor. They proved their worth most of all, however, in the war against Friedrich II of Prussia and Napoleon I.

Bertha's father and his three brothers also grew up in the family's military tradition, and all became generals. These four Kinsky generals belonged to the elder branch of the family, the counts (von Chinic und Tettau), the "wild Kinskys," about whom people in Prague told rather fantastic stories.

The Kinsky Palace in Prague was the residence of the princely branch of the family and anything but a quiet refuge. It resembled far more a gigantic hotel where the numerous members of the family who happened to be in Prague stayed and gave their parties during the "season." The real residences were the magnificent Kinsky country castles in Bohemia. Bertha's father, however, did not own any of these since he was not an heir in right of primogeniture, but only a "third son," who was limited to pursuing a military career. He lived with his family in one of the many apartments in the Prague Palais. There, and not in the lordly main wing, is where little Bertha was born.

One would think that beginning a life with such a name and being born in such a place would have been exceptionally advantageous and auspicious. Far from it, since the newborn child was fatherless. Shortly before Bertha was born, Franz Joseph Kinsky died at the age of seventy-five. He left behind a widow who was almost fifty years younger. Sophie Countess Kinsky had a serious defect that was to mar Bertha's future: she was a commoner, and as such she did not have equal status as a family member.

Bertha remained silent later on about these domestic calamities. She also had nothing to say about her father, not even from the stories her mother told. In her memoirs she merely quoted her certificate of baptism which, however, did offer people in the know some revelations about the extent of her family's difficulties. None of the princes or counts among their relatives appeared as godparents. Her sponsors were her elder brother Arthur Kinsky (who was six years old at the time) and the chambermaid, Barbara Kraticek.[2] The church where she was christened, the beautiful St. Mary of the Snow (Maria Schnee), was not the church traditionally used by the high Bohemian nobility for christenings. It was a monastery church. There was no denying the fact: a "bastard" of the Kinsky family had been baptized here.

This lineage constituted an indelible flaw in Countess Bertha Kinsky's social reputation. During her entire life, she never managed to cope with the dilemma of being an aristocrat on the one hand and a commoner on the other. She was proud of her name and later, even long after she had become famous as Baroness Suttner, she had her visiting cards printed with a mention of her noble background, "Baroness Suttner, née Countess Kinsky."

There is always a clear feeling of inferiority that comes through in Bertha's diary when she writes about her relationship with the pure aristocratic Kinskys. In each confrontation with a relative, she points to her own inferiority, which she then goes on to say is due to no fault of her own but solely to her deficient family tree.

Later Bertha writes about it:

> The Austrian nobility . . . is afflicted the least by the modern age. It does not recruit new members from the bourgeoisie like the English peerage does; here the ten thousand are more caste than class. To them, the blue of their blood is an article of faith. An abyss lies between them and the middle class. It is they, however, who do the work, both manual and intellectual; and since every cultural advancement is only the result of work, it is quite clear that the ideas that influence the times emanate from the middle class. These ideas do not reach those living on this side of the ten thousand clearly, but rather like the noise of the surf, somewhat unpleasant because it is menacing.

In general, there reigns in the world of the high aristocracy "a blessed ignorance of all the things that move our century."[3]

Despite all the merciless criticism she heaped upon the Austrian aristocracy during the entire span of her life, she was never able to conceal her admiration for the old values the aristocracy embodied, for example, when she wrote about one of the aristocratic residences:

> There are the galleries with portraits of crowned ancestors; there is the armory with weapons that were once carried by the members of the house who led armies; there are the rooms where royal guests stayed; there are entire museums of precious objects, parchments, and documents which give witness to the historical magnificence of the house; everything speaks of power, fame, and glory. From the highest turret on the tower where the flag waves in the colors of the coat of arms, all the way down to the deepest vaults where century-old ribbing rests in stony coffins: everything declares the majesty of the dynasty that reigns here. The respect which age instills; the devout thrill awakened in every soul by visible traces of long forgotten times; the esteem for the melancholy but awe-inspiring majesty of the past—this tribute of feelings

which the splendid, tradition-steeped castle wrests from every viewer, the owner pays to his own birth which made him heir to and representative of all the honors heaped upon his house. This self-respect is called pride—but does not piety also lie within?[4]

Regardless of all the animosity from the outside world, mother and daughter had a very close relationship. Bertha mentions "the great, natural love of this mother for me and my love for her, which was so great that if she drove to Vienna for two or three days, I sobbed for hours as though my heart were broken."[5]

Sophie Kinsky had, according to Bertha, "a somewhat impassioned, eccentric nature." At the age of eighteen this daughter of a captain in the imperial cavalry married the old Count Kinsky. In doing so, she made a "good match," but gave up her great dream of becoming a celebrated singer.

A short time after Bertha's birth, Sophie Kinsky left the Prague palace and, provided with a small fortune and a widow's allowance from the Kinsky family, she moved to Brno in Moravia, where Bertha's guardian lived. Landgrave Friedrich Fürstenberg took in his charge and her young mother. The somewhat sickly boy, Arthur, entered a military school and became alienated from his mother and sister.

Landgrave Fürstenberg was fifty years old when Bertha was born, that is, twenty-five years younger than her father. "To me he seemed ancient, but awfully nice," wrote Bertha. "I worshiped him, regarded him as a higher being to whom I owed absolute obedience, respect, and love which I also happily conferred." His image filled her "entire childhood and early youth" with a "friendly light."

She also explains why her guardian never married. "The reason was that he harbored warm feelings for a woman who was the widow of an aristocrat but by birth was not presentable at court. As far as he was concerned, marriage to her was simply out of the question. He did not want to cause annoyance within his family, and in the end it would have been an annoyance to him, too, since everything that lay off the beaten track, outside tradition, beyond 'correctness,' went against the grain with him." The fact that this lady was none other than her mother, Sophie, is something Bertha discreetly avoids mentioning.

There in Brno Bertha spent a sheltered if lonely childhood. English and French governesses, the chambermaid and godmother Babette, the somewhat effusive mother inclined to song, and the grandseigneur Fürstenberg provided company for the child who did not know any other children. Brief excursions to the country, playing the piano, singing, and the card game between her mother and guardian she was allowed to watch twice a week were her pleasures. Entertainments centered around "society," the elegant aristocracy which, as far as the field marshall was concerned, was "the only class of people whose lives and destinies interested him."

In this closed world, the young girl became a typical little *comtesse,* who went into raptures over Emperor Franz Joseph, always had problems with clothes, and was convinced that the world was keeping "fairy tale happiness" waiting for her. She had no interest in the outside world. "The workings of the world were only the machinery whose wheels all turned for the sole purpose of making me radiantly happy."

Bertha was barely twelve years old when her cousin Elvira, almost the same age, became her companion. The two mothers, both widowed, were sisters and lived together from that time on.

Elvira's father was a wealthy private tutor and his daughter "grew up in the paternal library, so to speak."[6] Even from childhood, Elvira knew the writings of the great philosophers such as Kant, Fichte, and Hegel. She had also read Shakespeare along with the authors of her day. "The result of this kind of education was naturally a little bluestocking," writes Bertha, who idolized her because she was well read.

From the time she was eight years old, Elvira also went in for writing poetry of her own. "She herself, Aunt Lotti, and I were absolutely certain that she would become the greatest poetess of the century," wrote Bertha, who for her part, wanted to "become a grand lady and take everybody's heart by storm." Thus, the roles were divided, making jealousy impossible, and now Bertha read and worked together with Elvira. Through her she got to know the great writers and with her she dreamed of the future. It was with Elvira that she also experienced her first great journey—to Wiesbaden.

The reason for the trip was certainly not to take the baths, although that is what the two mothers told the guardian Fürstenberg. The truth of the matter was they wanted to try their luck at the gambling casino in Wiesbaden. They were convinced that their clairvoyance would enable them to divine the winning numbers, and they created the most wonderful fantasies of what they would do with the millions they were sure to win. They would buy the most magnificent castle of all, the neo-Gothic "Eisgrub" (Ice Hollow) in Moravia, from none other than the incredibly wealthy Prince Liechtenstein. They even planned the furnishings.

With a "starting capital of a few hundred gulden" they "worked" mornings in the casino at roulette and cards—without the girls. Afternoons all four enjoyed the social life of the resort. Bertha was thirteen and Elvira fourteen years old when they went to their first ball here. Eight days later one of Bertha's dancing partners, Prince Philipp Wittgenstein, asked for her hand in marriage. In view of the girl's youth, he was turned down in a friendly way. Bertha said, "For me the whole thing was a pleasant little triumph, but I didn't take it to heart."[7]

The capital they brought along and that which they sent for later was soon gone. The two ladies had to return to Brno. In her memoirs, Bertha does not reveal what "Fritzerl" Fürstenberg said to these escapades. Only one thing is certain. The two sisters left Brno with their daughters and moved to Vienna.

It was three years before the two mothers dared to try their luck in Wiesbaden again. They took the two girls, now sixteen and seventeen, with them as before. It was the summer of 1859, which went down in history because of the bloody battles of Magenta and Solferino, as a result of which Austria lost wealthy Lombardy. Bertha: "But I know exactly, the event meant absolutely nothing to me then, simply did not exist, just as I would be indifferent today if I heard that a volcano had erupted on a West Indian island whose name I had never heard before. A momentous event at a great distance. That was the war in Italy for me. We had no one close to us in the war on whose behalf we could be afraid."[8]

Parties and festivities in Wiesbaden: that's what interested the ladies. Bertha got to know and like life in the elegant world, a world where she dreamed her future would take place. She observed the leaders of society and characterized the "groups of international high life" later as "a completely nomadized people who drag their tents to all the places of pleasure and who feel at home everywhere where they meet others like themselves and where life is led '*á grandes guides.*' These are the gypsies of luxury. Wherever sounds of operatic music, hoof beats, clinking champagne glasses and flirtatious giggling sound forth; where crests and crowns, fans and riding whips, powder puff and hunting rifle are the insignia of the profession; where people play baccarat, duel with the sword, wear two-thousand-francs outfits, go skeet shooting, take a drive just to be seen, rush to a rendezvous in a veil, date their ancestors from the crusades, or estimate their assets in millions: that's where one of these luxury gypsy bands has pitched its camp."[9]

Since the longed-for winnings did not materialize, admission to these circles was refused the ladies' quartet. "All the systems, methods, gifts of intuition and divination had proved to be illusory, and there were solemn oaths that from now on an end had been put to the green table forever."[10]

Big sums of money were lost. Bertha's mother had to limit expenditures drastically, give up the Vienna apartment, and move to a cheap country cottage in Klosterneuburg near the city. "We were to spend two years there in extreme seclusion and economy."

The girls were content. Elvira wrote and Bertha tried to emulate her. The result of "envy and the urge to imitate," as Bertha later admitted, was the novella, *Erdenträume im Monde* (Earthly dreams on the moon). She sent it to the modest women's magazine, *Die deutsche Frau,* and, surprisingly, the story was printed. The editors encouraged her to write more. But Bertha did not think very much of it and later called her novella a "celestial lunacy."[11]

The two years until Bertha would come of age were to be spent in rural seclusion and with as little expense as possible. A girl could not be introduced into Viennese society until she was eighteen. Meanwhile, Elvira, who did not nurture such high-flying dreams as Bertha, married a young midshipman for the imperial shipping line in Pola, whom she had come to love as a pen pal.

In 1861 the time had come at last. Bertha was eighteen and would very soon find her "future happiness" in the form of a rich, cultivated, and, needless to say, handsome young aristocrat. The question of clothes, which took on immense importance at this moment, was discussed at great length. Later Bertha argued against the passion for finery customary in her circle. "What treasures in time, in intellectual power, were wasted by women then on their most rewarding and honorable goal, to get to be, or at least appear to be, beautiful, is incalculable. 'Clothes' was the name of a whole cult, whose liturgy was called 'fashion.' It demanded constant obedience and constant change; and an army of slaves and priestesses and high priestesses was engaged to serve it. A cult which, like the Moloch of old devouring sacrifices, made innumerable fortunes go up in smoke on its altars and to whom health and honor were slaughtered."

There was practically nothing else young girls could do except enhance their beauty by any and every possible means, since "beauty presented those qualities which offered the greatest chance of catching a husband." And further: "Yes, *excite,* inflame with desire, . . . that was the highest female merit. And the fair sex contented itself with holding the rank of odalisque."[12] Yet Bertha pleads for understanding. "*Wanting* to please was a bitter accusation made against those who had been brought up to *have* to please."[13] For after all, there was only one "recognized profession" for a woman: marriage.

For Bertha's debut a "*picknick*" was chosen, a smaller kind of ball.

This meant that not only the high aristocracy of court society would be represented—or Bertha herself would not have been admitted because of her bourgeois mother. In addition to the *"crème,"* other "lesser elements," young people who did not have an impeccable family tree, would also come. Just the right thing for Comtesse Kinsky, who was accompanied by her bourgeois mother.

If one thinks how carefully this ball was planned, how many years mother and daughter waited for it and what enormous expectations they attached to it, then Bertha's profound disappointment becomes understandable. Even many years later she still mentioned it again and again with bitterness, "I entered the hall full of happy expectation. I left it full of offended disappointment." She, who appeared to herself to be so very beautiful in her ball gown strewn with rosebuds, had found practically no partners to dance with. "The mothers of the high aristocracy all sat together, my mother sat alone; the *comtesses* stood around in packs and gaggled with one another—I didn't know anyone; at supper jovial little groups got together, I was left alone."[14]

Later she tried to explain this humiliating defeat, "If you stay away from society all your life then you cannot suddenly burst into its midst, you lack everything: manners, jargon, the art of dressing—you look incongruent, or to put it plainly, you look ridiculous"—and this was not only true of the high nobility, but even of the lower nobility, "a clique somewhat less proud of name, but all the more proud of money."[15]

Bertha realized all too clearly in this moment that the world "would not grant a penniless girl issued from a *'mésalliance'* a particularly cordial reception." Never would she be able to marry into the top-ranking Viennese society she had dreamed of without money and without the prescribed sixteen aristocratic ancestors, that is, aristocrats exclusively back to her great-great-grandparents. Her mother also felt "a hurt remorsefulness, she had a genuine guilty conscience, not to have been born an aristocrat and . . . to have spoiled the lineage by her interference."

Already on the way home, the disenchanted girl declared that she was prepared to marry an older man who had proposed to her only shortly before. He was after all one of the wealthiest men in Vienna and his promises sounded tempting, "He wanted to surround me and my mother with the greatest splendor—villas, castles, palaces. I was blinded and said, 'yes.' I do not attempt to gloss over this situation. It is an ugly thing when an eighteen-year-old girl wants to give her hand to a much older man she does not love just because he is a millionaire! It means—to use the proper name—selling oneself."[16]

In her memoirs Suttner is discreetly silent about the name of this first fiancé. It is not until later diary entries that we discover his identity. It was the fifty-two-year-old Baron Gustav von Heine-Geldern, the extremely wealthy owner of the newspaper, *Fremdenblatt,* in Vienna and the younger brother of Heinrich Heine.[17]

Because of his connections to members of the government and his generous public donations, he was granted a number of distinctions and finally the title of baron. Thus he, the scion of a northern German Jewish family, moved into the second row of Viennese society, the class of those only recently raised to nobility, the industrial barons of the Ringstrasse period, the group that ruled Vienna's intellectual life to the end of the monarchy and which produced almost all of the intellectual and artistic greats of this time. Gustav von Heine-Geldern was a powerful figure in public life. He had political power because of his successful and widely read newspaper and business power because of his financial independence.

The baron did everything to pamper his young bride-to-be, gave her expensive jewelry and drove through the city with mother and daughter to buy magnificent wardrobes, carriages and horses, and the furnishings for their home.

In her memoirs Bertha describes the first time they were alone. "'Bertha, do you know how enchanting you are?' He throws his arms around me and presses his lips against mine. The first romantic kiss a man ever gave me. An old man, a man I did not love. I tore myself away with a suppressed cry of disgust and an impassioned protest welled up inside me—no, never . . ."

Against her mother's protests, Bertha terminated the engagement the next day and returned all the gifts. The girl displayed an unbendable will in this situation. "Soon the whole episode lay behind me like a bad dream. I found waking from it a relief."[18]

Soon after that she received her next proposal of marriage. It came from another elderly man, a Neapolitan *principe,* but was turned down. Then there was a winter in Venice, which at that time belonged to Austria. Bertha wrote: "I was feted because of my intellect—I was feted to such an extent during this season in Venice that I felt like one of their queens. It was, of course, a lovely feeling; it went to my head something terribly and I used this pleasant exuberance to pass out a few hearty refusals."

What made Bertha different from other girls her age was her upbringing. She did not at any point attend one of the usual convent schools for young aristocrats. She had governesses from whom she learned French, Italian, and English. Later she penetrated further into literature. She was spared the traditional literature for young girls of the aristocracy, which consisted of stories of the saints and classics that had been cleansed of the "bad" places to keep innocent girls from having unchaste thoughts. Bertha read the classics and the moderns in the original, unabridged.

For Bertha, books were a consolation and a constant source of learning throughout her life. "Come to think of it, I have always, under all circumstances and in every situation, led two lives, my own and that of my reading material—I mean to say, what I experienced and the events that were described have enriched my memory equally. The people I know from my associations have been augmented by the heroes of my authors."[19]

Being well read, however, did not improve her chances of marriage in "good society." "Learned" women were thought of as "bluestockings" regardless of how attractive or good-natured they might be. The "weak" woman was desirable, the "affectionate" woman who "looked up to a man." A lack of education was not taken as an offense since ignorant women were considered charming, feminine, virtuous, and chaste.

The fact was, there were already other countries during the 1860s where women were allowed to study. In France, for example, women had been admitted to all branches of study except theology since 1863, and four years later Zurich University had followed suit. But the innovation did not make its way into the Danube monarchy. There was not even a girl's gymnasium, the type of secondary school that led to a university education, and the attitude toward women who studied was marked by moral indignation.

> Gawked at, laughed at, maligned, derided: the female student. Most of the candidates came from Russia. And since nihilism also came from that same country, an idea took shape for most people that was a mixture of these concepts, nihilism and female student; a connection of ideas that was all the more natural because both were based on the principles of liberation and the advocates of both directions took to wearing their hair cut short. And so it came about that for timid souls who clung to all that was traditional, the picture of a female student of medicine awakened the same kind of disgust as one of a corpse hanging from the gallows.[20]

The better educated she became, the more young Bertha distanced herself from the girlish ideal of her class and time, and the more her chances for making the "match" she longed for dwindled. Unfazed by the Austrian-Prussian war against Denmark, mother and daughter spent the summer of 1864 in Homburg, whose casino was considered the citadel of gambling at the time. Here they got to know the Princess of Mingrelia, who was to become extremely important to Bertha.

The forty-eight-year-old Ekaterina Dadiani was the widow of the Prince of Mingrelia and the daughter of a Georgian prince. Bertha was very much drawn to her: "The oriental, the exotic mixed with the Russian and the Parisian worldliness, seasoned with romance and framed by the glitter of wealth, it exerted a magic of its own on me, I was truly happy over this relationship. For me she was the fulfillment of indistinct, long-cherished dreams."[21]

Although Mingrelia was placed under the protection of Russia, up to the 1860s it was a small, independent country. Under the rule of the widow Ekaterina, it experienced stormy times during which she proved herself as a sovereign.

> Warred against by the Turks, the spirited woman actually led her troops against the Turks herself once (how I admired this trait when I first heard of it!) and received a medal of bravery from her protector, the Russian czar. But it would be wrong to imagine the Mingrelian princess as a kind of mythological amazon because of this. Ekaterina was brought up by French governesses, lived a great deal in Petersburg, and was the very picture of a lady of high society, full of feminine charm and dignity. Harassed by enemies from without and within, the young regent saw herself forced to ask for Russia's help. With her three small children, she left the country, which was then administered by a guardianship appointed by the Russians, and went to Petersburg where she was accepted at court with all the honors due a reigning monarch. The princess remained in Europe for a number of years, spending the winters in Petersburg, Italy, or Paris, the summers in the German spas.[22]

Bertha, the young aristocrat, attached herself to the princess with downright rapturous admiration and through her got to know the "grand world." Thus, she was present when Czar Alexander II visited Homburg. At the princess's side, he took a walk through the gambling hall, bet a gold coin at roulette and lost it.

Bertha fell in love with the princess's melancholy, handsome nephew, Prince Heraclius of Georgia, who owned a palace in Tblisi and an old castle in the mountains. She studied the history of Caucasia avidly and waited for a proposal that never came. The prince departed and left the infatuated girl behind in Homburg without an explanation. Once again Bertha's dreams had gone too far.

Meanwhile, Bertha Kinsky was twenty-one years old and had still not made a "good match." Her prospects diminished, since the best time to marry—the age of eighteen—was long past and there was still no fortune from the gambling table. Failure arrived all along the line, and now the added necessity of having to save rigorously to pay for the gambling losses.

The older Bertha became, the more insipid society's entertainments seemed to her and the more self-assured she became.

Firmly supported by her mother, Bertha now wanted to become "the greatest singer of the century." Since there was no money available for parties and pleasure anyway, Bertha concentrated on her great career (which she firmly believed in) with four hours of singing lessons every day and many additional hours of practice. "Nothing from dawn to dusk, nothing all through the long months of autumn, of winter, of spring but notes—sung, played, read, written notes and yet: it was a world in itself, full of sweetness and beauty, full of enthusiasm, full of proud satisfaction. I do not know if a successful career as a prima donna (I never achieved it) really brings as much happiness as one experiences in the study-filled, confident preparation for it."[23]

A famous singing teacher in Baden-Baden, Pauline Viardot Garcia, was to complete Bertha's training within one and a half years. Bertha did not pass the audition. "You really can do nothing at all," said the artist. "Your voice is not bad, but also not exceptional."[24] Later, Bertha blamed this failure on her intractable stage fright.

By now she was twenty-three and still unmarried, and hopes for the great singing career were also clouded. Thus, she was in a despondent mood when news came of the deaths of her cousin and friend, Elvira, who had died from a "disease of the chest," and of her guardian, Fürstenberg. From him Bertha inherited no less than sixty thousand gulden, which would assure her an annual income of three thousand gulden, a sum that was comparable to a university professor's salary. Mother and brother Kinsky did not appear in the will at all, all of which points to the possibility that Fürstenberg may have been Bertha's real father.

Mother and daughter did not notice the biggest catastrophe, which was political and military: Königgrätz. The frightening news of Austria's defeat in the war against Prussia did not get as far as the two ladies, who spent the summer in Homburg once again. Although Bertha "showed more melancholy and resignation" and "did not expect much of life anymore," she spent her days as usual.

The fact that she had become twenty-three years old in the meantime and had remained completely unmoved by the war is something she mentions expressly in her memoirs, and she sees herself as one example of many who had no evil intentions but had simply not arrived at certain realizations yet: "When I encounter an obstinate lack of understanding for the peace movement today in certain circles, when arguments for the natural existence and the historical necessity for the scourge of war are held out to me, in the course of which anger and disheartenment threaten to take hold of me, I only need to think of my own past for ire to dissolve and courage to rise again."[25]

That winter the two ladies went to Paris and took a small apartment there. Bertha resumed singing lessons with Master Duprez. Since the Dedopali's family also lived in Paris during the winter and the World's Fair was also going on there, entertainment and distraction were well provided for.

The high point of this Paris stay was the wedding of the Dedopali daughter Salome and Prince Achille Murat, a scion of the Bonaparte dynasty "and known at the time as the best-looking and most terrific man-about-town in Paris."[26] Bertha was maid of honor at all three of the weddings: the civil wedding at the registry office, the Catholic wedding at the Tuileries in the presence of Napoleon III and Eugenie, and the Greek Orthodox wedding. The ensuing festivities and balls made a big impression on the girl. Her enthusiasm for singing diminished noticeably.

The summer season of 1868 found the two ladies in Baden-Baden again. Bertha took singing lessons from the famous Madame Viardot and enjoyed the social life. "The most dazzling spa society one could imagine." Bertha still went into raptures about it when she was old. "Judging from the names, a lot of French, who regarded '*Bade*' as a suburb of Paris in those days. King Wilhelm I and Queen Augusta; the duchess of Hamilton, whose daughter, the lovely Lady Mary, had just become engaged to marry the crown prince of Monaco; Pauline Viardot—surrounded by singing pupils—and her friend of many years, Ivan Turgenev, who was just writing his novel, *Smoke*. The recently married Queen Margharita of Italy, resplendent in her wonderful beauty."[27]

King Wilhelm of Prussia was staying in Baden-Baden, and the twenty-five-year-old Bertha had the satisfaction of finding that he enjoyed talking to her: "Actually, as an Austrian, I should have harbored patriotic resentment against our vanquisher; but I admit that I felt nothing of the kind, only an enormous respect for these very victories. Ever since the days of my history lessons, the term, 'victor of battles,' 'conqueror of lands,' was the epitome of all that was great, all that was glorious."[28]

When she saw the procession of German troops in Berlin returning home from the victory over France three years later, she still did not have any anti-Prussian feelings against Wilhelm I, who was now emperor, not even aversion to war; quite the contrary:

> It made an enormous impression on me: the rejoicing, the flags, the dazzling uniforms—and the awareness that "this is a historic moment!" Not *one* hint of the idea that the world would be more beautiful if there were no triumphal arches built upon death and destruction, not even a trace of the notion that a different kind of world could even be *possible*. It's true—just as the Bible says: one has ears and does not hear, one has eyes and does not see; and we could rightly add: one has a brain and does not think. If someone had approached me with the impossible suggestion that I enter a peace organization (since there were some . . .), I would have turned away from the situation with a barely less indifferent shrug of the shoulders, with a barely less uncomprehending countenance than the faces I have to confront in many places today—when I appear as a recruiter.[29]

Winter, 1868: they returned to Paris again and another engagement to marry. The talk was of immeasurable wealth in Australia. That was a consolation for the fact that the groom-to-be was a rather puny young man. The supposedly immensely rich father invited Bertha and her mother for a drive on the Champs Elysées to select a *palais* to buy. Bertha's choice fell to the Hotel Paiva, which Graf Henckel-Donnersmarck had once set up for his mistress. Afterwards, they went to a jeweler in the Rue de la Paix. Precious jewelry was brought out but not purchased because the father supposedly owned far more beautiful diamonds at home for Bertha's wedding diadem.

Later Bertha wrote: "I am still glad that I made this drive through Paris. It allowed me to experience a sensation very few people are able to have—namely, the awareness that you possess immeasurable wealth and that you need only nod to have anything, absolutely anything that money can buy." Like her mother, Bertha longed all her life to be rich. But they were disappointed once more.

Father and son disappeared suddenly, never to be seen again. The millions had never existed. Ashamed, Bertha had to admit that, for a second time, she had been on the verge of "selling" herself to a rich man she did not love, like the situation with Gustav Heine-Geldern earlier.

The singing lessons continued, this time in Milan with Master Lamperti. Finally, in the summer of 1872 in Wiesbaden (Bertha was twenty-nine), a new fiancé turned up, and this time a real romance came of it. Adolf Prince Sayn-Wittgenstein-Hohenstein was also a singer and was also working toward a career that would bring in millions. He, too was poor; being a younger son, he did not have a share in the family fortune. The two discovered each other while singing love duets.

Things soon got to be very complicated: the young man could not bring himself to decide on marrying. There was a lot of vacillation, misery, promising and prevaricating. He wanted to go to America to make a quick career and a lot of money.

Bertha offered to go with him. She asked her mother to accompany her since it was absolutely impossible for a respectable girl who wanted to marry a prince to travel alone with him. But her mother refused to go along with such highly uncertain plans.

Bertha did not know the true reasons behind Adolf's trip to America. He was the black sheep of the noble family and had been under a guardianship for seven years. The big German newspapers even printed the following notice in 1865: "Prince Adolf zu Sayn-Wittgenstein-Hohenstein, by a judgment of July 4, 1865, has been declared a profligate." In June 1872 a warrant for the arrest of the thirty-four-year-old was issued in Kassel, again for enormous debts his father was no longer prepared to cover. Alexander Prince Sayn-Wittgenstein then wrote to a relative, "The best thing is without question to expedite him to America as soon as possible, as he himself wishes, even better to Australia, never to return again."[30]

This was the situation when Bertha and Adolf fell in love and made their plans for marriage. In August Adolf reported to his father from Bad Homburg:

> I have made the acquaintance here and also earlier in Wiesbaden of the Countess Bertha Kinsky, daughter of Lieutenant General Count Kinsky, who has also devoted herself to art. The same is also determined to go to America and has received very excellent recommendations for New York from Baron von Rothschild here. Countess Kinsky is a great pianist as well as singer, was trained in Milan by Lamperti, speaks perfect Italian, English, French and German. The lady is thirty years old, her mother is still alive, but is very corpulent and cannot walk; she also has a fortune of 50,000 gulden, from which she draws interest annually! I regard it my sacred duty, dear Father, to tell you that I love the Countess Kinsky and that she returns my love.—If you and dear Mama would give your permission for a marriage, it would make me extremely happy to be able to undertake the journey to Amer-

ica afterwards with Countess Kinsky. . . . Both of us would then make
our own fortune with our talents.[31]

And to emphasize the bride's importance, he added, "Our King [Wilhelm I] sent her a very warm letter in his own hand."

The father, who had already had to listen to a good many of his son's fantastic stories, was unimpressed and did not want to hear of marriage. Now Adolf had to explain the fact that he wanted to go to America alone to his unsuspecting "bride." She was deeply hurt.

Adolf's father was resolute. He did pay for a first-class ticket, but advised utmost thrift and remarked unequivocably, "Regarding your intentions to marry, which you have since quite sensibly given up, I point out that no one who is placed in the custody of a guardian can marry; take care not to carry out such a project in America; I solemnly distance myself from all consequences."[32]

Adolf saw Bertha less frequently and wavered this way and that. Bertha groaned, "It is indescribable the amount of vexation the so-called 'ingrate' causes me—leaves and stays here and leaves again, stays after all and leaves anyway—and all the time my heart is tortured—since his leaving fills me with anxiety and separation with pain."[33]

In mid-October 1872 he actually did leave—without Bertha. He died on the crossing to America, probably from overexertion due to constant seasickness. His body was buried at sea, his estate settled with a bankruptcy.

That was the end of Bertha's youth as a budding member of high society. It is astonishing how ruthlessly she describes this youth that had so little to commend it. Later, when her closest collaborator, Alfred Fried, read this chapter in her memoirs, he was very unhappy about it and thought these accounts were detrimental to the esteem that was held for the "Bertha of Peace" and, as a result, also harmed the peace movement itself. But Bertha answered very resolutely, "The fact that you do not like the first part is justified. It is, however, the truth. Such a shallow, tawdry, *small* youth I had. Such unlovely things happened in it, like the trips to gambling spas to get moneyed proposals. I did not have to tell about it, but while I was writing, I found myself under a kind of spell: be truthful, completely truthful!—That's the only source lessons can flow from."[34]

2

Governess and Secretary

Countess Bertha Kinsky went through all the eager searching for a good match and the illusions of a great career only to wind up becoming an "old maid." She was thirty years old. Her mother's small fortune was exhausted, as was Bertha's Fürstenberg inheritance. All that remained was her mother's widow's allowance. Since Bertha could hardly count on a marriage of the kind that was prescribed by her day—what man would wed a penniless thirty-year-old girl—she had to reconsider the path her life would take.

There appeared to be only two possibilities for an educated woman like Bertha Kinsky. The first was to stay with her mother and live modestly from the widow's allowance. Bertha would have continued to be dependent on her increasingly eccentric mother, who had so far not been much of a help to her anyway. In fact her mother's unrealistic, overly ambitious plans had been more of a handicap than anything else. But the two women would have gotten along without having to work. Many women in Bertha's situation would have chosen this quiet, secluded life and spent their days reading, playing the piano, and doing needlework, a lifestyle that would certainly have been more in keeping with the reputation of a countess than taking on paid work in an independent situation.

Even if Bertha had still been in possession of the Fürstenberg inheritance, which would have ensured her a livelihood in keeping with her social position, the moral notions of her time made it impossible for her to live alone. An unmarried woman had to be under the "protection" of a mother, aunt, or other relative in order not to lose her good reputation. The second possibility was to move to another family and find work that would support her.

Of course she had no profession, but she was in a better position

17

than most other girls: she had acquired a great deal of knowledge through the years from constant reading, mastered three foreign languages perfectly, played the piano exceptionally well, and could—by amateur standards—sing very well.

These were the best possible qualifications for finding a position as a governess. Besides, the fact that Bertha was a countess would add to an employer's reputation, making it easier for her to find a job. It would also keep her from falling into the usual misery governesses had to endure at the time. A teacher had no social benefits or protection whatever, could be fired from one day to the next, and was entirely at the mercy of her employer's moods.

In 1873 Bertha took a position as governess and companion to four half-grown daughters in the house of Baron Karl von Suttner.

And she was very lucky. In her employer's house, she found a new direction in life. "Blessed be the day that led me to this house. It was the bud from which the centifolia of my happiness unfolded. The day that opened the gate through which the Bertha von Suttner was to walk who . . . is the person I feel I am today, whereas the Bertha Kinsky, about whom I have talked before, appears to me as a character from a picture book, whose experiences I know in vague outlines, but which do not touch me."[1]

The big family lived in a *palais* near Karlskirche in Vienna. Bertha's description in her memoirs shows how wealthy her new hosts were, "The apartment—I can see it before me: entrance hall with tapestries on the walls, a succession of three salons: a green, a yellow and a blue one; Mama's bedroom in lavender, Papa's writing room, which also served as a smoking room, with leather furniture and wood paneling on the walls. Then two more rooms for the girls . . . next to them my room."

That was the second floor. The mezzanine, the floor between the ground and second floors, was occupied by the youngest son, Arthur Gundaccar, who studied law more or less, and the oldest, Karl, with his young wife. Richard, the second son, was also married and lived at the manor in Stockern.

A suitable staff of servants also belonged to the Suttner household: valets, hunters, servants, ladies' maids, chambermaids, cook, kitchen maids, coachman, doorman, and now the noble governess. Additional status symbols were the carriage and the box at the opera, which Bertha used about twice a week with her charges. This enabled Bertha to introduce the girls to the great operatic literature in addition to what they learned in the daily music lessons she gave them.

The Suttner family did not spend the summer in Vienna, but went to their country castle, Harmannsdorf, about eighty kilometers north of Vienna.

This former moated castle from the seventeenth century was enlarged by Baron Suttner to forty-four rooms. A small private theater and an attractive orangery stood in the old French garden, which opened into an English park and finally into forests and fields.

Eighteen seventy-three, when Bertha entered her service, was the year of the Vienna World's Fair, a year of enormous financial speculation, and, when the gigantic profits failed to materialize as expected, also the year of the stock market crash. Many of the "industrial barons" lost their fortunes overnight. That Baron Suttner also lost enormous sums at the time and that his financial situation was no longer able to keep pace with the family's opulent lifestyle neither Bertha nor the Baron's wife and children knew. It was not until many years later that the Baron's will revealed his secret, and the family learned that the year 1873 had ushered in a time of economic worries he hid from them.

Although Bertha had no experience in bringing up young girls, she had no difficulties at all. The four sisters, 20, 18, 17, and 15 years old, quite obviously loved their new companion even though their studies, especially in languages and music, took up several hours a day. "I did not play up the dignity of my 30 years. Or the authority of my position. The five of us were playmates," and soon Bertha was no longer called "Countess Kinsky," but only by her nickname, "Boulotte," or Fatty, because of her jolly plumpness.

Sometimes their brother Arthur joined the happy circle. Arthur was the sisters' favorite and soon the teacher's as well. In the memoirs Bertha wrote after Arthur's death she pays homage to his memory, "I have never known a single person, not one, who was not enchanted by Arthur Gundaccar von Suttner. As rare as white ravens are the creatures who radiate such an irresistible charm that everyone, both young and old, high and low, are spellbound; Arthur Gundaccar was such a person. . . . He had an inexplicable and irresistible magnetic and electric power. . . . The room became twice as bright and warm when he entered it."

In short, Bertha fell in love with her charges' brother, who was seven years younger than she, and he returned her love. "The sisters gave us their happy blessing. The parents did not know a thing—there could be no talk of marriage since they would have put an end to the business at once. . . . And so we kept our secret and the sisters kept it with us."

The idyl lasted three years. Sunday excursions, opera twice a week, almost daily visitors for tea or dinner, lessons in a friendly, cheerful atmosphere—and again and again, Arthur took part in the entertainments.

The high point of the year was the summer in Harmannsdorf, with hunting and dancing parties, harvest and wine festivities, excursions in the donkey cart with the big picnic basket, and theatrical performances: "In the park there was a big theater with a stage and dressing rooms. We put on various shows and comedies there, not only for the Harmannsdorf public and the neighboring castles: the peasants from the surrounding villages came in droves and filled the auditorium." And again and again "the stolen hours of intimate *tête-á-têtes*."

But after almost three years of secrecy, Arthur's mother finally noticed what was going on between the now thirty-two-year-old governess and her twenty-five-year-old son. "With icy coldness, but with great tenderness, she gave me to understand her position. I had always known that there was no hope of getting her permission for marriage. I had also not considered it myself." Resolute, she told the Baroness, "I shall leave the house. Couldn't you give me a recommendation in London; I would like to find a position there—far away from Vienna."

The Baroness had already had similar ideas and was prepared. She showed Bertha a newspaper advertisement with the following text: "A very wealthy, highly educated, older gentleman who lives in Paris, seeks a lady well versed in languages, also elderly, as secretary and for supervision of the household."

Of course, answering a newspaper advertisement was considered impossible in the best Viennese society. But here, too, Bertha nonchalantly placed herself above the rules of society. Forty years later she thought back on this episode as one of a number of times when she had done something "one" should not. Her commentary: "Oh well. But who knows?—One shouldn't reply to advertisements—is a rule. All the same, what if I hadn't answered the Nobel ad?"[2] For the gentleman from Paris was the "widely acclaimed and famous inventor of dynamite, Alfred Nobel."

It began with correspondence between Nobel and Bertha: "He wrote intelligently and wittily, but in a melancholy tone. The man seemed to feel unhappy, to be a misanthrope, very broadly educated, with a deeply philosophical far-sightedness. He, the Swede whose second language was Russian, wrote German, French and English with the same correctness and elegance."[3] Nobel also used these languages in his letters, probably to test the job candidate's knowledge.

The first exchange of letters between Bertha and Nobel has unfortunately not survived. But a letter to a later private secretary allows something of a reconstruction of the tenor of the lost letters to Bertha. "Am a misanthropist and yet extremely well wishing," he wrote, "I have a few loose screws and I am over-idealistic . . . digest philosophy better than food . . . My demands are terrible: excellent English, French, German and Swedish, stenography . . . etc., etc., but I am not one who demands the impossible, and if I like somebody I let different demands of mine fall like a house of cards. . . . [T]hat comes from the fact that I, although a kind of worthless grumbling instrument myself, am still able to recognize and acknowledge the value of others."[4]

The value of Countess Bertha Kinsky was something Nobel was able to recognize already from her letters. All her life she was an extremely gifted letter writer, witty and brilliant, and besides, she would have given special effort to these letters that were to decide her future. She got the job and broke tent at the Suttner house in the autumn of 1875.

Bertha writes that at the last tearful secret meeting, Arthur knelt before her and humbly kissed the hem of her dress: "My only, my royally generous one, I thank you, thank you from the depths of my soul. Through your love, you have allowed me to know a happiness that will consecrate me all my life. Farewell!"[5]

Filled with lovesickness and the pain of parting, Bertha set out for Paris. Alfred Nobel met her at the station, a gesture toward a new secretary that was by no means common procedure for an industrial magnate. He took her to the Grand Hotel on the Boulevard des Capucines, "where . . . rooms had been ordered," that is, not a single room but at least two, also very unusual.

Bertha's admiration for her new employer can still be felt in her memoirs:

> Alfred Nobel made a very likeable impression. An "old man," like the advertisement stated and like we had all imagined him, gray-haired, frail: that he was not. Born in 1833, he was forty-three at the time [that is, ten years older than Bertha], of somewhat less than medium height, dark beard, neither ugly nor handsome features, a rather dark expression, softened only by gentle, clear eyes; his voice had a melancholy or alternatively, a satirical quality. Sad and cynical, that was his manner. Is that why Byron was his favorite poet?[6]

The two had already discussed poetry in their letters.

These letters also kept them from meeting as strangers. When Nobel came back to the hotel after a short rest to pay a visit, the conversation was "immediately carried out in a lively and stimulating manner." Nobel's liking for the countess was unusual, considering his normal reticence and shyness. Judging from photographs, Bertha was a very attractive if already somewhat stout woman with a cheerful, spirited temperament and a "magnetism," as she herself called it, which she sometimes very consciously used in confrontations with other people.

Nobel was born in Stockholm in 1833, the same year his father, a technical inventor, went bankrupt. The father emigrated to Russia and left the mother behind in Sweden with three small sons. She earned her livelihood with a grocery shop, and the eldest son sold matches. Nobel's later charity had its foundations in this very bitter experience with poverty.

When Alfred was nine years old, the family moved to the father in St. Petersburg. The Russia of Czar Nikolaus I was extremely friendly to foreigners and made it possible for them to amass great wealth. Nobel senior made his fortune with the invention of land and sea mines, which he produced in his own factories with more than a thousand employees. He even built Russia's first steam-powered battleship.

Nobel's sons got an excellent education from private Russian tutors. The very delicate Alfred was especially attracted to English literature, but he became a chemist—without attending a university. When he undertook a two-year study trip through western Europe and North America at the age of seventeen, he was already a cosmopolitan and spoke five languages: Swedish, Russian, German, English, and French.

On this journey Alfred made contact with the most famous chemists of his day. In Paris he got to know the Italian, Ascanio Sobrero, who had invented an explosive oil, nitroglycerin. Later Nobel did his own work based on this invention.

Following his return to St. Petersburg, Alfred Nobel worked in his father's factory together with his brothers, but after the Crimean War, was sent back to Europe, this time to raise capital. Meanwhile, he had become twenty-three years old. While the two older brothers stayed in Russia, built up the Russian oil industry in Baku, and became wealthy there, Alfred went to Sweden to carry out experiments in his homeland. In the big "Nobel explosion" in Stockholm, five people died, including Nobel's youngest brother, Emil. This and several later accidents contributed a great deal to Nobel's melancholy.

In 1867, when he had just turned thirty-three, he registered the most important of his 355 patents: dynamite, or "Nobel's Safe Gun Powder." The production of this dynamite in his own factories made him one of the wealthiest men of his time, since it was this new explosive that made the important building projects of the nineteenth century possible, such as the Panama Canal and numerous railway tunnels.

Within a very short time, the Nobel undertakings grew into an international imperium. Nobel himself led an unsettled life as a commuter to his factories and laboratories scattered all over the globe. He became famous as the "richest hitchhiker in the world," without a private life, without social contacts, shy, distrustful.

He was forty years old when he bought his first house, the magnificent *palais* on Avenue de Malakoff (today Avenue Poincaré) in Paris, near the Arc de Triomphe and the Bois de Boulogne. The house was furnished very luxuriously; the marvelous winter garden was especially famous. Nobel set up a laboratory in the courtyard but was not able to carry out experiments of any kind because of the danger to the rest of the neighborhood. He loved his Parisian *palais* all the same and felt at home there, at least for the short periods between journeys.

This was the situation when Nobel met Countess Bertha Kinsky. He was a man who had worked all his life and longed for a house and family. And Bertha—attractive and highly educated, ten years younger, warm hearted and open—was exactly the kind of woman who could have drawn this lonely person out of his cage of mistrust.

On the first evening after Bertha's arrival in Paris, Nobel drove her through the Champs Elysées to exactly the place where she had once so enthusiastically chosen a *palais* with her Australian fiancé.

In the light of her earlier ideas, she could have felt that she had reached her goal now at the side of one of the wealthiest men in the world, who courted her in his own shy way. But by now, she had distanced herself too much from the ideals of her youth. Having known love, she was not in the least interested in making a "good match," not even in view of the enormous liking that bound her to Alfred Nobel.

She could not forget Arthur even in Nobel's presence. She spent the many free hours she had at her disposal in Paris giving in to her grief. "I was unhappy. Simply miserable. Homesickness, longing, the pain of parting made me suffer in a way I did not think possible. . . . When I was alone all I could do was weep or write home [to Harmannsdorf] or groan with lovesickness."[7]

Nobel managed to spend one to two hours a day with his new secretary even though he was a very busy man. The fact that he took this time at all, just to talk and not do any work, can only be explained by a special personal interest in Bertha. In her presence he overcame his shyness completely. "He was so fascinating when he chatted, told stories, philosophized, that his conversations held my attention in total captivity. Talking to him about the world and people, about art and life, about the problems of time and eternity was a great intellectual pleasure."

Nobel also explained what he wanted to achieve with his inventions:

increasingly efficient types of explosives. "I want to be able to create a substance or a machine with such horrible, enormously destructive capabilities that wars would become absolutely impossible."[8] Inspired by his poet-idol, Shelley, Nobel had already begun to concern himself with pacifism and, as paradoxical as it may sound, had placed his inventions in the service of the pacifist movement. Bertha, by contrast, knew practically nothing at this point about the pacifist movement and showed no noticeable interest in the subject. She does not appear to have contradicted Nobel, apparently having no opinion on this topic that was so important to her later.

The question that keeps coming up, whether it was Nobel or Bertha who gave the decisive impulse to pacifist work, has a clear answer. Nobel, ten years older and confronted with the problems of armament since childhood, examined the issues of war and peace critically in 1876, albeit as a general theme and not in respect to an "organized" pacifist movement. Completely in line with the Darwinian theory of evolution, he imagined a process of "refinement of human society." "New knowledge, new discoveries, ideal works of art should enrich and beautify the world, and the basic prerequisite for the guarantee of all these products of all progress: peace."[9]

The following would have to contribute to creating this peace: "on the one hand the dispersion of human stupidity and baseness with the help of art and knowledge; the defeat of misery by the progress of technology that produces good, and on the other hand waging war *ad absurdum* through its own hellish development."

Bertha was deeply impressed by Nobel's idealism: "He placed complete trust in the abstract ideal of a higher human being to come—'when the people with better developed brains are finally born'—but full of mistrust for most of the people of the present since he had had occasion to meet so many of low, selfish, insincere character."

"He was also mistrustful of himself and shy to the point of timidity. He thought he was repulsive, believed he could not inspire liking in anyone; was always afraid that people flattered him because of his enormous wealth. That's why he never married. His studies, his books, his experiments—that filled his life. He was also a writer and poet, but never published any of his poetic works. He gave me a manuscript to read, a poem a hundred pages long, composed in English—I found it absolutely magnificent."[10]

It was the poem "The Riddle," which Nobel wrote at the age of eighteen, in the style of Shelley. Unlike most of his other poetry from this period, this was one piece he did not destroy. The poem displays strong autobiographical traits, describes the childhood of the weakly boy, Alfred, in particular his love for a girl who is torn from him by death. Even at that age, Nobel avoided company and idle pleasures and decided "from now on to dedicate my life to a nobler cause."[11] The long poem showed the basic features of Nobel's attitude toward life, the sensitivity and vulnerability hiding behind an occasionally exaggerated cynicism and his loathing for the frivolities of society, which he exposed as an "ugly face with make-up."

It was a very great sign of confidence for Nobel to show his new secretary these personal verses, to discuss them with her, and to let her share in his ideals and desires.

Twenty years later in a letter to Nobel, Bertha mentions these days of getting to know each other in Paris. "What an odd little novella—since it wasn't a novel—more like material for a psychological study: a thinker, a poet, a human being, bitter and good, unhappy and cheerful, with a brilliant flight of thought and terrible mistrust, who passionately loves the great expanse of the human world of thought and deeply despises the pettiness of human stupidity, who understands everything and expects nothing: that is how you appeared to me. And twenty years have done nothing to erase this image."[12]

In her memoirs, Bertha is exceptionally discreet in her treatment of Nobel. After all, they did come close enough for him to notice that she bore a "hidden sorrow" and to ask her, "Is your heart free?"

Bertha said no. "He pushed farther and I told him the whole story of my love and my renunciation."

Nobel replied, "You have acted bravely; but be totally courageous, break off the exchange of letters. Then let a certain time pass . . . a new life, new impressions—and you will both forget—he perhaps even sooner than you."[13] But give up the last shred of contact was precisely what Bertha could not do.

Her grief overcame her when Nobel had to go away eight days after her arrival and she was left alone. "The longing for the man of my heart became so great it was unbearable," she wrote in her memoirs. She knew from the Suttner girls that Arthur was also in a bad state. "The sisters wrote that Arthur was unrecognizable, did not speak a word; it was as though he had totally succumbed to melancholy."

Then she got two telegrams, one from Nobel in Stockholm, "Arrived safely, be in Paris again in eight days," and the other from Arthur in Vienna, "Can't live without you!"

Bertha decided against Nobel and for Arthur. She decided against the "good match" for a life of uncertainty and adventure, since Arthur would be cut off without a penny if he married against his parents' wishes, and he did not have a profession to fall back on. At the side of a man like this, Bertha would never be able to lead the usual kind of life for a woman of the nineteenth century. In this union she, who was seven years older, would have to take over the main responsibility. She was determined to do it.

She thanked her friend Alfred Nobel in writing, "for all the trust and friendship shown," and explained that she could not accept the position as his secretary.

Nobel's romance with Bertha had not lasted more than eight days. He had opened his heart to her as to no other woman, had entertained hopes. Despite the disappointment, Nobel's attachment to her continued to be one of friendship and admiration. The strong tension that was apparent between the two lasted for decades, until Nobel's last letter to the meanwhile famous pacifist Bertha von Suttner a few days before his death.

Several weeks after Bertha's flight, Alfred Nobel plunged into an affair with a twenty-year-old flower seller in Baden near Vienna. A relationship resulted that lasted several years and also provided what he, the misanthrope, had always expected from other people. Sophie Hess exploited him shamelessly and was a source of constant irritation and great disappointment. Nobel never did marry.

After turning Nobel down, Bertha sold a valuable diamond cross that she had inherited from her guardian Fürstenberg. With the proceeds she paid her hotel bill so that she would not be indebted to Nobel, bought a ticket, and took the next train to Vienna. "I behaved as though I were in a dream, as though under an irrepressible compulsion. The idea that it might be folly, that I might be running from fortune into the arms of misfortune, did flash through my mind, but I could not, could not do anything else, and the bliss I expected from the moment of reunion outweighed everything that might yet come—even if it be death." Using a disguised handwriting, she summoned Arthur to a hotel room in Vienna. Her happiness was complete.

They decided to marry in secret since permission from the Suttner family was not likely. "And then out into the world! We can get through somehow: work, exploit our talents—find a job. . . . Off to Caucasia!—was my suggestion. I had powerful friends there." Bertha's hopes were not directed toward the Mingrelian nobles, but straight to the court of the Czars: "Through my connections with the Russian emperor it would be possible to find a position in the Russian civil or imperial service."

Arthur made the preparations for the wedding in utmost secrecy. He got the papers, but had to look for creditors. This turned out to be the hardest job since he had no security and he did not want his family to know about these debts. After the couple fled, no less than six creditors sent their demands for a total of 4,250 gulden to Arthur's father.[14]

The young couple's desperate efforts to get money together took a long time, more than half a year, a fact Bertha glosses over quickly and without closer details in her memoirs. During this extended period, the Suttner family was not supposed to find out that Bertha had returned from Paris. We do not know if she took a job during this time to cover her living expenses. Later, she writes only sketchily that she hid with a family in the small Moravian town of Lundenburg during this time. From here she wrote the Princess of Mingrelia, relating "our whole novel" and announcing their visit. "A friendly welcome was telegraphed back to us."[15]

Their bitter poverty did not seem to bother her. But as an old woman, Bertha sighed with a little envy when she saw the magnificent trousseau of a young couple she was related to: "I always envy people for their trousseaus . . . having everything all together: 12 dozen dozen— and the jewelry and the clothes and the housemaids and the bridegroom and one's own youth and suddenly becoming a woman and the white train and the sweetly trembling 'alone at last.' . . . Oh well, let's not begrudge them this."[16]

On June 12, 1876, Arthur and Bertha were married in a secluded church on the outskirts of Vienna before discreet witnesses. What little importance Bertha attached to the church ceremony (they appeared already dressed in their traveling clothes) is reflected in the fact that she lists the wrong church in her memoirs. She was not married in the parish church of Gumpoldskirchen as she herself writes, but in St. Giles (St. Ägyd) in Gumpendorf.[17]

3

In the Caucasus

Filled with soaring dreams and a lust for adventure, the young married couple started out on its journey. "We were terribly enchanted over our being together, our bold prank brought us such an enormous feeling of happiness; everything so far had gone '*sur des roulettes*,' so that we looked to the future as a continuous enhancement of our feeling of good fortune. Someday we would return home in triumph; but we would not want to return for a long time yet; for the moment out into the wide, beautiful, rich, strange world—we'll get ourselves the golden fleece. And didn't even need it—that was the most beautiful thing about it."[1]

It was Arthur's first big trip. Bertha: "I was intoxicated with his youthful exuberance and became just as childish as he." Since the railway had not been built yet, the journey went down the Danube to Galatz and from there to Odessa with the postal carriage. Then they boarded the boat for Batum on the Black Sea. Here they entered Asian, Georgian territory.

According to legend, Georgia was the site of paradise. It possesses enormous treasures of natural resources and natural beauty. The fertile soil and mild subtropical climate allow tangerines, grapes, tea, cypresses, and palms to thrive. Later, Bertha would recall with rapture entire roads lined with blossoming mimosas.

Georgia is the Colchis of antiquity, home of Medea and land of the golden fleece. Wonderful antique gold and enameled works are still unearthed there every year. The enamored couple had no doubts: in this land of ancient culture and incredible wealth, to which Princess Ekaterina herself had extended her welcome, great fortune awaited them.

The Dadianic family estate took up almost half of the country of

Mingrelia. According to Bertha's account, it held "such treasures from mines and forests hundreds of years old, that they could, if properly administered, produce an income of a million rubles, but unfortunately they are in the hands of Mingrelian officials—and not properly administered."[2] The young couple thought they had a good chance of getting a position of trust there.

The Caucasus, or Caucasia, was, however, not a very suitable place for a honeymoon then, since it was a political crisis area of the first order. The country, for years a bone of contention between Russia, Persia, and Turkey, was restive, particularly because of the battles Persia supported beween Christians and Moslems. In order to counteract the Islamic tendencies, the last princes of Georgia and Mingrelia had accelerated the spread of European culture in their countries and settled large numbers of foreigners, including many Germans, in the Caucasus. Finally, however, they were forced to give up their political independence and place themselves under Russian protection.

By forcefully preventing further religious wars, Russianization brought about greater legal security and rapid economic development. All the same, one had to be prepared for new crises at any moment, since in practice, Russianization was far from having been completed. Imperialism had an entirely different character in Russia than it did in the other European superpowers: the spread of Russian rule did not apply to areas abroad. It covered the east (Siberia), the south (toward Amur and Ussuri), and central Asia (the Caucasus, Turkestan, Samarkand, and Tashkent). Thus, in the middle of the nineteenth century, the biggest geographically connected colonial empire in the world was created.

Worrying about politics in Caucasia was tiresome for the young Suttners. Besides, they had no other refuge to go to. They entered their adventure with courage and curiosity.

The beginning was like the description Bertha later made of the whole country: "Picturesque—oriental—somewhat theatrical."[3] One of the Princess's envoys met them at the dock and took them first to Poti, a marshy harbor from where the journey by land was to continue. The messenger "wore the costume of the region: a long caftan, cartridge cases against his chest, a bashlik on his head, dagger in his belt."

The first stopping place in Caucasia looked hardly less adventurous than the princely messenger. The beds were full of vermin so that the young couple slept on chairs. The only tin washbasin in the house "and the towel (and in what condition besides!)" were carried from one room to the next, as needed.[4]

"In a good mood, still unmarred" they traveled on. The temperature was very hot. "But everything we saw and heard—and smelled was so exotic for us: the foreign people, the foreign costumes, the foreign construction of the buildings and—as far as smells were concerned—a very peculiar, not unpleasant scent of sun-dried buffalo manure. The buffaloes themselves, here used both as beasts of burden and dairy cattle . . . , were an exotic sight for us."

A second messenger accompanied them from Poti to Kutais, the capital of the Georgian province of Imereti. There they were received by a friend of the house, the Comte de Rosmorduc, who originally came from Brittany.

He introduced the couple to the high society of Kutais. "Here we saw women in their national dress and witnessed a performance of the national dance, the *lesginka*, for the first time. Also took part for the first time in a festive meal where the fiery Cachetin wine was poured from slender silver pitchers into huge drinking horns, where someone who had been elected to the honorary office of 'fore-drinker' proposed the toasts—on this occasion, to the health of the guests from Austria first." Finally, Arthur sat down at the piano "and played several of the waltzes he composed himself. . . . To close the party I did my best with an Italian bravura aria and then the 'Laughing Song' by Auber . . . the sung laughter was contagious and the whole business ended in a chorus of laughing."

At last, in a troika, the three-horse carriage notorious for its discomfort, they drove from Kutais to the prince's summer residence in Gordi. Prince Nikolaus received his guests personally, waiting at the "Bridge of Pompey," the border to Mingrelia, with an enormous entourage. They had breakfast there in a tent and then rode seven kilometers on horseback along precarious serpentines, "surrounded by a troop of princely escorts, who provided a wonderful show, wearing their picturesque uniforms and performing all sorts of equestrian stunts in their high saddles, jumping up and down along steep mountain walls."

Aside from a few summer months in Gordi, Prince Niko lived in St. Petersburg as an adjutant of the Czar. He was married to the daughter of a Russian minister and gradually became just as Russianized as his principality.[5]

The guests occupied one of the small frame houses near the prince's castle. In the evening the princess extended invitations for dinner in the extremely elegant flower-decorated apartments. It was just like Paris: "I found the same chic, the same artistic nonchalance, the same splendor of ivory, porcelain and bronze bric-a-brac in the Mingrelian mountains; also the same scent of orange blossoms that clung to every object that belonged to the princess, every room she lived in."⁶ After dinner they went "out to the plateau that lay there in bright moonlight, and now dances were also performed, rockets flew into the air, choruses were heard and it was after midnight before we retired. That was our reception in Gordi."⁷

Despite the declaration of renunciation, the Mingrelians regarded the Dadiani family as their rulers. "The Mingrelians are respectful and thoroughly loyal-minded. The homage I saw paid to Prince Nikolaus and his mother by both the high and the low of the land . . . is not extended to many European monarchs. . . . All addressed the latter with the title 'Dedopali,' which means approximately the same as *queen* in Georgian. And just as the queens of classical tragedy were never allowed to enter the stage without a big following, the Dedopali in Mingrelia also never took a step outside her house without a few members of her court following at a respectful distance." Prince Niko was also constantly "in the midst of a whole troop of natives . . . who received every word that passed his lips with rejoicing."⁸

But the Suttners' hopes of getting a high position at the Czar's court soon vanished. And as pleasant as life at the prince's summer residence was, it came to an end after a few weeks. Prince Niko went back to St. Petersburg, the Princess to Paris.

The young couple stayed behind and moved to Kutais. A few well-known aristocratic families lived there, and the two Austrians were able to work as teachers. Bertha gave music and French lessons, Arthur who was not nearly as well educated, could only teach German.

They could expect no financial support from Arthur's parents, who were still not willing to make a reconciliation. We do not know anything about the details of the family quarrels. The many letters the couple wrote from Georgia to Arthur's family, also to Bertha's mother and "Aunt Lotti," have not been found.

This striking lack of reports on the Georgian period can only be attributed to Bertha herself. When she wrote her memoirs, she sifted out her papers and only saved what supported her own, rather idyllic portrayals. She prepared the material her future biographers would have to work with very knowingly. The bitter details of the Georgian years—the disappointment after all the grand expectations, the fear connected with their economic situation, the homesickness—were something she did not want to disclose in the immediacy of a letter or a diary. The biographer has no other choice but to depend upon the two sources provided by Bertha's embellishing pen, her memoirs and the marriage novel, *Es Löwos* (a nickname referring to Arthur's thick, curly hair that resembled a lion's mane), but at the same time, it is her responsibility to point to the lack of immediate sources which would surely have given a more somber picture.

One thing is certain: aside from casual invitations from their Caucasian friends, they could expect nothing, absolutely nothing.

"And that's how our school of life began," she writes later full of pride. "Work, study, the simplest secluded existence mixed with deprivations and, on the other hand, a cheerful mutual satisfaction with ourselves. Here we learned to share in the questions of humanity, here the need awoke in us to gather *knowledge*."[9]

Despite the worry, they persisted in their happiness, at least retrospectively in the memoirs: "But our inner cheerfulness was invulnerable."

Barely a year after their arrival, the Russian-Turkish War broke out. The Caucasus became a theater of war. "I don't remember having been afraid. And I sensed just as little a feeling of protest against war in general as I had in the years 1866 and 1870. Arthur also saw only the elemental event in the war that just broke out, albeit one of particular historical importance. Standing in the middle of it lends you a certain reflected importance."[10]

Her sympathies belonged to the Russian side. "The aim was to liberate 'Slav brothers'; that was the motto cited all around us, and we accepted it credulously." It was the slogan of Pan-Slavism that showed itself for the first time in this war. There was, however, another slogan in the Caucasus that belonged to the Moslems: "Revolt—Shake off the Russian yoke."

The situation was dangerous, especially for foreigners who spoke the language of the land, Georgian or Mingrelian, poorly, just as poorly as the official state language, Russian.

"Of course everybody who stayed behind was seized with Red Cross fever, making bandages, transporting supplies of tea and tobacco, refreshing passing regiments with food and drink, collecting money, planning and carrying out charitable events—all for the benefit of the poor soldiers."

The Suttners wanted to work in the military hospital as nurses' aides but withdrew their offer when they found out that they would not be allowed to work together. Thus, they were spared the experience of caring for the wounded. Instead they took a very active part in arranging charity events in aid of poor soldiers. One example of these was a garden party:

> lamplight, orchestral music ("God Protect the Czar," a potpourri from
> Glinka's "Life for the Czar," "Balkan March," Slavic songs, etc.), booths
> where things were sold, and a raffle. A big painting was put up between

two trees, strongly lit, portraying a touching battle scene; in the fore-ground a very beautiful, benevolent Russian nurse with tears on her cheeks, gently bent over a wounded Turkish soldier whose head she lifted so that she could give him refreshment; in the background a tent, gunpowder smoke, dead horses, and bursting grenades. Standing in front of the picture, I shed a tear myself.[11]

In her memoirs Bertha describes how the unsuspecting and gullible "subordinates" were misled by the politicians. She admits that she had believed these rallying cries herself and even spread them further. It was not until much later that Tolstoy's book, *Christian Belief and Patriotism*, enlightened her about the true motives of big politics. Tolstoy writes that the so-called liberation of the Slavic brothers had been a mere pretense for the military struggle for power and the suppression of Turkey. The patriotic phrases, propagated by the press, were aimed at strengthening the willingness to fight. "The enthusiasm of the mob is usually artificially created by those who need it." But it was not until ten years later that she got to know Tolstoy's writings and took up correspondence with him.

The war had a drastic effect on the young married couple. Practically no one was interested in music or French lessons. There was very little money. "We even got to know the ghost, 'hunger,' on certain days back then."[12] But their love stood firm against their worries, and they made the best of things.

At this point Arthur tried his hand at writing. He sent the news-paper, *Neue Freie Presse,* reports on the events of the war in the Caucasus. At first they were also printed, but later turned down. Arthur was too sympathetic to the Russians, and the *Neue Freie Presse* took the side of the Turks. All the same, he had discovered his talent for writing.

The war lasted a year. The Russian troops advanced almost to Con-stantinople. Turkish rule was badly shaken. Among the areas the Russian empire gained in the peace of San Stefano were parts of Armenia with Kars, Ardahan, and Batum. This meant that Russia increased its power in Asia and succeeded in countering the strong Moslem opposition in Caucasia.

Arthur sought new topics for his newspaper articles and chose the obvious: reports on life in the Caucasus, descriptions of the landscape, local customs, all sorts of everyday incidents. One of these articles was printed in Europe, for a fee the household desperately needed.

"Was it envy, was it imitative instinct? I wanted to see if I couldn't write, too."[13] Bertha wrote an essay entitled "Fans and Aprons" and sent it to *Die Presse* in Vienna. A copy of the issue it was printed in and twenty gulden came by return mail. "Then I wrote a second piece (called 'Foolish Stuff') for a family publication. It was also accepted. From then on I wrote constantly, in the beginning at longer, gradually at shorter and shorter intervals."[14]

The young couple was able to recuperate during the summer after the war ended. They were guests of the prince's family in Gordi, and here they led a carefree life in the style of Russian high aristocracy. Bertha wrote a play in French for the theater in Gordi, a society comedy in one act for four actors: the two Suttners, the Prince of Mingrelia himself, and Count Rosmorduc.[15]

Then they tried their luck in Zugdidi, the capital of Mingrelia a hundred kilometers away from Gordi, where the Dadianis had a winter residence. The Murat family also had a house here. Bertha was able to give the Dedopali's grandson, Lucien Murat, German lessons, and Arthur was to oversee the construction work on the new palace.

There were other big plans besides. Together with an acquaintance, Arthur wanted to found an agricultural community in the environs of Mingrelia. His idea was to bring in foreign farmers who would do a better job of cultivating the land and would teach local farmers modern agricultural methods. But his plans proved to be an illusion again. Too late, he thought about the fact that it would all cost a lot of money. No financial support came from the big Russian landowners or from the Prince of Mingrelia.

Then Arthur tried dealing in wood, but had no success there either. His good nature was to keep him from ever becoming a good businessman.

They continued to live from teaching and writing newspaper articles and remained childless. Bertha admitted being "rather glad about it," since "taking care of a pack of hungry children might have spoiled the good mood that has never left us during our life's duet."[16]

She frequently emphasized how steadfast her defiant love was. "The worse off we were, the closer we snuggled together—one consoling the other, encouragingly, cheeringly—although we did not really need comforting, were certainly never unhappy."[17]

"There were days, not very many but a few, when we did not eat a meal at noon, but days when we did not joke, caress and laugh—there were none of those."

Their kind of living together was not the usual patriarchal arrangement of the time. Bertha took the dominant role in the marriage, not only because of her age, but also because of her energy and her strong will. Still, she avoided anything that made this superiority all too obvious. She always emphasized the quality of partnership in her relationship with Arthur.

At the same time, this picture of a perfect marriage must be seen in the light of one particular consideration: Bertha would never have revealed anything negative. Yet she had fought too hard for this marriage for anyone to blame her for worrying about aspersions being cast upon it. Still, the fact remains, we know this blissful Caucasian marriage only from her own descriptions of it and are forced to believe her when she writes: "It was a rich life that we led in the secluded farmhouse where we sometimes heard the jackals howl in the night. Rich, although our income was the most minimal . . . rich in adventures and experiences even though for weeks at a time we saw no one and nothing really ever happened—the source of our experiences were our books and our hearts. We had the rarest of mortal privileges: complete, firmly anchored happiness."[18]

They did not mourn their former, grander life. "I would not give up a single one of my present joys for the fun of my youth. The delight I experience when a shipment of new books and newspapers brings me news in my solitude of the great world of thought outside and creates a sudden brightness—like a bolt of lightning that lights up a new horizon—this delight I would not exchange for [former] pleasures . . ."[19]

With their earnings they could just barely pay for the rent, their meager meals, and the installments for the piano that they did not want to live without since music provided what was usually their only entertainment. Toward the end of their Caucasian stay, they made music on a zither. Bertha accompanied herself in sentimental songs, Arthur played lusty Austrian country dances and attempted waltzes in the Georgian style.

The main expenses were subscriptions to western magazines and books. For them, books were a home and a consolation. Bertha admitted to having a "passion for the up-to-date." She liked modern authors and their new publications far more than the classics. "I love my contemporaries—something like the way one loves one's compatriots. It is not only the space, it's also the time we are born in that makes up our homeland. Rooted in time just as much as in our native soil are the thousands of customs, habits, and forms of speech that are so familiar and dear to us, and that is why I feel as good and at home with the books of my contemporaries as I do in the company of my compatriots who speak my dialect and who live in my area."[20]

They read the great authors on the new theory of evolution, especially Darwin and Haeckel. They concerned themselves with the new science of sociology and immersed themselves in the writings of Herbert Spencer. "And most of all, the book that was a revelation to me: Buckle, *History of Civilization*."[21]

This book of Buckle's created a sensation in the educated world in the 1860s and 1870s because it expanded the laws of the theory of evolution in a dogmatic and materialistic sense to cover the events of history.

Like their great examples, Bertha and Arthur also believed in a constant development of man into a nobler being. This belief that man developed continually according to natural law from vice to virtue, from hatred to love, from bestiality to humanity, gave Bertha an unshakable optimism. Later, skeptical contemporaries would frequently use a less friendly term and dismiss this optimism as naïveté.

The Suttners always read together. "I had the advantage of having read more works on natural sciences than he, he had the advantage that he loved nature more passionately than I. . . . [W]e helped each other rise to new heights. He taught me to enjoy nature, I helped him understand it. This taking possession of a new truth together made the possession doubly secure, the possession doubly clear."[22] And at another place, "We got to know two joys that we would not have wanted to do without; the joy of being together cozily and the joy of intellectual endeavor."[23]

They also wrote together at a common desk—as they did all their lives—to make money. At first they hid their identity. Arthur wrote under the name "M. A. Lerei" and Bertha as "B. Oulot," short for her nickname, "Boulotte."

Bertha had a much easier time of it than Arthur because she had a much livelier, wittier, and more pointed style. Arthur was often verbose. After the feature stories, she dared her hand at serials, sticking to the current style set by women's literature. The plots were always set in aristocratic circles and always had true or false love as their theme. A typical example was the serial story, "Taken from Society. Pages from the diary of Countess X," with detailed accounts of the daily events at a secluded country estate: card games, knitting, reading from pious books, gossip, playing the piano, and for high points, country excursions and evenings of dancing. Problems of the heart added excitement.[24]

The publication of her first novel, *Hanna,* as a serial in the *Gartenlaube* was a great triumph which brought in eight hundred gulden. Bertha: "In addition to the honor, there is also no small joy in the money. People who have never suffered deprivation, who have never been in the position of not knowing what they would live from the next day, what they would pay their urgent debts from, such people know nothing about the elation a sum that turns up unexpectedly causes, and one earned so honorably besides!"[25]

Bertha never referred to her Georgian surroundings in her novels, as Arthur did in his writing. In her primitive Georgian frame house, she dwelled on memories, probably homesickness, too. Georgia was an almost oriental country; the woman whose activities were confined to the house saw her responsibility in bringing up sons. Bertha's writing could not compete with this. Contacts were limited to a few western European families. Of necessity, she spent almost the whole day at home, concentrated on her work and her marriage, which was all-important for her happiness. "We were, as far as our emotional bond was concerned, also on a kind of island, a pretty, blossoming, cheerful little island of love, about whose existence the huge ocean liners beyond had no idea."[26]

Arthur had far more contact with the local inhabitants—with construction workers, craftsmen, tradespeople, and artists. As a man he was able to pursue a job and move around the country freely, a freedom that was not permitted his wife.

Even if one takes account of the social contacts with several aristocratic families, among whom Bertha assumed a more or less subordinate rank as a language instructor, one can speak of the couple's isolation in Georgia.

In any case, the Suttners left practically no mark on Georgia's intellectual life. Georgians at large did not find out until much later, when Bertha became famous all over the world because of the Nobel Prize, that she had lived in the Caucasus for years.

Bertha progressed well with her writing. She was industrious and wrote several pages a day. The search for newspapers and publishers proved to be difficult, however. Long distances by post and a lack of personal contact with editors in western Europe demanded a lot of patience and a great deal of tenacity and optimism, of which Bertha possessed more than enough. She did not allow herself to be discouraged by refusals and always made another try. Later she advised a colleague who was close to despair over refusals, "Even if a contribution is returned by five or six papers, it can still be accepted by the seventh. I have published highly acclaimed novels that had been been sent back by several editorial departments."[27]

The long years of disappointment, hard work and worries about a livelihood finally demanded their tribute. Bertha became seriously ill, and she, who always made the best of everything—at least in the retrospection of her memoirs—regarded this illness as a blessing. "Still it was a wonderful time, God knows. I was overcome by a half-dazed weariness, lying down gave me a good, satisfying feeling of rest, and the attention and care and tenderness of my [husband] cradled me in a deep, quiet awareness of happiness. That lasted about six weeks. Then I was well and, once again, we had come to love each other even more."[28]

At some point during these years, Arthur also took ill—from malaria. Just fourteen days before his death in 1902 he attributed his sickness to the "old Mingrelian reminiscences of malaria."[29]

Studying together and discussing together intently led Bertha and Arthur toward a liberal weltanschauung. "Our code word in all things pertaining to thought and actually to everything is: freedom. We despise all chauvinism—love, progress and happiness are our dogma."[30]

This stand was reinforced by the extreme internationality in Georgia, which rested on a tradition of tolerance and which also expressed itself in a very open attitude toward its different religions. Tbilisi, the capital of Georgia, had seventy-six churches at this time; thirty-six of them were Georgian and Russian Orthodox, twenty-six Armenian; there were two Protestant and Roman Catholic each, two mosques, several temples, and various monasteries.

The Suttners could not make friends with the Roman church's claim to be the one and only redeeming church—as it was held to be in Austria-Hungary, at least. They were freethinkers, filled with respect for all religions. Sometime during this period, Arthur became a member of the Order of Freemasons.[31]

In the battle between church and science, carried out at the time by unreconcilable opponents, the Suttners clearly took the side of science and "truth" against "metaphysics" and were for the provable versus the impalpable.

They were also firmly planted in the liberal political camp, not only in regard to constitutional issues and the necessity for further democratization. Although they were aristocrats, they upheld the bourgeois virtues: achievement, education, and competence. They thought that "Both kings and peasants will have to become members of the middle class in order to be likable, in order to work for progress."[32]

In August of 1882 Princess Ekaterina of Mingrelia died in Gordi. She was buried with great pomp in the old crypt in the Marthwili Monastery. Bertha mourned her deeply. The "Dedopali" had been a last refuge, since there was little contact with the younger generation of the family.

The Suttners left Mingrelia and moved to Tbilisi, 350 kilometers away. At the time, this capital of Georgia had a hundred thousand inhabitants of various nationalities. "Tbilisi is a half oriental, half western European city. In the European quarter, the same kind of life goes on as in our big cities. European dress, European customs, French cooks, English governesses, *jours, soirèes,* conversation in Russian and French."[33]

Arthur found a job working for the owner of a French wallcovering factory and construction company. For 150 rubles a month, Arthur kept the books and drew wallpaper designs and later even construction plans. "I can't understand to this day how he managed to do it," Bertha wrote proudly. A number of houses in the Tbilisi area were actually built to Arthur's plans.

Arthur, "who was so pampered at home and lazy to a vice," had to get up at five in the morning. While he worked in the factory, Bertha gave lessons. Starting at six in the evening, however, they became members of high society, dressed up and went to elegant places where they were invited, at least at the beginning of their stay in Tbilisi.

"They knew our novel, they also knew about our close relationship to the Dadiani family, and in their world we were not treated as factory employee and music teacher, but as a kind of aristocratic emigrant, not only on the basis of equality, but with the special courtesy that was customarily extended to illustrious strangers."[34]

How long this "special courtesy" lasted, we do not know. In any case the Suttners remained extremely poor, and the genteel invitations soon lost their appeal. "We accepted the invitations so that we would not grow completely wild, to get connections; we went out into the world for all sorts of reasons, but certainly not in search of pleasure."[35]

One handicap was and always had been the language, since they spoke just as little Georgian as they had Mingrelian in Zugdidi. And there were still difficulties with Russian. Besides, the Russians in Tbilisi were mostly military people and civil servants, and as such did not interest the Suttners.

Astonishingly enough, they also took very little notice of Georgian and Russian literature. Aside from the Russian newspaper, *Westnik Ewropy,* they mostly read French and German publications which they borrowed from the English consul or one of their Swedish friends.

Their writing ambitions grew. Now Bertha wanted to write more than her shallow love stories. She wanted to progress, to learn at and for writing and to profit for herself and her education. In a self-portrait that she sent in to the *Neue Illustrirte Zeitung* in 1884 she professes, "One thing only has become clear to me: that in taking up the writing profession, I have to live up to the difficult task, to go forward incessantly, to expand my scope of thought, in short—despite my mature age—to learn, to learn, to learn."[36] The fact that she succeeded is demonstrated by the increasing variety and improving quality of her writing and by the more demanding themes she treats in her books, in contrast to Arthur's many novels that continued to be limited to Caucasian themes.

Bertha delved intently into the modern literature of realism, especially Zola's works. And at least her essay on the purpose of art in modern times ("Truth and Lies") was given a prominent place by the Munich author, Michael Georg Conrad, in his new magazine, *Die Gesellschaft,* "a realistic weekly publication for literature, art, and public life." In her article, Bertha criticized "old" art as the art of the lie.

For the Suttner couple, truthfulness that did not hide ugliness also became a criterion for the new art, realism their new ideal. "There is only one supreme principle of morality . . . and that is: truth. All honor and honesty rest upon adherence to what is true."[37]

At the beginning of the 1880s Bertha began writing her ambitious book the *Inventory of a Soul* (Inventarium einer Seele), in which she deals with her own weltanschauung and quotes her great teachers, especially Buckle and Spencer, as one would in a philosophical work. In this inventory of her own soul she states that the basic principles of her life and her work are: "a steadfast, cheerful belief in progress. Absolute rejection of fatalism. It is clear to me that if I pass by a powder keg while smoking, I can put out the burning pipe or throw it into the keg, and this—not irreversible predetermination—is what the prevention or cause of an explosion depends upon."[38]

She extolled progress in endless raptures: "No matter where I look, everywhere, I see it confirmed, this marvelous principle. I see it in my garden where the scent-laden *malmaison* developed from the wild Scotch rose; I see it in my classics, in whose works the first babbles of human speech have grown to poetic majesty; I see it in the heavens where the cosmic mists concentrate themselves into suns. The eternal becoming is simultaneously an eternal ennobling: the striving toward expansion, toward embellishment, toward perfection is a vital force inherent in all things."

She compared progress with the suffering "of ruthless ancient times," when "our poor ancestors lived in mud huts, with an incoherent intellect, undeveloped mind, knowing no greater joy than that of delivering a blow to an enemy's skull with a club."[39]

Bertha's involvement with the problem of war and peace grew out of this ideology of progress. Already in *Inventory of a Soul* she put forth the demand for disarmament as the natural consequence of general progress.

She argued against the attitude that war lay in the nature of mankind. "That is a simple confusion of terms—the law is battle, not war." And fighting battles was not only possible with cannons, but also with the

> weapons of the intellect, of beauty, of skill, of any kind of ennoblement at all. And this way one can very easily imagine the battle of increasingly stabilizing mankind against barbarism through the course of time: a gradual extermination of the tribes that wage war by peaceful nations; an extinction of hatred among nations through the spread of cosmopolitan ideas; a reduction of military honors in the face of the growing glory of knowledge and the arts; a union of world interests growing into a closer and closer brotherhood as opposed to trivial, dwindling special interests; and in this manner the lawful eternal battle can and will achieve eternal peace.[40]

No one would need war anymore to achieve glory. "Fighting the elements, which frequently confront us as enemies, fighting sickness and suffering also demand their heroes. Blasting mountains, building dams, extinguishing fires, visiting hospitals, healing, helping—these are not cowardly deeds. There is enough to fight against anyway, without hitting about on command. Illnesses, floods, avalanches, misery, insanity, wild animals—and wild people, those are all enemies, against whom, fighting can satisfy quite a lot of the lust for battle."[41]

"In technology, art, science, charity, everywhere, more beautiful goals than those on the battlefield beckon to ambition. I would rather be named Edison than Hannibal, Peabody rather than Radetzky, rather Newton than Wellington."[42]

According to Buckle, humanity's future peace was to be the "arithmetic result of mathematically arranged facts," and Bertha concluded from this that peace was a condition "that would necessarily result from the progress of culture."[43]

There were different theories on how the goal of peace could be achieved. Leaning on Buckle's theses, Bertha thought that "apparently unconnected motives in the interests of peace" would advance peace more than justice and gentleness; for instance, the discovery of an efficient gunpowder. "And it can be hoped that someday the discovery of increasingly powerful instruments of destruction, which would finally, by way of—who knows—an electrodynamic or magnetic explosive device, be able to destroy entire armies at once, and thus eliminate the whole strategy and make waging war totally impossible."[44]

This passage clearly shows the influence of Alfred Nobel. And of course, Bertha sent him a copy of her book. A warm letter of thanks showed her that Nobel had retained his friendship. "I am still completely under the spell of your wonderful book. What style and what philosophical ideas, borne on profound feeling! . . . Along with my respectful homage, also accept my deep devotion, inspired by an unerased and unerasable recollection and admiration."[45]

The *Inventory,* published in 1883 in Leipzig, reaped some excellent reviews, but no money. It was easier to earn money with serial novels than with philosophical books that did not even satisfy the highest philosophical and artistic demands by any means.

The Suttners tried everything in their power to build up their connections with authors in western Europe. In their letters they introduced themselves as cowriters, chatted a little about their lives, and more important, expressed their appreciation—usually in a rather original manner—for the work of the other. Almost all of the writers they wrote to answered. A longer period of correspondence resulted with some, such as with Friedrich Bodenstedt, who had spent several years in the Caucasus himself, Robert Hamerling, and Conrad Ferdinand Meyer.

Especially important were the connections with writers who were also editors. Of course, the Suttners wrote these letters partly because they were able to generate enthusiasm and partly for intellectual contact, which they needed so badly in their Caucasian isolation. But most of all, they needed connections that would help them publish their work.

In 1882, still living in the Caucasus, they joined the German Writers Association in Berlin and eagerly read all the information about their colleagues in Europe in the association's magazine. Then they planned their return to Europe. For their last project in the Caucasus they worked on translating the Georgian national epic, *The Knight in the Tiger's Skin,* by Shota Rustaveli, into French and German. The idea apparently came from Arthur's friend Meunargia, whose mastery of French was severely deficient and whose German was nonexistent. They agreed that Meunargia would translate the Georgian verses into French literally, and the Suttners would then put them into poetic French and German. Jean Mourir, another friend of Arthur's, helped, and the Hungarian artist Count Michai Zichy, who was living in Tbilisi at the time, supplied the illustrations.

The project was announced in a big way. Arthur wrote a six-part series on Rustaveli and the planned translations for the Georgian newspaper *Droeba* and an article on the same theme, almost forty pages long, for the Russian *Iveria*. According to modern Rustaveli specialists, Arthur's works are still very valuable today and are one of the first appraisals of the Georgian poet by a European.[46] Arthur showed great intuitive understanding of Georgian history and literature.

Bertha writes about the translation work: "It opened up a completely vanished world—the world of the thirteenth century in this distant corner of the earth. An epoch the Georgians are proud to look back upon because it was the golden age of their land—the epoch when the great Queen Tamra reigned."[47]

Bertha's mother died in solitude in Görz in 1884 while this work was going on. Bertha dedicated the novel *A Manuscript,* which appeared in Leipzig that same year, to her. In it a mother writes to her daughter who has married and gone to live in a foreign country, and Bertha clearly shows her guilty conscience. "Only someone left behind knows the real sorrow of separation. When the hour of tearing away is over, the person who strikes out on the journey knows nothing of the isolation, the desolation of the other." Bertha praised her relationship with her mother as being "so sisterly and intimate, at the same time almost passionate, and so absolutely trusting."[48]

The estate had to be settled, and it turned out that there was nothing to inherit but debts. The promissory notes she signed and the interest due on them were a burden to the couple for decades. Ten years later they still had 2,400 gulden of debts incurred by Sophie Kinsky to pay.[49] The death of her mother made Bertha's homesickness greater.

The translations took longer than expected. As usual, the biggest problem was money: they could not find a publisher. Meunargia asked the French writer, Ernest Renan, to mediate, but Renan got out of it by answering that he did not know enough about Georgian literature.[50] Bertha wrote Friedrich Bodenstedt about the German translation. He, at least, would be capable of judging Rustaveli's importance accurately. He sent Bertha his best wishes for the project but offered no help in looking for a publisher.

Zichy, who had finished his drawings in the meanwhile, was pushing for publication. In December of 1884 Meunargia wrote the literary specialist Niko Nikoladse, who was also impatient, that they still needed two to three months. He said he wanted to retire to his country house in Zaischi (near Zugdidi) for Christmas to work undisturbed together with Arthur (and of course Bertha, whom he did not mention but whose French was the best of the three).[51]

But as industrious as they were, the undertaking proved to be impracticable. Translating a highly complicated poetic text by these methods was simply not possible.

Bertha and Arthur had spent many months on this work without any kind of remuneration, and now they did not know how to meet their living expenses. Apparently, they had been living all these months in Meunargia's house—and at his expense.

In the hope that a fee of 440 francs mailed from Stuttgart had arrived, they made a trip to Batum in the middle of March. From there they wrote Meunargia an urgent letter on March 23 asking for money. Their fee had not arrived; they were stranded because they did not have the price of a ticket back.[52] There is no doubt that they were in a desperate situation at this point, and Bertha's relationship with Meunargia was, for one reason or another, already tense.

On top of it all, chaotic news came from the Balkans: Prince Alexander, who had succeeded to the Bulgarian throne with the help of Austria, had been driven out of the country. The Russians took over power in Bulgaria. War threatened to break out between Austria-Hungary and Russia. The anti-Austrian mood in the reports that came mostly from Russia, increased the worries of the homesick Suttners. They were afraid they would be regarded as enemy aliens. The situation appeared untenable.

Now, after so many years of what had often been desperate attempts to make a living in Georgia, they gave up and broke tent in frantic haste. There was not much to pack anyway, a few Caucasian carpets and weapons that had been hung above the sofa for decoration according to the practice in the Caucasus, a few souvenirs that the Suttners would later proudly display in their "Caucasian Room," and most important, their crates of books.

By this time Bertha was forty-two and Arthur thirty-five years old. They had written a number of books and made a name for themselves in literature. They had not acquired the fortune or the position at court they had hoped for, but they had gained a healthy self-assurance which they now displayed. "The parents who now realized how loyally and happily we held together, how bravely we fended for ourselves without asking for their help, gave up their stubborn rancor and invited us to Harmannsdorf. We had meanwhile achieved an independent position in life and could therefore go back home without humiliation."

We learn about the journey home from Bertha's article for the *Neue Illustrirte Zeitung.* "It was a marvelous spring afternoon when we boarded ship. The Vice Governor of Batum, Prince E. and his wife, who had given us a farewell dinner, accompanied us on board, where many other of our Caucasian friends had also gathered to wish us a happy journey. For us this journey is 'happy' in the truest sense of the word—

you can imagine: after so many years of absence to finally be heading for our own country—for home!"

The trip across the Black Sea from Batum to Odessa aboard the Russian steamboat *General Kotzebue,* with stops in all the small harbors, lasted five days. They visited Yalta, the "Russian Nice," and Sebastopol, which still showed traces of devastating battles thirty years after the bloody siege by French and English troops in the Crimean War. "Sebastopol, although long since reconstructed, still looks sad with its bombed barracks standing there like a landmark, the big cemetery lying within sight, where bones of the French, English, and Russian soldiers who fell here rot by the thousands."

Then they made a stop in Kerch, the former capital of the Pontic Kingdom where the tomb of Mithridates is located. Bertha's commentary on the importance of the ruler who was given the epithet, "the Great": "Oh, yes, 'the Great'—after all, he conquered Roman Asia Minor where he had all the Romans, some 80,000 in number, murdered. That is the standard by which the greatness of a king was measured in ancient history: the murdered masses, the enslaved peoples, the ravaged lands, and burned cities; and the amount of praise and honor bestowed upon the conquerors was equal to the amount of fear and terror they generated." How close Bertha had meanwhile come to the Tolstoyan idea of peace without even having been influenced by him, is revealed in these sentences.

In the report on her journey, she describes the passengers on board in caricatures, and she includes the people first-class passengers usually overlook. "It is cold and rainy outside; in the salon for tea and grog, cards and 'flirtation,' it is rather cheerful. On the deck where third-class passengers—families of Greek emigrants, poor monks, soldiers, and country folk—have to hold out through the dark, cold night, crowded together, many a sigh probably mixes with the cold wind and gives expression to the quiet complaint that life is hard to bear."[53]

The very difficult years in Caucasia had awakened Bertha's social awareness. She had come a long way from the life of a young aristocrat in Vienna. She knew now that it was not merely the occasional individual "who lived in want. The occasional ones were rather those who were able to lead what we think is a dignified existence," and that did not apply only to Russia.[54]

Despite all the deprivations, the nine years in the Caucasus were a "High School of Happiness" for Bertha, as she writes in retrospect. And because she had been so happy, she felt she had a responsibility to help those who were not. "Then through such happiness—namely, where it rests upon deep, devoted love—you turn gentle and mild. You cannot bear the thought of pain, of want, of violent death afflicting another, because you always involuntarily imagine your own beloved being among these 'others.'"[55]

During the Balkan crisis of the next few years, in which Russia was always the enemy of Austria-Hungary, Bertha stood up against a denunciation of the Russian people as Austria's archenemy. "They don't *know* each other. Imagining the Russian people as a warmongering folk is a complete mistake. On the contrary, they are one of the most peaceful, best-tempered people there are."[56]

4

The Writer's Life

Bertha and Arthur returned to Austria in 1885 as established writers. They settled down in the Suttner house in Harmannsdorf in the Waldviertel region north of Vienna—and had to get used to life in a big family after knowing only a cozy twosomeness completely isolated from their surroundings.

Arthur's parents and two unmarried sisters lived in Harmannsdorf. The four married brothers and sisters also came for frequent visits with their sizable families. The Suttner lifestyle was more modest than it had been at the time when Bertha was still a governess in the house, but even a relatively small castle needs servants. A large number of people lived together there. There was a big kitchen, there were common meals, common leisure activities, in short, a common life. Everybody knew practically everything about everybody else.

In her memoirs, Bertha saw her life in Harmannsdorf in a positive light. "The homey and companionable life left nothing to be desired in respect to coziness and liveliness," she writes, albeit with the important addition, "Nevertheless, we rescued many hours for working together alone. We continued with our academic studies, always read the same books together, and also wrote together."[1]

A visitor described their study: "The great high-ceilinged room with high, gabled windows. The furnishings are not inherited, they are the result of lived experiences and every little thing is a story in itself. The Tbilisi decade the writing couple went through gives this quiet corner of great creativity its main character." The two desks pushed together in front of the window are also mentioned: "*One* lamp symbolically illuminates both places of work. . . . And next to the desk is the library. Not numerous . . . but select. Buckle, Darwin, Marx, Bebel, the whole spectrum of the rainbow in this intellectual direction."[2]

Their writing was definitely not merely a hobby for well-to-do coun-try aristocrats. It was just as necessary as ever since the couple's earnings were badly needed as supplementary income. The Suttner quarries were making bigger losses than ever. "They changed managers, changed direc-tors, they negotiated with agents about companies—but nothing got better. Just the opposite, the business deals they planned led them to false hopes and made them take risks. When these later fell through, everyone was a bit worse off, but then they pounced upon the next hope-ful situation all the more gullibly. And—there was a touch of recklessness in the entire Suttner family—they shrugged off their worries and took the good things the day had to offer."[3]

In addition to the congeniality, there was also a lot of quarreling in the big family about the lack of money, about religious beliefs ("The grandparents are what you'd call feudally pious," the Suttners wrote to a friend.[4]), about politics, about the question of war and peace, and many other issues. Bertha complained that "[I] find myself in a circle of terribly unmodern people. . . . If the two of us . . . did not have each other—we would *suffocate*."[5]

The castle was secluded. The little town of Eggenburg was an hour away by carriage, three-and-a-half on foot. The train to Vienna left from Eggenburg. The long winters in this rather chilly place, cut off from the outside world, were especially hard to endure. Arthur's aged parents be-came a bit odd. "The parents . . . somewhat spooky in their manner-isms."[6] And soon the objection, "And life here is really *boring*. I've never known boredom so easily before, but this family life offers quite a share."[7]

Only a year after their return from the Caucasus, Arthur asked a friend for advice on how to get Swiss citizenship. Apparently they wanted to emigrate, a topic Bertha did not mention in her memoirs. But the plan fell through.[8]

In spite of all its problems, Harmannsdorf did offer them a home. So they remained but swore to themselves and their friends "the fact that the circles we now move in do not exactly sympathize with our ideas will not keep us from holding on to the truth outspokenly."[9]

They remained anticlerical and freethinking in a piously Catholic mi-lieu, progressive and liberal in an archconservative environment. And they continued to be interested in social issues, although the very men-tion of the workers' problem was "a blasphemous intervention in the divine order of things."[10]

Both Suttners were to be liberals for the rest of their lives. Arthur never did formally join any of the liberal parties. Bertha, as a woman, was prohibited from taking this step anyway.

The party spirit is pitifully restricted everywhere, and although everyone pretends to demand the common best, the welfare of all, everyone is still more or less intent on preserving their own or the state's interests, and even the individual person who is really enthusiastic about the interests of all in common, lacks the possibilities for being effective within today's political structure; he wastes all of his energy fighting the special interests that work against him; his views and goals are incomprehensible to his opponents, and they accuse him of having the same motives they themselves nurture.

Under these conditions, it is impossible to achieve the high ideal of social progress. "As long as politicians carry on feuds with each other instead of working together toward a clearly recognized goal; as long as cleverness used for personal means is considered statesmanship, the representatives of the people will not achieve anything beneficial to the people."

Of course, the household in Harmannsdorf was not interested in either liberalism or literature. Bertha complains about this sometimes in her diary, but she also consoles herself:

It is not hard for me to do without the sympathy of the other members of the household. In fact I prefer for them to ignore my work entirely, far better than if they—from their point of view which is so utterly opposed to mine—wanted to enlighten me with opinions, advice, questions and conclusions. Literature is a field that is stranger to them than the crater landscape on the moon. They have no idea that a contemporary body of writing exists that is imbued with the modern spirit. They concede the fact that Homer was a great poet, that Shakespeare possessed genius and that there are admirable German classical writers who are worth reading—even though they have not read them themselves. Beyond that, one might look at a serial novel printed in the feuilleton section of a newspaper now and then, but these are supplied by the writer to satisfy the general drive to kill time, in the same manner that bread is supplied by a baker to still hunger. . . . But the fact that there are people who create books and other people who read these books and who welcome the expression of the zeitgeist in them, the motor of progress—that's all extremely far-fetched to them.[11]

Now that Bertha had gained distance by living abroad, the way of life and weltanschauung in this extremely conservative aristocratic circle interested her so intensely that she made it the theme of her next novel. In *High Life* she gives a critical description of the way the Austrian aristocracy lived and gets some of her anger off her chest.

> In the atmosphere here, there reigns a blessed ignorance of all of the things that motivate our century. The development that social science is beginning to make is being placed among the list of crimes in the category of "socialism," and it is taken for granted that a few special laws will take care of the matter. . . . To want to change the world—what blasphemy! A world that is so beautiful, so orderly, so harmonious, so blessed by tradition and led by Providence! And virtuous! Aren't we—we, the representatives of the status quo—aren't we brimming over with virtue? Loyalty, piety, bravery, the spirit of sacrifice, patriotism: we know all about that . . . so leave us in peace with your eternal cravings for change and your accusations.[12]

Mercilessly, she criticizes the mistakes and the undeserved privileges of this class, the representatives of the older generation that divided the great offices of the monarchy among themselves and the representatives of the younger generation, "the lieutenants of the cavalry, members of the jockey club, patrons of the ballet and sportsmen," who, "thank God, think about things that are more fun than political and social theories are. Of course, they are also conservative, since who would not want to conserve such a beautifully privileged life?"

And then she comes to the conclusion: "The aristocracy in Austria still assumes a highly privileged position indeed, as far as the prestige it enjoys among the lower classes is concerned, and the homage it pays to itself. I found the English aristocracy proud, the French vain—but the Austrian is arrogant."[13]

In the novel, the representative of the modern day is an American, and for him the "pomp of crowns and tiaras" is "like an oriental costume play."[14]

Bertha also condemns the big military maneuvers the Emperor himself so admired as an "ugly comedy," in which

> princes and generals . . . high to horse, under fluttering plumes of feathers, with golden braid, with moirè sashes, decorated with thickly strewn Grand Crosses . . . have the various machines and machinists of destruction file by in front of them. That is only the dress rehearsal for the play; but it is easy to imagine just how the real event would go, if one's imagination added flowing blood, the scream of pain through the rattle of death, skulls bashed in by hooves, swelling intestines, the dying in the ditches, parched with thirst, and the living buried in the ditches.

The festive day of maneuvers is closed in "brotherly friendship" with "a dinner in the company of sweet princesses."[15]

These quotations also show how Bertha saw her position as a writer. She wanted to be "modern" and at the time, that meant writing in a realistic style without the "old fashioned" concern for subjects taken from antiquity. For her a modern writer was one "who abandons the well worn paths of school, who does not draw from books and create them over again to write anew what has already been read, and instead studies *life* itself in order to capture on paper the moods, the details, the impressions as they arise from it, still fresh and alive, drenched with reality."[16]

In order to remain true to this ideal she could write only about things she knew through and through: about life and living conditions among the Austrian landed gentry from "master" to servant. For us today, Bertha's detailed, realistic accounts are an important source of everyday life led by the Austrian nobility in the nineteenth century and are a treasure trove for sociologists.

Her novels also contain enormous amounts of authentic autobiographical material since she did not convert her problems into coded "modern" literature. When she wrote her memoirs later on, she was able to draw her own quotations from her diary and her novels alike: both were life as it had been lived.

The ideals of literary realism required that a work be true to life and be honest, qualities that Bertha supported especially in her *Schriftsteller-Roman* (Writer's novel). In modern literature there is a

> longing for liberation. Liberation from the set pattern, from aesthetic hypocrisy, from spinsterly prudishness, from routine and the lie. Claim is laid to the right to write boldly and truthfully. One wants to speak to an audience of men or highly rational women, not to a knitting society of squeamish aunts or the upper classes of a girls' school. One does not want to produce only for the Romans and Egyptians, only for the traditional Italy-traveled painters and "presidents" of a "small residence" but to people one knows and sees; who live in Vienna, in Berlin or Munich, who speak and feel as you and I, who make mistakes and hesitate and are not paragons of virtue.[17]

The great model of literary realism was Emile Zola. And it was none other than Zola's books Arthur's mother found in the house that caused her to stage an auto-da-fé. She burned all of them—merely one example of the family conflict.[18]

Suttner did not think very much of the aestheticism of the late nineteenth century and certainly less of "*l'art pour l'art.*" Her ambition was to enlighten with her books, to teach, to start something rolling and not just to enjoy the beauty of art. "Do you really believe," she has a character say, "that an author has done enough when he has pleased—for instance, with a successful stage set or a pretty lady's gown at a ball? He should fill a need, elevate, make someone happy—he should serve truth, justice, and beauty, vanquish prejudices that restrict joy, help destroy superstition and darkness."[19]

She freely admitted to one colleague "that novels offered a better chance to smuggle in one's ideas."[20] This all hints at her heading toward the novel with a purpose: the kind of novel by which the American, Harriet Beecher Stowe, set such a successful example with her antislavery book, *Uncle Tom's Cabin*.

Just at the time when there was so much talk of "genius" in Vienna's artistic life, Bertha von Suttner kept her feet on the more solid ground of craftsmanship. She had a low opinion of the Bohemian life that produced brilliant ideas from time to time and preferred a disciplined schedule, working regularly several hours every day. In the *Writer's Novel*, she countered the argument that "art is not a craft, one cannot deliver a certain amount of 'masterpiece' every day on demand," with the answer, "One can take great pains to do one's best during this time. *Nulla dies sine linea* (no day without a line) was Victor Hugo's motto, and he wrote mountains of masterpieces. Writing little does not, by any means, speak for the excellence of the writer. Of course there are people without talent who write a great deal, but there are more lazy dilettantes who have never gotten beyond two or three worthless volumes, and some who never got further than their first work."[21]

One thing was clear. Even though Arthur had to spend part of his time now taking care of the estate, they still wanted to return to their earlier lifestyle. They wanted to be writers and felt the need to take up contacts with others who thought as they did.

They got to know personally several of the people they had corresponded with for many years and were able to deepen these friendships. Bertha contacted others, such as the philosopher and liberal politician Bartolomeus von Carneri, through the letters of homage that had already proved so effective in Caucasia. Carneri answered with compliments for Bertha's *Inventory of a Soul*. Between these two very different people (Bertha was forty-six years old, Carneri an almost seventy-year-old widower, crippled and ailing) a deep friendship developed that was reflected in a very extensive exchange of letters.

For the next ten years, Carneri stood by Bertha as an incorruptibly critical but lovingly admiring friend who made a number of important decisions in her life easier. Whenever he was in Vienna for a session of parliament as the representative from Styria, "a circle of parliamentarians" gathered around him at the Meissl und Schaden hotel, and the Suttners joined them. This resulted in growing contacts with the liberal members of parliament, who would soon be such a big help to Bertha in the organization of the Inter-Parliamentarian Union.

Count Rudolf Hoyos also became a close friend. He was a man who had little sympathy with the members of his class and devoted himself entirely to his belletristic interests, wrote poems, and was an extreme anticlerical liberal and democrat. The Suttners liked that.

The friends, Rudolf Hoyos and Balduin Goller, also wrote for the *Illustrirte österreichische Volkskalender* (Popular illustrated Austrian calendar), which Bertha edited in connection with the *Volksbuch zur Unterhaltung und Belehrung* (Popular book for entertainment and instruction). In this very traditional, even old-fashioned type of folk literature she published rather undemanding novellas of her own and her friends, embellished with pleasant illustrations. With this work, she acquired organizational skills in running a magazine that would soon be very useful to her.

In October 1885 the Suttners went to Berlin to the congress of the German Writers Association. Bertha writes about her first impressions in her memoirs, quoting her *Writer's Novel:*

> Whenever a name is mentioned which has a great sound in literature, it moves me with the same joy that comes when the winning number is called out in a raffle. Only there's one thing that can be a bitter disappointment: sometimes their appearance does not suit the picture you've created in your own mind of the particular author. . . . What, these perfumed love-songs, these rapturous fantasies were penned by that brutal-looking fat man? And those sophisticated elegant images of the fashionable world were written by this awkward, ordinary little man? What—those essays, dripping with experience and wisdom were written by the youth over there with the downy beard who looks like a grocery store attendant?[22]

It was the first club meeting the Suttners attended. "Suddenly an understanding opened up to me for something that is certain to take on greater dimensions for mankind of the future—namely, the awareness of solidarity. That is an awareness that has a stronger effect than the commandment 'Love thy neighbor as thyself.' For true solidarity is identical with oneself from the very outset."[23]

The fact that club life as practiced in the Writers Association was also far removed from this ideal was something Bertha learned painfully. She was astonished and angry when she found out that nothing was being done here to improve the life of the writer. Instead there were endless discussions about principles, statutes, and membership dues; and finally it was decided to abolish the club publication, that very magazine the Suttners had always longingly awaited in the Caucasus and which was for them an important connection to the German-language literary world. "The whole thing disappointed me terribly. I had hoped that we would come from these discussions enriched—and I feel I have grown poorer."[24]

Even the reduction of the membership dues from fifteen to ten marks brought no consolation, especially in view of the reason behind the decision. It was thought that lowering the dues would bring in more members. "And there you have my third loss: the loss of the illusion that we are proud of our qualitative greatness, and meanwhile it seems increasing the quantity is the main objective. In the Académie Française there are only forty members at any one time—and that's enough for them. . . . Adding *one* great name does more for our image than winning hundreds of little ones."[25] In Bertha's opinion, an organization of writers ought to try to get proper remuneration for capable authors instead of bothering with people who call themselves writers but do not achieve enough. The Writers Association should not be a "charity institution for incompetent scribblers."[26]

Bertha knew very well that in expressing this opinion she was bargaining for accusations of being unsocial.

> I answered that if there was ever a group of people who had the right to aristocratic exclusivity it was this organization of writers, which does in fact belong to the finest and most promising aristocracy, namely, that of the intellect. . . . Anyone with no talent should not be called a writer at all; the mere act of taking up a pen does not automatically bestow a claim to the title of author, just as using a paintbrush does not make anyone a painter. An organization of artists would take care not to welcome all the house painters in the country into their midst, and it would not come closer to the ideals and material goals of painting in the least, if the various artists' collectives were to be converted into provident funds for jobless house painters.[27]

Apparently Bertha, in her isolation in the Caucasus, had created an all too idealistic notion of the writer's status. Now she was often disappointed when she met cowriters in the editorial offices of Vienna and at the congress in Berlin who did not fit into this elevated picture.

Her attempts to modernize the German Writers Association soon failed. In 1895 she and Arthur finally cancelled their membership.[28] A short time later they founded the "Austrian Literary Society" in Vienna, and its first publication was Bertha's novel, *Vor dem Gewitter* (Before the storm). "Over champagne, a great future was prophesied for the undertaking, but—Austria is not fertile soil for literary foundings—only a few years later the thing disbanded."[29]

After a series of more or less important attempts at novels, Bertha tried her hand again at a more demanding book, *Das Maschinenzeitalter* (The machine age). Writing it "was a great joy. . . . In it, I shook off all the grudges and suffering over present-day conditions and the embers of hope for the promising future that had gathered in my soul."[30]

She gave the book the subtitle, "Lectures for the future about our day." She placed her nine lectures in the future and described from that point of view the period of 1885–86 with all its backwardness in various fields. Behind the deplorable state of affairs, however, she sought out the signs of better worlds and for this she used the analogy of "autumn leaves in April." In April the trees are still full of withered leaves, but the young shoots are already pressing for growth. It is a transitional period in nature: "Also in history: the epoch our course is concerned with was an April of autumn leaves. . . . [I]f we look at the outmoded customs, laws, attitudes that were spread all over Europe at the time, and the way their yellow plenty covered all the shy green sprouts, then let us think—autumn leaves in April!"[31]

She was especially harsh in judging the nationalism of the 1880s that passed itself off as "patriotism." "For at that time patriotism was considered the noblest of all virtues; ethnic altruism was still unknown. Placing the national ego above everything else, to praise it to the point of idolization, to elevate it by belittling, despising and—when necessary—destroying the national neighbor, was the citizen's primary duty. . . . Not yet mature was the realization that ethnic altruisim represented a great advancement over national egoism, just as neighborly love among individuals is far superior to individual self-interest."[32]

Suttner argued fiercely against what she thought was a totally outmoded school system. Students' desire for knowledge was being restricted rather than encouraged and was, moreover, being exhausted by too much knowledge that had long been obsolete, "and their childhood and youth soon became the most tormented and agonizing time of their lives: the overexertion brought on hundreds of physical and intellectual defects—bent backs, weak lungs, short-sighted eyes, dull brains—we shudder at this calamity!"[33]

She settles accounts harshly with the way history was taught: "If you look at the historical gossip which tells of insignificant events, empty sayings, all the love, marriage, and murder stories, then it is no better than the gossip of old wives' coffee klatches."[34]

More than anything, however, she criticized sexual prudery:

> With the utmost severity, they made certain that young people would not find out anything about the workings of nature that precede the reproduction of life, and least of all the occurrence of blissful feelings connected with them;—but of the many ways life is destroyed amidst agony and pain, about that, they could not say enough, and no detail of the wanton gratification of cruelty was too sophisticated not to be allowed to embellish the reports of prehistoric battles. That immorality lay hidden *herein,* one that was certainly more dehumanizing than the eroticism despised as "animal-like," was an idea that this period in time was not aware of. Everything that belonged to sexual life was declared undignified—as though it had come from pigs—but one overlooked the fact that the acts of pure bloodthirstiness are actually more befitting wild animals of prey.[35]

She underlined her accusations with examples of brutality taken from history books.

In this same style, she continued her accusations against outmoded governmental institutions, against discrimination directed at women (see chapter 13), against the church, and more. And she spoke up for freedom and truth.

After the manuscript was finished, the Suttners decided to use the fee to finance a winter in Paris. Of course, Bertha announced her arrival to Alfred Nobel, who wrote, "How happy I am to know you are happy and satisfied, returned to a country you love, all your battles behind you, the extent of which my affection can very well imagine. What should I say about myself—a shipwreck of youth, of joy, of hope? An empty soul whose contents are a blank page—or a gray one."[36]

There was no doubt Alfred Nobel was unhappier and more melancholy than ever, despite his success, and Bertha wanted to see him again. Eleven years had passed since those eventful days when Nobel and Countess Kinsky had made friends and separated. Now Bertha brought her husband with her to see Nobel on Avenue de Malakoff. "I found him unchanged, only somewhat gray, but more deeply engaged in his work and inventions than ever."[37]

Although Nobel was very unpretentious himself, nothing could stop him from pampering his guests. Bertha went into raptures over the "exquisite dinner." "For example, fruits straight from Africa—with names I'd never heard of before and the rarest vintages of Château Yquem and Johannisberg to go with them—he only drank a little 'reddened water' himself."

They gazed in wonder at the palace interiors, the green reception hall with malachite furniture, the red music room, and especially Nobel's study: "The bookcases were filled exclusively with the works of philosophers and poets. Byron's complete works had a place of honor; he could recite whole pages of this, his favorite, poet from memory." Conversation with Nobel was "a great intellectual delight."

"He did not receive many people and went out into the world only rarely, this diligent, somewhat antisocial man. He detested vacuous salon babble—in fact, his great love for the ideal humanity in the abstract was mixed with a great deal of contempt, bitterness, and distrust against real people in general. Certain forms of shallowness, of superstition, of frivolity filled him with downright angry disgust. His books, his studies, his experiments: that was his life."[38]

Nobel introduced them into the famous salon of Juliette Adam. She was the publisher of the important literary magazine *La Nouvelle Revue* and as such was "a little potentate." "Young talents force themselves upon her," wrote Bertha. "Anyone who succeeds in reading a manuscript in her circle achieves a kind of name for himself from this alone."

Bertha, who placed great value on elegant clothes, noted with pleasure that Adam was one of the best-dressed women in Paris, "a feature which is very highly regarded there and which benefits a woman author especially, since bluestockings have a reputation for dispensing with feminine charm."[39]

Adam's active political interest, however, irritated Bertha. "How can a woman concern herself with politics so much, I thought at the time. How much trouble and sometimes even ridicule she brings upon herself by it! And how can anyone torture herself with bringing out a revue to boot!"[40]

The special feature of this salon consisted in its being "both a political and a worldly salon at the same time. . . . Leading statesmen meet there and discuss the fate of the republic." Since the hostess was an ardent patriot and revanchist, the talk was mostly of French retaliation for the defeat at the hand of Germany in 1870–71.

At the end of the 1880s, not only the French, but other peoples of Europe all believed that a German-French war would break out soon. Bertha, on the discussions at the Adam house, wrote: "That was a lot of political twaddle! Everywhere you went there was the question: will it take place? In the newspapers and even more in the air there was the expectation of some kind of a great happening."

The intellectual brilliance of the society that came together at Juliette Adam's salon was not able to blind Bertha. She reacted with considerable distance to the rhapsodic patriotism that broke out in this gathering. "Prophecies that something was bound to happen next spring were pronounced with confidence, a situation that in no way detracted from the cheerful mood and probably even aroused lovely hopes in the housewife burning for the glory of her fatherland. I was no longer so unresponsive to these things as I had been in my youth. I already hated war with a passion—and this frivolous dallying with its possibilities appeared to me to be unscrupulous and uncritical."[41]

The Suttners also gained entry to the salon of the Buloz family. It was a meeting place for people who worked for the renowned monthly magazine *Revue de deux mondes,* "this ancestress of all revues," which, considering its ambitious presentation, had an extremely high circulation of twenty-five thousand copies and had made its owner, Buloz, wealthy. Among the guests of this salon were numerous members of the Académie Française. As a result the mood here was less political than academic—stiff, puristic, learned. "The same tenor that wafts through the pages (that so frequently remained uncut) of the treatises in the old revue."[42]

It was painful for Bertha in Paris to realize how poor Vienna's intellectual life was. There was not a single big salon in Vienna anymore that could compare with the salons of Paris. It became one of Bertha's unfulfilled dreams to possess so much money that she could have a truly great salon of her own in Vienna.

She thought the barriers lay in the deep, and as it seemed to her, unsurmountable chasm separating the aristocracy and the intellectual elite. In one of her novels she has an aristocratic woman complain about these problems:

> Our usual society would have been very unpleasantly surprised to see nonaristocrats here and would not have found the proper manner for dealing with these people. And they, too, would have found my salon unbearably boring with its *comtesses* and sportsmen, its old generals and old canonesses. What part could men of intellect and knowledge, writers and artists have taken in these eternally identical utterances: where they danced yesterday and where they will dance tomorrow— whether at the Schwarzenbergs', the Pallavicinis', or at court—what passions the Baroness Pacher indulges in, what match Countess Palffy rejected, how many estates Prince Croy owns, what lineage the young

Almassy was born to, whether a Festitics or a Wenkheim and if *the* Wenkheim, whose mother was a Khevenhüller, etc., etc. That was the subject matter of most of the conversations going on around me.[43]

The relationship between the Suttner couple and the writer Max Nordau also got its start in Paris. Nordau, who was later one of the leaders of the Zionist movement, was a correspondent for the *Neue Freie Presse* in Paris in the 1880s and already famous as an author of books, especially for *Die konventionellen Lügen der Menschheit* (The conventional lies of mankind). "There were several unforgettable hours we spent discussing the marvelous world of God and the conventional, false world of man," writes Bertha about meeting him.[44]

One of the high points of her stay in Paris was the meeting with Ernest Renan, who had been denounced by the church but was highly admired by liberals, the author of the *Life of Jesus*. Paying a visit of tribute to Renan was tantamount to making a liberal profession of faith and would hardly have met with conservative applause in Austria.

"I had expected Renan to have an unattractive appearance since it was a well-known fact, but this went beyond all my expectations: short, fat, pallid, with a wide beardless face . . . , a monstrously bald skull— thus the writer of the *Life of Jesus* gave me a first impression of being the ugliest man I had ever seen. After ten minutes, when he began to speak, this impression was blotted out. He not only looked reasonable to me, he seemed to be in the possession of a genuine magic."

Discussions with Renan also turned to "the threatening cloud of war" between the current archenemies, Germany and France. Ludovic Halevy, the historiographer of the war of 1870–71, a famous patriot and member of the Académie Française welcomed "with some pathos, the day of retaliation that may be nearing." Renan contradicted him vehemently. "He makes no secret of his loathing for the slaughter of whole peoples, but what especially hurts him, the thinker, is the hostility between his nation and the 'nation of thinkers.' He admitted having learned a great deal from German philosophy and spoke with great respect of its exponents from earlier and recent times."[45]

The Suttners also met with a hearty reception at the house of the poet Alphonse Daudet. In Daudet, writes Bertha, "power is joined by intellect, by fiery, easily flowing speech, and even a beautiful outer appearance. With his sparkling black eyes, his thick curly head of hair, his fine mobile features, Alphonse Daudet would have to have been appealing to everyone even without being Alphonse Daudet."[46]

Princess Tamara of Georgia also lived in Paris with her children and was happy to see the Suttners again. They met mostly in Russian society. However, *société* was no longer the most important thing during this visit to Paris, as it had been for the young Countess Kinsky. Now she was intent on getting together with French intellectuals and literati. And Bertha was a master at making contacts.

All their lives the Suttners held fast to the practice of assimilating new impulses, making friends, and escaping their monotonous family life in Harmannsdorf. They needed a stimulating intellectual life, at least from time to time, and they needed international contacts. And so they became what Bertha always held up as her ideal: citizens of the world and people not caught up in national pride:

> People who are well traveled, know a number of languages and are well read in these languages and through this have assimilated the best of the spirit and character of different nations, shake off their national flaws even in external characteristics, and become like Englishmen who are not stiff, like Germans who are not ponderous, like Frenchmen who are not superficial and vain, like Italians who are not histrionic, and like Americans who are not vulgar. Refined in every direction, they present a type which belongs to a newly forming nation which must one day conquer the world: the nation of world citizens.[47]

5

Lay Down Your Arms

I have often been asked, 'Tell me, *how* and for what purpose and why did you come upon the idea of writing *Lay Down Your Arms* and forming a peace society?' I always lacked an answer. At best I could reply, I didn't come upon the idea, the idea came upon me—but why? I don't know anymore. . . . [C]ertainly some passage in a book or some word I heard provided the first germ for this direction in ideas—but in what book the place was, when that word was spoken? That I do not remember. I definitely did not act according to a set plan or an impulsive decision. It all happened 'by itself,' gradually and altogether differently than I had thought."[1]

And Bertha emphasized—contrary to all legends—that her pacifist activities did not go back to her war experiences. "I personally have never suffered from war, I myself was never exposed to its dangers, it never even caused me loss of property nor did it cause me any harm . . . and if I choose to attribute my aversion to war to an event, then it cannot be something that *happened* to me, but only something I read."[2]

How ripe she was for the idea of the peace movement in 1888 is shown by those passages in *The Machine Age* that she wrote before her trip to Paris. In connection with Darwin's theory of evolution, which she so ardently defended, she described war

> as the most reprehensible crime, as the height of depravity. Aside from the hundreds of thousands of slayings—which compare with murder in a relationship of 100,000 to 1—war is the negation of evolution in all directions. It prevents further development and destroys the fruits of culture previously attained, and the height of its immorality (judged according to the ethical principles that have been recognized recently)

61

is: it turns the most excellent means of natural evolution—selection by survival of the best and the fittest—into the exact opposite; it selects the best for death, namely, the young, strong, competent, and leaves the old, weak, and lame to reproduce their incompetence. In short, a reversed natural breeding selection—artificial degeneration. A gigantic offense committed by men of today against men of tomorrow. And the height of stupidity.[3]

Bertha learned of the existence of an organized peace movement in Paris at the home of Alphonse Daudet. "What, such a group existed—the idea of popular justice, the attempt to abolish war had taken shape and life? The news electrified me."[4]

She tried to get additional information and learned of the London Peace Society under Hodgson Pratt, of the French counterpart under Frédéric Passy, the Italian under Ruggiero Bonghi, and of the Danish pacifist, Frederik Bajer. In Germany there were small pacifist associations in Württemberg, Frankfurt, and Berlin (here, moreover, with the famous physician, Professor Virchow). There were also small groups in Hungary, Norway, and Sweden; in Geneva there was an "International League of Peace and Liberty." However, the pioneers of the peace movement were the Americans: in 1886 there were thirty-six societies there. The oldest went back to 1816.[5]

The movement was splintered, consisted mostly of small private associations, and had no central organization. Suttner heard about a call from Hodgson Pratt to "form a big league with branches in all the European cities" with the objective of enlightening the population and winning them over to the idea of the peace movement. This would prevent additional wars "through the irresistible power of a sufficiently informed and energetically organized public opinion."[6] The implementation of an international court was proposed for settling conflicts between countries.

Bertha was for it heart and soul. And like everything that made an impression on her, she wasted no time in exploiting it in a book. Upon her return from Paris she found the proofs of her new novel, *The Machine Age,* waiting for her, and she quickly added another chapter on the international peace movement. "Since *I* hadn't known anything about it, I assumed my readers were also ignorant of this new phenomenon."[7]

Then she confronted the old saying *si vis pacem, para bellum* (if you wish peace, prepare for war), critically, that is, the principle of keeping peace by deterrence and constant armament. She called this principle, which she had come across in full force in her discussions with the dynamite producer, Alfred Nobel, an "ancient Roman idiocy."

In contrast to the people's love of peace,

militarism . . . in the machine age achieved the same degree of importance and development that the power of the church had in the Middle Ages . . . a collapse of the growing insanity of armament in the near future was unavoidable. That point when everything that is must stop—the point of unbearableness—was not very far away for the world's armament load. All the wealth, all the power of the people, all *life* aimed at one target—destruction: in the end, such a system must destroy either humanity or itself. How high the ability to destroy could climb was unforeseeable. From the original stone hurled with a slingshot to the newest cannon, what a long way! The way was much shorter that lay between the weapon firing 500 shots per minute and an *electrical* killing machine that could exterminate an entire army with *one* blow—the melanite or other still unnamed explosive pellets which would rain down from the sky to smash a city in a few seconds.

And why? What for? What then? Perhaps these questions would be asked after all by those driven to their deaths before they blew each other up. "For the greatest good of mankind"—this popular phrase for driving the war forward would lose its meaning if there were not only no more good left after the battle, but also no more people. The self-sacrifice of the few for many, may well appear to be virtuous and desirable, but the sacrifice of all for none? That would be the height of madness![8]

She pointed to the gigantic dimensions of a war fought with modern weapons. "In *one* future European war it would be possible to pile up an amount of killing, devastation, and degeneration that was not accomplished in a hundred battles of antiquity," and she continues in more detail, "Instead of spears that flew only a short distance, instead of the shot from a gun that hit the opponent at a few hundred paces, now deadly bombs whizz through the air for miles; long before the two opponents can see each other, the advance guard covers the field."

And when is such a war over? Who would be the *victor,* who the *vanquished?*

A beaten, retreating army? There is no such a thing anymore, since there are no armies left to recall, there are only the people, all the people. They went at each other because of a strip of land, and the *whole* land was devastated—depopulated and ravaged on both sides. All the seed trampled, all the work stopped, all the homes destroyed, only *one* scream of pain from border to border—and still no end. Every village a fire, every city a heap of rubble, every field a graveyard and still the war rages on. Beneath the waves of the ocean, torpedo boats are shooting in order to draw mighty steam ships to the bottom of the sea; armed and manned airships climb to the clouds heading for another aeronautic troop, and from a height of a thousand meters mutilated warriors snow down in bloody flakes—mines are detonated and bridges with their entire freight of people, horses and wagons plunge into the torrents, gunpowder magazines explode, long railway trains derail, hospitals go up in flame and still there is no end. . . . Army, reserves, territorial reserves—the aged, the children, the women—all murdered one after the other; the few still alive will be the spoils of starvation and inevitable contamination and then the war is over—but without having been won.[9]

She follows with concrete and practical advice about the peace organizations that existed then and a quotation from an appeal by the London society "To all those who want international peace."

In order to understand the very basic and very genuine fear felt by Suttner, who spoke for many others of her time with similar feelings, it is necessary to take the political situation in central Europe of 1888–89 into account. Great upheavals were taking place. In Germany the ninety-nine-day rule of the liberal Emperor Friedrich III, who was mortally ill with cancer, was followed in June 1888 by the reign of Wilhelm II, then twenty-nine years old, with pithy remarks and threatening gestures against the archenemy France. There, War Minister Boulanger called for "revenge" and was very successful in the elections with this cry. The spread of the idea of revenge, even among intellectuals, was something Bertha had seen enough of in the salons of Paris. In the Balkans there were constant, dangerous entanglements between Russia and Austria-Hungary.

The atmosphere was tense everywhere. Fear of a big war spread, and Suttner's warning about the monster, militarism, was not an isolated occurrence. Fear of war even took hold of the crown prince of Austria-Hungary, Rudolf, and caused him to make a desperate plea to avoid a German-French war by changing the Austrian alliances—and drove him to the hopeless despair he was in when he put an end to his own life in January 1889 in Mayerling.[10]

Resignation, despair—these were certainly not the reactions of a Bertha von Suttner. She was full of vigor, of optimism: a means had to be found to counteract this peril. Everyone, especially she herself, would have to contribute to the well-being of mankind. She saw an organized peace movement as the way to do this.

For an ally in her battle against war, Suttner counted on the social democrats most of all, since their platform included: "the brotherhood of peoples at the top of the list; and the Bebels, the Liebknechts in Germany—the heads of parties in other countries—have worked enthusiastically for the idea of peace among peoples. But what good did it do: the power was not yet *theirs*. On the contrary: governments were suspicious of them, and one of the main reasons for maintaining an armed service was to defend themselves against *their* attacks."

As long as the power lay in the hands of monarchs and parliaments alone, pressure would have to be exerted on them. Of course, she did not conceal the fact that there were differences between the peace movement and social democracy: what was the whole platform for the one, was only a "subparagraph in the party platform" of the other. The friends of peace did not want to have to "create a whole new state first, in which militarism would be only one of the issues, but because of the immediate and existing circumstances, they wanted to help abolish *one* evil—in their eyes, the greatest evil of all."[11]

In *The Machine Age,* Bertha also confronts one other related movement, the Red Cross, founded in 1864 by Henri Dunant to provide better care for wounded soldiers. "How could the flag of the Red Cross compare with the white flag of peace? To heal a small fraction of wounded soldiers was possible for the former, but for the victims of a coming war, to make all the impoverished rich again, all the sick healthy, all the dead alive, that was what the latter would be able to do by eliminating the coming war itself."[12] While she was writing her book, she was supposed to have avidly read the files of the Society of the Red Cross and Florence Nightingale's accounts of the Crimean War, which strengthened her in her opinion.[13]

The Machine Age was successful and had positive reviews. The extent of Bertha's talent for publicity became increasingly obvious. She was clever and not at all shy in promoting her own books—and as a result, the ideas she wanted to spread. For instance, she wrote the parliamentarian Carneri, "At this opportunity I would like to tell you, my friend, how you could perform a good service to my *Machine Age*. Make an allusion to it in a speech in parliament. Then it will make all the newspapers, all the political talk in the pubs and coffeehouses—the name of the book or the quotation will take wing and then popularity is achieved." As an example, she mentioned Nordau's *Conventional Lies,* which had a fifteenth printing after being mentioned in parliament.[14]

Carneri complied with her request when he was the spokesman for the liberal opposition in the budget debate. Carneri wrote to Bertha: "Do not expect much, but you will find parliament open to your cause,

the most important thing for you. You will laugh at the transition I
devised to get from the so-called Bohemian compromise to *The Machine
Age*."[15]

The next day, the *Neue Freie Presse* reported on Carneri's speech and
even made a friendly commentary: "The thinker Carneri sees militarism
not unjustly as the main cause of the exigency that is spreading throughout Europe today, creating painful convulsions everywhere and from
which this great movement has sprung."[16]

Bertha rejoiced and proudly included the parliamentary coup in her
memoirs; but she described the event to make it appear as though she
had no idea how it came about, and she was silent about how cleverly
she had arranged it all.

Bertha asked other writers she knew to review her works, but protested when one critic said that with her idea of peace, the author was
crashing through doors that were already open. "I wish it were true—
but the militarism I sought to fight is no crashed door; instead—unfortunately for the spirit of mankind—it is still the gate of a fortress, barri-
caded tenfold."[17]

A chapter in *The Machine Age* was not enough to storm this gate.
The book addressed itself to intellectuals and could not count on a great
propaganda effect. Suttner now put her proven methods to work for a
new book that would be devoted solely to the movement: she wrote a
novel with a message intentionally directed to a mass public, especially to
the readers of women's novels. "I did not want to put only what I
thought in my book, but also what I felt, passionately felt; I wanted to
express how the pain of war as I imagined it burned into my soul. Life,
pulsating life—I wanted to show reality, historical reality, and that could
only be done in a novel, preferably in the form of an autobiography."[18]

The two-volume work *Lay Down Your Arms* (Die Waffen nieder)
tells the story of an aristocrat (Martha) as an autobiography. Her fate is
being determined by war. Her first husband dies at Solferino in 1859 in
the war in Upper Italy. She fears for her second husband (Baron Tilling—a portrait of her beloved Arthur) in the war Austria and Prussia
fight against Denmark in 1864, and again in the war between Austria
and Prussia in 1866. This second husband, the "hero" of the story, is
finally shot in 1870 in Paris by French nationalists because he is a
German.

> In order for the historical events I used to correspond with reality,
> for the descriptions of the battle scenes to be authentic, I had to do
> some studies beforehand, collect material and documents. . . . I read

thick volumes of historical works, hunted through old newspapers and archives to find reports by war correspondents and military doctors. I had my acquaintances who had been to war tell me about their battle experiences and during this period of study, my revulsion for war reached a painful intensity. I can assure you that the suffering my heroine felt through me, I myself also suffered during this work.[19]

Suttner deliberately told stories about war that "compare with the usual veteran's tales . . . as the reality of the wretched life a shepherd leads does to Watteau's paintings of shepherds."[20] Her love of truth compelled her not to show battle in terms of heroic deeds, but to put human suffering in the foreground, as she does in an example of a battlefield on the morning after the battle:

> Now, for the first time, you can see the massiveness of the bodies lying around: on the streets, between the fields, in the ditches, behind the ruins of walls; everywhere, dead people everywhere. Plundered, some naked. The wounded, too. Despite the medical orderlies working all night, a great number of wounded are still lying all around, look pale and destroyed, green and yellow with a fixed, vacant look in their eyes, or buckling with ravaging pain, they beg everyone who comes near to kill them. Swarms of carrion crows perch in treetops and announce the tempting banquet with a loud cawing. . . . Hungry dogs come running from the villages and lick the blood from the wounds.[21]

She describes how hurriedly and inadequately the dead were buried. "They throw one or two feet of earth over a heap of corpses. It looks like a tumulus then. A few days later it rains and the covering gets washed away from the rotting corpses." Some of the wounded, stiff with spasmodic seizure, were buried alive. A few rescued by chance told about it. "But how many are there who weren't able to say anything? When a few feet of earth are lying on top of your mouth, then you have to hold your tongue."[22]

How outrageous expressions like "honor and glory," or "joyous hero's death" sound to her. "When a soldier is lying with smashed limbs on the field after a battle, and, since he goes undiscovered for the next four or five days, dies from thirst, hunger, and unspeakable pain, rotting alive—and all the time knowing that his death has not helped his fatherland, but has only brought desperation to his loved ones—I would like to know if he is glad to die with the cry ['For the Fatherland'] going on the whole time."

Then the objection comes from the older generation, "You are committing blasphemy. . . . And besides, you speak in such harsh words—totally unseemly for a woman."

And Martha (alias Bertha) energetically replies, "Oh, yes, the truth—naked reality is blasphemous, is indecent . . . only the cliché, sanctioned by being repeated thousands of times, is 'respectable.'"[23]

Martha speaks staunchly about terrible mutilations, even emasculation. And when the conservative environment reacts with moral indignation, her patience gives way.

> Oh, your prudery; oh, your squeamish respectability: all the abominations are allowed to *happen*, but no one may mention them. Delicate women must not know anything or say anything about blood and filth, but they are allowed to embroider the flags that will wave above the bloodbath; girls must not know that their future fiancés could be made incapable of receiving the rewards of love, but they are supposed to promise them this reward as a goad to battle. There is nothing indecent about death and killing as far as you are concerned, you well brought up little ladies—but you must look away, blushing, at the very mention of things that are the source of the reproduction of *life*. That is a terrible morality, do you know that? Terrible and cowardly! This looking the other way—with a physical and a spiritual eye—is the cause of the persistence of so much suffering and injustice![24]

Mercilessly, Suttner reveals the hypocrisy of a society that trivializes and exalts war as a test of a man's worth and courage. She castigates the flippancy with which the mighty risk a war to rescue their so-called honor. She criticizes the church that blesses weapons and the naiveté of the belief that God would help in war: the opponent calls upon the same God.

The progress of technology demands a rigorous reorientation. New inventions should not be misused to divide peoples and destroy life. "Look at our railway lines, look at our telegraph lines—'we are civilized nations,' we boast to the wild people and use these things to multiply our lack of civilization a hundred times."[25]

Despite all her condemnation of war, it did not occur to her, the daughter of a field marshal, to say anything detrimental about soldiers. "Contempt for soldiers is something that does not occur to me," she has a fighter at Königgrätz say already in the *Inventory*.

> My good, poor Austrian brothers, whom I saw fall next to me—and my good, poor German brothers who fell over there in the enemy lines—and my good brothers in humanity all, who stayed back on the French

and Russian and Italian battlefields—I lower my sable to you in greeting. Your memory, the memory of your brave sacrificial death is something I did not want to insult with a shadow of a disrespectful thought,—but the barbaric custom, whose compelling force unleashes us against each other and lays upon us such undignified responsibilities, I can say out loud, is something that fills me with disgust![26]

The "gullible" soldiers were blinded by the "nice-sounding title" of "defender of the fatherland"—and used for other purposes than defense. Bertha's accusation: "Why does his oath bind him to hundreds of responsibilities of war other than defense? Why does he have to attack, why—when the fatherland is not threatened in the least—does he have to risk those very goods, life, and home, simply because of the quarrels about property and honor between some strange, isolated princes, as though it were indeed a matter of defending the endangered life and hearth—as the justification of war maintains?"[27]

She attacks the politicians and high-ranking military leaders, partly because of their supposedly imperative armament campaign. The novel tells about the eve of the Prussian-Austrian War of 1866:

Thank God! Austria declares that all the rumors that are circulating about secret armament are false; it does not occur to Austria to attack Prussia. Therefore it demands that Prussia halt its measures for the preparation of war.

Prussia replies: it would not think of attacking Austria, but the latter's armament makes it necessary to prepare for attack.

Thus the duet alternating between the two sides continues along these lines:

> My arming is for defense,
> Your arming is for offense,
> I must arm because you arm,
> Because you arm, I too, arm,
> Therefore we arm,
> We arm and arm and arm.[28]

Because of these experiences, the hero of the novel reaches the decision to fight war with every means. "I shall take up service in the army of peace. Admittedly still a very small army, whose soldiers have no other defense or weapons than the idea of justice and their love of mankind. But everything that ever became great had a small and unremarkable beginning."

Whereupon the author has Martha object in the old style of the woman's novel, timidly, femininely, "Ah . . . it is a hopeless beginning. What do you—an individual—want to achieve against the mighty bulwark defended for thousands of years by millions of people?"

> TILLING: "Achieve? I? . . . truly, I am not so foolish as to hope that I personally will bring about a change. I only say that I want to enter the ranks of the army of peace. When I stood in the army did I ever hope that I could save the fatherland, that I would conquer a province? No, the individual can only *serve*. Even more: he must serve. Anyone burning with a cause has no choice but to work for it, but to risk his life for it—even when he knows how little this life can contribute to victory. He serves because he must; not only the state—one's own conviction, if it is enthusiastic—can impose military conscription."

The loving wife, who wants to fight loyally at his side, relents, "You are right. And when this compulsory military service finally becomes sufficient for millions of enthusiasts, then that bulwark, deserted by its defenders, must fall at last."[29]

There were problems having the manuscript printed. The weeklies that had previously published Bertha's novels in serial form returned her manuscript with regrets. The reason they gave was that "large numbers of our readers would be offended by the content," and they pointed out that despite all its fine qualities, it would be impossible "for the novel to be published in a military state."

The book publisher hesitated, too, and suggested that "an experienced statesman" look through the manuscript to strike out anything offensive. Bertha rebelled against this solution. "Letting such a work which . . . after all has the merit of being deeply felt and unrestrainedly frank, be cropped in this diplomatic-opportunistic manner, and reshaped according to the rules of the most despicable of all arts, namely, the art of making it suit everyone: no, better to throw it into the fire. Then I should at least change the title, the publisher suggested. No! The title puts the whole purpose of the book into [four] words. Not one syllable of the title may be changed, either."[30] Finally, Bertha's persistence succeeded. *Lay Down Your Arms* appeared in 1889 through her Leipzig publishers, Pierson.

In this particular book, Bertha's concern was not art; it was the effect the book would have on the public—and for that reason she was uneasy about it.

She asked journalists she was on friendly terms with for support and also called on her old friend, Alfred Nobel. He replied immediately, *"Lay Down Your Arms,* so that is the title of your new novel, about which I am very curious. But you ask me to publicize it, that is a bit cruel. Because where do you want me to sell my new [gun] powder if there is universal peace? I would at least have to change over to *'poudre de riz'* [a cosmetic powder] in order to add more dust to those who are already all too dusty. Next to *Lay Down Your Arms,* give a little room instead to *Down with Misery, Down with Old Prejudices and the Old Religions, Down with the Old Injustices and the Old Disgrace, the Old Jehovah,* who is all too disgusting and another one whose reputation is all too overestimated, the Holy Ghost, who is absolutely not holy, and this whole collection of worm eaten antiques."[31]

But when he read the book, he was enthusiastic:

> I just finished reading the text of your admirable masterpiece. They say there are two thousand languages—that would be 1999 too many—but certainly there is no language into which your wonderful work should not be translated, so that it can be read and thought about. How much time did you need for this miracle? You will tell me when I have the honor and the luck to press your hand, this Amazon's hand, that so watchfully wages war on war. All the same you are not right to cry, *Lay Down Your Arms,* since you yourself make use of weapons, though of course, yours—the charm of your style and the greatness of your ideas—go much farther and in a different manner than those of Lébel [weapons], Nordenfelt [cannons], de Bange [guns], and all the other tools of hell.

He closed the French letter with an English phrase, "Yours for ever and more than ever. A. Nobel."[32]

The breakthrough to the big success was brought about by a critique in the *Neue Freie Presse,* written by Bartolomeus von Carneri. "Never has militarism been so described in such drastic terms before, how much suffering it spreads around it and how beautiful the life it disregards can be." He commended the "book, that ennobles in every direction in the most beautiful sense of the word." The book's natural quality comes from the author's idealism, "the moral indignation over the deceit of society."

Carneri also thought disarmanent would be "the dawn of a better time. There are already millions who realize that today. . . . Hail to the prince who plucks up the courage and grasps the white flag! The more gallant he is, the easier it will be, if a noble woman holds it out to him.

And even if no one takes the dare: this flag will not stop waving, since the height from which it waves is the welfare of mankind."[33]

Many other reviews followed this prominent one, many of them were argumentative. But that only made for a more heated discussion.

Then Bertha experienced the satisfaction—this time totally unexpected and unsolicited—of having Finance Minister Dunajevsky mention the book in parliament. "Very recently a German lady—it was not a parliamentarian—described war in a story in a very moving way. I ask you to devote several hours to this work, and if anyone still has a passion for war afterwards, I truly feel sorry for him."[34]

Suttner proudly quotes this statement in her memoirs. But she does not tell us what the finance minister went on to say afterwards. He did not attribute as much importance to the pacifist book as Bertha would have us believe. He merely stated that a repugnance for war was "a well-known sentiment that is stirring in all the countries of Europe." To ensure this peace, however, Austria-Hungary needed good weapons: "Situated as it is in the middle of the great continent, subjected to all the trends and passions and all the impulses of the public spirit and the effect of all the material and scientific tendencies which often contradict each other, our state, as things look now, must want and work for peace, but truly: arms at the ready. There is no other way."

Lay Down Your Arms was one of the most successful books of the nineteenth century. Its influence can be compared with that of Harriet Beecher Stowe's *Uncle Tom's Cabin*. Just as the latter did more for the abolition of slavery than all the scientific arguments put together, so did Suttner contribute more to the spread of the pacifist idea throughout the world than what the pacifists had hoped for in vain for decades. The book was translated into all the civilized languages and discussed extensively. The subject of the "International Peace Movement" became a major topic overnight.

Bertha von Suttner had become one of the prominent personalities in the peace movement without even personally knowing any of the pacifists in other countries. Their praise and recognition made her especially happy. "Hodgson Pratt conveyed the thanks of the English arbitrational society to me and asked for the authorization for an English translation."[35]

Writing to Nobel, she equated the success of the book with the success of the idea: "If the majority of the people were of belligerent views they would certainly not welcome a work of fiction with the title, *Lay Down Your Arms!*"[36]

As long as she lived, she explained the book's appeal as the result of a propitious moment and drew her optimism for her work in the peace movement from it. "I think that when a book with a purpose is success-ful, this success does not depend on the effect it has on the spirit of the times but the other way around, that success is the result of the spirit of the times. If someone accidentally hits upon the expression of an idea that is in the air, that is slumbering as an idea in untold minds, as a longing in untold hearts, then his book is a hit, as the current expression goes. . . . The stroke of lightning is only possible if the air is loaded with electricity."[37]

She was very glad when Karl Liebknecht, the German socialist leader, asked for permission to print the novel free of charge in the so-cialist publication *Vorwärts*. She wrote to Carneri proudly, "Of course I have nothing against it. . . . I am even very proud that the social demo-crats who thus far disdainfully pushed the peace movement aside as being bourgeois and impotent, are now coming closer to us because of my book—and that the head of the great party of the people is also one of Martha's conquests now. In *this* respect, namely, the matter of the peo-ple's peace, we are going along together with this party, and it would be wonderful if all the parties (with the exception of the regressive ones) would come together on our platform."[38]

The importance of the sociological aspect of peace had concerned Bertha for a long time. "Yes, I see it already," she wrote to Carneri, "the *social question* is what will bring about a solution to the questions of war and peace because it will permeate all other matters; while on the other hand, getting rid of the military burden would also facilitate the possi-bility for economic justice; so everything will have to work together and for each other—each 'flying towards the center along its own rays.'"[39]

Finally, though, she felt there was something eerie about the over-whelming success, and she tried to put things back in proper relation and balance them. She admitted "that my last two books made much more noise (in relationship to other German books) than their inner value war-ranted. It just shows how an avalanche works: in rolling, it becomes irresponsibly larger—I already want to stop it and I ask everyone: do not overestimate me!"[40]

It took a while for her to get used to her sudden fame. In 1891 still, she wrote her friend Carneri from Venice, "I just happened to find friends from that period again [before her marriage]—they are all very astonished that I have become—what they call—a 'famous writer.' Am I one really? It simply will not sink in."[41]

In view of all her successes, the author was angry because there was no international agreement on translation rights. Foreign publishers re-printed her book without paying the slightest royalties. Infuriated, she complained of "piracy. . . . Our grandchildren will see a time when intellectual property is protected internationally."[42] When German-American publications also printed her novel in serial form without paying her anything, she wrote to Carneri, "Isn't that annoying? If there were an agreement with America and the northern countries, then *Es Löwos* would already have his villa. And these stupid writers form their societies where they work to get 75 *pfennig* a week as an old age bonus!"[43]

For years reprints also appeared in the German-speaking area, and Suttner remarked in 1893, four years after the first appearance, "It is strange that the book has still not stopped selling well. Proof that it corresponds with a need that lives in the time and heart."[44]

She followed the international response to her novel closely and the spread of the pacifist idea that went hand in hand with it and that was defended with so much temperament. She observed with satisfaction that it was not only the United States and western Europe that discussed the book; even Czarist Russia had brought out no less than five translations. "The peace *feuilleton* of the Petersburg paper is encouraging," she wrote to Carneri, "and shows that there are sensible people there, too—and that the idea of the abolition of war is continuing to spread irresistibly."[45]

Through her extensive correspondence with pacifists all over the world, she was well informed about the movement's next plans, and before she noticed it, she was not only the harbinger of the peace ideal, she was also one of the organizers of this, for her rather new, movement.

Thus, she also came into contact with Leo Tolstoy. She had the Russian edition of her book sent to him and wrote him a letter explaining the meaning of the peace movement and her place in it. "The movement is taking on a favorable and encouraging shape. But great is the ponderous slowness of the masses, great is the irony of the disbelievers and great the resistance by the war party. . . . We will reach our goal, and those who are the great, the good, and at the same time also the mighty, could help us speed up our progress." And of course her request follows, "You, master, you are one of those whose word is heard in Europe." He should be so kind as to "write two lines, *one* line saying that you support the tendencies of the peace league and that you believe in the possible realization of these wishes." She wanted to publish this "precious word," and expected to win over a large number of followers for the sacred cause with it. "And that is what it's all about—the large numbers are needed to make the manifestation for the principle impressive."[46]

Tolstoy actually answered with a letter Suttner proudly quoted a number of times. "I admire your work very much and think that the publication of your novel is a good omen. The abolition of slavery was preceded by the famous book written by a woman, Mrs. Beecher-Stowe; God grant that the abolition of war follow your book." Then he turned to the peace movement Bertha praised so highly and raised the objection, "I do not think that the court of arbitration is an effective means for hindering war." But the congress in Rome would contribute to "spreading among the public the awareness of the obvious discrepancy Europe finds itself in—the discrepancy between the warlike condition of the people and the Christian and humanitarian principle they profess."[47]

That was exactly the declaration of sympathy Bertha had hoped to get.

But as great as Tolstoy's approval might have been, he was not impressed by the book's artistic value. He wrote in his diary, "Evening, finished reading the book *Lay Down Your Arms*. Well formulated. One feels the great conviction, but untalented."[48]

Like Tolstoy, Vienna literary circles also thought the artistic merits of the Suttner book were inferior. At a time when aestheticism was celebrating grand triumphs in Vienna, a "utilitarian work" like that of Bertha Suttner's received little attention. Even though writing was little more than a means to an end for her, and her artistic ambitions were limited as a result, Bertha was hurt for the rest of her life by her literary colleagues' turning up their noses in disdain. When she wrote *Martha's Children*, the sequel to *Lay Down Your Arms*, in 1902, she already anticipated such criticism. "The terrible tirade against 'tendentious' writers will be lowered upon me again. The *intent to do good* is thought to be so very unartistic."[49] During the next few years Bertha had to endure a good deal of mockery—most of all from Karl Kraus, prominent essayist and playwright.

But it was not only for artistic reasons that Suttner's book ran up against rejection. She had made her position all too clear as a liberal, an anticlerical, and as a follower of Darwin's theory of evolution, and this irritated many conservatives. The fact that a woman took such a belligerent and aggressive approach to a cultural matter, made the anger of her—mostly masculine—opponents burn even hotter.

We still have malicious caricatures of "Peace Bertha," and Suttner must have become well acquainted at an early date with the fact that her work for peace exposed her to public ridicule. There were times when the constant derision was hard to bear, when she made an effort to show up the comic side of these attacks. She quoted a newspaper remark with downright pride: "Who's calling *Lay Down Your Arms*? A hysterical blue-stocking started the cheeping."[50] And she wrote to Carneri in 1892, "The latest editions of the humorous magazines have worked me over again thoroughly, but I find it fun and it helps make the cause popular, doesn't it? The peace movement has the most dangerous state—the deathly quiet state—behind it."[51]

Suttner felt the strong reservation of her relatives and the aristocratic neighborhood of Harmannsdorf. She admitted to her friend Carneri that her novel had been condemned "in certain circles." "Our neighbors here, whom we see frequently and intimately, do not mention my scandalous act with a single word. This intentional and unnatural silence shows that terrible things have been said about the book in that clique, and now they are embarrassed to say anything about it to me. Oh well, a number of things that are sacred and dear to me were bound to fall along with militarism."[52]

She could not count on the support of her aristocratic relatives for the peace movement—quite the opposite. Later she complained, "Unfortunately the aristocrats are still our enemies in the peace movement. I find the greatest opposition to my propaganda among my cousins. Generals, courtiers, treasurers, wives of officers all think this is about nihilism and anarchism because it talks about changing old customs. For them, everyone who wants to reform today's society-state (a state that offers them so many advantages) is criminal or insane."[53]

The success of the book improved the Suttner's financial situation enormously. The couple, used to drab times, enjoyed their new prosperity to the full. They granted themselves an old wish and spent the winter of 1890–91 in Venice. They rented a small *palazzo* on the Canale Grande and a gondola with two gondoliers, one of whom also functioned as a valet. They had a cook and a maid. "We were so happy," Bertha wrote in her memoirs and dreamed from then on of being able to move to Venice someday and live in their own *palazzo*.[54]

In the morning they worked at their desks as usual, afternoons and evenings belonged to "society." Princess Tamara of Georgia happened to be in Venice at the time. An old friend from Bertha's youth was there; she was married to the Marquis Benjamino Pandolfi and kept a grand house. Pandolfi was a member of the Italian parliament and belonged to the Roman division of the peace society and the Inter-Parliamentarian Union (IPU). Through him Bertha found out about details connected with these peace organizations and related movements.

The English member of Parliament Randal Cremer and the French parliamentarian Frédéric Passy, both leaders in the peace movement, had founded this special union for parliamentarians in 1888, that is, three years previously. Their main objective had also been to force the formation of an international court of arbitration and to work for limiting the arms race. "The fate of the people lies in the parliaments, after all. If they were to press for disarmament, the governments would not be able to do anything but give in," said Bertha hopefully.[55]

Like the stay in Paris, the winter in Venice also became an important landmark on Bertha's way to becoming a pacifist. Now it was easy for her, the famous writer, to get the contacts and information she needed. Not a word of complaint that she would never be able to work in the IPU because she was a woman. (Women then did not have the right to vote, let alone the right to run for office.) As usual, she made the best of the situation. She contributed privately and, most of all, she did what she had mastered to perfection: made contacts and publicity.

There in Venice, Bertha got a visit from the English pacifist Felix Moscheles. He came to her, "First, as a friend of peace to thank the writer, and second, as a human being to offer his condolences to the poor, broken widow." He had taken her novel for an autobiography and reacted to the sight of Arthur, whom he assumed was Bertha's third husband, somewhat accusingly. "We explained amidst laughter that the two dear departed military gentlemen were merely products of the imagination."[56] That was the beginning of a lifelong friendship.

Moscheles' plan was to establish a local peace group in Venice, but he had not met the right people. Disappointed, he had been on the verge of leaving. Now Bertha became active. She introduced Moscheles to Pandolfi at a party. "While distinguished Venetian society and vivacious young people danced and amused themselves in the big dining room, a long discussion took place in the host's study between the Marquis, Mr. Moscheles, and the two of us. The result was that Pandolfi not only promised to help with organizing the approaching conference, but also to prepare invitations and letters immediately for the founding of a peace organization in Venice itself."[57]

A meeting was called within a few days. Thanks to Pandolfi, everything went perfectly. "The next day, all the Italian newspapers wrote about this event and for a while it was the topic of conversation in our circles," Bertha wrote, but adds the qualification, "Of course, the way salon conversation customarily handles a new movement that strives to create a big upheaval: with an expression of prudent doubt and reservation, gentle ridicule, condescending recognition of the noble cause—and all of that against a background of unmoving, rigid indifference."[58]

Felix Moscheles drew Bertha completely into the international peace movement, and she became an active participant. On her very first eve-

ning back in Vienna, Bertha attended a meeting of the liberal parliamentarians at the Meissl Hotel. Still "under the enthusiastic impression of
what had been experienced," she spoke about the Venetian peace society
and the Inter-Parliamentary Union, with the intention, of course, of
bringing an interparliamentary group together in Vienna. Her friends
"listened with interest, but with skeptical expressions. Joining—no one
considered that."[59]

Bertha was not discouraged that easily. She had meanwhile established a lively correspondence with the leading pacifists of the world. Her
knowledge about the peace movement became more thorough. More
and more she felt obliged to participate, not only with her pen, but also
in organizational work. It got to the point that her friend Carneri cautioned her and tried to hold her back with his constant skepticism. "You
are immortal because of your novel and your devotion to the cause of
peace. Leave the striving toward an arbitrational court to others. It will
only be possible in the intended form when the current nationalist questions have died down—in a hundred years . . . that is, if the people,
whom eternal peace requires, are possible!" And as far as Darwin's evolution was concerned, one should not be too optimistic. "A world of only
good people is an absurdity; therefore the world will always improve,
but so very slowly, that no one notices it."[60]

But Suttner did not stray from her firm belief in progress. Her first
concrete goal was to create an Austrian peace society and get the Austrian parliamentarians interested in the Inter-Parliamentarian Union.
Very quickly, the author of a best-seller became an activist for the international peace movement. Her excellent knowledge of languages, her
aristocratic background, her impeccable social conduct, her self-assurance
and her optimism—all that was rich capital.

The Viennese writer, Felix Salten (the author of "Bambi"), later tried
to explain this phenomenon of success:

> Some female writer or other from a lower class would have been able—
> with more or less artistic talent—to portray the horror and absurdity of
> war well enough to let the publicity for eternal peace speak passionately.
> A successful book. And that's all! Among all the high-born ministers,
> regents, diplomats, who would have listened to the ordinary middle-
> class woman? Who would have let her come forward? To get through
> to any of these mighty persons in the audience, to hold a conversation
> which would be measured and granted by the minute, she would have
> had to spend more energy, work, and strength of nerve than is needed
> for the writing of three such novels. . . . No matter how much presence
> of mind she had, how eloquent, how could she have made an impres-

sion on the high aristocracy who lie in wait for the mannerisms, the tone, the gestures of the commoner, with more acuteness and amusement than for the meaning of her words? Then it is better to put Suttner in her place: baroness, a born countess, and a writer besides.

Salten compared Bertha von Suttner with Theodor Herzl, who also began his Zionist movement with a book (*The Jewish State*). "The enthusiasts (like Suttner and Herzl) start with a book, always go beyond their own work, are lifted from their work, torn away from it, carried off. They hurl their work into the river, jump in after it, bring it back, supersede it."[61]

There is no doubt that during these years Bertha was at the height of her creative power and her belief in a better future, which she wanted to help create. She was forty-seven years old when she admitted to the writer Hermann Rollett, "By the way, I myself—the matron (inspiring awe in no one)—feel like a 25 year-old through and through."[62]

6

Founding the Peace Societies

She had to reach the age of forty-six before she found her life's mission, before the powers slumbering within her found their release and made the dallier into a person of the times," Alfred Hermann Fried wrote later about the upheaval in Bertha's life following the success of the novel *Lay Down Your Arms*. He points up the fact that Bertha "was not a pacificist yet when she wrote her burning accusation against war. Her own book made her into one. The movement it released also dragged the author into the machinery that did not let go of her again."[1]

Suttner herself liked to talk about the "calling," the "vocation," that she suddenly felt for the peace movement. "There is no cause in the whole world that approaches the greatness of this one. . . . That is a conviction that lies so deeply and devoutly within me (one likes to call that a vocation) that I cannot subscribe to it often or loud enough. Even though I know very well that nine-tenths of the educated world still have a low opinion of the movement and ignore it—and one of these tenths even bears ill will against it—it does not matter—I appeal to the future. The twentieth century will not end without human society having shaken off the greatest scourge—war—as a legal institution."[2]

For her, the first step on the long path was the foundation of the Austrian Peace Society and the participation of this society in the next International Peace Congress (IPU) in Rome in 1891. Since a conference of the Inter-Parliamentarian Union was also scheduled in Rome for the same time, she also worked for this meeting as well, even though she was not a parliamentarian in the strict sense of the word. Except for her private activity in Venice, she had had nothing to do with the IPU.

The hurdles on the way to Rome were not few in number. The first—and for Bertha the hardest to overcome all her life—was the matter of money. Even if she succeeded in founding an Austrian Peace Society, becoming its president, and being elected the delegate to Rome, how was she supposed to finance the trip for herself and Arthur, and how was she to send other delegates to Rome without money? Before she promoted this trip, she had to be certain that there would be some kind of financial assistance.

In 1891 Bertha turned to her friend, Alfred Nobel. She had an unshakable trust in his love for peace and his fondness for her, and hoped that this friendship would also hold up in money matters.

She was not disappointed. Nobel sent her the remarkable sum of two thousand gulden. Bertha thanked him affectionately: "And now I very formally insist that you inform me of your next visit to Vienna. I have the right to want to see you, to say with my own mouth, my eyes looking in your eyes: thank you and thank you for the enormous service you have done."[3]

From this point on, Bertha looked upon Alfred Nobel as a party to her cause, even though he only donated to her privately and did not lend his name for publicity. Her goal was to make this particular man, the world famous maker of explosives, a fighter against war. "Remain true to us. It would be so wonderful if the inventor of war explosives were to become one of the supporters of the peace movement."[4]

Nobel continued to be generous. During the years to follow, Bertha often had reason to thank her friend for considerable sums. These either went to the Austrian Peace Society or directly to Bertha, usually for traveling or for special wishes. She provided him with information and newspaper clippings "in small doses, since I know you have no time for reading a long article. . . . I only ask you (but this with my whole heart) not to throw them in the wastebasket, but to pay attention to them."[5]

With Nobel's money behind her, Bertha could now dare to start her publicity campaign for the Inter-Parliamentarian Union. In many, many imploring letters, she urged the liberal parliamentarians she knew best and thought would be most likely to support the formation of an Austrian group of the IPU, to speak out for a court of arbitration for international disputes. The answers she got were friendly refusals. Most of the parliamentarians were skeptical and did not believe that an international court of arbitration would have the slightest chance of coming to be.

The social democrat Engelbert Pernerstorfer warned her to use caution regarding peace acclamations from his coparliamentarians: "This friendship is definitely only a very platonic one which does not go beyond pathetic affirmations and sentimental phrases." From his own sad experiences, he warned Suttner of too much optimism, "Apparently, your judgment of the Austrian parliament is far too cordial. The thoughts that rule this house are of a purely practical and frequently very egotistical nature. Efforts on behalf of ideals are regarded here as ideology, and moral indignation is not taken seriously."[6] Support for the court of arbitration was something she could not expect from these members of parliament.

But after many, many refusals, Bertha's stubbornness was finally rewarded with success. Full of satisfaction, she wrote to Carneri in June: "And now for the surprise. Yesterday I received a letter from one of the people I have tortured [the expression is apt, since she had afflicted the parliamentarian with a number of rather strongly worded letters], Baron Pirquet, saying that my wish has been granted—that he has put his name on the list of parliamentarians who are going to Rome. Exner and Kübeck did the same. Others will follow. 'We men must not stay behind,' he added, when women march ahead and call to us so bravely: lay down your arms.—So, thank God! Austria will *also* be represented. Germany has accepted as well. . . . [T]he French parliament has 70 adherents."[7]

After the formation of an Austrian IPU group became reality, Bertha could proceed to the next goal: the founding of an Austrian Peace Society. The public call appeared on September 3, 1891, in the *Neue Freie Presse*. Bertha had composed the long proclamation without consulting others and sent it to the newspaper without much hope of its being published. She was suprised that it appeared in print so soon. And she was happy about the editorial remarks, "To speak out in the name of the friends of peace, there is no one in Austria better suited than the author of *Lay Down Your Arms*."

Suttner wrote: "It's like this: armies of millions, divided into two camps, rattling weapons, hesitate for just an instant before throwing themselves upon each other; but the trembling fear of the immeasurable terribleness inherent in this menacing outbreak provides something of a guarantee for its postponement. However, putting off is not calling off."

She wrote of "an armed system of inspiring fear," which had little to do with true peace. What was necessary was to ensure peace by abolishing, not postponing, war. War had become, "a moral and physical impossibility in the evolution of culture. Morally impossible because men have lost something because of their wildness and disregard for life; physically impossible because the technology of destruction that has developed over the last 20 years" would make the next military campaign "something quite new, different, no longer able to be described by the name *war*." And further:

Another few years of 'maintaining' peace like this, of inventions for machines of murder—electrically detonated mines, air torpedoes loaded with ecrasite—and on the day of declaring war, all the dual, triple, and quadruple alliances will be blown to bits. The explosion can come any second.

Fortunately, those who hold the weapons in their hands are cautious. They know that, with such a supply of gunpowder, the consequences would be horrible if they were to fire carelessly or wantonly. In order to increase this charitable caution, the supply of gunpowder is steadily increased. Would it not be simpler to get rid of the guns voluntarily and unanimously; in other words, disarm? To institute international law . . . and establish a union of the civilized countries of Europe.

It was high time for the peace-loving masses to work for peace—not for "the fearfully extended peace, rather for a secure, guaranteed peace." "Anyone waving the white flag has a following of millions behind him."

Then Suttner told of the activities of the peace movement abroad and of the coming peace congress in Rome. To create a broad peace movement it was necessary "everywhere where followers of peace exist, for people to declare themselves as such in public and to participate in their activities with all their might. . . . The invitation to send names and addresses to the author goes out to all those who want to join."

The success of the project was enormous. Hundreds of declarations of affirmation came in. Totally surprised, Bertha wrote to Carneri, "What I started on September 3 is unpredictable; all over Europe the article was reprinted and commented upon. . . . What a poor monster I am!"[8]

Even Alfred Nobel responded, albeit with his usual skepticism:

My dear friend! I am happy to see that your eloquent appeal against this horror of horrors, war, has found its way into the French press. I fear, however, that ninety-nine percent of the French readers are infected with chauvinism. While it is true that the government here almost has its wits about it, the masses are drunk with success and vanity. An amiable way of poisoning, less damaging than wine or morphia—when it doesn't lead to war. And where may your pen be headed for now? Now that it has written with the blood of the martyrs of war, will it show us the prospect of a future fairyland or the less Utopian picture of an empire of thinkers? . . . My sympathies tend in this direction, but my thoughts usually ramble into another region where silenced souls are impervious to misfortune.[9]

Her friend Carneri also remained skeptical, and Bertha defended herself, "We are not going to the capitol to lead the politics of Europe or to decree the abolition of the armies. We are going to declare the *will for peace*. Everyone may do that without being unpatriotic; monarchs do it themselves in every speech from their thrones. . . . Times change and the desire for peace grows stronger. . . . [T]oday a 'feminine' appeal suffices to make the most important paper in the country open a column to it."[10]

She also feels the necessity to defend herself against the reproach that she is vain and makes a lot of fuss. "To have made such a terribly loud appearance in (the political) public, as I just did, is *not* a pleasant thing for me to be aware of—and the burden of additional responsibilities for action also lies heavily on my shoulders, but I *had to do it*. Rome asked me to—could I do otherwise? Other than *try?*"[11]

It is hard to imagine the load of details this work placed upon the forty-eight-year-old woman. There was no organization of any kind so far, no helping hand. Suttner had to take care of practically all the work herself: enormous correspondence and all the practical jobs, even seeing to railway tickets at reduced rates for wives and daughters parliamentarians wanted to take to Rome with them.

She also did all of the press work—with amazing success. She succeeded in getting the complete support of the editor in chief of the *Neue Freie Presse*. That meant that this most distinguished Austrian daily would print the calls for peace and news of the organization from then on.

Tirelessly, she asked prominent like-minded people for help. To Peter Rosegger, whom she did not even know personally, she wrote,

> Highly honored poet,
>   During his time, Viktor Hugo placed himself at the head of the peace movement; in Sweden Björnstjerne Björnson led the war against war—and now that the friends of peace are declaring themselves in Austria, the first and best should also be named. You will give your name, won't you?!—and even more—your participation? When you hold a lecture again, speak to the people whom you love, if you include a word for the goals laid out in Rome—what an enormous help that would be for our cause. I say "our" because I know that you are a foe of barbarism.
>   Perhaps you have not seen the article which refers to the matter I ask you to lend your name to; I therefore include it herewith. Looking forward to a concurring line, I remain
>
>   Your admirer Suttner
>
> P.S. I have received a large number of acceptances: professors, lawyers, learned people, aristocrats . . . but I need a poet—I need our poet.[12]

Peter Rosegger answered immediately:

> Highly honored lady! If there is something that can warm my heart, then it is the great cause in which you do such excellent work: war against war! In this cause I also lust for war, as I have often shown according to my limited writer's powers and hope to show again from time to time. Of course you have my name, most honored lady; it has probably never stood in such an honorable place as it will among the friends of peace. Abolition of war is apparently one of the most distant ideals and is nevertheless achievable because it lies within the power of united humanity. People will have peace when they want it.[13]

Bertha sent the poet a copy of *Lay Down Your Arms,* for which he thanked her immediately: "An hour ago with the mail received *Down Arms!* Have already forged ahead to page 69. You are a wonderful woman! My greatest admiration! Rosegger."[14]

And a few months later, "Dear lady, I admire you! Please do not be angry with me for telling you straight to your face. I always have to get things out right away, otherwise I choke on them."[15]

Rosegger, however, did not think he was in a position to work on the administration of the peace society himself, but, "As a poet and writer, my pen is devoted to peace at all times, and I shall emphasize this in the future even more often and more enthusiastically. . . . Nothing in my life has inspired me so much as this idea that you are reawakening and championing in Austria so bravely." He also placed his magazine, *Heimgarten,* at the disposal of the peace society and allowed Suttner to use his name for appeals.[16]

Encouraged by so much affirmation, Bertha called a meeting of her followers at an inn at the end of September, to prepare the statutes for an "Austrian branch, to be properly registered" in preparation for joining the international society.

This evening at the *Stephaniekeller* was Suttner's first public appearance, although still within a very small circle, of course. "How they honored me, it was absolutely insane; they rose from their seats, held speeches of gratitude for the initiatives, etc., etc. . . . I have so much to *do* that I shudder," she groaned to Carneri. "With a unanimous vote of confidence I was appointed to . . . put together a committee . . . among my friends."[17] "In all it should comprise only ten names, but names that have a *high standing.* The committee will not have to *work*—Es Löwos and his secretary [she probably means Arthur here] will take care of that by themselves—but it will lend *prestige.*"[18] This was told to each of her chosen friends right at the beginning to allay any fears. And they accepted the honor, just like Peter Rosegger: the prominent geographer, Carl Ritter von Scherzer; the physician, Professor Freiherr von Krafft-Ebing; the member of parliament, Freiherr Pierre von Pirquet; the Suttners themselves (Bertha signed with Suttner-Kinsky); and two aristocrats, Count Carl Coronini and Count Rudolf Hoyos.

All her life, Bertha thought highly of using prominent and aristocratic names to advertise the peace movement. It was not only because of social ambition, which certainly did play a role, but it also had something to do with the pattern she took over from London. The "International Peace Association" in London, which the new Austrian branch joined, could point to the best addresses among its officers. In addition to Hodgson Pratt as president, there was also the duke of Westminster as vice-president, and besides him there were an earl, a marquis, and the bishop of Durham. This set an example for Bertha. But even her incomparable energy was never able to succeed in winning over Viennese "society" to the peace movement in the same degree. Only a few aristocratic friends joined in, such as Duke Elimar von Oldenburg, a retired high-ranking military officer, whose participation Bertha rejoiced over in a letter to Carneri. "Oldenburg . . . Just think—a colonel *à la suite*—I'll get a third of the retired army with this. He's shown them how they can follow their better instincts—a prince and a colonel have made a public example."[19]

The duke of Oldenburg and Prince Wrede were taken into the committee somewhat later, although neither was prepared to work actively, being willing merely to supply their splendid names. This composition in the committee did not exactly attract followers of the social democrats, whose support the society was hoping for so badly, but Bertha, blinded by the brilliance of aristocratic names, did not think about this. Her optimism knew no limits. "I am confident in the hope that the congress will turn out wonderfully—that the conference and congress will be held in *Vienna* in 1892, and in '93 in Chicago the *governments* will meet to conclude treaties. I'm not saying that wildly: *I am up to date on the plans.*"[20]

During the next few months Carneri got a lot of these success reports. "Soon we will be the elite of Europe! Not only Europe, but also America, Libya, and Bohemia."[21]

And she continued to collect proof of sympathy in the form of donations of money, declarations of membership, and publicity for the movement. She wrote friends who were writers and asked for letters of endorsement that could be published in support of the cause. She was successful with some—Leo Tolstoy, Max Nordau, and Conrad Ferdinand Meyer—whose letters she proudly published in her memoirs.

But there were also skeptical letters, like those from Alphonse Daudet and Paul Heyse: the latter wrote that he was reluctant "to talk about pious wishes, which are taken for granted among a nobler, humane minority, in solemn protestations which I cannot hope will bring any practical results. As long as European civilization is still threatened by semi-Asian barbarism which never subjected itself to arbitration and will only bend to force, I even hold the *ceterum censeo* of such congresses to be a danger, like everything else that, in the name of world peace, impairs our indispensable fitness to fight."[22]

In a long letter composed in wobbly, outdated handwriting, the seventy-five-year-old "Wise man from Emmersdorf," Adolf Fischhof, one of the great leaders of the Viennese Revolution of 1848, gave his complete support. He enclosed his two most important writings ("Die Reduktion der kontinentalen Heere" [The reduction of the continental armies], from the year 1875, and "Österreich und die Bürgschaften seines Bestandes" [Austria and the guarantees for its existence], from 1870) in which he had pushed for an international peace movement and disarmament a considerable time before Suttner—albeit without success. Now he wrote to the more successful and energetic successor, "As you will see from the two enclosed magazines, my ambition in 1875 was to be the flag bearer of the idea which you, Baroness, have defended during the last few years in literature and journalistic articles with superb talent and admirable energy. My aspirations were never satisfied, and it will be an honor for me to follow the banner whose bearer is a noble and brilliant woman."[23] Truly, this was a patent of nobility for the Suttner peace effort.

She passed over the setbacks, and only occasionally complained, as here to Carneri: "Oh, what a load I have on my shoulders. But I have taken the dare—now I also have to carry on to the end."[24]

She admitted to having moments of weakness and fear and asked her friend, "Carneri, my Carneri, do not abandon me! Many will ridicule me and hate me—I need those who love me."[25]

And it was true: the troubles the old skeptic Carneri prophesied began to show up even before the peace congress began. They were the same problems that arose again and again later on whenever the issue was not concerned with demonstrating for the great peace, but was focused on concrete political differences between countries. German and Austrian parliamentarians refused to go to the conference in Rome because the president of the IPU, the famous scholar and former Italian minister of education, Bonghi, "published an article in some review or other, in which a remark made on the Alsace-Lorraine problem was sympathetic to the French standpoint."[26]

The Austrian member of parliament, Haase, wrote to Suttner indignantly, "What Mr. Bonghi wrote about the position of France on Alsace-Lorraine, ought to make him be in favor of *this* war at least if France declares war on Germany. And therein lies, for him, the logical impossibility of condemning war at all, and if he does anyway, then he enters a contradiction with himself." Haase called for a boycott and swore to the friendship of Austria-Hungary for the German Empire.[27]

Italian parliamentarians had similar reactions. They did not want to meet with the Austrian delegates in Rome for fear of getting into difficulties over the "Irredenta," the annexation movement of Italians living in Austria.

National conflicts could not be abolished overnight simply because all the participants at this conference wanted peace and disarmament. The problems had not surfaced at the previous two IPU conferences because up to this point, it had mostly been French and English delegates who took part. Now, however, through Bertha's efforts, the circle of participants was much wider. The fact that the members of the IPU belonged mostly to conservative, usually nationalist parties, whereas the international-minded social democrats were against the IPU from the very beginning and did not take part, made the situation even more difficult. These quarrels between peace-lovers, carried out in the open, naturally gave cause for scorn and derision. Bertha von Suttner saw her work threatened. One after the other, her followers tried to back out, giving various excuses.

Alarmed by these incidents, she lamented, "Oh God, oh God! National ticklishness when the concern is international understanding—political considerations where we are supposed to be practicing *supra*-politics."[28] But then she became active and fought back. She gave the news of the newly founded Austrian Peace Society and a list of its members to the *Neue Freie Presse*. This made it impossible for those who were faltering to back out. Suttner rejoiced in a letter to Carneri, "Look, I do not want to be overly modest, but I am a genius, there's no doubt about it. By sending the communiqué to the *Neue Freie Presse* (it belongs to *me*) right in the middle of the Bonghi commotion when one after the other was breaking away, the Austrian branch was *born,* presented to the world as a living thing and introduced with *such names*. Now the acceptances are arriving again. . . . If I had hesitated at that moment, not led my little troop gathered around me, the cause would have run aground. . . . The cause is advancing *splendidly*. . . . The way I'm working now—a Moltke has no idea . . . there is simply not enough time. 'My peace is gone.' But my heart is glad."[29]

She had an answer to well-meaning criticism (the peace movement was utopian and did not have a chance, that was obvious from the quarrels prior to the congress). "The purpose of the congress is only to *make preparations* so that the principle of treaties on a court of arbitration will be recognized by governments and then carried through. When all countries decide to disarm *together* then no patriot will have to vote for military budgets anymore; *without* concerted action, no one can be expected to vote for making *his* fatherland defenseless."[30]

After long discussion in the open, Bonghi was finally compelled to declare before the IPU conference that neither the matter of the "irredenta" nor that of Alsace-Lorraine would be mentioned. In addition he handed over the presidency of the IPU to someone else while holding on to the presidency of the peace congress.

During and despite the international stir, an important event occurred. On October 30, 1891, at the Altes Rathaus in Vienna, the Austrian Peace Society was founded; president: Baroness Bertha von Suttner; membership: two thousand.

But Bertha could not afford to rest on her laurels. She had to put together an Austrian delegation to the Roman congress and prepare herself for the meeting. Again, she had to write Alfred Nobel an urgent letter for money. "Now or never, you can show whether I can call you a friend or not. Do you want to give me moral and real [meaning financial] support as a friend in this most burning and most treasured task in my life?"[31]

He answered rather skeptically, "I don't entirely understand what great tasks the league or the peace congress might carry out." He enclosed eighty pounds sterling anyway. Still, he did not think much of the peace movement and cautioned his friend, "I think there is less a lack of money than platform. Desire alone does not ensure peace. The same thing can be said of big banquets with big speeches. It is necessary to be able to lay an acceptable plan before well-meaning governments. Demanding disarmament is almost like making yourself ridiculous without helping anybody. Demanding that a court of arbitration be established immediately, means butting against thousands of prejudices and making an enemy of everyone with ambition."

How thoroughly Alfred Nobel had studied the peace movement in the meanwhile is shown by his suggestion:

> One should be satisfied with more modest beginnings in order to achieve success, and do what they do in England when success appears doubtful: they content themselves with passing a provisional law, lim-

ited to a period of only two or three years. I think only very few governments would refuse to consider so modest a proposal if it were supported by reputable statesmen. Would it be too much to ask of European governments to commit themselves for the period of one year to take every difference that comes up between them to a court established for that purpose; or, if they refuse, to postpone any hostile act until the end of the period prescribed by treaty? That would appear to be little, but it is when you are content with little that you achieve the big success. One year is so little in the life of a nation, and even an aggressive minister will tell himself that it is not worth it to break an agreement of such a short term with force. And when the period is over all the countries will hurry to extend their peace agreements for another year. Without upheaval and almost without noticing it, they will enter an extended period of peace. Only then will it be meaningful to think about arriving little by little at the disarmament that every decent person and almost all governments want. And assuming that a conflict breaks out between two governments, don't you think that in nine cases out of ten during the binding cease-fire they have subjected themselves to, they will quiet down?[32]

In her answering letter, Bertha did not acknowledge any of these objections; she thanked Nobel for the donation and explained what money was constantly needed for: "Big parties are being organized for the Italian committee and that costs a lot of money. . . . Besides, funds are needed for publicity, correspondence, circular letters, etc., etc."[33]

It was clear: without Nobel's help, Bertha's successes would not have been possible. Before membership dues would have been able to supply the enormous sums of money they needed, the congress would have long since been over.

The Inter-Parliamentarian Conference and the third International Peace Congress met in Rome in the middle of November 1891. Bertha took part in the congress as president of the new Austrian Peace Society and as a world-famous writer for the peace effort. She enjoyed these days thoroughly: "The affirmations of peace at the reception prepared for us by the once so warlike Rome were both festive and solemn. Flags decorated the square, on the steps of the open stairs were Michelangelo's two rows of City Guards with drawn swords; in addition the sounds of the wedding march from *Lohengrin*, the *fedeli* in their rich Renaissance costumes."

She anticipated possible objections. "Do not say it is theatrical, pointless pomp. All pomp is the expression of esteem rendered . . . to the peace congress, which was previously ignored if not scorned, such superficial, official homage is a sign of the times, not to be underestimated."[34]

The congress met at the great council hall at the capitol. Bertha von Suttner tells of gilt chairs, a large number of Italian and foreign journalists, and of festive speeches. After the deputy of the mayor of Rome and President Bonghi made their speeches, she spoke—in Italian. It was her first speech in public, and not only that—it took place in the capitol where no woman had ever spoken before.

Only a few years before (at the congress of the German Writers Association in Berlin in 1885) she had made the following remark when other women delivered speeches: "I can't understand it—how can they have the courage to speak like that in public?"[35]

Now all these misgivings were gone—and with them the stage fright that had once hindered her in her career as a singer.

> Very calmly, without embarrassment, joyfully elated, I said what I had to say . . . quite fearlessly, with the assurance of a messenger who had specific and happy news to impart. I was able to relate that in a big central European country where no peace association had existed six weeks ago, today, at the first appeal of a powerless woman who had no other merits than to have written a sincere book, two thousand people have already gathered together to have themselves represented in Rome; and if two thousand cofighters had responded within a few days, then there would be twenty thousand members of the Austrian peace group to be represented at the next congress.

Optimism always was one of Bertha's qualities.[36]

Here in Rome, Bertha met "both of the two peace veterans," Frédéric Passy and Hodgson Pratt, along with Frederik Bajer, Elie Ducommun, Moneta, and many other leading international pacifists, who now became her friends.

The business was carried out with only minor differences of opinion among the delegates from seventeen countries. The pacifists encouraged each other, exchanged information, made new contacts. The feeling of international solidarity, even though it was in a rather limited society, made a big impression on Bertha, "Oh, the wonderful togetherness . . . in one community—in the community of love for humanity and human dignity." The "congresses so despised by 'practical' politicians" were in her opinion "places for cultivating and practicing the feeling of community among peoples which had not arisen until this modern time."[37]

It was decided to establish a central office of the peace societies in Bern to improve organization and publicity. It was subsidized by the Swiss and Norwegian governments and by private donations. The president was the Swiss, Elie Ducommun, the vice-president, Suttner—a job which brought her even more work, but it also brought satisfaction and worldwide recognition.

There were a lot of suggestions for improving international peace work. There could be international brotherhood festivities at universities. Calls for support went out to women's clubs, teachers, workers' associations, and students. They should all work for peace and against war, each according to his or her abilities. And they should join the peace associations.

The possibilities were limited for both the societies and the congresses, as Bertha admitted: "Abolishing war only needs the will of whoever has the power in his hands. The rest of us can do nothing except provide proof that the need for this abolition exists—therefore our most important, almost our only responsibility is *propaganda*."

Frightened by the national conflicts within the peace movement, Bertha added, "And above all—no politics! No party! Politics *separate*, we want to *unite*—the parties have colors and colorations, nuances and shades, our color is that of unbroken light, is that of our flag, *white.*— We must keep our eye on this *one* goal alone, as our unwavering guiding light: *arbitration instead of war*. Away with the giant death penalty that is imposed upon entire peoples! . . . Our objective is manifestation: the will to peace becoming articulate, concentrated, in places where it is shy and scattered, and education, too, where it is lacking."[38]

Despite all the work, the congress was a big international social event that Bertha and Arthur enjoyed together. Special trains went to Naples and Pompeii for sightseeing, there were receptions and gala performances. "Being together casually, in an elated mood combined with cheers from the people, flags waving, bands playing music: all of that almost brings about more brotherhood and understanding than the congress business itself."[39]

Alfred Nobel, who had contributed so much to this journey, got an enthusiastic report:

> I was a success—a perfect success. I don't know where I got the courage to speak in front of the full capitol, to mix into the debates and to succeed in warding off the whole question of Alsace-Lorraine they wanted to bring up and that would have made enemies rather than friends. This courage is probably the awareness of the great responsibility that has been given me. If I had failed in the capitol, the young Austrian society would have failed, too. This responsibility, this burden, is something I must continue to carry. And for that reason I am grateful, from the bottom of my heart, to all those who encourage me and who are my friends.[40]

Alfred Nobel proved his generosity again and soon made official donations of considerable size to the Austrian Peace Society. Bertha: "It makes me *so* happy that you direct your interest toward our cause!"[41]

The congress in Rome made one thing clear to her: from now on, she was a fighter for peace—on the frontline. Everything else had to be secondary, even her writing. The success of her lectures had also been a positive experience, and she wanted to continue with this, as inexperienced as she was. She wrote to Carneri, "Well, I'm almost afraid that now the *responsibility* of giving lectures will descend upon me; since the living word makes more proselytes than the written."[42] "It's amazing what a Löwos can become! I now feel it is my responsibility to sow every seed for peace I possibly can."[43]

Her next task was to create an organ for the new peace society to keep its members informed and publicize its activities. First, Bertha tried using a cheap publication that appeared right after the Roman congress, the *Mittheilungen der österreichischen Gesellschaft der Friedensfreunde.* But another possibility opened up soon. Alfred Hermann Fried, a twenty-eight-year-old book merchant originally from Vienna but now in Berlin, had written Suttner a glowing letter of admiration after the appearance of *Lay Down Your Arms.* Since then they had exchanged letters. He decided to place himself entirely at the service of the peace movement—beginning with the publication of a magazine that was to appear under the title, *Lay Down Your Arms,* and have Bertha von Suttner as its publisher.

The relationship between Suttner and Fried began with quarreling. Each thought the other was wealthy. Fried was surprised when Bertha demanded a fee for publishing the magazine. "You reckoned 3,000 marks for paper and printing expenses," she wrote him angrily. "You'll have to add another 2,400 marks for editor and author. For these to cost nothing is not correct."[44] And when Fried, whose financial resources were extremely limited, did not give in, she insisted, "I am not rich—we exist on what we earn with our pens, my husband and I."[45] Finally, they agreed on a monthly fee of 50 marks, which would soon fail to appear anyway. Bertha: "As it is, I make *so* many sacrifices for the cause. . . . I would not have regarded myself *paid* even with the fee I asked for."[46]

Then Fried confessed his unfortunate financial situation. He was a Jew, came from a poor background and because of this, had not been able to study. He had no connections or backing. At learning this, Bertha tried to cheer him up: "But since you are still so young, you can hope for fire and action—and since you are *self,* the *made* will soon put in an appearance, too. Grow—that is what lies at the bottom of all greatness and strength; the big things that fall from heaven (by birth, wealth) often stay the same, if they don't shrink."[47] Fried's enthusiastic willingness spurred the already hardworking Suttner on even more during the next decades; it even developed into a true motor for the woman twenty-one years his senior.

The magazine, edited in Vienna and printed in Berlin, was supposed to be more than a club organ. It was to be "a general paper for support-ing the peace idea" and a pathfinder for the intended German peace soci-ety. They reckoned with five hundred subscriptions, but their excessive expectations were soon disappointed. Bertha wrote Fried, "I am very ashamed about the subscriptions. It seems we have both been too san-guine. . . . [E]veryone is behaving so indifferently, waiting to see what will happen. . . . I don't have to worry about brilliant contributors, only about brilliant subscription results, that's difficult to achieve."[48]

Finally, Fried had 370 copies printed for the first issue in February of 1892. And even these few were not sold. Suttner tried to cheer up her young publisher: "So, a deficit? That's the way the *Revue de deux mondes* started, too. We *will* work our way through. . . . And the thing that gives the magazine its own peculiar value is the fact that it appears in Berlin (*la citadelle du militarisme*)."[49]

Again Suttner found prominent people who supported the maga-zine. Carneri, Rosegger, Tolstoy, and numerous other pacifists re-sponded as authors. There were also a number of refusals—for instance, from Ibsen, who confessed "that he does not know anything about peace matters and therefore cannot write about them." Nobel, too, restricted himself to making a public declaration of sympathy for the peace move-ment and giving money.

Bertha wrote a long article for every issue of the magazine, took care of answering the letters to the editor, and the encounters with peace opponents.

The magazine was rather amateurish and was even criticized by Bertha's closest friends, including Bartolomeus von Carneri, who objected to its rather childish optimism. He wrote his friend, "You are caught up in a great mistake if you think state leaders do not know that people want peace; and the expectations you attach to making this known are unfounded. First, the possibility for a sturdy peace has to be created; then the court of arbitration will have a place. We are not so far away from that, but you don't have to try to force it inside a two-year period."[50]

His criticism of the second issue was also acute. "That thing must not look like an advertisement created just for you," he cautioned his friend, "and, more important, it should not always concentrate on the one thing."[51] Suttner agreed: "[T]he advertisements and the market cries about the eternal Bertha von Suttner annoy me. In *my* house, I have to greet my elevated guests with the proper distance and not trumpet the merits of Bertha von Suttner's literary products."[52]

She wrote something similar to Fried, whose accolades put her in the foreground far too much. "The magazine should not be an advertising institute for the publisher," she reprimanded in reference to the many advertisements for her book. "If *I* already feel offended by the repetition of this name, others will feel it even more." Then she protested against Fried's writing that Bertha von Suttner stood "at the head of the move-ment." "The Pratts, the Virchows, the Pirquets, the Bajers, etc., will hold this presumptuousness against me in no small way. . . . Things like this make a person unpopular. And if you want to run a movement like this one especially, you have to make yourself popular, have to see to it that you are excused if there is too much noise made about your name—not add to it yourself."[53]

The faster and better she herself worked, the more impatient she became with the slow, deliberate coworkers in the peace society. Every-thing was too slow for her, too afraid and careful.

She hated the trivial business of keeping receipts and similar jobs; it went against her chaotic sense of order. She constantly had trouble with things like this.

She also loathed long discussions in the society. "If I had had to let my press article, which brought the whole 'society' into being, be cen-sored by a committee of twenty, it would probably never have been pub-lished at all," and she explained why she never thought of her paper as the official organ of the peace society: "[S]o that I can run it indepen-dently, without questions and without making the others responsible."

Carneri looked upon this hectic situation with concern, and warned her "not to break" the peace cause "over her knee." "I judge people dif-ferently than you do. You see them from the viewpoint of the socialists who think it is possible for mankind to achieve perfection at the twist of a wrist. I am convinced that we are still very far away from a time that can abolish war."[54]

Suttner answered with unaccustomed sharpness, "This time your let-ter really hurt me because it showed that sympathy for the movement is not very strong, not only 'in your circles' but in you yourself. When I say 'sympathy,' I mean trust.

"You do not *believe* in the possibility of people coming to their senses *before* the great horrible war of the future, and stopping *it* is the ardent desire of those who come together in peace societies and congresses. If we also thought that the goal could only be achieved after the sixth or seventh generation, then we would also be wise enough to leave the trouble to that generation."

One had to fight for the good cause and not stand aside skeptically. That would show the opponents were right.

> *Then,* in a few years, the war would have to stop by itself, and we would not need to strain our energy and our minds—the destruction of all peoples through armament would make rearming impossible; the electrical death machines would be so highly perfected that there could be no duels between peoples, only double suicides between peoples, and then—perhaps even earlier—strikes will also break out among soldiers. . . .
>
> When my best friends, including friends in our peace movement, criticize so sharply and moreover have so little faith—what can I expect from the indifferent, what do I have to fear from the opponents?[55]

Carneri is very precise in his answer. "You say yourself that above all, truthfulness must reign between us and I, too, cannot imagine our friendship any other way." He had not made the reference to the seventh generation, that is, the distant future as being the time for realizing the peace idea "because I listen to hot-headed people who want war but because I cannot come to any other conclusion due to my own knowledge, as far as it covers history and the nature of man . . . and all I want to do is to place a little damper on you. I mean it for your own good."[56]

Bertha's conciliatory answer, "Everything is all right again!"[57]

No prominent person was safe from her ideas. "I met Johann Strauss recently," Bertha reported to Carneri. "He asked me for permission to dedicate his next waltz to me, with allusions in the title to the peace cause (which he is very enthusiastic about). The premiere should go to Bern. . . . That should bring some spirit into the business."[58] But once again, her optimism was too great.

Two years later she tried her luck again with the highly popular Waltz King. She wrote him that she had learned "that you are writing a new waltz suite. If this is so, then I remind you of your promise that is so very highly supportive to our sacred cause. Wouldn't 'Rustling Palms' or 'White Doves' be a nice title? Or 'New Goals.'" Then she added somewhat sadly, "*Lay Down Your Arms* or *Peace Waltz* ought not to be used, because military officers would not dance then and military bands would not want to play it."[59]

But the master had his wife Adele reply that he "had the best intentions," and wanted to devote "the first free hour" to the "peace waltz." "Only the pressing load of urgent work . . ."[60]

And if she had no luck with the Waltz King, at least she did with a representative of the "silver Viennese operetta," Franz von Suppé. He wrote a piece for men's chorus, "Lay Down Your Arms," which was performed for the first time at the congress in Bern. Bertha wrote Fried, "This is a brilliant piece! The Suppé men's chorus is marvelous. Can become a popular melody."[61] (With which she probably wanted to make the extremely simple melody and choral setting appear more attractive.)

She worked on other prominent personalities with similar stubbornness, going all the way to the "police president himself," whom she asked to take part in a meeting of the peace society. She knew very well how annoying she was and called herself a "vampire" who clung "to the neck, brutally sucking blood" from the person she was courting.[62]

Just about every prominent person who held a lecture in Vienna and could even vaguely be thought of as like-minded was asked by Bertha for a public sign of peace. Fritjof Nansen was one of these. He actually wove the following sentence into his talk on polar exploration: "The time of great wars of conquest has passed—the time of conquests in the land of science, of the unknown, will endure, and we hope that the future will bring further conquests and thus bring humanity forwards."[63]

When Mark Twain was in Vienna, he accepted Suttner's invitation to a demonstration for solidarity with Emile Zola in the Dreyfus case, but expressed his doubts in a letter dated February 17, 1898: "I am indeed in *sympathy* with the movement, but my head is not with my heart in the matter. I cannot see how the movement can strongly appeal to the selfishness of governments. It can appeal to the selfishness of nations, possibly, but nations have no command over their government, and in fact no influence over them, except of a fleeting and rather ineffectual sort."[64]

A half year later, she even succeeded in getting the famous author to make a short, improvised speech. He spoke in English and amiably declared that he was prepared to disarm immediately, although a penknife was the only thing he carried with him. The newspapers did not let the joke slip by—and so there was publicity for both sides: for the peace cause and for Mark Twain.[65]

When newspapers published the sensational news in 1895 that Henri Dunant, the founder of the Red Cross, was not dead, as everyone thought, but living in dire poverty in Switzerland, Suttner contacted him immediately. She wrote him a letter of homage, organized a collection (which produced a very meager sum of money) and asked him for contributions for the peace magazine, which he in fact supplied. From the very first letter, she tried to make it clear to him, that he was one of them: "[T]hat means a pacifist, an enemy of war and militarism . . . Your movement was the predecessor of ours." She did not want to compete with the Red Cross, she wanted to work together with it.[66]

Then she got it into her head to win over the best-known Viennese actor, Joseph Lewinsky, to her cause. He was an "intellectual," a very educated and ambitious actor and was even admired by Empress Elisabeth, who allowed him to read Heine and Goethe to her in a very intimate circle. An appearance of this particular, extremely popular person had enormous propaganda value; Bertha knew that very well—and, when Lewinsky declined at first, she insisted "at the danger of being unpleasantly obtrusive—once more with pleading hands I ask you: take part in our peace evening (the 29th)! There will only be artistic things, no club speeches—but it will give us new impetus, and supply us with additional funds for our exhausted treasury. I know that my imposition is no small one, no modest one—but I *am* not modest and am not shy when it comes to service to this cause."[67]

Finally, Lewinsky accepted, and even got his wife, the great actress Olga Lewinsky, to agree to join him in performing for the peace cause. Both were a big success.

It took seven letters in May of 1892 to get Peter Rosegger, who was ill at the time, to come to Vienna from Graz for a meeting. Finally, he capitulated and made the difficult trip. "I alarm myself with my obtrusiveness," she wrote the "highly honored poet," and said, "under no other circumstances would I torment an honored friend who does not feel well with such an imposition—but when it comes to our dear, right, and unfortunately still so insecure cause—I overcome all scruples."[68]

Rosegger gave a lecture with the title, "My Opinion on the Justification of the Friends of Peace."[69] Bertha got all of her admirers together for this meeting and for the pleasant gathering afterwards at the Imperial Hotel.

In addition to Carneri, Alfred Nobel was also filled with sympathy for Bertha but skepticism for her peace work. She worked as hard as she could to allay his doubts.

> All these things are as small as seed-grains. I admit this—at the same time the world's monstrosities of war, the Caprivi [the German *Reichskanzler,* or chancellor] speeches, the anti-Semitic practices and reactionary intrigues everywhere look enormous; but the seed-grains, as small as

they are, carry the shaded forest of the future within them, and the big thousand-year-old trunks are rotten and will soon collapse. The battle against malice is hard, but it is an enormously gratifying feeling to know you are one with the best and the most benevolent and the clearest of judgment in your time. We want to fill the few years we still have the strength with the work of slaying the dragon—perhaps we will see the day of victory dawn![70]

The closer she worked with the young Fried, the more she allowed herself to be caught up in his enthusiasm, if such a thing was possible, considering her own activities—and the more she distanced herself from the increasingly skeptical, constantly warning Carneri, who praised her only very rarely.

If Carneri tried to hold back his younger, too tempestuous friend, tried to get her to think things over quietly, Bertha was soon having to do the same thing with her associate, Fried. He was tempestuous, over-enthusiastic, and very unpopular with colleagues and book merchants because of his brash manner. He even got into repeated quarrels with his coworkers for peace. Bertha calmed him down as well as she could in letters, but became more adamant when Fried wanted to include an anarchistic article in her magazine. "That contradicts the dignified, quiet appearance we have always made," she protested. "So, away with that paper immediately."[71] Fried obeyed. Soon the following remark to Fried turned up in the midst of business letters: "I just want to mention in passing that I am very fond of you."[72]

The magazine continued to have problems. The number of subscribers was still small, and the deficit grew so much within the first few years that Fried was no longer able to keep the paper. He asked Bertha to cadge some money off her rich friends. But she, who had financial worries of her own, shied away from this humiliating step. "It sounds so easy to collect such a relatively minor sum of money from one's friends, but it is not easy. One can have reasons—reasons that lie outside—for not being able to do this."[73]

A serious quarrel arose between the two, and even Arthur von Suttner interceded with a strong letter to Fried. "The entire burden lies upon our backs," he wrote. "Put yourself in the situation where you are close to the breaking point and are supposed to take on a few hundred kilograms more. I think I owe you this explanation, since you are probably laboring under the mistaken idea that we lead a paradisiac existence."[74]

Fried had no way of knowing that there were pressing money problems in Harmannsdorf at this time. But Bertha succeeded at least in getting her Leipzig publisher, Pierson, to take the magazine over from Fried. However, she did not get a fee from Pierson, either.

The next goal was to found a German peace society in Berlin. Up to this point there had already been a few small, more or less private circles of pacifists and a small interparliamentarian group there. But, "No real German peace society exists. Virchow originally consented but has said nothing since. Dr. Max Hirsch, a member of the German Reichstag, wants to found one now. Dr. Barth, the publisher of the *Nation,* is also one of us. And I think there is also an organization in Frankfurt."[75]

Founding a central organization for all of Germany ran into considerable difficulties. A lecture delivered by the famous author of *Lay Down Your Arms* was supposed to speed up the project.

Fried did everything in his power to make Bertha's debut as brilliant as possible. The high point was to be her lecture, of course, but a banquet with the intellectual greats of Berlin was intended to honor the leading fighter for the peace idea and create publicity. Bertha, carried away by Fried's enthusiasm, wrote Carneri, "Oh, my trip to Berlin. I'm quite beside myself. Hall sold out. Ticket agents selling to the highest bidder. Flowers from the audience."[76]

Despite the success, there was still the fear of not being good enough. "My reputation has grown far beyond my merits—that bothers me a bit," she complained to Carneri.[77]

To Fried she wrote, "Laying the cornerstone of a German peace society during my visit—that would be wonderful!"[78]

And cheerfully, she wrote, "A guardian angel is watching over this peace cause: ever since I have taken it in hand, everything has gone perfectly."[79]

Again—just as she had for the founding of the Austrian society—she sought important names to support the peace idea and was soon forced to admit that the really prominent men in the Berlin of Wilhelm II were not enthusiastic about her cause at all.

All of the gala speeches resounded with the desire for founding a German society. Despite all the effort, this goal was not reached in Berlin at this time.

The work continued but was centered in Vienna again. Fried and Dr. Max Hirsch made regular reports to Bertha on new projects, and she herself wrote letters diligently, gave instructions, and urged Fried to hurry. "A German society *must* come to life before Bern (the venue of the next peace congress)."[80]

The main problem was Alsace-Lorraine. How was the peace movement to get the representatives of the traditional enemies, Germany and

France, to work together? The pacifists took the political stand held by their own governments, and each laid claim to the area along the Rhine.

Suttner wrote long, imploring letters emphasizing the fact that an international peace movement without Germany was worthless, since the question of war or peace pivoted on German politics—especially where Alsace-Lorraine was concerned. "The whole world knows that the danger of war, all of the current armament, rests upon the different interpretations of Alsace-Lorraine ownership. Starting out by declaring the German interpretation to be the only right one [as many German pacifists demanded] does not require a peace society; *para-bellum* politics does that, too. It stands on the same level with the French peace parties that say, Alsace-Lorraine back first, then peace." She said it was absolutely necessary "to have a sister society in Germany, too, otherwise this movement's international effectiveness is crippled."[81] The German peace society would also have to be "above politics" (primarily, that meant not nationalist).

The Fourth International Peace Congress in Bern in 1892 had to take place without German representatives. But a national problem came up all the same. A Polish member of the Austrian parliament demanded that Poland be reinstated as an independent kingdom. He was placed "out of bounds" with the explanation "that the congress cannot possibly take up the revision of Polish history. The justice of the future must be prepared; the individual incidents of injustice in history cannot be canceled since all of the existing distribution of land is based on violence; new laws, new systems—and they should be worked toward—have no retroactive power."[82]

As long as she lived, Suttner never tired of advocating this view, and she repeatedly impressed upon her coworkers "what a peace society cannot do—namely, establish peace *itself,* wipe out the political causes of war."[83] This job is incumbent upon governments alone.

Suttner did not give up her struggle for founding a nonpolitical German peace society—nor did Fried. Every day, sometimes even several times a day, she wrote him, and of course the other German friends of peace as well, such as Father Südekum, Professor Wilhelm Förster, and Dr. Max Hirsch.

When the news finally came from Berlin in November 1892 that a founding committee had been formed, Suttner was overjoyed. "I have not experienced a greater joy for a long time," she wrote to Fried. "That is wonderful. The part you played in it is immeasurable—if you had not worked on untiringly, it would not have come about—at least not for a long time yet." She said she would get her Austrian peace workers to send greetings to the founding meeting in Berlin. "Then we Germans and Austrians will work 'shoulder to shoulder'—but not in the old manner, baring our teeth toward east and west."[84]

But the German peace society in Berlin was and remained a source of annoyance and trouble. The Alsace-Lorraine problem continued to be the main issue and refused to be banished. All the beautiful ideals of supranationality and of cosmopolitan ways of thinking about peace could not suppress German nationalism. Following Bertha's intentions, Fried fought hard, sometimes unrestrainedly and insultingly, against the "political," "national" peace followers in Berlin, and in the end he resigned under protest from the German Peace Society he himself founded. Now he planned to found a new central organization in Frankfurt, a plan that was thoroughly justified historically, since one of the oldest peace societies was situated in Frankfurt. Yet Berlin, being the capital of the German Empire, was the center of all activity, and attaching Berlin to a central organization in Frankfurt was unthinkable.

The plan would have meant a split, which Suttner warned the heated members against. She advised Fried to make up with his opponents, something he did not do.

The constant aggravation—not only because of the "enemy," militarism, but also because of some among their own numbers—embittered Bertha to such an extent that she seriously considered giving up her involvement in the movement and working as a writer again. It took a great deal of effort on Fried's part to cheer her up.

So she took up her work again, together with Fried, whom she needed more than ever since he worked for the peace movement without tiring and without pay. She knew that he had financial problems and helped him despite her own precarious situation. By now, the Austrian Peace Society had eight thousand members, but "far fewer than a thousand *pay* and most of them only after the third reminder."[85]

Again and again, it was the lack of money that made it impossible to carry out peace activities that were necessary. In 1894 Suttner wrote Fried, who had urged her to take a trip to Paris, "The idea of Paris is not without merit. We could do something there, but we would also have to 'be able' to. What that means is: there's no money. Despicable money."[86]

Then America beckoned, the cradle of the modern peace movement. "I am as well known in America as a counterfeit coin," she wrote to Carneri in 1892. "Got instructions from the president of the Chicago Exhibition (Department of Congresses) to take over the organization of the Peace Congress.—Thanks so much."[87] Not that she had lost the desire for organizing. But she lacked travel money, a situation she did not admit to her friend. Nor did she tell Alfred Nobel, who had just donated a large sum of money for the peace society. Besides, she had to write another novel very quickly, for which a large fee had been agreed upon. It is hardly surprising that these novels written in the greatest haste became worse from year to year and her reputation as a writer declined.

Usually the Suttners were able to find a patron to cover the travel expenses to the annual peace congresses: sometimes, a newspaper Bertha would write congress reports for; sometimes, a friend like Alfred Nobel or Baron Leitenberger; and sometimes, the Austrian Peace Society even had enough money to send its president on a journey. Bertha von Suttner was the center of attention everywhere she went, was celebrated and highly honored. On congress photographs she was always placed in the center of the first row, usually next to Frédéric Passy—and was extremely elegant, very dignified, even majestic to look at.

Her role at these congresses went far beyond representational duties. There were almost always quarrels between various countries to mediate, usually because of sudden, acute, political problems that also had to be straightened out among the pacifists. "Congresses are hard work," she wrote Fried. "It is easy to lose your patience and become angry."[88] It often required all of her strength and persuasive powers to reconcile the fighting cocks. She had authority and was accepted as a *consiliatrix,* as a mediator, by all sides. This was due to her merits, her personality, and no less to her strong international position as vice-president of the Bern Peace Bureau.

The activities of the international organization were varied and provided satisfaction along with the occasional annoyance. Bertha wrote to Nobel: "Do you know the Bern bureau just got the official support of the Danish government? That's a step forward. Peace budgets—that is something new. They are beginning to attribute our institution with a character of 'public usefulness.'"[89]

In the course of the years it became apparent that the Austrian Peace Society, founded in 1891, had trouble speaking for all of Austria-Hungary. It became all too clear that neither the Hungarians nor the Bohemians (not to mention the other nationalities) felt they belonged to this central organization in Vienna and therefore stayed away. Bertha von Suttner was faced with the neccessity of founding at least two additional peace societies in Austria-Hungary, namely, one in Prague and the other in Budapest.

In the autumn of 1895 she took a lecture at the Concordia Press Club in Prague as the occasion for putting her plans for Bohemia into action. After all, she was born in Prague, grew up in Brno, and had many personal attachments to the Bohemian lands, even though she did not speak Czech.

Her lecture was extremely successful. The *Bohemia* reported that in the "German House" in Prague, she "talked to the best German social circles" about the great fighters for peace and also praised the contemporary Czech writers, Svatopluk Cech and Jaroslav Vrchlicky. She also recited a Vrchlicky poem in the German translation she had done herself. In another place she praised these poems as "a brilliant collection of jewels," and said: "This book should be hurled at the skulls of the *Ur-Teutons* who babble about the 'inferiority' of the Slavs."[90]

She firmly believed that the peace idea would also bridge the national problems of the Austrian-Hungarian monarchy but met with strong opposition from the Germans in Prague. Soon, even she saw no chance for building up a common Bohemian peace society made up of both Germans and Czechs. The national antagonisms and the hatred on both sides were insurmountable.

Since 1882 there had not been a common university in Prague. Instead, there were separate German and Czech universities, and their professors and students fought each other furiously and occasionally even bloodily. Societies for everything from gymnastics to singing were either Czech or German, never "Bohemian."

Although Bertha basically held on to the idea of a single Bohemian organization, she suggested having two national branches as an interim solution. "Where could the reconciled cooperation of two nationally separated groups be better achieved than in the supranational realm of the peace movement? If the current situation in Prague really demands that for a start two branches work separately in order to avoid language conflicts, their members will have a feeling of solidarity with each other in one of the greatest cultural issues, because of their common goal. They will work next to each other in complete accord, take part in the congresses together . . . reach agreement on the issues of humanity."[91]

But these were hopes that could not be reconciled with a Prague reality that was filled with hatred. The Bohemian peace society did not materialize, even though Suttner had several important friends in Prague, such as the philosopher Friedrich Jodl, the enthusiastic pacifist Vrchlicky, and the novelist Sophie Podlipka.

In contrast to Bohemia, Hungary held a strong, preferential position within the empire and was dominated nationally by the Magyars. Founding a peace society there, in December 1895, was easy. Bertha celebrated a genuine triumph in Budapest. In a letter to Carneri, she wrote, "The Budapest episode surpasses everything that has ever happened. Terrific!" And further, "Storm in the Pest newspapers: in *every* Hungarian and German paper, four to ten columns!—And besides, an executive board with two former ministers." And: "Vienna compares to Pest like ice to fire."[92]

No less a figure than the most famous poet in Hungary, Morzi Jokai, placed himself at the head of the Hungarian Peace Society. The Hungarian aristocracy, which had a strong liberal tradition (in contrast to the Cisleithan nobility), was represented with prominent veterans, first and foremost Count Albert Apponyi.

The Suttners were even received by the prime minister, Baron Banffy, with exceptional kindness. All this was cause for optimism and joy and the occasion for a long letter of jubilation to Alfred Nobel. Banffy had told her that the Hungarian government would "not only go along with us, but would go ahead of us."[93] Nobel promptly donated, more or less in congratulation, a thousand gulden for the next international peace congress. It took place in 1896 in Budapest.

The president of the Congress was General Türr, the grand old man of the Hungarian Revolution and international pacifism. Bertha wrote Fried, "Having such a great *military* big shot be one of us is worth a lot."[94]

Suttner gave her congress address in French.

She used the fact that Hungary was very active in the movement as an opportunity to confront several prejudices. "The Magyars are a brave, proud, fighting and yet egalitarian people. If they enter the peace movement, they do so in a totally different spirit than that of battle-shy, lamblike meekness, which is mistakenly taken to be the foundation of the peace league—it happens in the spirit of courageous opposition to a barbaric, ancient institution that oppresses culture and enslaves mankind. The Hungarians have recognized the war against war for what it really is and have joined it with fiery boldness: a war for freedom."[95]

It was the Budapest congress that showed that Bertha von Suttner had meanwhile become an undisputed leader in the international peace movement. Frédéric Passy called her *"notre général-en-chef."*

It became increasingly clear that the movement's great boom in 1891 had been a flash in the pan. Only a minority still showed any interest. Even confirmed friends of peace were no longer prepared to work actively for the cause. The membership dues failed to come in. Bertha had reason to complain to Fried of overwork and financial worries: "Quite apart from the millionaire—or the million followers we need, couldn't you manage to extend the day to 47 working hours and raise my moral capacity to work by a hundred horsepowers? Then I might be able to achieve something—as it is, I often sit here at a loss and let my wings droop."[96]

More and more, she doubted whether the work of the organization was really as important for the movement as she had believed in the beginning. Of course, the peace societies were an organization of international scope, a podium for numerous calls for peace directed to governments. They were supposed to provide the financial backing active members needed but were usually not in the position to do so. They were supposed to lighten the load, but in reality, especially for Bertha, they became an additional burden with enormous internal vexations. Only the International Peace Bureau in Bern and the international gatherings at the congresses offered real advantages.

Frédéric Passy, the grand old man of the European peace movement, saw the task of the fighters for peace this way: "Until the federation of states is established, *we* constitute the federation of workers for the future empire of justice and peace."[97] There were different opinions on whether this was done more effectively through an organization or by individual work, like that done by Fried. The older Suttner became, the more her faith in the efficiency of the organizations diminished and the more convinced she became of the success brought about by personal effort.

After ten years of peace work she said the peace movement "must get out of its state of club fanaticism if it is to become a popular movement. The organizations were only a beginning, as they once were for the women's and workers' movements. Today feminism and socialism have their power—now it's pacifism's turn."[98]

What was lacking was the consolation brought by success. No matter how great their efforts were, war still existed. The outbreak of the Spanish-American war in 1898 affected Bertha so deeply that she was sick for two days.

She had the next political commentary in *Lay Down Your Arms* set with a black border for mourning. "What makes our sorrow greater is this: America, the cradle and stronghold of the peace movement . . . America, which knows no militarism—it has to be America where war was unleashed." And again she warns that once a war has started, it is hard to limit it. "This may have given the signal for a world war, since who can foresee the consequences? The fire has started: the flaming rafters are flying and all our roofs are covered with straw—straw soaked in kerosene."[99]

She was almost defiant in her letter to Fried: "But we will *not* let the flag be lowered! The scorn of the unbelievers must not be allowed to harm us. Progress in liberating and ennobling the world has made another terrible backwards spiral—but maybe the peace movement will increase its pace after this pressure. . . . Darkness all around. The tiny lights are lights all the same and must not go out voluntarily. Courage, my cofighters. *Our* voluntary corps, our expense of millions will also come. Perhaps we will live to see it. . . . Let us remain at our posts!"[100]

7

The Fight Against
Anti-Semitism

A second organization ran parallel to the peace movement in Austria, and it, too, was substantially supported by the Suttners, especially Arthur. The Association for the Resistance to Anti-Semitism was seen as a complement to the peace society. Arthur: "Before we are able to achieve peace abroad, we will have to establish peace within. We and they [the pacifists] are working at this task and we complement each other."[1]

Anti-Semitism broke out in the 1880s after the mass immigration of poor Russian Jews to western Europe. At first the Suttners experienced this trend, that struck them as barbaric, from a distance. In Georgia they read with bewilderment the reports of speeches by the court chaplin in Berlin, Stöcker, and about the response this anti-Semitic campaign awakened in the public. The Suttners thought this movement was a "backslide into the Middle Ages." For them racial hatred was a manifestation of dark times that had long since been surmounted, and its reappearance went against their belief in the progress of humanity from barbarism to "ennobled mankind."[2] Like many of their contemporaries, the Suttners thought that assimilation and intermarriage would eliminate the Jewish problem. The progress of humanity would wipe away ethnic differences, overcome nationalism and religious intolerance, and finally reach its culmination in the birth of the free-spirited cosmopolite.

The Suttners regarded the terrible Jewish pogroms under czarist rule as relics of former times, a barbarism that only seemed possible in a country as backward as Russia. But the flow of Russian emigrants

poured over Poland to Berlin, over Galicia to Budapest and Vienna—
and suddenly anti-Semitism also burst into flame there. The Suttners
thought everything possible had to be done to combat it. They had great
faith in the value of public opinion, and their aim was to mobilize
it against injustice—also against the unjust treatment of poor Jewish
emigrants.

In 1882 the "First International Anti-Jewish Congress" met in Dresden, and its manifesto demanded a battle against the Jews. Governments
were called upon not to admit any more Jewish immigrants.

Bertha was so incensed by this still new phenomenon that she composed a reply to the anti-Jewish manifesto, in which she refuted the arguments of the anti-Semites at length and spoke out for "justice"—that is,
for upholding the rights of these poorest of the poor, whose fate she
clearly deplored:

> In my mind I see this mass of poor people who have fled from wild
> mob persecution, who have lost everything they own. They are dispar-
> aged, tired, and marked by tears. For some of their most beloved—the
> youngest child perhaps, perhaps the aged mother—have fallen under
> the blows or been left lying on the way. They have reached the border
> of the distant German land and will have to see to establishing a new
> home here. Rise! Ye Christian brothers! Is there no one with a spear to
> push back the Jewish riffraff?—Perhaps there is a Christian living at the
> border who remembers his Master Jesus and the parable of the Good
> Samaritan, who will take in the unhappy flock and give it food and
> consolation. But the border guard jumps in just in time and saves the
> Aryanized culture!—The unhappy people over there fall into each
> other's arms weeping. Now there is only one alternative left: to die. . . .
> But since the issue here is not one of beating back attacking enemy
> hordes, but one of eradicating a group living peacefully in our midst,
> the proposed fight cannot be called war, it must be called slaughter. O
> Jesus—Thou gentle, mild one, impassioned with the love of man—and
> this in *Thy* name!

Bertha did not lay the greatest blame for this offense on anti-Semitism's riffraff, but on its eloquent spokesmen:

> Of course they will not lay a hand on anyone themselves, the pastors,
> the owners of knights' estates and parliamentarians, who are the spokes-
> men here, but the fact that their word unleashes fanatic devastation and
> puts the use of throwing stones and lighting firebrands into action, they
> take as "the one and only completely satisfying solution to the prob-

lem," as the fulfillment of an "incontrovertible cultural mission of the Christian world." A good portion of self-control is necessary, considering the horror that is borne in the paragraph quoted here, to continue with objective calm and to take a serious look at the phenomenon being examined here. One's heart is seized with compassion for those who are threatened, with indignation against the threateners. Revulsion wells up inside us.[3]

Bertha and Arthur wrote several articles of this kind in anger. They were bent on making these atrocities known to the public in newspapers as a means of fighting anti-Semitism. But all the articles connected with anti-Semitism were returned for reasons such as these: "It would do the cause too much honor . . . is unpleasant . . . will be disproved by itself among reasonable people . . . is already at the point of waning . . . the attention would only add more strength and support . . . we do not go into this subject in principle and request that you avoid any reference to it in your esteemed articles," or, "In Austria there is no anti-Semitism, and if something of it should be transplanted to us from Prussia, the only correct thing to combat it with is: disdainful silence."[4]

It was not long before a new anti-Semitism arose in Austria-Hungary with undreamed-of characteristics. German-nationalist circles (not only those surrounding the "pan-German" Georg Ritter von Schönerer, but also more moderate representatives of the German-Austrians) allied themselves with Magyar, Polish, and other nationalists, with leaders of a militant Catholicism, and above all with the Christian Socialist movement surrounding Karl Lueger (who was later to become the mayor of Vienna) and his followers.

The conflicts became more and more serious and did not only take place between Jews on the one hand and anti-Semites on the other, but to an increasing degree within Judaism itself. The almost completely assimilated and frequently nonreligious Jews in big western European cities now saw themselves confronted with a mass of poor, orthodox, eastern Jews and were abused along with them by the anti-Semites. Afraid that now, with the outbreak of such hatred of Jews, they would lose their status as accepted Germans or Hungarians that they had worked so hard to achieve, some of them took a stand against the Jewish proletariat. And even those who showed solidarity and provided genuine aid, despite all the differences that had grown up during the previous centuries of western and eastern Judaism, were extremely insecure and felt threatened.

Many of the Jews who had been in Austria for generations were integrated into the "second society" in Vienna. This class was clearly set apart from the "first society" of court nobility but was open to the "third" society of the bourgeoisie. It consisted of the new aristocracy of "industrial barons," civil servants, military officers, and the artistic and intellectual greats of the Viennese fin de siècle who are still considered today to have made the main contribution to this splendid cultural epoch of Vienna.

The Suttners belonged to this "second society," and they saw their closest friends suddenly exposed to spreading anti-Semitism. The problem they had seen as a purely humanitarian issue in the Caucasus took on very personal aspects at home. Anti-Semitism could not be passed over in silence: everyone in this increasingly aggressive climate was forced to take a position—either for or against.

There was no question about the Suttners' decision. Their cosmopolitan, liberal, and anticlerical views ran absolutely contrary to both nationalistic and Catholic anti-Semitism. And since neither Bertha nor Arthur passively allowed injustices to take place, they felt it their responsibility as non-Jews to fight this barbarism with all their might. "One must resist . . . injustice . . . there is no alternative. Silence exists, but although it pretends to express disdain, it is itself disdainful. It is not enough for those affected to react, it also befits those who are not involved to revolt against injustice wherever they see it. Their silence bears part of the blame and is usually based upon the same motives as the silence of the afflicted, namely, fear."[5]

Already in *The Machine Age*—in a clear reference to the leader of the Christian Socialists, Karl Lueger—Bertha had pointed to the monstrosity of making anti-Semitism part of a political platform. "How could . . . the animosity against a fraction of the population provide a banner under which the good of the people as a whole was supposed to be accomplished?"

And "what was . . . this idea [meaning anti-Semitism] doing in the midst of the law-making bodies of the 19th century, where the principle 'all are equal before the law' provides the foundation of the law?" With "amazement and indignation" some contemporaries of the machine age asked themselves, "How is this possible in our humanitarian and enlightened century? . . . It's a disgrace to our century . . . a remnant of barbarism, of religious mania."

According to Suttner, anti-Semites claimed "to have nothing in common . . . with the blind fanatics of the Middle Ages. . . . [T]hey wanted to give their standpoint a certain appearance of being enlightened and scientific, and hit upon the following cliché: not religion, race was the target of their attacks. For the would-be intellectuals among them, this tenet was entwined with endless, meaningless ethnographical phrases swarming with Aryans, Turanians, and Indo-Europeans."

She reacted angrily to expressions of anti-Semitism within "good society" and described a field marshal who turns out to be a "raging Jew-eater" and "calls himself humane because he is against *violent* persecution—but wants all Christians to plot—just as he has done—never to buy anything from Jews or to sell them anything—to treat them as air, contaminated air—what lovely humanity. And thus make life impossible for fellow citizens with equal rights. O logic!"[6] And: "Whether you starve the Jews by imposing a ghetto or systematically withdraw their source of livelihood (not buying from them, excluding them from everything, etc.), whether you say Jewish swine in a drawing room if you are a cavalier or strike him bodily if you . . . belong to a mob, it's all one and the same thing."[7]

In her novel, *Before the Storm* (*Vor dem Gewitter*), she has a good citizen say appeasingly, "The Jews should not be maltreated." The reply to this is: "As though whipstrokes were the only form of maltreatment, as though a blow to a person's honor and feeling for justice did not often hurt much more than a blow on his back—as though the deliverer of the blow did not display just as much brutality in performing the act?"[8]

Bertha always protested when her Jewish colleagues accepted anti-Semitism all too calmly and generously. "If anti-Semitic, then I have lost my trust from the very beginning," she wrote, for instance, to Moritz Necker. "Racial intolerance, just as unscientific as the religious, points to something small and narrow in the mind and in the heart. I do not agree with you that one could be a *dignified* thinker and an anti-Semite at the same time."[9] She told him, "I'm toying with the idea of writing a novel on this subject.—I would be grateful for material. . . . I have to get the resentment I have accumulated against *this* barbarism off my chest by writing something, after all."[10]

Necker replied with an argument that was typical of Viennese Jews of this time. He advised against writing such a novel on anti-Semitism, because:

> First, it is probably a bit too late: the movement is ending. Second, it is only usable in a literary work as episodical material, it is not enough for a main theme. Though its manifestations are very easy to feel, anti-Semitism is just too stupid and tasteless to be taken seriously; a detailed portrayal could even be embarrassing. You would also have to describe the shortcomings, or let's say, the peculiarities of the Jews, a worn-out

subject which would neither please the Jews nor the anti-Semites. As a novelist, I would either pass up the subject altogether, let anti-Semitism wear itself out like influenza or, at most, mention it in passing. The fact is that with a treatment of the Jewish question which has been discussed to death, you will not create a public; neither here nor there.[11]

But Bertha was not to be talked out of her opinion that all unbiased people should finally begin to rise up against anti-Semitism:

> Not only those affected, all people who are pained by the screaming injustice that is being done to their fellow citizens who have the same rights, their fellow human beings, ought to pull themselves together for a loud protest. They have been standing on the sidelines for too long, much too long; the more wildly and loudly the others baited and incited, the more quietly and contemptuously they turned away in the mistaken idea that the doings, which break both the law of the state and of reason, are bound to disappear by themselves. And also out of a certain sense of decency, not wanting to injure the insulted class by taking notice of the insulters, the non-anti-Semites have behaved passively.[12]

Above all, she exposed the motives of the petit bourgeois Christian Socialist anti-Semites mercilessly:

> Nothing is easier than baiting, nothing easier than awakening hatred and distrust among the uneducated masses. Therefore the large following anti-Semitism has found among the populace, namely, on the flat plains, is no proof of its justification. And one other thing: people are so happy when they can regard some class or other as inferior, second-rate beings; it gives them distinction in their own eyes. When an ordinary workman or servant can say of the Baron So-and-so driving by in his four-horse carriage, "That's *only* a Jew," he feels elevated to a kind of nobility himself. And for all of the others who suffer under the pressure of the economic situation, it is a pleasure to imagine they belong to a class of people who can unload all their rancor and hope for an improvement in their repression.

In the parliamentary elections of 1891, the anti-Semites won a radiant victory—the liberals were thoroughly beaten. Bartolomeus von Carneri also lost his seat in the Reichsrat (parliament) to an "unknown anti-Semite," and Bertha complained, "We have lost all the halfway intelligent people of Austria, I mean all the free and clear-thinking people. . . . [These] we have lost."[13]

During the election campaign violence broke out between followers of the liberals and the anti-Semites. "The indignation my husband felt boiled over. 'Something has to happen!' he decided. And he sat down and wrote statutes and first draft and proclamation."[14]

An association was to be founded as a counter movement to anti-Semitism. Arthur presented his plan to Count Rudolf Hoyos and found in him a coadvocate. The textile industrialist, Baron Leitenberger, also made a spontaneous decision to join immediately. The next day, the famous physician, Hermann Nothnagel, also joined. A call to form an association to resist anti-Semitism was printed in all the daily newspapers—and several hundred Viennese responded.

The founding of this organization was based on the model from 1890 provided by the Berlin Association for Resistance of Anti-Semitism, to which only non-Jews belonged. It recruited members from similar groups, such as the Berlin pacifists. Thus, the famous physician Virchow belonged to both movements.

Just as they had come together some time before in Georgia for their writing, Bertha and Arthur worked together in the 1890s in their respective organizations: Bertha in the society for peace, Arthur in his anti association. Of course, each did a lot of work for the association of the other. Euphoria was the God-parent at both of the foundings. "The great Jewish rescue makes enormous demands on us—the thing is developing marvelously," Bertha wrote Carneri in May 1891;[15] and when the first newspaper articles about the project appeared in Vienna, she triumphed, "The success of the whole thing is truly magnificent—no one would have believed it. Even if nothing else happens—the mere fact *that* such an association could come to life, supported by such names, is an enormous gratification. . . . There will be a lot of work to do, but the satisfaction is sweet."[16]

As in her youth when she rescued herself from one dream into the next, and even under the worst of omens always saw everything in a rosy light, she had illusions about the success of the anti project.

Many prominent people could be won over for the association, people whose names would draw others: the aristocrat Count Edmund Zichy; the geologist and early liberal member of parliament, Eduard Suess, who had had to give up his office as Rector of the Vienna University in 1888 because of an anti-Semitic riot; the physician Krafft-Ebing; the engineer Wilhelm Exner; the architects Hasenauer, Fellner, and Helmer; the writers Peter Rosegger and Ludwig Ganghofer; the couple Ebner-Eschenbach; the painter Olga Wisinger-Florian and—the Waltz King, Johann Strauss. It was almost the same list of names that helped in the foundation of the Austrian Peace Society. This shows how close the fight against anti-Semitism was to the peace movement.

There was some discussion over naming the new organization. Peter Rosegger said it would be better to call it the "Battle Against Nationalism," because he saw the greater danger in this evil. Professor Nothnagel argued, "Let's stay with anti-Semitism. It can be cured. The nationalist sickness is incurable."[17]

Bertha tried very hard to underline her husband's achievements and his importance to the association at every opportunity. When Bertha thought Baron Leitenberger, who gave the association a large sum of money, had held the presidency much too long, she grumbled in a letter to Carneri, "Everyone seems to have forgotten that it was actually Arthur who called the whole thing into being. That's the way it is."[18]

Whether Arthur really possessed such great capabilities is rather doubtful. When he delivered the first speech of his life during these few weeks, Bertha, who normally paid tribute to her husband with exaggerated praise for every little thing, was strangely reserved in her comment. "In the end, Arthur gave his maiden speech—without stuttering and with applause."[19]

Before this, Arthur had written novels that sold very badly and for which he had a hard time finding publishers, succeeding only because of secret intercession by his wife. Otherwise, he had spent his time carrying out his duties as caretaker of Harmannsdorf, here too, with great difficulty and no success. Now he had his hands full with the anti group, suitably admired by Bertha.

The anti-Semitic papers sold extremely well. Schönerer and Lueger were highly popular. Bertha wrote: "How can it satisfy anyone to have such an enormous following—if it's all rabble?"[20]

On July 2, 1891, the first meeting of the association was held in Vienna. Full of pride, Bertha quoted in her memoirs Arthur's essay that appeared the next day in the *Neue Freie Presse:* the association had made it its task to "combat anti-Semitism by holding public lectures, discussions, circulating instructive writings, possibly by founding an official organ." Arthur felt that

> In a time when associations are founded to protect animals—and quite rightly so—it is, I think, only logical also to finally take a stand against the maltreatment of fellow men, all the more so since it has not stopped at attacks against honor, but has come to acts of violence which have given our Jewish fellow-citizens every reason for fearing for their safety. I remember those heroes in outlying areas of Vienna who smashed the

windows of Jewish women and called out threats of murder to them: those schoolboys who ran a knife into the eye of their Semitic comrade. Those are a few examples drawn from many; one alone would have been enough to cause all principled people to make a great outcry of indignation.

In contrast to the rude tone of the anti-Semitic press, their own camp should "preserve a sense of decency. . . . Our two weapons should be reason and a feeling of justice, with which we will be able to face any attack."[21]

To counterbalance the powerful anti-Semitic papers, the opposing association planned its own newspaper. Bertha made lofty plans in advance: "*not* a leaflet, a big, distinguished literary daily newspaper which should only keep to the *spirit* of anti-anti and at which there will be no Jewish editors, to prove that Aryans also think along the same lines as the so-called Jewish liberals, that is, progressively and without prejudice."[22]

In her novel *Schach der Qual* (The restraint of agony) Bertha laid out a grand plan for such a paper, which was supposed to be distributed free of charge for the first year and influence no less than a hundred thousand readers daily in a peaceful spirit. The editors of this newspaper would have an exalted mission: they would have to "see a kind of priesthood in this job" and feel the responsibility for "such a use of power," since "Influencing a hundred thousand spirits, isn't that incalculable power?" Then there would finally be an antidote to the anti-Semitic smearsheets, against which no state authority and no courts would take action. Bertha wrote angrily, "A cautious health department goes to the marketplace every day to make certain that the public is not getting harmful . . . milk. But every morning many hundreds of thousands of editions of spiritual food filled with poison to the mind and heart, adulterated with lies, come from the newspaper deliveries and are strewn among the people with no objection."[23]

The main problem with all these beautiful plans was, as usual, money:

> Incomprehensible, actually, that to this date it has not occurred to any great benefactor—like Peabody, Carnegie, Baron Hirsch—to create a philanthropic institute through which an independent, noble, and also brilliantly done newspaper could prove itself. Hospitals, asylums for the blind, old people's homes—what is all of that compared to a nursery for matter that ennobles intellectually, which would paralyze the extensively concocted poisons? Will those capable of sacrifice, the generous, the

enthusiastic, the bold men in this country not find their way to start such an undertaking?[24]

Finally, Baron Friedrich Leitenberger from the textile industry was prepared to furnish the money. He had already donated generously in 1886 for a newspaper opposing anti-Semitism, namely, for the *Wiener Tagblatt* published by the journalist Moriz Szeps. No less a personage than Crown Prince Rudolf had worked for Szeps and against anti-Semitism at the time. But the money was soon lost. Now Leitenberger tried a second time to set up a resistance paper. It did not appear every day and also not in a circulation of 100,000 as Bertha had dreamed, but once a week, starting in April 1892. It was called *Freies Blatt,* and was done in the style of the *Unverfälschte Deutsche Worte,* that is, it intentionally appealed to simple people. It wrote up articles against anti-Semitism that were frequently very aggressive.

Prominent people were asked to participate just as they had been doing for Bertha's peace newspaper. Carneri wrote articles, and so did Peter Rosegger. Jewish journalists, of all people, sent in refusals, among them Theodor Herzl, who lived in Paris then as a correspondent for the *Neue Freie Presse.* He criticized the resistance paper sharply: "The *Freies Blatt* is not a newspaper, it is a circular—that does not circulate. . . . I do not think that it has any practical value whatsoever."[25] Herzl's letter, in which he laid out his ideas on how such a paper ought to look, was twenty-two pages long.

But Theodor Herzl did not only criticize the newspaper, he attacked the resistance effort as such. He said in a letter to Leitenberger that he did not want to make any accusations against the organization. "On the contrary, I have a great deal of esteem for this effort. It shows that your heart is in the right place and that you are a healthy and just man." However, the organization came ten or twelve years too late: "The time when you could do something against it [anti-Semitism] using friendly and modest methods is over."

Carneri still had his doubts as well, and on many occasions Bertha von Suttner felt she had to defend the project and emphasize the overwhelming effect the organization was making. The association "has provided the proof that there are a lot of highly admirable people who are raising a loud protest. . . . And even if the association has not converted one single anti-Semite or rendered one harmless, it has still safeguarded the peace of mind of those who have felt that they have been scorned and insulted by anti-Semites."[26]

Just at the peak of anti-Semitism, a converted Jew became the archbishop of Olmütz and the anti-anti association celebrated it as a sign of a new, better time and a result of the association's efforts. Suttner wrote to Carneri with optimism, "The new Archbishop Dr. K. [Theodor Kohn] might not have made it without the anti-anti association. Ducking from anti-Semitism has gone out of style because of this."[27] Whereupon the philosopher Carneri coolly and a bit mockingly put the brakes on her enthusiasm somewhat. "If Dr. K. has the anti-anti to thank for his election, then you are experiencing eternal peace."[28]

The association sent a delegation to the president of parliament with the request that he do something about parliamentarians making inflammatory anti-Semitic speeches, and it presented him with a written protest from the association. But parliament proved to be powerless against the anti-Semitism of its own members.

In the Lower Austrian parliament, the great liberal Eduard Suess had to fight heated battles with the anti-Semites. With great satisfaction, the *Freies Blatt* printed a short conversation between Emperor Franz Joseph and Suess in 1892, expecting that the head of state would make a decisive statement against anti-Semitism. The emperor told Suess, "You have gone through difficult days in the Lower Austrian Parliament. It is a disgrace and a scandal the way things are going there. One does not know what to say about it." Suess replied, "There are lines drawn before the educated in parliamentary debate, beyond which we cannot go. We can express our indignation, but we cannot answer scandals with scandals."[29]

The anti association staged a protest gathering against the anti-Semitic outrages of the Christian Socialists in the provincial parliament. "They disgrace the Christian part, they misuse the socialistic." But the increasingly urgent request to the state and church "to fulfill their responsibility" and "use all their energy" to do something about "the spread of a movement which is leading to the brutalization of the people and the disregard of all the principles of humanity and justice," echoed in a void.[30]

In her novel *Schach der Qual* Bertha describes this session of the Lower Austrian parliament, using original quotes. The debate centered on the appointment of a Jewish doctor to the provincial insane asylum. The anti-Semitic parliamentarian Gregorig protested with this argument: "The public has to be reassured. This reassurance is not given if Jews are employed there. We know that a Jew is susceptible to anything as a rule. People will be locked up who are not insane, and it is dangerous when Jews are employed who are more susceptible to such doings than Christian doctors are. Jewish doctors should be dismissed wherever possible, and the Christian people be protected from the practices of Jews and the morals of the Talmud." Karl Lueger, the leader of the Christian Socialists said, "One may be an anti-Semite or not, but one has to admit that a Jew cannot be used in an insane asylum. No educated person can doubt that."

And the parliamentarian Schneider even wanted to prove the Jews were a "species of their own" with their supposedly "peculiar construction of the spine." "Just look at a Jew. He is actually different from us. His long arms, his curved legs and flat feet—the way the head, the eyes sit . . . it is a total difference. . . . I go so far as to say, that a chemical analysis of Jew and non-Jew would have to result in a different spectrum." (Resounding laughter from the anti-Semites.) And finally, "If a Jew wants to have a Jew for a doctor, as far as I'm concerned he can let himself be poisoned by one; the faster the better."

Gregorig said: "May consideration for the Christian population finally be shown, so that it will not lose its patience; and drive out the Jews . . . Yes, drive out the Jews and confiscate all the Jewish property. May that happen soon. God grant it."

The hero in Bertha's novel, *Prince Roland,* listened to these inflammatory speeches with bewilderment and, as a parliamentarian, tried to speak out, not against the anti-Semites, but against all those who had let these infamous remarks go unchallenged. "My enraged, reproachful astonishment is directed toward those who have heard everything that has been said here and in response are—silent. All of you who do not think as the speakers do. . . . All of you allow such incitement of hatred, such threats, such—monstrosities to go unchallenged into the minutes of your meetings, unrefuted into the morning papers all over the world."[31] Prince Roland is so long-winded in the novel that his speech is finally cut off by the president—certainly not an optimal end for a novel.

In the fight against the "Jewish protection corps," the anti-Semites were not squeamish in their choice of means. Schönerer, for instance, did not shy away from printing excerpts from the land register of Harmannsdorf to show how much the estate was in debt. The *Unverfälschte Deutsche Worte* regretted quite sanctimoniously that the Suttner family was "forced into performing protective services for the Jews."[32] Bertha reacted to all these attacks calmly and wrote to Carneri, "The size of the debts should prove—what? More likely the opposite of what it is supposed to prove—why didn't the protected Jews cancel [the debts] immediately? But what do you think of this method of fighting."[33]

When Professor Nothnagel called anti-Semitism a "plague of the soul" in public and one of "the most serious accusations against the human heart," riots broke out during his lecture. The intruders "broke out in noisy death calls and began to stomp with their feet." Nothnagel's students tried to outshout the disrupters.[34]

Wherever the members of the anti association appeared publicly, they had to reckon with such incidents. Bertha also got to feel the reactions of anti-Semites. Already in October 1892 she wrote to Carneri, "Now I get anonymous letters of abuse frequently. Usually permeated with an anti-Semitic spirit . . . and along with it, always the friendly pointer to cooking pot and knitting needle."[35]

Several of these letters still exist. One of them contains the remark, "that your *shameless, treasonable action,* in which you debase yourself to become a tool of a people that apparently wants to force all other nations into slavery and destroy them, fills me with shame and pain."[36]

All too soon, it became clear that the fighters against anti-Semitism, the so-called vassals of the Jews, "are just as unprotected and just as exposed to abuse as those whose rights they want to see protected," wrote Arthur, but, "in our hearts we have the awareness that we are representing a position every person who feels and thinks justly should take. This awareness is sufficient for us to keep up our courage."[37]

And Bertha wrote to Carneri, "That is exactly the proofstone of the matter: there, where the ultimate step becomes frightening and it would be more tactful to remain silent, the whole thing becomes abominable. As a result, the anti-Semites have to keep silent about their ultimate conclusion, killing the Jews—and *we* on the other hand, we friends of peace, can openly state our final goal."[38]

The triumph of ignorance, of meanness, aroused "disgust" in Bertha. "People with this kind of education—way below zero—with this kind of base-mindedness: *they* belong to the wheels of the machine that weaves the fate of a great empire!"[39]

"Physical disgust joined the moral. The young men puffed on Virginia butts and spat on the floor every few minutes; when they put their beer glasses to their mouths, one could see their unwashed hands and their chewed fingernails which were as good as never cleaned.—A happy state of affairs, a dignified existence for all?—Yes, that is the goal, but it also means worthy people have to be enlisted—morally and physically pure people. To put it in another way, a people must be beautiful to deserve to be happy."[40]

Even though Bertha created the impression in her memoirs that Arthur organized the resistance group alone, accompanied only by her sympathy, she helped considerably in the background. In 1893, for example, she wrote the preface for the rather militant book by F. Simon, *Defend Yourselves! A Call of Warning to the Jews,* and justified herself to Fried, "because I fight the anti-Semites just as I do war—after all, they represent the same spirit."[41]

This time it was not Christians who were being called upon to resist, it was Jews expressly, especially assimilated, urban Jews. No good came of it, wrote Bertha, when the Jews kept silent in the early 1880s, as anti-Semitism was spreading like wildfire, regarding defense as beneath their dignity and counting on justice.

She asks herself:

> How is one to face them and say, "Such treatment is shocking, cannot be tolerated any longer," when the maltreated keep an even-tempered face? No, a decisive "I will not permit it!," a "holding someone responsible" for any, even the most minor legal violation to the last and highest court, is absolutely necessary here if anywhere. The law still offers generous protection. But the persecutor and persecuted act as though the Jews' deprivation of rights set as a goal from the very beginning was already a fact. And so it can be: a legal paragraph which is not used, dies, and an action that becomes a custom demands and gains entry into the lawbooks.

In her opinion, Jews should also sue for their legal rights. "No one who has had the vaguest insult of 'You are a Jew,' hurled at him, should overhear it, but press the accuser against the wall: 'Yes, I am, exactly like you are a Christian . . . and what of it? What else are you accusing me of?' It should be looked at and examined."

The resistance group offered all insulted Jews legal assistance free of charge. Previously, "the silent endurance of the injustice" was "the general custom . . . but their blows should no longer remain unparried, for the solution has now been proclaimed: defend yourselves!"[42]

Of course, Bertha took part in all the resistance meetings and gave a number of speeches, such as the one in 1894 in which she took a position against idealizing women. According to Professor Nothnagel, women's inborn love of justice made them immune to anti-Semitism. Just as Bertha was convinced of the peace cause, she was also convinced of the equality of man and woman in the question of anti-Semitism. "I would like to emphasize the urgent importance of the task [fighting anti-Semitism] that has been given to my sisters; I cannot, however, accept on behalf of all, the praise that has been accorded us, accept even less because I come forward as an accuser of women."

She accused many women of being "the fiercest friends of militarism and war" and by no means friends of justice by nature. For they had

resolutely followed the call of the Christian Socialist, Prince Liechtenstein, "Do not buy from Jews!" and taken this disgraceful slogan "from
that meeting back to their families." Fighting back, she opposed the anti-
Semitic saying with a slogan that was no less clear. "We women can
achieve a lot, despite this. We hold the means for selective breeding:
those whom we choose to honor must avow our goals. I would like to
impress a word upon all my sisters: do not make love with anti-Semites!"[43]
This call for a sexual boycott caused enormous excitement and gave
Bertha, who had been known as "Peace Bertha," the new name: "Jew
Bertha."

Suttner implored women not to fall for the anti-Semitic fairytale
about a collective Jewish guilt, since guilt should "only be applied to the
guilty." She supplied women with counterarguments to use against anti-
Semitic slogans, and she called them into active participation. Above all,
they were told to raise their children to have a sense of justice. "It befits
mothers, especially when they notice that their half-grown sons are in
danger of being infected with this poison, to protect them, since no
mother should be indifferent if her child nourishes and expresses opinions that are based on cruelty and injustice, on arrogance and darkness,
that brutalize the disposition and constrict the intellect."[44]

Because of her activities in the resistance fellowship, Suttner was
soon held to be "dangerous to women," as a grotesque episode from the
year 1896 shows. The Catholic newspaper *Das Vaterland* sharply criticized the fact that among the one hundred books that had been donated
as prizes for a lottery in support of a home for women teachers, there
were writings that endangered morality, such as *Brehms Tierleben* (a work
on animal life by Brehm, who was a Darwinist), *Meyers Konversationslex-
ikon,* novels by Heyse and Franzos, and also by Suttner and Ebner-Eschenbach. It criticized the fact that the latter two were "true types of
intellectual feminism alienated from God." Bertha was so amused by this
that she sent the newspaper clipping to her friend Nobel.[45]

The members of the resistance organization attracted enormous dislike from the anti-Semites—and failed to reap the enthusiastic approval
they had expected from the Jews. Here, too, there were two battlefronts:
the new Jewish awareness resulting from Zionism became stronger, the
Freies Blatt called it a new nationalism and argued against it, placing itself
on the side of assimilation and against the eastern orthodox Jews. The
resistance organization lost followers and persuasive power since it could
not show any success in the fight against anti-Semitism—quite the contrary.

Theodor Herzl observed this process very closely and commented in his diary, "Not the least bit is achieved with declamations on paper or in closed circles; it even seems comical." However, he did admit, "At the same time, there are also some very bright people on such 'relief commit- tees' in addition to the pushy and the simple-minded. They resemble the relief committees set up after—and before!—floods, and do about the same amount of damage. The noble Bertha von Suttner is making a mis- take—of course, a mistake she holds in high esteem—if she thinks that such a committee can help."[46] He sought a different way to fend off the distress of the Jews.

The Vienna municipal elections in 1895 ended in a victory for the anti-Semites under Karl Lueger. But Emperor Franz Joseph did not con- firm Lueger's election and was thus able to prevent Lueger's becoming mayor for two years—much to the displeasure of the voters. Bertha, in her memoirs, wrote: "A high Austrian official and aristocrat told me that he was in court society when the news came that Lueger had not been confirmed. 'Oh, the poor emperor!' cried the duchess of Württemberg (daughter of Archduke Albrecht), 'the poor emperor—in the hands of the freemasons!' And when, a year later [should be: two years] in the same circle, where my informant happened to be present again, news arrived of Lueger's confirmation, the same duchess raised her eyes and her folded hands to heaven with the words, 'God be praised—the em- peror has finally seen the light!'"[47]

Lueger's failure to be confirmed by Emperor Franz Joseph twice was explained away at that time, just as it is today, with suspicions that the emperor was jealous of Lueger's popularity in Vienna and wanted to hinder him for that reason. This explanation is too simple. The fact that the emphatically Catholic emperor differed in his opinion in this case from the prevalent clerical, anti-Semitic position was more likely con- nected with the basic principle of his rule: to preserve justice—and that went for all his subjects, whether they were Jews or Christians. Lueger was a politician who did not let this same justice apply to all citizens. He preached hatred of the Jews and made them second-class people. Franz Joseph could not support a man with Lueger's political convictions, even if this man acted with the approval and in the name of the Catholic Church and was democratically elected.

Nevertheless, the emperor avoided making a clear denunciation of anti-Semites in public. Embittered, Arthur von Suttner wrote in the *Neue Freie Presse:*

A clear, a decisive word from above, spoken at the right time instead of evasive, circumventive phrases that could be stretched and turned around like the ancient oracles, could have held back what had to come today—no, not had to—what was allowed to come. And that section of fellow citizens who are defenselessly exposed to the wildest offenses and threats, contrary to all the state order, has a right to this specific, clear, unequivocal word, which for all purposes has been outlawed. This clear word is: anti-Semitism is an extremely dangerous movement in writing, word, and deed, which seriously damages the character of the state order and the basic laws of the state. It cannot be tolerated by a government anymore than anarchism or other activities can be, which result in disturbing the inner peace by measures of force and bringing on a civil war.[48]

When Lueger was confirmed as mayor by the emperor in 1897 after all, Bertha was beside herself with indignation and even wrote to Alfred Nobel, who had very little interest in Vienna's municipal politics, "Lueger, the idol of bigoted anti-Semites, soon the mayor of Vienna, has been received in an audience with the emperor, victorious in a word— and basically, it is human stupidity which is victorious. And because I know how you despise stupidity, I thought of you immediately, and thus I am airing my anger at the address in San Remo [where Nobel was staying]."[49]

Suttner thought the Christian Socialist movement surrounding Lueger was the main danger to Austria's inner peace, and most of all to justice in respect to Jews. As a matter of fact, the movement later made an enormous impression on Adolf Hitler and actually became his demagogic model. In her diary Suttner complained of the astonishing power of the "Gentleman of Vienna" and his "brutal anti-Semitic regiment."[50] She also regretted the helplessness of the few Lueger opponents and the lack of support for the Jews.

The *Freies Blatt* folded in 1896 after appearing for four years. Baron Friedrich Leitenberger, who had lost a great deal of money with the newspaper, gave up.

The paper that followed distanced itself from its predecessor and promised its readers "not to appear at the scene of battle for freedom and equality in kid gloves, but in boxing mitts. . . . [R]udeness can only be answered with rudeness."[51]

This kind of fighting was revolting to the anti-anti society. Conflicts arose. Arthur von Suttner felt forced to publish a paper of protest. Finally, this newspaper also closed down after a year.

No matter what kind of fighting was chosen, there was never a method that could combat the power of anti-Semitism effectively.

Despondent, Bertha wrote in her diary in 1897, "Evening, annual meeting of the anti-anti. Meune speaks very well, Nothnagel somewhat pessimistic. Gathering despressingly small. For Lueger, thousands—unbelievable!"[52]

The appearance of Herzl's novel, *The Jewish State,* came during this period of resignation. Herzl himself sent his new book to Bertha von Suttner along with a friendly rejection: he could not participate in the peace society. "Of course, I have been following your magnanimous efforts for years with admiring attention. . . . If I cannot join you openly, there is a reason for it: I have just been drawn into an 'insane' war. You will be able to see what I am foolishly fighting for in my writing, *The Jewish State,* which I am allowing myself to send you. In sincere admiration, your devoted, Th. Herzl."[53]

The book, a novel with a purpose, like *Lay Down Your Arms,* made Zionism well known throughout the world. Herzl demanded a new Jewish awareness: not assimilation anymore, not baptism, not humble conformity, but a return to Judaism. "I do not hold the Jewish question to be a social or a religious issue, even if it is colored this way or that. It is a question of nationality."[54] And the goal of this Jewish nationalism was a Jewish state without "Jewish distress," a refuge for oppressed comrades in faith in the Promised Land of Palestine. Herzl gained emphasis for his ideas by founding the magazine *Die Welt* in 1897.

Bertha hesitated when Herzl asked her to contribute to the *Welt.* "The specimen issue of the *Welt* and its whole procedure fills me with respect," she wrote to Herzl. "It has heart, there is openness, clarity, deep firm will—the vision directed toward something great and helping." But Zionism was for her what the peace movement was to Herzl. "Respect and doubt. 'God speed you,' one says to a boat—but one cannot sail with it, *may* not, because on both sides, our ruddering needs the whole person."

She did not try to hide the fact that, in her cosmopolitan, supranational way of thinking, she had trouble understanding the new Jewish nationalism. "And I really don't know whether assimilation would not be better than founding a new state and nationality. I wanted for all reasonable people to assimilate themselves in a higher category of 'European,' 'cultural being' that is in the process of formation now and that is *beyond* national, religious, or social self-importance and fanaticism."

Herzl's "fellow tribesmen" could contribute "so many valuable specimens" to this new, worthwhile type of "European" without national conceit, "wouldn't it be a pity to direct them into a separate bed?" She did not want to express her doubts openly, "because I tell myself that I can be quite wrong and that in the current state of the world situation and human development, perhaps it is *your* plan that would be the more beneficial." Herzl printed this letter in the *Welt*—with Bertha's permission.[55]

Arthur Suttner's reaction was much warmer than his wife's, and he congratulated the new paper. These friendly words did not prevent Herzl from arguing against the resistance organization in his second issue, however. "There is assistance that shames. The Association for the Resistance to Anti-Semitism humbles the very Jews who seek a final refuge in their unbroken self-respect during these hard times. These words should not be interpreted wrongly; they contain absolutely no arrogance or harshness, which would of course be inappropriate in respect to men like Suttner, Nothnagel, Suess, and all the others." According to Herzl, Jews of no character did not deserve the efforts of the organization's members. "However, the Jews who are upright men want and have to defend themselves, and that alone will help raise their opponents' opinion of them a little. The organization for resistance can still do something good for us: it can disband. . . . We will only be able to thank these noble men without being ashamed when they are no longer banded together on our account."[56]

Bertha overcame her doubts and finally reached the conclusion that Zionism was not "a condition of being infected with the prevailing frenzy of nationalism." Instead, "I now understand the erection of the Kingdom of Zion as a deliverance from misery and persecution, as a proud rearing up against the outrageous insult that has been perpetrated, and above all as a creation of a place of refuge." It is a comfort to her, "that anti-Semitism will be defeated by Zionism."

The peace movement did not want to fuse nationalities, rather "to unite" them in a "federation of autonomous states" and for that reason was not against national identity, only against chauvinism. "The Jew who avows world citizenship today—and most of the progressive Jews are on this level—serves the idea of world citizenship only very little because of it, since he is accused of taking this standpoint because he does not have a fatherland; if he has a fatherland, an independent and recognized homeland, *then* he can say: I have grown beyond the interests of my country, I feel like a European, a civilized being." Zionism was "a product of rebellion, and at the same time of self-elevation and rescue" and thus complied with the spirit of the peace movement.

She explained Zionism to the American diplomat, Andrew White, as "the practice of national pride," corrected herself then with, "Pride is not the right expression—affirmation of national dignity—self-respect."[57]

The Suttners' work for Zionism was primarily a personal effort on behalf of their friend and colleague, Theodor Herzl. At the first Zionist congress in 1897 in Bern, Arthur assured Herzl of his fullest sympathy.

Herzl's convictions were "exactly the same as those that inspire us at our peace conferences. I can therefore prophesy to you that these beautiful impressions, this awareness of heartfelt solidarity will increase with the coming congresses, because your cause is just as good and full of vitality as ours. Hearty congratulations, therefore! The ice is broken, the cause *must* go forward now."[58]

For his part, Herzl defended Bertha against accusations that she was a utopian, a charge that was also made against him. The peace movement was "seen by 'practical' people as silly or foolish activities," he wrote in the *Neue Freie Presse*. "How these practical people turn up their noses if someone wants to build heated rooms in summer. But when winter comes and there are no heated rooms, who is the fool then?"[59]

Added to the disheartenment caused by the almost triumphant success of Austria's anti-Semites was the discussion about anti-Semitism in France in 1897. Emile Zola demanded the reopening of the Dreyfus case and the rehabilitation of the Jewish officer who, he thought, had been sentenced unjustly. In fiery newspaper articles, he branded anti-Semitism, drawing the hatred of the anti-Semites toward himself.

Bertha dealt with the events in Paris and their equally hateful echo in the Viennese papers in letters, articles, and, most of all, her diary. She complained to Carneri, "The Dreyfus affair is horrible. Oh, everywhere, where the anti-Semites and chauvinists are at work with their terroristic and deceitful actions, one could doubt humanity. That's why I say—keep away from them."[60]

The international peace movement placed itself clearly on the side of Emile Zola. In one of her lectures, Suttner proudly quoted a letter Zola had written her in 1893, "What I promise you, Madame, is to work with all my might in my little corner for the reconciliation of peoples."[61]

Of course, her indignation was all the greater when Zola was sentenced to a year in prison and fined three thousand francs. Bertha wrote: "One ceases to feel at home in the world." "This Dreyfus story has torn the mask off the face of modern France in a terrible way. The world is sick with cowardice."[62]

"The brutal victory that militarism—arm in arm with anti-Semitism—has carried off in Paris makes me truly lose faith in humanity—I see that a much, much larger percentage than I thought is still stuck in barbarism. People who stand for justice and moderation have to hold together and push ahead all the more firmly and actively. No one who holds a torch may lower it to the ground. The trial will have done some good after all by uncovering the ugliness of the system of hatred to so many people."[63]

She pointed to this particular combination of anti-Semitism and militarism again and again. But what good did it do? Lueger was the "Lord of Vienna," and to the rejoicing of his followers, he declared, "Dreyfus belongs on the Devil's Island and all the Jews with him!"[64] The anti society's protests against this pronouncement fell flat.

Meanwhile, the organization could not even get the money together for the monthly rent on the office. At the beginning of November 1900 Bertha wrote sadly in her diary, "The dying anti-anti organization is canceling the apartment, and because of this, the not-yet-dying but very weary peace organization is also losing its shelter."[65]

All the same, she continued to fight anti-Semitism in articles and novels like *Daniela Dormes* and *Schach der Qual*. Theodor Herzl recognized her good intentions. "Your goodness shatters me," he wrote, but after reading *Schach der Qual*, he added, "However, I do not want to hide the fact that I am going through a crisis again, in which I do not believe that one can improve people with magnanimity and noble thoughts."[66]

Of course Bertha still believed that anti-Semitism was "heading toward an end." After all, it contradicted the law of progress.

The barbarism of anti-Semitism, however, did not develop according to the rules of the theory of evolution. It became stronger rather than weaker, "acceptable to the drawing room and the court," as she complained, had become a "fashionable attitude."[67] And news came again and again of terrible Jewish pogroms in Russia. "The massacres in Russia make one ashamed to live in our time. And the Viennese Christian Socialists still want to breed anti-Semites in the schools—even though they see what the last step of their teachings looks like in practical terms. Scandalous! Anyone who does not become indignant over certain baseness, must be base himself."[68]

In view of the catastrophic situation of the Jews in Russia, Theodor Herzl tried everything he could to make direct contact with the czar. He asked his "magnanimous and highly respected friend" Suttner to write the Russian foreign minister, Muravyov, whom she knew, and to ask him to arrange an audience with Nikolaus II.

Herzl wanted Bertha to emphasize in her letter that "Zionism wants to create a home for the Jewish people that is guaranteed legally. For Russia, this cause which I hold to be humanitarian, is politically interesting for a number of reasons." Since in Russia:

> The Jewish question [is] an unsolved and very embarrassing matter. . . . The czar cannot possibly deny his support for a peaceful, humanitarian solution. The Jewish persecution that breaks out from time

to time in Russia, and at the same time creates grave disturbances of the peace in general, would then cease forever. By no means would all the Jews leave Russia, any more than they would any other country: only a surplus of proletarians and desperate people supported by their prosperous ethnic comrades, would find a new and permanent home, and at the same time could enlarge the cultural substance of the civilization in the Orient considerably. A weakening of the rebellious parties would go hand in hand with this increase of culture and order. It should be pointed out emphatically that we are in battle against rebels everywhere, and as a matter of fact we are heading off young students and Jewish workers from socialism and nihilism by unfolding a purer national ideal in front of them.

Without Zionism the desperate Jews would have to "all become anarchists." Herzl even anticipated the question of to whom the holy sites in Palestine would belong then and wrote that this problem "could surely be solved by exterritorialization agreed upon by all the great powers."[69]

Suttner agreed willingly. "I shall write Muravyov today. I totally agree with you that it would be a wonderful thing worthy of the czar of peace, for him to support Zionism." In addition, she offered to make it possible for Herzl to be received at the Russian embassy in Vienna.[70]

Herzl's audience with the czar did not take place. Jewish persecution in Russia increased. No alleviation of the "Jewish need" was foreseeable. In his desperation, Herzl tried again in 1903 after the massacres of Kishinyov and wrote to his friend, "I am getting disastrous news from Russia. The Jews are beginning to despair because of the defenselessness demonstrated in Kishinyov. Something like a panic of anxiety threatens to break out among this unfortunate mass of people. Fifteen- to sixteen-year-old children, young girls and boys, are listening to nihilistic temptations." He did not give up hope that the czar would speak a decisive word. "My audience would have a calming effect. The Jews would not feel so deserted, and the lower authorities would know that their villainy would not go unnoticed." "Now, limited enough as the leader of the Zionistic movement, I am demanding an audience through legal channels . . . [b]ecause today it [the massacre] has become a nasty administrative embarrassment, and the government itself ought to be grateful to me if I can contribute to soothing those who are desperate. It is impossible to have seven million people murdered."[71]

In addition to this official approach, he also asked Bertha to write a personal letter to the czar and an accompanying letter to the Russian ambassador in Vienna. He even sent her envelopes in various sizes, "because there might not be a paper merchant in Harmannsdorf."

Bertha was startled at the idea of writing to the czar personally. But on the same day she made a note in her diary: "I'll do it. It is the height of presumptuousness, but I'll do it."[72]

She wrote the letter in French and composed it according to Herzl's suggestions, except for the one sentence, "It is impossible to have seven million people murdered." She called upon the ideal of peace that the czar still strove for and asked for the favor of an audience for the "head of the Zionistic movement, Theodor Herzl."[73]

The answer was a polite letter from the Russian ambassador—an audience was not granted. Persecution of the Jews in Russia increased even more.

Herzl, worn down by too much work and excitement, died suddenly in July 1904 at the age of forty-four. "Herzl could have been the King of Zion and had to die in Edlach from a heart defect. Death is a fool."[74]

In her letter of condolence to Julie Herzl ("Dear lady, poor sister in sorrow") Bertha assured her that, "the way this blow, which has deeply shattered those who belonged to him, has painfully, angrily saddened the others, too, the distant ones who knew and appreciated him. Yes, angry—at the stupid, brutal fate that prematurely carries away *such* people who would have had so much usefulness, happiness, brilliance still to give. . . . Irreplaceable, irreplaceable—not only for you—for us all. Some of the richness of our time is lacking now that Theodor Herzl—the king of Zion, the king of the feuilletonists, the dear, good, dignified human being has been taken from us."[75]

She and Herzl both worked for a better world and a distant goal that could be reached only in the future. The strong parallel she saw between Herzl and herself is apparent in a letter she wrote during this time to Fried, whom she already had her eye on as the administrator of her literary estate and her successor. "I like Herzl's wish for his body to be taken to Palestine. It is a proud Zionistic statement. I shall emulate him and give instructions for my urn to stay in Gotha [where she wanted to be cremated] until such time that it can be taken to the first temple of peace."[76]

Herzl's wish was fulfilled after the founding of the State of Israel. Bertha's temple of peace never became reality, nor did the peace she dreamed of.

Again and again, she compared the peace movement with Zionism. "I knew from the imposing spread of Zionism . . . [that it] has a great deal of similarity with the peace cause. Also in the false judgment made by the world.—But Herzl's death will hurt badly . . . so much depends upon the individual people."[77]

She had practically no relationship with Herzl's successor, Max Nordau, but continued to offer the Zionists the assistance of the peace movement. When a new bloody wave of anti-Semitism flared up in 1905, she wrote to Fried, "Nordau asks where the European conscience is?—Now, on the pacifists' stage. Why don't the people thirsting for conscience join together?"[78]

She had long given up hope of an active protest against anti-Semitism by an Austrian politician and was now betting on the New World. "America protested against persecution against the Jews in Rumania. 'Humanity'—*this* word for the first time in a diplomatic note. It will cause a revolution."[79]

When Jewish students asked her to write an article against the Jewish riots in Rumania, she did it immediately. The Jewish question must

> be tackled and settled in the open and with absolute determination in a way that is worthy of proper, just, and humane people, that is, by creating legally ensured equality—and the equal respect that results from it—for the Jewish people everywhere. The fact that there are people somewhere in civilized countries who have to weep and plead for their human rights, proves that these countries—and I do not mean Russia and Rumania exclusively—are not fully civilized, but are to one extent or another, overshadowed by medieval darkness. . . . When a whole section of the population of a country is stamped as a class without rights, upon which hatred and defamation can be heaped without penalty, then in the time of famine and pestilence, at times of any kind of uprising, those people will be fallen upon first: one holds them to blame because one has learned to hate them from time immemorial.[80]

In Bertha's opinion, militarism and toleration of anti-Semitism destroyed Austria-Hungary's credibility where the mediation of human rights violations in other countries was concerned, for instance, in the Armenian massacres in Turkey. "How can countries who are themselves divided into two camps that distrust and threaten each other, who devote most of their energy to the cult of mass slaughter, who, even if they do not persecute Armenians at home do persecute Jews—how can they, in the name of humanity . . . intercede with authority?"[81]

Suttner's fight against anti-Semitism harmed the reputation of the peace organizations. They were increasingly denounced as "Jewish clubs," as un-German, unpatriotic, internationalistic, and heathen.

At first Bertha had tried to keep anti-Semitism away from the peace movement by advising the Jewish pacifists, such as her Berlin colleague Karpeles, to exercise restraint. In 1892 at the founding of the German Peace Society, she wrote Alfred Fried, "Karpeles is quite right not to want to join; he should join in the activities, provide people for the committee, but not sign up. As things stand, the initiative should not depend on too many Jews—or it will be classified immediately; and by the same token should also not be too social-democratic, etc., etc. The Austrian caricaturists are showing me as the leader of Polish Jews as it is."[82]

Fried also became a target for anti-Semites. Suttner could not and did not want to do without him of all people, her most avid associate. When the attacks got out of hand—under the pretence that Fried had allegedly printed pornography—she stood up for him before her group, defended him before other German pacifists, and held him back when he wanted to give up the peace publication.[83]

From this point on, Alfred Fried was frequently called upon more or less discreetly by his copacifists to make a sacrifice for the cause and convert to Christianity. A pacifist from Stuttgart, the parish priest Umfrid, made an "intimate suggestion" to Fried in 1909 to go ahead and take this step since "being Jewish" was "a hindrance in propagandistic work."[84]

Fried gave a very clear answer to these unreasonable demands. "It is not the religious community that binds me to Judaism, since I learned practically nothing about Jewish beliefs in my upbringing, and my weltanschauung is infinitely far away from Jewish belief. What makes me want to endure is Judaism's present social position. To separate myself in this time of oppression and persecution from the community to which I belong through birth and lineage is something I would regard as desertion in a time of war. . . . [A]s an intellectual I believe I have the responsibility to hold out with the oppressed minority."

He doubts the advantages of conversion for the peace movement

> because I would always be the Christened Jew, the renegade. I could very well profit personally, since my being Jewish was always an obstacle in my career, and always will be. But I think desertion for personal motives is especially abominable. No! I know that in order to achieve recognition, we Jews have to work, to endure, three or four times as much as our Christian fellow citizens. But I would never have become a pacifist if I did not immensely enjoy fighting and swimming against the current, if I did not feel the calling within me to defy the medievalness that still dominates in our time.

And besides, there were not many Jews among the leading pacifists anyway:

> With the exception of Heilberg, I cannot think of a single one. In France there is only Moch, who is having just as hard a time there as I am here. Otherwise, I know of no one. What damage can that do to the movement. It does not hurt social democracy for Marx and Lassalle to have been its creators. Suttner is fortunately entirely free of suspicion of Jewishness and Jewish ancestry.[85]

That did not keep the anti-Semites from attacking "Jew Bertha." After receiving another vicious anti-Semitic letter, Bertha wrote Fried angrily, "strange, how ordinary this caliber of anti-Semites are; they cannot find anything more powerful to bring up than *Jew, Jew*. The militarists and the anti-Semites insult the pacifists as Jewish, and the pacifists accuse Jewish speculators and journalists of warmongering."[86]

8

The Hague Peace Conference

Suttner looked forward to the turn of the century expectantly. Like many of her contemporaries, she hoped it would introduce a new and better time. She was quite certain that the twentieth century would also bring the fulfillment of the great goal: an international court of arbitration and a peace conference of all governments. In 1894 she wrote Alfred Nobel, "I have one conviction: it is that the six years that separate us from the new century could make way for the official conference to bring peace to Europe, if the work of the pacifists is energetic enough." She connected this congress to the great World's Fair planned for 1900 in Paris.[1]

Bertha thought influencing people in power would be her best chance: "I ought to talk to Queen Victoria, to the new czarina. These could all be seeds that would sprout around 1900."[2]

She compared the congress she dreamed of with Henri Dunant's organization of the Red Cross, which became a powerful political institution through the participation of official governmental bodies. She wrote to Nobel, "You will see, we will succeed in bringing about a diplomatic conference for peace and disarmament, the institution of an international court—just as Dunant succeeded in bringing about a Geneva conference where all the powers were represented."[3]

She held the internationality of such a conference—like that of the peace movement in general—for an absolute prerequisite. "Either the peace movement is international or it is not," she repeated again and again in her lectures and newspaper articles. "The objection is rightly made against anyone who talks of disarmament: 'But we cannot make our fatherland defenseless in the midst of all our armed neighbors—go to the other countries with your suggestions—they should start.'—Start? That is something the others will not do either, for the same reasons. Such measures must be taken simultaneously and unitedly."[4]

She thought things were going "in the direction of gradual reduction of violence" anyway, although not fast enough.

> If things are left to their own accord, the new judicial system will estab-lish itself after immeasurably long periods during which the still domi-nant, still insufficiently regulated system will live out its course and finally die of its own hypertrophy; in other words, after the most terri-ble world wars between increasingly larger groups of countries, after revolutions and bankruptcies of unheard of dimensions, after distress and terror pile up to an unbearable degree—finally the establishment of "a universal peace organization embracing all states." *But should one, will one leave things to their own accord?*[5]

All her efforts went into accelerating this development, this "step from theory to experiment," finally culminating in an official and interna-tional discussion on securing peace.

Bertha von Suttner knew very well that the peace movement was not in a position to abolish war. "Only those who have the power in their hands—that is something the pacifists realize—can put the idea into ac-tion. But the idea, if it is repeated clearly, frequently, and unanimously enough, also possesses a power, namely, the power to affect the desire of the mighty to act. And that is what we want. Not we ourselves rushing to solve international legal problems; not we ourselves erecting the house of world peace . . . but may those who can, do it."[6]

Her belief in the establishment of an international legal system was unshakable.

> It has taken a long time for the single elements—individual, tribe, for-tress, city, province—to give up the privilege of settling their conflicts with their fists; but in the upward progress of culture, it has actually come to the point where individual parties have renounced war with the nearby tribes, neighboring fortresses, and neighboring cities in order to protect their mutual security and existence. With the exception of North America, however, the mode of unification has not progressed to the states; these—bringing false pride and defiance into play—are still living in the anticultural, wild condition of hostile separation glossed over with the name of "sovereignty."

Against the much used argument of "noninterference" in the affairs of other countries she argued, "My God, you have a certain independence in private life at home, too, and forbid outside interference. But if cries for help come from a neighboring apartment, if a lunatic is trying to kill a member of his own family, don't you rush to the rescue—or do you calmly respect the internal affairs of the deranged neighbor? No, you call the police."

And to the objections "What police should nations call? The soldiers? That is armed intervention, that is war. And that is to be avoided, isn't it?" Bertha answered:

> Armed people who step in to protect are not wagers of war, they are guardian policemen. The united civilized world does not need offensive armies aiming at each other anymore, but it does need an allied and armed army of protection. It cannot be sent out to kill, plunder, but only to bring murderers, robbers, and the lunatic under control. . . . No, neither the lust to conquer nor the lust for revenge may motivate intervention made by the future world army; it must simply bring help and protection. Wherever the oppressed, the tyrannized, the starving raise their cry of lament, there it hastens to intervene, because it is not an internal affair, it is a humanitarian affair.[7]

She demanded the "expansion of the legal body" that would finally seal the "solidarity of interests of all civilized peoples," and she never tired of condemning violations against the principles of international law, whether they were connected with the Cuban crisis, the Japanese-Chinese War, or the Italian campaign against Abyssinia in 1896. "What a terrible self-contradiction Italian patriotism has gotten into; it has based its pride on shaking off the foreign yoke, and in order to bring the adventure to an end now that it has started, they will have to subjugate entire peoples in the most gruesome manner."

Aside from its "moral untenability," this war forces Italy into such enormous expenditures "that *no* conquered area, no matter how large, will be able to replace the losses connected with its acquisition. *Maintaining* a region conquered by force and at great sacrifice requires additional force and additional sacrifices. If Italy were to conquer all of Ethiopia, it would not be able to enjoy this possession in peace, unless a country's ownership of mere kilometers were capable of creating happiness in its citizens."[8]

More and more, Suttner became a voice of political conscience, an absolute champion of morality in politics, even in the face of the "modern" and celebrated imperialism. "In Madagascar a state of siege has been proclaimed—because the natives are rebelling. New expeditions will therefore be necessary. If only the European countries would colonize, clean up, and Christianize themselves first!"[9]

And she waited longingly for the mighty who would understand the signs of the new times and the new century and who would give the impulse for a new international agreement on war and peace and legal order. At first she placed her hopes in Emperor Franz Joseph, who celebrated the fifty-year jubilee of his reign in December of 1898. Something truly special should come of this great occasion—perhaps even the ardently desired "peacemakers' conference" she dreamed of in her novel *Schach der Qual,* written in 1895. In the book she wrote, "At the initiative of one of the most powerful heads of state in Europe and after the approval in principle was given by all the other governments for this purpose, this meeting was called—and almost all the countries, the great and the small, with very few exceptions, gave their approval and are represented here."[10]

She also placed her hopes in the young Czar Nikolaus II, who ascended to the throne in 1894. "A lot speaks for a 'new human being' having come to power, who also has the new ideals in mind."[11]

In a number of newspaper articles, she claimed that precisely in Russia, "in addition to, or perhaps even because of the immense preparations for war, the idea of an international legal system is already at an advanced stage," thanks to the famous legal expert at Moscow University, thanks to the sociologist and pacifist Novikov in Odessa, and above all, of course, thanks to the untiring work for peace of the Russian member of the State Council, railway industrialist and writer, Johann von Bloch. He was one of the leaders of the European peace movement and had always been a generous donor to the cause.[12]

The two Russians, Novikov and Bloch, nourished Bertha's hopes in the young czar. She was convinced the czar would not close himself off to the arguments of the pacifists, and she sought for an opportunity to make personal contact with the ruler.

When the czar paid a visit to a relative in Darmstadt in 1897 (the czarina was a princess of Hessen-Darmstadt by birth), Bertha asked an acquaintance of the czar's mother-in-law to smuggle the Suttner book, *Schach der Qual,* in with his visit. She also made a second attempt to reach the czar. She inquired at the court marshal's office in Darmstadt whether she could present the czar with a painting that glorified the peace idea. The czar had an answer sent that was a refusal but was friendly and even mentioned the "great idea of world peace."

She saw her great expectations more than fulfilled when the Russian foreign minister, Count Muravyov, presented a peace manifesto to all the accredited foreign ambassadors on August 24, 1898, at the order of the Czar. According to Suttner, it was "the most splendid peace document that was ever issued . . . a new page of history was turned."

The document stated, "The maintenance of universal peace and a possible reduction of the excessive armament that burdens all nations present an ideal in the current situation all over the world, upon which the efforts of all governments ought to be directed. The humane and noble striving of His Majesty the Emperor, my exalted Sirs, is entirely devoted to this task." The financial burdens of arming had struck "the welfare of the people at its roots." "The development of national culture, economic progress, the creation of values has been lamed and led astray."

The czar regards it his responsibility "to put an end to this incessant armament and to seek the means of preventing the disaster threatening the whole world," and to this end he proposes holding a conference that would be "a favorable omen for the coming century, with God's help." He called for a "unanimous consecration of the principles of law and justice upon which the security of the states and the welfare of the peoples rest."[13]

For Bertha von Suttner, who was completely weighed down by material and personal worries at this time, the manifesto was a deliverance from all adversities, like the dawn of a new, long-awaited, peaceful time. She wrote in her diary, "And *such* a powerful event today—like a bolt of lightning—but wonderful: peace manifesto from the czar! That will push our movement thousands of miles forward. Joyfully excited—sleepless night! For once, sleepless with joy. *Now* there'll be a lot to do. Telegrams."[14]

"Enchanted, astonished, shaken, enraptured," she wrote to Fried in Berlin. "Isn't it wonderful? *Schach der Qual,* page 194, the whole Russian move is already sketched out." In her self-assurance, she speculates, "Who knows whether it was not read at the highest place in Petersburg. . . . It fits into the discussion of what should be talked about at the conference, anyway." Fried was to try to print the chapter again.[15]

It soon turned out that Nikolaus was indeed influenced by a pacifist, namely, by Johann Bloch and his six-volume work that appeared in 1892 and was translated into all the civilized languages: *The War of the Future, Viewed from the Technical and Political Standpoint,* a standard work of pacifism. In it, the author describes the economic and social consequences of a modern war and reaches the conclusion, "War will come to an end because the military machinery will fail for economic and social reasons." The new technology of war, including Nobel's explosives, had created completely new conditions that imperatively demanded an international accord. A war could no longer be won by any side, primarily for economic reasons; a new consideration of the subject was therefore necessary.[16]

Suttner said of Bloch's work:

> The great Russian financier was no visionary, he was a thinking, practical man who drew conclusions according to scientific method and imparted them to the world. He did not demand to be believed. He said, go forth, inquire, study, reckon, and then admit that the war of the future can no longer be waged; because—first, the nerves of human beings will no longer be able to hold up to the effects of modern weapons that cause mass destruction from invisible distances. . . . [S]econd, the economic effects of a war would show up in universal ruin and misery long before it could end . . . and Bloch saw a third coming: before a war of the future between great powers could come to a decisive end, revolution and anarchistic killings would break out internally.[17]

Czar Nikolaus made Bloch's work "the object of a thorough study." "Shortly before the appearance of the work, he called for the author to present himself, and the latter found him in the midst of maps and charts from this work, spread out over a number of tabletops. Von Bloch had to give information on detailed questions and remarks for two hours; he was already very tired, but the emperor continued asking questions and making comments untiringly and with intense interest."[18]

The manifesto calling for an international peace conference was thought to be the result of the emperor's occupation with Bloch's work. Suttner wrote to Leo Tolstoy, "What kind of a northern light is this imperial word! What do you say? Certainly a trace of what motivates your writings has also reached that far. I am very happy. Because—what a turnaround that is in public opinion. This good word, coming from so high above, will move the entire world—people are starting to think."[19]

Bertha and her friends were convinced that the goal of the peace movement, an international court of arbitration for preventing war, was near, could even be achieved before the magic year, 1900. Messages of congratulation arrived.

Björnstjerne Björnson: "The czar has done something marvelous. Whatever comes of it, starting today, the air is buzzing with ideas of peace, even there where they never would have been found yesterday."

Henri Dunant: "This is a gigantic step, and whatever happens, the world will not cry, 'Utopia!'; it will not experience the belittling our ideas did; and if the realization of the congress . . . does not follow immediately, at least it has been set in motion."

The Russian writer Novikov, who knew his czar, cautiously hinted at doubt: "But what I think about it? First, all of us who are of one mind with the spirit of the manifesto should support Nikolaus II with all our might; not only against his opponents, but also against his own person. The undertaking is extremely difficult. He could lose his courage in the face of the obstacles. Then liberal opinion in Europe and the peace organizations, especially, will have to provide him with untiring, unwavering assistance."[20]

After reading the newspapers, Bertha stated with satisfaction: "The papers are full of the czar, thanks to Suttner. The star of the cause of peace is shining brighter than ever."[21]

The future conference would introduce a new cultural era and would be "a good omen for the coming century."

> Just as one is used to putting his house and his books in order on the last day of the year, to be able to begin a better and more beautiful life in the new year, now in this final year of the century, we have the opportunity to clean up the worst remnants of old barbarism (or at least begin energetically with this cleaning project), so that the coming century can be devoted entirely to working out happy cultural tasks, so that—exactly the same way some people resolve on New Year's Eve to become a new person from now on—the threshold to the 20th century can also be crossed by a new humanity. Not one that is changed through and through, a humanity that has become like angels, but simply one that has freed itself of the burden of an inhumanity that had long since become unbearable.[22]

All the same, the response from politicians and the press was marked by skepticism. Suttner, disappointed, said: "No fellow regent, no government answered the manifesto with more than politeness—not *one* heartfelt word was uttered."[23] Of course one would be prepared to send a representative to the conference. Much more readiness was hardly to be expected from a government.

Many newspapers reacted to the czar's manifesto with disdain and scorn. The peace manifesto belonged "to the realm of wild fantasies, in the area of bloodless, washed out, powerless, and effeminate *Suttneriades,*" wrote the *Linzer Montagspost.* "Only a dreamy cosmopolitan" could take it seriously, because it was just a "slyly planned move made by cunning, truly Slavic politics." "Under a hypocritical and dissembling mask of selfless friendship concerned only with the welfare of all peoples, the czar and his foreign minister are offering peace to all countries, writes a note to stand alongside and on a par with all the wistful lamentations of Bertha von Suttner's stamp, and places his hopes on his imperial and royal colleagues. The bear in sheep's clothing!"[24]

Moltke's famous remark was repeatedly used against the disarmament efforts: "Eternal peace is a dream and not even a beautiful one. War is an element in God's order." "Serious political idealism is not possible without the idealism of war," the *Deutsche Rundschau* argued. "By showing war as mass murder and by the abasement of the heroism of the army, the people's spiritual military capability is gradually poisoned and destroyed, so that when the war breaks out one day despite the peace congress, we may face a people fired by a warring spirit and find ourselves at the greatest disadvantage." Then the newspaper pointed to practical problems of international disarmament and its control, problems that could not and would not be overcome in many, many disarmament conferences even some hundred years after the czar's manifesto.[25]

Wilhelm II answered the peace proposals in his own way. Before the Westphalian provincial diet, he said, "Peace will never be better safeguarded than with a German army, powerful and ready for combat . . . like the one we have the opportunity to admire and be glad about now. God grant that it will always be possible for us to care for the peace of the world with this spirited and well-maintained weapon! Then may the Westphalian peasant go to bed in peace."[26]

Suttner wrote in her diary, "The czar's heavens are darkening a bit because the papers are writing such stupid stuff." "German professors are writing and saying the most awful things: do not understand the czar and want to countercheck him."[27]

But most of all, the socialists doubted the czar's peaceful intentions, a reaction Suttner took especially badly. "But the social democrats are behaving in an ugly and suicidal way over the manifesto. *Party* narrowness!"[28]

August Bebel answered Suttner's request for him to join other prominent people on a "committee to support public declarations in favor of the peace conference" by saying that although social democracy was favorable to the idea of the manifesto, it had reservations about the czar personally. "Even an absolute emperor is not omnipotent," and therefore he thought "that in our mutual interest it would be better in this matter to march separately."[29]

That was a clear rebuff to the conference, but at least it was formulated more politely than the derision of the socialist *Vorwärts,* which wrote about the "laughter of the world" over bourgeois hopes for peace. Suttner: "Watch out, that you won't have to regret that—not because of the laughter but because of the tears of the world!"[30]

For a long time, Bertha could not reconcile herself to the position held by social democrats, but she held fast to her own conviction for the rest of her life: "War and peace are *not* a matter of class." Everyone ought to work together, "the farmers, the workers, middle class, the poor, the rich, statesmen, and even (who would have dared to hope for such a situation before August 24, 1898) the very highest military commanders."[31] They would not have to wait for democracy to take effect: "At any rate, the realization of the peace ideals would be postponed indefinitely if they wanted to make them dependent on a complete upheaval of the social situation happening first."[32]

She felt very sorry for the "poor" czar. "He's not doing much better than we are—his proposals are being treated just as condescendingly as ours."[33] "It is really shameful how the Czar has not met with understanding, except from us, not to mention cooperation. Really, if people are so blind and mean that they slay all their good angels, they really do not deserve anything better than to be shot at. Only the innocent suffer with them."[34]

The general opinion among diplomatic and political circles was that, "Emperor Nikolaus was . . . entirely in the hands of his ministers, who, while flattering His Majesty's humanitarian ideals, were actually pursuing their own intentions to get other countries to stop arming until Russia finished building the Siberian Railway and succeeded in getting some more loans. The problems Russia has run into recently in its attempts to find money were the real reason for suggesting disarmament."[35] The main objection to the czar was that he himself—for instance, in his brutal and bloody policies toward Finland—did not by any means behave as though he loved peace.

Toward the end of October 1898 a telegram arrived with the news that the Russian foreign minister, Count Muravyov, expected to receive an Austrian delegation led by Suttner. The audience would take place in connection with a journey Muravyov was to make to the capitals of Europe to inform himself of the chances and possible objectives of the peace conference.

The meeting with Bertha von Suttner was not very productive, although she tried to attach as much importance to it as possible. Bertha reported Muravyov's first words to his guest: "[H]e was happy to meet an enthusiastic champion of the idea that had made the Czar and his government its apostles, an idea that he confidently hoped would gradually conquer the world." Success would take years: "For the time being a standstill in armaments, a pause in inventions is the first stage, it could not be hoped that the states would approve of complete disarmament or even a reduction of arms, but if they could agree on a pause in the 'race to ruin,' that would be the most favorable result."[36]

Bertha's commentary:

> It was a peculiar feeling for me to hear talk about war and peace the same way we are in the habit of talking in our meetings, and to remind myself that this was not a member of our organization but the chancellor of the most powerful military state, who was standing there in a semiofficial capacity—for I was not there as a lady of the world, but as a representative of the movement—explaining that from then on, it would be necessary to work toward putting world peace on a secure foundation since a European war of the future would be a thing of horror and ruin and actually a thing that was impossible.

All the same, there was no more talk of disarmament, only of a "standstill in armaments." "It had apparently become clear to him after conferring with various rulers and statesmen that for the time being there was no inclination to approve a reduction of troops or weapons or even the principle of abolishing war and the threat of war."[37]

Muravyov reacted rather peculiarly when Arthur von Suttner asked him "whether it would not be advisable to found a peace organization in Russia and hold a congress there." One would have to ask the czar first, said the minister, who thought "that such a founding was neither desirable nor necessary. Not desirable because in a country with such a young culture, with such a warm-blooded and easily excitable populace, rather a lot of awfully immature and unrefined elements that could be dangerous for the cause could get involved." Bertha cautiously contradicted him, pointing to the temperament of the Hungarians and their peace activities. But Muravyov kept to his opinion that a peace movement in Russia was not necessary, because "Standing at the head of the movement right now are the czar and the government themselves."

Bertha commented trustingly, "It is true. Does one need to light a lamp in a room flooded with sunlight?"[38] She summarized the conversation thus: "All in all, *odd* that we are being received. But unfortunately, a lot of diplomatic shrinking back."[39]

The meeting between the Russian foreign minister and the "Peace Bertha" caused a stir all over the world.

At the same time, the old fear of not being up to the immense task tormented her again. Fried "scolded" her then for having "stage fright on the stage of the world." Bertha replied:

> The expression is nice and suits me very well. You have stage fright when you feel that you've been given a role you're not up to, when you have to recite something you haven't memorized well enough, and when you feel that your costume and makeup are not good enough either. For *the* role that is being assigned to me everywhere now—leader of the movement—source of inspiration for the czar—speaker—literary personality—etc., etc., I *am* too weak; and besides, too old—I ought to be different personally, too—in short: flee, I wanted to flee out of (not *into*) the public eye, and if not entirely out of it, then have a small part like I had at the beginning, one I could *fill*, the role of a loyal, hard-working, enthusiastic participant.[40]

The product of Muravyov's fact-finding mission was a second circular to the government and the press, dated January 16, 1899, with a proposal for the conference agenda. "You can see how much water has been added to the drink of strong, fiery wine," commented Suttner,[41] because now the talk was mostly about regulating matters of war, starting with the prohibition of certain explosives and reaching to an agreement on the rescue of the shipwrecked. More and more, the Red Cross stepped into the center of the preparations for the conference.

Bertha wrote Henri Dunant:

> Your wonderful creation that has done so much good is—in the hands of backward elements—about to become an obstacle in the path of an even higher good. You will understand me: all the militarists, statesmen, and governments who do not want to hear anything about an end to war are retreating behind the Red Cross and the Geneva Convention in order to hinder the whole Hague conference. You will negotiate there on additional articles to alleviate future massacres, but not concern yourselves with means to prevent these massacres. That is also a way to announce to the world: see how good and humane we are, but we are too sensible not to regard war as unavoidable, and we will come to an arrangement about how it can be mitigated.

She appealed to Dunant to protest against these maneuvers. "Something has to be done. These men ought to know that the people are expecting something propitious and that the founder of the Red Cross himself is hoping for progress. You have always wanted the Red Cross to prepare the way for the white flag. The world has meanwhile progressed from 1859 to 1899." She called the efforts of the war alleviators a "trap that opens up in front of the feet of the pacifists,"[42] and stressed the point that abolition and alleviation of war were opposites like north and south and that "when the goal lies in the south, we should not pave the way to the north."[43] But all her efforts were to no avail.

Invitations to the conference were supposed to be issued by the Netherlands. Quarrels broke out immediately over which countries ought to be invited. Italy successfully opposed an invitation to a papal representative. The two South African states, Transvaal and Orange, were not invited owing to English opposition and to the displeasure of the Netherlands. Of all the countries on the American continent, only the United States and Mexico wanted to take part. The dissension generously and widely publicized in the press increased the ridicule directed toward the peace conference.

Then, what should burst into the midst of the preparations but the news that the Suttner novel *Lay Down Your Arms* had been banned in Russia, the very novel that was attributed with having made such a great impression on the czar. Somewhat uncertain, Bertha wrote to Fried, "I still don't know if the ban on my book is true. The fact that the opponents are exploiting this news, does not prove anything. . . . If Russia is going along with peace-Bertha, then that's an argument against Russia's seriousness; and if it is ignoring or even banning Bertha, then it's an argument against Russia's sincerity."[44]

The composition of the German government's delegation was a shock for the pacifists and a bad omen for the conference. Its members included the specialist in international law, Professor Stengel, who had only shortly before caused a sensation with a provocative antipacifist pamphlet.

Suttner put out a counterpamphlet and wrote an energetic preface for it.[45] The German peace society protested in vain against sending Stengel to The Hague.

The public derision, the rebuff of the socialists, and now the apparent resistance of one of the most powerful delegates to the goal of the conference was enough to dampen the pacifists' euphoria, but it also spurred them on toward greater activity. The English journalist W. H. Stead organized an international peace crusade in preparation for the conference, with big meetings in Europe's major cities. Suttner wrote: "The Stead pilgrimages are turning into something marvelous. By comparison, what's happening in Germany now—the expulsions, the imprisonments—awful!"[46]

Bertha was supposed to organize the reception of the peace crusade in Vienna, but the project failed. The only big crowd Stead was able to attract was in London. "It turned out that the other countries did not provide strong enough contacts or response. Especially Germany—there the motto was *rejection*."[47]

Stead persisted in publicizing his project. Pope Leo XIII had an answer sent to him saying the Holy See could "not wish for anything more than for all peoples to be united by a peace union and for justice to reign in relationships between nations. May the century that has done so much for the expansion and improvement of weapons of war do something noble before it closes, namely, create the ways and means to make it possible for the voice of reason to assert itself easily in international conflicts"—words that Bertha was to quote frequently.[48]

She admired Stead greatly and defended him vehemently against mockers. "Stead is admirable in his campaign—in my eyes a saint in the movement, and has such a power for work, it's inhuman. I feel so small next to him."[49]

But others were also to be inspired to activity by the conference. The wife of a Munich professor, Eleonore Selenka, collected more than a million signatures of women from all over the world, including that of Queen Elisabeth of Rumania, and presented the document to the president of the conference to assure the delegates of women's support.

The grand old man of the international peace movement, Frédéric Passy, wrote the eighteen-year-old Queen Wilhelmine of the Netherlands an open letter in which he urged her to prepare a welcoming surprise for the conference in The Hague. The most important point on the agenda was the court of arbitration, and Wilhelmine could conclude a treaty with Belgium or Switzerland even before the conference, to set an example. "If I were Your Majesty," wrote the seventy-seven-year-old Passy, "if I were the charming and highly intelligent Queen of the Netherlands, I would make it a point of honor to place in my crown this most precious of all jewels, which has so far not shone from a single crown, not even the most brilliant one." But the queen did not answer.[50]

Out of worry that the peace conference might fail because of the political differences of the day, some of the pacifists came up with rather weird proposals. Fried suggested in all seriousness that the superpowers should quickly agree on a partitioning of China before the conference, so that it would not be hurt by this problem as well.

The Chinese empire was about to collapse after losing the war it fought with Japan. The European powers intervened time and again with their troops and occupied Chinese territory. Suttner unequivocally branded the threatened division of China by the great European powers a crime. In August of 1897, together with Henri Dunant, she composed a call "to the peoples of the Far East," saying: "Our so-called European civilization comes from the Orient. You are several centuries ahead of us. Above all, we must recognize and admit with great sadness that for centuries our ancestors all too frequently behaved like barbarians toward you." She asked for participation in the international work for the court of arbitration and against war.[51] Contacts were actually established, and she exchanged letters with several East Asians until her death. This enabled her to be very well informed on events in this region.

The fact that her closest associate, Fried, of all people, was propagating imperialistic force against China in order to rescue the Hague conference, outraged her. She wrote a letter of protest.

> If Europe wants to unite to pursue *robber politics* in Asia and Africa, I am against it. Colonizing must also be brought into the realm of ethics, otherwise we will be contradicting ourselves. And there would be nothing to gain except that the whole horror over stretches of territory would be carried on in China and Egypt instead of in Alsace-Lorraine or the Balkans. . . . Our principles have to apply to colonial quarrels, too. *Defense* against wild peoples, certainly, but to go somewhere and *exterminate* under the pretense of acquiring a market—that is the same barbarism that we are fighting against.[52]

> The others of us, we apostles, do not have to make compromises with that which we are fighting. The moral element has to penetrate all questions of politics, only then can we win. . . . We must not become 'practical politicians.'[53]

Finally, she pointed out to Fried that his viewpoint would hardly meet with understanding from China's delegate to The Hague.

Suttner also brought up the question of morality when Fried, for tactical reasons, took up the German motto, "Increase the Fleet—the Way to Disarmament."

> I don't go along with you! . . . Those are the crooked, the opportunistic roads that world history does choose sometimes, but that *we* have nothing to do with: we must never leave the straight path. Should we join the fleet society because disarmament can be forced into being as a result of its goals? No, in Emperor Wilhelm's new idea, I see a direct

counteraction to the Emperor Nikolaus manifesto, and it remains our responsibility to point out that economic and moral arming at sea is just as, if not more, pernicious, senseless than arming on land.

Increasing the fleet was not a guarantee for a healthier economy, as the government wanted to have the Germans believe. "If a country gets into a war with a great sea power or even engages in a hostility that threatens war, it damages its industry more than conquering a colony can help it. . . . Wilhelm II is intoxicated with conquest, and the German nationalists with him."

Suttner had just as little sympathy with the much discussed continental alliance against England and America. "That would result in an all the more horrible catastrophe. We *need* the elements of peace in the great English-speaking peoples for our work—always an alliance between the law-abiding peoples against the peoples of force *everywhere*—but not categorized according to countries or continents."[54]

Fighters for peace streamed into The Hague from all over the world. They wanted to be present, if not as offical delegates, at least as observers, as informants, and do their best to enlighten and assist the various governmental representatives who mostly had little idea of what the peace movement was supposed to do or about the court of arbitration it was working for. They went to The Hague "like the legendary pilgrim kings of the Orient to Bethlehem," wrote Bertha. "We want to wait close to the council room, where the issues that have been the subject of our studies for many years, that have made up our propaganda work, that comprise our dearest ideals are being handled. We want to come into contact with the delegates personally. . . . We want to share our feelings, at least in the adjoining room, when the child of salvation, codified peace, comes into the world!"[55]

The same old obstacle stood in Bertha's way again. She had neither the money for the trip nor for the six-week stay. Naturally, she did not want to stay in just any cheap hotel room; she wanted to rent an apartment where she could receive guests and practice peace politics. She wrote to Theodor Herzl, the new feature editor of the *Neue Freie Presse,* "I would like to suggest that you suggest to the management of the *N.Fr.Pr.* that it suggest that I stay in The Hague during the six weeks that the conference will be meeting there. I have connections with various statesmen there, with the Russian delegate . . . know a number of conference members personally—would go out into the world there, attend the different banquets and receptions—would therefore be in a position to send interesting 'Letters from The Hague' back to the paper."[56]

But the *Neue Freie Presse* showed little interest in the peace conference, and Bertha complained to Herzl about it. "Tell me, for God's sake, what kind of a war-fury is this that's gotten into the *N.Fr.Pr.?*—On the eve of the *peace* conference in The Hague, to which all the eyes of Europe are glued: lead article, which already suggests at the outset 'that nothing can come of it'—articles that I send in, on the other hand, and that are certainly *expert*, get thrown into the waste paper basket." She complained that even the feuilleton only printed warlike articles, "And *you* are the feuilleton king! The 20th century is standing at the door—an intergovernmental congress announced, which is to bring in a new era—and the newspaper public is supposed to wallow in old reminiscences of the glory of war?"[57]

Eight days later she tried a new attack and also approached the subject of her fee. "As far as the 'delicate question' is concerned (by the way, I don't think there is anything delicate about it; everybody from the well-paid general to the newspaper boy gets paid), let me say from the very beginning that being able to spend six weeks in The Hague and receive all the various 'plenipotentiaries' in my salon will require an allowance of at least 1,000 gulden. An American newspaper would find a sum like that much too small."[58]

It took a third letter to achieve success, but along a different line. Herzl commissioned Bertha to go to The Hague for his newly founded Zionist paper, *Die Welt*, to send back reports and also to use this important international platform to work for Zionism. "As to the Zion interviews, I think your commission is very generous, and I will do my best to carry it out well. The various statesmen should bare their most intimate thoughts on Zionism to me, and if they don't have any, I will suggest some to them." Shortly before her departure, she wrote to Herzl happily, "So, *I* am going to The Hague, when are *you* going to Jerusalem?"[59]

As a tribute to the man who convened it, the conference was opened on May 18, the birthday of Nikolaus II.

Suttner was the only woman admitted to the solemn opening. "I shall always be grateful for the favor of this exception because the impression that was made on me here was like the culmination of many long years of hard work, the fulfillment of an ambitious dream," she wrote rapturously. "Peace conference: for ten years the word and the cause were laughed at; its participants, powerless private people, were thought to be Utopians and dreamers; now, however, the representatives of all the rulers and governments have come together at the call of the mightiest warlord of the earth, and their meeting bears that same name: peace conference."[60]

She knew very well that the people gathered here were not all pacifists: "The ignorant, the indifferent, doubters, and opponents are surely in this hall in larger numbers than determined followers. But the goal has been laid out, the message proclaimed. Words have been spoken that, although unheeded by many today, will echo, will remain written on the slates of history."

The First Hague Peace Conference convened from May 18 to June 29, 1899. In addition to the countries of Europe, the United States, Mexico, China, Japan, and Siam took part. Most of the countries sent diplomats, military heads, and international law experts. Work was done in three commissions: on disarmament, on working out laws of war, and on the court of arbitration. The press was excluded from the meetings, a situation Bertha lamented greatly.

The most famous pacifists were busy behind the scenes: Stead, Bloch, Novikov, Fried, Suttner. Since they were not admitted to the meetings, they saw their main work in supplying information about the peace movement to delegates, on the one hand, and to the international press on the other. Stead succeeded in getting minutes of the meetings from delegates who were friends of his. He had them translated into French and published them in the paper.

Bertha did press and information work. She was one of the most interviewed personalities at The Hague, and according to a comment made by Theodor Herzl, who arrived later, she was "the unofficial focal point, as it were, of the whole thing."[61] All the information came together in her. The hotel where she and a number of her friends were staying hoisted the white flag of the peace movement next to the flags of the participating countries.

Wherever Suttner was, there was also sociability in the aristocratic style, spiced with pacifistic bustle. In her salon, delegates met with pacifists from all over the world. An open-minded, international society came together there. Many had the feeling "that they were experiencing something unforgettable" and wanted to preserve the moments of international understanding for posterity. The most original idea for this came from Bertha herself:

Every guest should speak a sentence into the funnel of the phonograph. This lovely suggestion, however, called forth a general state of horror. No one wanted to be the first. Finally an Italian diplomat came forward and confided a compliment to the hostess in the phonograph. The French delegate, Léon Bourgeois, was supposed to be the next speaker. But it turned out that the recording had not been successful, and it was not possible to make the apparatus speak. . . . Someone . . . said, "Now that it is too late, I know what I could have said. This sentence: The phonograph fills us with the justified fear of posterity!"

Bertha always defended social gatherings. She thought that many things were easier to talk about in a relaxed atmosphere than they were at the official negotiating table, and many of the delegates at The Hague agreed with her.

Johann Bloch had four pamphlets printed as information about the ideas of the peace movement for both the delegates and the press. He also held lectures and discussions.

Theodor Herzl described the differences in Bloch's and Suttner's approach like this: "She is only against war for sentimental reasons, he only for rational reasons. She does not want war at any price, even if there were no problems with feeding the millions of troops." Bloch's motto was Beat Each Other, If You Can! But You Can't! Herzl then quoted a friend who was supposed to have said to Bloch, "I think the Suttner sentimentality is more effective for the cause than your calculations, which are certainly right. Because with calculations you appeal to reason, and that is wrong, because war is as a rule not fought because of reason but because of lunacy. Suttner appeals to feelings, and in the end she is right."

Suttner contradicted Herzl, "You always maintain that I only fight war for sentimental reasons. That is *not* so. But that is irrelevant. Being the opposite of Bloch's iron head sounds even better."[62]

Many of the delegates who were skeptical at first became more careful about their verdicts in the course of the talks and even began to believe in the possibility of an international agreement. In fact, a feeling of international solidarity gradually grew up among all the participants during the six weeks of working together. For most of them this was a new experience, since international congresses of this size had rarely taken place in politics before this one.

It was clear to almost all of them that the conference was the beginning of a process of development, even though the results were meager. The disarmament commissions failed: the Russian proposal for a five-year arms standstill was rejected. No concrete agreements were reached.

The second commission decided on a prohibition of dumdums, gas, and dropping bombs from balloons. (After a five-year period the latter prohibition was not extended, however, and also not renewed at the Second Hague Peace Conference in 1907—since the first airplanes were already flying, and this issue had become a question of real military importance.)

The Red Cross actually stood at the center of things. The Geneva principles of 1864, which applied only to war on land, were extended to cover war at sea.

Only the third commission took decisive, new steps. It signed a convention on the peaceful arbitration of international conflicts, opening the way for international courts of arbitration and mediating services by neutral countries in case of war. The delegates were able to build on the preliminary work done by the peace movement, especially in regard to the work of the Inter-Parliamentary Conference in The Hague in 1894.

For the rest of her life, Suttner never tired of quoting the Hague agreement and reminding countries of the responsibilities to which they had agreed. "In order to avoid the use of force in international relations as much as possible, the signatory powers commit themselves to use all their efforts to bring about arbitration of international conflicts by peaceful means." The "peaceful means" were: use of a court of arbitration, mediation, investigating commissions.[63]

Bertha complained about the role Germany and its allies played in the negotiations. "The fact is that the positive motions concerning the court of arbitration put forward by the delegates from Russia, America, and England were supported and promoted by France . . . and a number of other countries while the only thing Germany, Austria, Turkey, and Rumania did was to put on the brakes."[64]

The American delegate, Andrew D. White, described the motives of the German government in his memoirs. Count Münster, the most important man in the German delegation, had told him, "Courts of arbitration would only be damaging for Germany. Germany was prepared for war as no other country was; Germany could mobilize its army in ten days, something neither France nor Russia nor any other country was in a position to do. The Court of Arbitration would simply give every enemy power time to get prepared, and therefore would bring Germany nothing but disadvantages."[65]

Suttner gave Germany all the blame for the relative lack of success at the Hague conference.

"It is really outrageous *how* Germany was represented at the conference—and now German papers have the gall to jeer at failure, which, even if it were so, could only be blamed on them; luckily it is not so—*despite* Germany's behavior, something has been achieved. But one can only think what the success would have been like if the princes of the Triple Alliance had thought exactly the same way as Nikolaus, if the press had finally helped, and social democrats had not sneered at us!"[66]

One of the big innovations inside the peace movement following the Hague conference was the creation of the term "pacifism." In August of 1901, Bertha wrote Fried, "'Pacifist'—remember the expression and use it! Enough of *friends* of peace and their peace *movement*. From now on it's called pacifism—on equal footing with the other 'isms'; socialism, feminism, etc. The idea came from E. Arnaud, was launched in the *Indépendance Belge,* and I think it is so wonderful that from now on I shall only be a pacifist."[67]

When Fried hesitated and preferred Novikov's term, "federalism," she stressed her opinion all the more, "I prefer pacifism to federalism. The latter is a platform, but one that is too fenced in. The pacifists have quite different strings on their lyre." Even Bloch had already spoken out against Novikov. Bertha wrote:

> He says the federation is so far away and would only be created when everyone realizes the impossibility of a future European war. Therefore he would refuse to call himself a federalist, and among pacifists, he is one of the greatest. He doesn't like friend of peace either. Pacifism is of course a foreign word, but for an international cause, a foreign word is better. . . . Besides, it can be altered, "pacifistic," and such. Peace movement cannot be altered. You can say, "pacifistic declaration," "pacifistic correspondence," "pacifistic journalist," "pacifistic celebration." The word includes the movement and the doctrine in one term. "Peace" is something old, has been here often (between two wars).[68]

After a long struggle, Suttner won; Fried used the word *pacifism* in his newspaper, *Friedenswarte,* and made it popular.

Both old-fashioned "friends of peace" and modern "pacifists" waited for a long time without seeing any positive effects of the Hague conference. The German fleet project was supported in a way that seemed like a jeer.

"A real, systematic strangulation of the Hague conference has taken place on the part of the Germans. . . . A new conference of the powers ought to be called. *One* attempt at a start cannot be enough for such big matters," Suttner complained.[69]

As far as the pacifists were concerned, the czar had been conquered by Wilhelm II. Besides, all contacts with him had been broken off. Nikolaus did not even receive Bloch after the conference, even though it had been his work that supposedly motivated the czar to issue the manifesto. Suttner wrote to Fried: "Nikolaus did not receive Bloch? I suppose he is disgusted by the reception his noble impulse met with. Like us, he too overestimated the extent to which the peace idea had spread, the reputation of the peace movement."[70]

In the conflict with Finland, which began to escalate in 1899, Nikolaus proved to be the opposite of a "Peace Emperor" and practiced violent, authoritarian, and bloody politics. In his letter dated May 7, 1900, Mark Twain expressed the doubts that many of Suttner's closest friends felt: "I believed the Czar, now, as before the Finland episode; in which case I should hold it a pleasure and a privilege to be allowed to come and hear him praised. . . . I am not as young as I was. I realize it when I put the Finland tragedy and the Hague Comedy together, and find that I want to cry when I ought to laugh."[71]

In spite of everything, she hoped for a new initiative for peace from the czar. "The czar ought not to call a conference, he should preside himself."[72]

She accused the European press of concealing the czar's achievements: "Nikolaus II abolished the knout and all physical punishment. There is no mention of that. Moreover, the Russian clergy is urged to preach against anti-Semitism. Now, we have not come that far yet with the Christian Socialist clergy here." And when Björnson attacked the czar in a magazine, she was angry, "Aren't there anti-Semites and admirers of brutality living in other places, too—and more besides: at the helm? It is unjust to hold the czar alone responsible. And ungrateful of the friends of peace to do so. They should never forget what he strove for and actually *gave* the world. Hague—and the proposal for a halt to further armament."[73]

Suttner declared the day of the opening of the Hague conference, May 18, "Peace Day," and it was to be a yearly reminder of the court of arbitration.

The lethargy of the public regarding plans for peace disappointed her terribly. Of all groups, the ordinary people who suffered the most in war were caught up in nationalism and rejected the court of arbitration and a union of states as being unpatriotic. "But it would be the role of the *people* to demand a general union vehemently and to protest against the special alliances formed for the eventuality of war. But what are the stupid flocks doing? They just say baaa—even if it's in wise, full-sounding, political-diplomatic-publicistic-statesmanlike phrases—it's still only baaa."[74]

Of course, the newspapers did not miss the chance to show the obviously disappointed "Peace Bertha" in biting caricature. In the *Fackel* Karl Kraus also joined the chorus of mockers, "[T]he peace manifesto was a harmless proof of an absolute monarch's lyrical talent, and its results were just as harmless; except for the commotion in the press and the disturbance of the peace among diplomats, it left no damaging effects behind, for instance, in the form of reactionary laws."[75]

Depressed, Bertha had to admit defeat, as she did in a lecture in Munich, "and the intensified arming everywhere comes as an additional jeer. War fever, fleet fever, imperialistic fever. Instead of international understanding, there is fanatically nationalistic divisiveness, driven to the point of paroxysm. Now, all of this (we do not deny it) is resulting in a serious, momentary defeat for the peace fighters. It is the reaction. The new pushed too far forward—the old is taking its revenge and is going about it passionately, loudly, and powerfully."

The blame could not be placed upon the pacifists: "The organized peace organizations did what they could. But the fact is, they cannot do much. They know that their appeals and declarations rank only as declarations of principle. In order for these to be effective, they need to possess the means, need to have a stronger organization—something like the fleet organizations. People accuse them of this lack of power and forget that they—the people—are to blame because they have not helped."[76]

Ridicule of the pacifists reached a high point when the Boer War broke out only a few months after the Hague conference.

English nationalists used their fists against pacifists who protested at Trafalgar Square. Once again peace-loving people were berated as unpatriotic and were made to look ridiculous.

> The English nationalist is just as coarse and brutal a creature as the French—and as our anti-Semites. *One* mob across the whole world. They threw sticks, keys, knives at our speakers. Moscheles was hit in the ear with an open penknife. The newspaper *Sun* . . . agitated for this demonstration and is calling it a marvelous declaration of London public opinion. Everybody knows these obscure peace people are paid by secret Kruger funds . . . [they are being accused of being supported by the Boers]. If there had not been so many policemen there, the "patriotic" crowd of some 50,000 people would have lynched the few speakers. Our time civilized? Ridiculous! There are a few thousand civilized people, no more than that. *But they have to hold together*—and then their's will be the victory after all.[77]

After a renewed outbreak of English nationalism, Bertha wrote, "By the way, it's true that the English are behaving *disgustingly*. . . . They have smashed pacifists' windows in England again and wanted to throw a professor who was against the war into the water." However, she did not forget to add, "Of course, the imperialistic-minded fleet-Germans would be just as disgusting."[78]

In lectures and newspaper articles she spoke against the jeering commentaries. The Boer War was by no means proof of the senselessness of the Hague negotiations. The work of the pacifists did not have to be "hopelessly called off"; rather, "this work has to be carried on with twice the zeal and twice the speed." She called for help "in extending the international justice decided upon at The Hague." Incidentally, the English pacifists did not give up after the events at Trafalgar Square. On the contrary, they gathered fifty-six thousand signatures for a call that contained a message to the government: "We raise a solemn protest against appealing to force to regulate our differences with Transvaal before the principle of arbitrary process, approved by the Hague conference, is used and found ineffectual." "It is true: the court of arbitration, mediation, good services—all of these measures stipulated in the Hague conference have not been used to avoid the Transvaal war. But no one can say that these means have failed for the simple reason that they have not been tried. The fact that this has not happened is unfortunate but such means can only be declared unusable and hopeless if they have been tried exhaustively and zealously without bringing results."[79]

Pacifists all over the world tried to mobilize the international public against the Transvaal war. They clearly took the side of the Boers, who "from the beginning to the end, called for a court of arbitration," according to Bertha.[80] "Of course, the Hague convention only exists on paper—but it is there, it is a treaty, and if depended upon, everyone would have the right—even more, the responsibility to postpone the outbreak of war or at least to prevent its progress."[81]

All the appeals for peace were futile; a neutral mediator could not be found. The turn of the century they had placed so much hope in did not bring about a change for the better, quite the opposite. "It is disgraceful the way this last year has hurled us backwards. The Hague conference has shaken the system of the world and its powers out of its complaisance. It saw that it was threatened and took action."[82]

The war dragged on until the Boers were defeated. In a letter to Fried in September of 1902, after peace was reached, Suttner wrote, "The great Boer begging crusade now shows what the results of the war were. What kind of chaos would be created if a big war were to break out in Europe? Could something like that ever be put right again? Thirty million pounds sterling were needed to alleviate the African misery. Nobody spent anything to prevent it. Stupid world!"[83]

Meanwhile, the great trouble spot in China flared up again. In the

Boxer Rebellion, the Chinese fought against foreign rule. The big powers advanced against the insurgents with a combined army led by the German General Waldersee, spurred on by such sayings from the German emperor as, "Even a thousand years from now, no Chinese will dare to look at a German suspiciously," and "What the Russian emperor was not able to do in The Hague, may succeed now with weapons in our hands." Bertha's commentary was, "Hardly. And who was to blame for not succeeding in The Hague? Wilhelm alone. Discord is still all that sprouts from seeds of discord."[84]

At the beginning, Bertha was prepared to welcome the "protective" European army stationed in China as a harbinger of a new age in European solidarity: "The thing itself: united troops, French, Russian, etc., under the command of a German general, belonged to the new conditions that were in the preparatory stage, but the way it was carried out showed the old spirit."

This "old spirit" expressed itself in the fact that the army was by no means called out for protection alone; it exercised "revenge, cruelty, and pillaging." "Descriptions of the atrocities Europeans performed against people who were not even fighting, against the innocent, made your blood stand still."[85]

The "Czar of Peace," Nikolaus II, was especially cruel inside his own sphere of interest, Manchuria. In this point, the peace organizations held back with their criticism—and in doing so, lost some of the good will they had gained. One of the first members of the peace society, Baron Joseph Doblhoff, resigned in protest in 1901. He regretted that pacifism "had not managed to hold a protest meeting yet against the hypocrite; on the contrary it is upholding its homage to the czar! . . . I shudder at the blood that the crowned protector of peace spills in his piety.—I request that my resignation from the Austrian Society of the Friends of Peace be acknowledged. I do *not* render homage."[86] Others followed him.

Bertha lost a lot of sympathy during these months, since she held the German emperor responsible for all the atrocities. Her hatred was so great that Fried finally asked her to refrain from mentioning the emperor so often, at least in the articles for the *Friedenswarte,* published in Berlin. He was afraid, probably rightly, that he might be thrown out of Berlin. Bertha's response was: "It is absolutely impossible to write chronicles on war and peace without mentioning, and I mean critically mentioning, the person who holds all the strings of the war marionettes in his hands."[87]

The conflict with Fried was so serious that she actually stopped contributing to the *Friedenswarte* for several years.

The disappointments during and after the peace conference left deep marks upon Bertha. Added to these were serious financial difficulties and personal problems, about which even Fried, her closest associate, did not have the slightest idea (see chapter 9).

The failure of her *Hague Diary,* written with such great hope, joined all these adversities. "Peace literature is now an article that sells poorly in our world of topical newspapers and also among the public," she wrote to Fried.[88]

The reviews, when they were obliging, recognized the historical source value of the book, but justly criticized its form and content. Even Theodor Herzl, despite all his praise and understanding for the peace movement, made objections that could equally be applied to Bertha's memoirs: she includes "quite a few ordinary things, a lot of parties and dinners, conversations with people who had nothing to say, explanations that did not mean anything, letters that had nothing in them, transcripts that were signed without being read." Herzl made excuses for "the poor famous woman" as having been overworked in The Hague: "She was observed so much that she barely got around to observing," he wrote in a very subtle Viennese way, expressing the negative positively.

> She kept her diary hastily because she always had to think about her social responsibilities, visits here and there, breakfasts with the delegates, dinner with an ambassador, afterwards a reception at the little queen's [Wilhelmina], and in between, twenty letters, fifty cards to leave, nineteen conversations with journalists, beginning with the *Mississippi Messenger* and ending with the Eskimo's daily and the *Corriere di San Marino,* and finally the proofs of newspaper articles she had written herself. It is said that she was also photographed several times a day, sat for painters and sculptors, but that sounds highly unlikely.[89]

These are statements made by someone who knew Bertha well and appreciated her. They make it all too clear that her excessive activity also had a negative side: her unconcentrated, much too superficial accounts that frequently bogged down in an empty rattle of words. Quite apart from their poor literary quality, the Suttner books probably sold very poorly also because their message was not expressed strongly enough. And, since Suttner was subject to public ridicule anyway, this all created a welcome cause for criticism.

Her optimism clung to trivialities like the czar's having accepted her *Hague Diary* through his ambassador and even having his "sincere thanks" conveyed to her. She immediately attached hopes of a new peace initiative by the czar to this episode.

With every international crisis, Suttner hoped for the implementation of the Hague Court of Arbitration, and she suffered renewed disappointment every time. When the Venezuela crisis needed mediating, she complained: "The big powers *do not want* the Hague Court of Arbitration in the Venezuelan affair. Quite right—they are resisting the system that could rob them of the 'might' of their rule."[90]

Again she tried to talk to an Austrian politician and, embittered afterwards, she wrote in her diary: "Long visit with Dr. Steinbach in the Palace of Justice. Cowardice and halfway measures! Very nice with his "most gracious Countess"—but an official cannot dare to speak up for The Hague, out of respect for his most gracious warlord."[91]

And eight days later, relieved, "Venezuela is sorted out— *without* The Hague—Wilhelm II is terribly afraid of The Hague. And rightly so: The Hague means the end of militaristic doings, as the first locomotive meant the end of the postal carriage."[92]

The enterprising French pacifist and justice of the court of arbitration, Baron d'Estournelles de Constant, finally took the initiative. On a lecture tour of the United States, he was received by President Roosevelt, and on this occasion he urged the president "to wake The Hague's 'Sleeping Beauty' from its slumber by turning over some unsolved quarrel for a judgment." Roosevelt saw the justification for the request; he had "a difference with Mexico dug out from the American records" and submitted it to the Hague Court of Arbitration, which would now function for the first time.

Bertha, full of enthusiasm about this step, remarked: "So the devotion of an individual, supported by the activity of a mighty person, set the machinery in motion. Proof was given to the world that it *can* work. Of course the opponents are saying that the case submitted was very unimportant—as though unimportant cases had not already led to war! It's not the case that's important, it's the method."[93]

After this, the work of the international pacifists concentrated on expanding the regulations regarding the Hague Court of Arbitration. Their objectives were to have compliance with the decision of the court in international disputes made mandatory, to open the court to all countries of the world, and to make it a permanent institution.

In the meanwhile, the "Czar of Peace" was not doing honor to his name. Bertha, in her diary: "The czar wants to remain an autocrat. . . . Police states. Laws against revolution." As ever, she did not lay the real blame upon the czar, but on his reactionary environment: "[M]y dear czar . . . was forced into the role of the tyrant: he is being abused and reviled."[94]

She thought the loud outrage of western Europeans over the Russian atrocities was hypocritical: "Oh my western Europe, beat thy breast. Racial hatred, the worship of brutality and force are ruling everywhere. . . . As far as the massacres of the Jews are concerned: are our charming anti-Semites reading about them with a smile and only regret that if something similar were to be attempted by fanatic mobs in our area (there's certainly enough baiting) the authorities would not only be on the side of the perpetrators? Who may find fault if their own countries forcefully Germanize, Magyarize, and Czechize?"[95]

In December of 1903, the east Asian conflicts that had been growing for years escalated to the point that there was a danger of war between Russia and Japan. Suttner tried desperately to continue her defense of Nikolaus and affirm his love of peace, which she claimed was being "opposed by a very warlike clique." Together with pacifists all over the world, she appealed to governments to offer to mediate in the conflict between Russia and Japan and in doing so, prevent the war.[96]

Diplomatic relations between Russia and Japan were broken off in February 1904. In response to this situation and prompted by Fried, she took a desperate, much ridiculed step. As the president of the Austrian Peace Society, she sent the American president, Roosevelt, a telegram calling on him to mediate. "There is little hope that the European powers—perhaps you cannot either—will offer to mediate, whereas the modern state system of the Union appears to be excellently suited for carrying out this task. Mr. President, the fearful but trusting gaze of those who see the era of international justice dawning is directed to you especially, because you supported the realization of the Hague Convention so energetically." She also spoke as the vice-president of the International Peace Bureau in Bern and believed herself "to be the representative of millions of people."[97]

However, this telegram was already out of date at the moment it was sent. The Japanese attacked Russian ships in Port Arthur on February 9, 1904, without declaring war. Her friend d'Estournelles tried to calm the totally distraught Suttner and said, "For the last thirty or forty years, despite our efforts, Europe has tried its best to militarize Japan; it has instructed Japan in the art of war, it has turned Japan away from all its traditional industries, it has armed, exalted, pulled her along, and now is surprised that this good pupil is burning to do honor to the master."[98] Efforts to prevent the war had failed. Now the objective was to end it quickly. There had to be another attempt at getting the European powers to mediate. Suttner went to Prime Minister Körber with a delegation from the Austrian Peace Society. She handed him a resolution that challenged the government "to leave its former passive attitude behind, and take the cause of peace and humanity in its hands by providing energetic mediation for the two warring sides." The neutral powers were supposed to "seriously employ the rights" with which the Hague conference had endowed them.[99]

But success was not to be had in Austria-Hungary or in any of the other countries where pacifists had been active. The international peace societies did what they could. They issued public calls to be signed for ending the war. They held lectures and wrote articles against the Russo-Japanese War.

The pacifists became very depressed when the news came that the painter Vasily Vereshchagin had died. He was on board the battleship *Petropavlovsk* to sketch the horrors of war and shake the world out of its apathy. A mine sank the ship with its crew of eight hundred men.

Soon even Bertha began to notice how much the constant news of horror had become an everyday affair. "The East Asian war is awful. But we are getting used to it. That's the worst thing about times of war, this numbing of our most noble sensation—merciful compassion."[100]

Rumors that Emperor Franz Joseph planned to mediate between Russia and Japan were denounced. Suttner's commentary in her diary:

> It does not occur to the man who is a soldier with heart and soul to interrupt these so interesting and instructive and professionally fulfilling events. There should be at least one more big battle. Some 50,000 people still have to die to see whether Russia can acquire another bit of military glory and prestige. That is the mentality of our leaders and newspaper response. And all the time, the most horrible news keeps coming from Russia today: although the headlines do not say so, the revolution is wreaking havoc. Burning factories, 280 workers shot without being sentenced, a massacre in the streets of Baku, petroleum set on fire . . . railway connections between Vienna and Warsaw interrupted . . . and the countermeasure from the government: a ban on all foreign newspapers.[101]

Learning about a mass demonstration by Russian workers on January 21 gave her hope. "Demanding constitution and a stop to the war. Want to talk to the Czar himself. That is revolution." "The events are happening so quickly that all the petitions and projects for peace come too late. Perhaps they will be forced into peace, or there will be absolute chaos. Shots fired at the Winter Palace yesterday. Did the czar live through it? If only he had remained the emperor of peace and freedom!

He would have been the greatest ruler that had ever lived. He was not strong enough."

On this "Bloody Sunday," January 22, 1905, the Czar's government had the demonstrators in front of the Winter Palace in St. Petersburg shot down. There were more than a thousand dead.

The first Russian revolution, triggered by the unfortunate course of the war, raged for months. Bertha, in 1905, wrote: "Now the Caucasus, Mingrelia, etc., too, in full rebellion."[102] "We can't keep up, we can't keep up! The events in Odessa overshadow everything else. . . . Humanity, you disgust me. We, with our slow sowing and tilling, what are we supposed to do against this storm, this hurricane. And everything we write is obsolete within the hour."[103]

On August 20, 1905, she was finally able to see some success: "Russian constitution is here." A parliament, the Duma, took up its work on May 10, 1906—and its representatives were received with great optimism at the next Inter-Parliamentary Conference in London in 1906. But just as the Russian delegate was supposed to hold his welcoming speech, news came that the Duma had been dissolved. The Russians had to leave London without having achieved anything. "But oh, the Duma dissolved, and the terrible revolution . . . the czar could have saved everything still, but the wisdom of force (which also rules in our circles) won out—and woe, what will follow now."[104]

The Second Hague Conference was postponed because of all this horror. Bertha became restless and wrote letters to politicians all over the world to keep the idea of the peace conference alive. In April of 1906, she also turned to the man in whom she placed her greatest hope: the American president, Theodore Roosevelt. She enclosed her book on the First Hague Conference:

> Mr. President,
> The world's peace is sure to come—but only step by step. These were the words you said to me on the day—the 17th of September, 1904—when you so kindly received me in the White House. Of those steps in the advance of humanity's greatest ideal, you, Mr. President, have promoted the most vigorous and the most far-reaching. You have awakened the sleeping Hague Tribunal to action; you have brought to a close the tremendous war of the Far East; you have given the signal for a second Hague Conference; you offer arbitration treaties to every nation, and the golden words you addressed to the deputies of the Inter-parliamentary Union and pronounced on the subject in your last message to Congress, represent a whole treatise of peace, a whole system of its loftiest principles and surest methods.

Will you then permit me to inscribe your name in this volume, which I venture to offer as a token of the deep gratitude and fervent admiration with which your sentiments, backed by your actions, fill the heart of its author? This book, too, was meant as a step, however small, toward the goal toward which your energy and your power, Mr. President, are taking such mighty strides.

Very respectfully
Bertha von Suttner[105]

Theodore Roosevelt did not disappoint her. In 1907, he took the initiative, but this time, too, he let the czar call the conference officially.

Suttner developed new interest in her work. She tried to get the problem of minorities—anti-Semitism and also the Armenian issue—on the conference agenda. "Such heaviness must be lifted from our breast; the idea that it is still possible in our day for wild hordes to fall upon poor unfortunates who have done nothing wrong except belong to a different faith and a different tribe: this idea, to which pictures of the deepest barbarism on the side of the henchmen and the greatest desperation on the part of the victims are attached—we have to get rid of these at last, but in some other way than through the cold, cowardly, empty phrase of mollification."[106]

She made an open call for donations so that she would be able to carry out her publicity campaign for the conference. The results were disgraceful—and so were the results of the conference.

The opening was already sobering. Bertha wrote in her diary about the "ceremony which is only that. Two speeches with stereotype phrases, and unfortunately phrases denying peace, and that's it."[107]

As she did at the First Hague Conference, Suttner gathered journalists and pacifists into her improvised "salon." She helped William T. Stead publish the daily conference newspaper and held more than ten lectures. But the work of the diplomats and lawyers annoyed her more than ever: "Nothing but mitigations and arrangements are being handled in the commissions and even these are not getting through." And when one associate scolded with, "Whoever thought up the name 'peace conference' for this one here, deserves a slap on the face," Bertha answered just as angrily, "No, whoever falsified the character of the congress, deserves it."[108]

The disarmament issue was choked off immediately, mostly by the German government and Austria-Hungary, which was becoming more and more politically dependent on Berlin. The Austrian representative in The Hague, Baron Merey, received a letter of thanks from the foreign minister, Count Ährenthal, for the fact "that the preparations and the course of the plenary session at the conference, in which the disarmament issue was taken care of in a harmless resolution, was completely in accordance with our wishes," and he was decorated with the Grand Cross of the Order of Leopold.[109]

The reason why hopes for disarmament fell apart was the fact that preparations for war were being made in all the countries of Europe. Hardly anyone thought that war could really be averted, and everyone intensified the armament process.

Suttner had the impression "that the world is looking at the gathering of the delegates as a kind of trial in which 46 opponents or a number of opposing groups are using cunning and trickery to lay traps for each other, conclude all sorts of alliances, or postpone or destroy them—all with an eye toward improving their own power advantages in the ever present possibility of future war."[110]

In the end the Hague conference was again left with nothing but matters of international law and humanitarian problems to solve. Merey said to Suttner, "It is inevitable that war will break out between England and Germany." Bertha's horrified reaction, confided to Fried, was, "And *that* from our Hague representative! . . . The Quadruple Alliance between Germany, Austria-Hungary, Rumania, and Turkey was given the task from the very beginning to turn the peace conference into a conference on the practices of war. They've already succeeded to a great extent."[111]

In retrospect, Bertha called both of the Hague peace conferences "Conferences for consolidating war. For that is truly what they were. . . . The second conference corrupted. Now the work of the pacifists has to be done in entirely different fields and with ten times as much energy. The job is no longer to show that governments are working with us. Although masked, they have decidedly worked against us."[112]

Between the first and second peace conferences, armament increased by 50 percent—and airplanes gave war an added dimension. "And there's something else—a nightmare: the war of the future. The delegates themselves here at the conference stated how it was to be declared and how it was to be conducted. So, they see it coming and are not 'doing everything' to prevent it."[113]

Christian   Franz   Carl   Anton

1

1. The Kinsky family had a strong military tradition: Bertha's father (second from the left) and three of his brothers were generals in the imperial army. Courtesy Prince U. Kinsky.

2

2. *Countess Bertha Kinsky in Bad Homburg. Courtesy Historical and Ethnographical Museum, Zugdidi, Georgia.*

3. *Baron Gustav Heine-Geldern, one of Bertha Kinsky's three fiancés. Courtesy Austrian National Library, Portrait Collection.*

4. *Prince Adolf zu Sayn-Wittgenstein-Hohenstein. Courtesy Prince B. Sayn-Wittgenstein, Laasphe.*

5. *Alfred Nobel at age forty-three, when he met Bertha Kinsky. Private collection.*

6. *Baron Arthur von Suttner at the time of his return from Caucasia. Private collection.*

3

4

5

6

7. Entrance to Harmannsdorf Castle, the Suttner family's summer home in the Waldviertel. Private collection.

8

8. *Bertha as a young wife in front of her wooden house in Caucasia. Courtesy United Nations Office at Geneva, Library, Suttner-Fried Collection.*

9. Bertha in her Caucasian surroundings, with the typical weapons and rugs on the wall. Her later comment was, "I don't look like this. Also, my favorite emblems are not here; I love neither pistols nor rifles." Courtesy Historical Museum of the City of Vienna.

10

10. A successful and self-confident writer: Bertha after the appearance of her novel, Lay Down Your Arms. *Private collection.*

11. The niece, Marie-Louise von Sutt-ner. Private collection.

12. Bartolomeus von Carneri, the skeptical friend. Private collection.

13. Bertha's closest associate and her successor, Alfred H. Fried. Private collection.

11

12

13

14

14. *Bertha as a widow, at the time of the Nobel Prize award, with the frequently used dedication, "The future belongs to goodness—most of all, it belongs to young people." Courtesy Austrian National Library, Manuscript Collection, Arthur von Suttner.*

15

15. *As a prominent pacifist, Suttner held an important place at all the peace congresses. Here next to the white-bearded Frédéric Passy in the second row. Courtesy United Nations Office at Geneva, Library, Suttner-Fried Collection.*

16. *Andrew Carnegie, patron of Suttner in later years. Private collection.*

17. *Suttner and Prince Albert I of Monaco at the Opening of the Peace Institute in Monaco in 1902. Courtesy United Nations Office at Geneva, Library, Suttner-Fried Collection.*

18. *Postcard that Suttner sent home from Monaco, showing Alfred's greatly envied oceanographic museum. Private collection.*

16

17

18

19

19. *Honored by the American women's clubs: Suttner with the wife of the news-*
paper magnate Randolph Hearst, seated. Standing between them is Mrs. An-
drea Hofer-Proudfoot, the organizer of the United States tour in 1913. Courtesy
United Nations Office at Geneva, Library, Suttner-Fried Collection.

20. *Untiring at the age of seventy, Suttner still went on lecture tours to warn people of the approach of the great war. Private collection.*

21. *Abroad, Suttner appeared before her large audiences dressed in widow's veil, mourning jewelry, leather gloves, and very elaborate dresses. Courtesy United Nations Office at Geneva, Library, Suttner-Fried Collection.*

22

22. *At home on Zedlitzgasse, she sat many a night at her desk next to Arthur's portrait decorated with peace palms and wrote for peace. Private collection.*

23

23. *One of the last photographs of Bertha von Suttner. Private collection.*

9

Human, All Too Human

Her enormous success with the novel *Lay Down Your Arms* and her role in organizing the peace societies made Bertha von Suttner a well-known personality in public life. She was honored and ridiculed and had to learn to get along with both the light and the dark sides of her popularity. Hardly any of her contemporaries had the slightest idea how great the discrepancy was between public fame and private hopelessness at the time of her greatest successes. Only her diary reveals the details of this private life for posterity: "Fame for the future—oh, what it looks like at close range," Bertha complained in 1897.[1]

One of these big problems was the Suttner family's desolate financial situation. Bertha, who proudly gave "Harmannsdorf Castle" as an address in keeping with her social status, and who put up a very elegant and extremely dignified appearance, was in fact as poor as a pauper. The castle belonged to Arthur's aged parents. The estate farm and the quarry, which had not shown a profit for years, swallowed up new sums of money regularly to fend off ruin and the scandal of bankruptcy. It was money the parents could not provide and had to be taken from Bertha's and Arthur's writing income. When Bertha started working for the peace movement, income from her writing decreased rapidly. And being active in the organization also cost money, but did not earn any. The financial pressure increased.

For that reason Bertha was forced to write novels and serial stories for weekly magazines—in addition to her time- and nerve-consuming pacifist activities. She wrote in haste, without concentration and on subjects she did not really care about. And she had no illusions about the literary quality of this work.

Every new novel cost her agony. Since she usually had an advance paid to her due to a shortage of funds, she was always under pressure of a deadline and needed a great deal of strength to "cover the daily allotment. That's certainly not an *artistic* way to work."[2]

She would have preferred to write only newspaper articles at this point, covering topical issues from the position of the peace movement and to satisfy her growing interest in politics. But these articles did not bring in enough money. Moreover, she was doubtful about her journalistic capabilities. "I do not write quickly, or easily; if I could I would be someone else besides Bertha von Suttner."[3]

Her lack of success as a writer increased the need for money, and the need for money made peace activities harder. Suttner wrote to the equally impecunious Fried in 1895: "Well, the ministers of war are above all financial worries and can spend all their energy on their satisfying work; those of us who want to work for peace are hemmed in on all sides by want and private problems."[4]

She admitted to her younger friend, who repeatedly asked her to help him out with money (which she usually did although she herself was in need), "We, too—you probably don't know that—we Suttners have serious money problems. So I sympathize all the more acutely and understand what it means to be in the position you appear to be languishing in at the moment."

Arthur was having an even worse time with his novels. He could not find a publisher anymore and in 1901 was even forced to take part, anonymously and unsuccessfully, in a competition for novels. Even his newspaper articles were not printed, and were frequently not even returned anymore. Bertha complained bitterly about this treatment to the feature editor of the *Neue Freie Presse*, Theodor Herzl: "Beneath the mask, you are the only one with feelings, and that is why I am writing this complaint to you, to ask you to step in with a storm that will clear the air. Quite apart from the literature, we, being people of society, are used to being treated with a certain politeness."[5] Resigned, Arthur decided to give up writing. "It truly is a bad profession—overfilled," said Bertha in her diary.[6]

A new generation of writers was creating excitement in Vienna—Hugo von Hofmannsthal, Arthur Schnitzler, Peter Altenberg, Karl Kraus. The Suttners could not keep up, not only because they wrote in an "old-fashioned" manner, but also because they were artistically inferior to the young writers. The Suttner novels, with their messages—pure utilitarian art—did not fit in at all with the new aestheticism of the Viennese fin de siècle.

"The two of us are just plain excluded from literature now. *Place aux jeunes*," Bertha complained, after another of her novels had been sent back by the publisher.[7]

She read the "new" literature, went to see Schnitzler's plays, got excited about Ibsen's *The Wild Duck*, and wrote Alfred Nobel, "Have you read the novels of your countryman, Strindberg? I just paged through *The Confessions of a Fool*. It's simply awful."[8]

In her diary she noted, "Strange, how far away from ours the style of the new writers has developed. Is it beautiful? I don't know. Fascinating? Yes."[9]

Arthur tried desperately to find a permanent job as an editor. This alternative was closed to Bertha from the beginning because she was a woman. With a salary as security she could have carried on her peace work much more easily. She did not succeed.

During the mid-nineties, Arthur hoped to be put up as a candidate for parliament by the liberals, to no avail.

The situation in Harmannsdorf had by then become so bad that objects of value, from paintings to furniture, had to be sold, and even worse, legal seizure was a constant threat. Bertha knew that everything depended on her achievements alone, since the other residents had no possibilities for earning money. "Who am I dissatisfied with? With Bertha Suttner. Because she does not work quickly, which would be the only means of rescue, relief, and satisfaction."[10]

The peace work was not very satisfying at that particular moment: "The work I ought to be doing and am not doing, the whole feeling of 'not living in the present'; always having to do something for the future—but which one cannot get finished—as if in a bad dream."[11]

Added to this was the certainty that even if she worked constantly, she would never be able to raise enough money to prevent the Harmannsdorf estate from going bankrupt.

Bertha turned to Alfred Nobel in 1893, very cautiously, but also very clearly: "We will probably lose our home. Harmannsdorf is to be sold, that is, it will actually be a forced sale. It is a pity since it will definitely go for much less than its value—and the big unexploited industries (quarry, cement) will not be counted in the price . . . I only tell you this so that you will not [be] surprised to find out about it if you do after all happen to come to Vienna in the near future. And then, who knows: perhaps *you* would like to acquire property in Austria? That is *not* a request; I am only telling you in case it all happens to come together by chance and so that you will not be able to say to me, 'why didn't you tell me that before?'"[12]

Nobel's answer is not known. It is certain, however, that he did not buy Harmannsdorf. But in countless other situations he proved to be a helper in need. When he died in 1896, Bertha lost a truly good friend.

Life in the big family at Harmannsdorf became more and more difficult, as less and less money was available for the household. The old parents, the aunt, the sisters-in-law, the niece Marie Louise, the servants—a maze of relationships, of sympathies and antipathies and finally, of blaming each other. The parents-in-law got Harmannsdorf into this hopeless situation by their generous lifestyle. Arthur was not a clever overseer. After all was said and done, Bertha remained the outsider who had married into the family and did not behave the way the landed gentry expected a woman to.

The situation became so difficult that she could not even afford to go to Vienna anymore. Even the postal connections were bad and expensive. Mail went via the post office in Eggenburg, in winter an arduous route for which the postman expected a tip, especially for extra services such as telegrams. And by now, a gulden tip was a painful expense.

The Suttners felt more and more cut off from intellectual and social life. Visitors rarely came because the drive was so tedious. Bertha wrote in her diary, "We feel so slavishly bound to this piece of soil!"[13]

On trips and at congresses she always led a lifestyle appropriate to her station. For her it was unexpendable. For Bertha was thoroughly convinced that she had to play a role as the representative of the peace movement. There were only a few women at the time who were active in the international peace movement, and everywhere Bertha appeared she was the center of attention. She enjoyed it and noted all her triumphs in her diary, as she did the Bern peace conference: "There were posters everywhere saying: 'Proletarians of the world, listen to the lectures of the famous pioneer of peace.'"[14] Cutting back her usual standard would, in her opinion, have damaged the image of the movement.

Her return from such trips brought the realization of the desperate Harmannsdorf situation back again. "At 11 o'clock, a lovely surprise: . . . Seizure commission.—But I have to finish writing the review for the *Friedenswarte*. . . . Clerk Peters . . . arranges things in a friendly way and even eats semolina *strudel* with us. *Another* Suttner bankruptcy."[15]

When their need got to be so great and unbearable, Bertha took refuge in daydreams: "In our plans for the future (literary prize or some such) we have decided to buy a *palazzo* in Venice."[16] "Joy over *things* is also a real joy, and what bliss it would be for me to be able to buy a stock of linens and things like that."[17]

Aside from the financial worries there were far more serious personal problems. These were connected with Arthur, for whom marriage to such a successful woman was not easy. The difference in age became a problem, too: Bertha was nearing fifty, Arthur had just turned forty. Bertha hinted at her suffering in very discreet terms to her old friend Carneri, clothing her worries in apparent concern for Arthur's poor health: "What a terrible blow one is subject to when one really loves the people who belong to him!"[18]

The tone of her letters to the always lovingly critical Carneri became increasingly irritated. He felt all too clearly how unhappy she was, but did not know anything about her private difficulties. He thought her sadness came from resignation over the world's lack of willingness to create peace. He preached to her to stay calm, have patience, and wait. But she saw only the dark side of everything and even took offense at her old friend for many things she would have accepted earlier with good-natured protest. The letters they exchanged became sparser and shorter.

Long-restrained differences also broke out into the open. Carneri had always had reservations about Arthur. For that reason Bertha could never have told him about her marital problems. Finally, after years of being blind, Carneri died in 1909 at the age of eighty-eight, little mourned by his friend.

In all of her public statements, Bertha praised the unmarred happiness in her marriage, described it as a constant source of strength for the toils of her work. She never gave reason to doubt her relationship with Arthur. Later, Fried described the dignified distance she always kept in her dealings with friends from the peace movement: "She always showed her nature dressed in its Sunday-best; even to her most intimate friends, and even the women among them." She knew how "to keep a distance even in daily activities, something the narrow-minded bourgeois does not understand and finds annoying, like a shirt collar and jacket in the heat of the sun. The aristocracy, as I understand it in this respect, scorns life in shirt-sleeves. The aristocracy, as I understand it here, is self-discipline of the individual, aimed at realizing a higher, a more artistic life-style."[19]

The real problem in the late phase of the Suttner marriage was the pretty, vivacious niece, Marie Louise Suttner. She was fourteen when she came to Harmannsdorf after the death of her father, and from the very first day on, she attached herself to her beloved "Onkeles" Arthur. Bertha loved the girl, too. When "Mizzi" reached marriageable age, none of her admirers were good enough for her: she preferred to stay in Harmannsdorf. Her relationship with her uncle became closer and Bertha's family relationships harder. Only too frequently, quarrels broke out between them, and Arthur was always in the middle. Then both of the women accused him of having taken the other's "side." One of Marie Louise's letters of complaint, addressed to "My beloved Onkeles," has survived among Bertha's belongings: "The only thing I hold against you is that you sacrifice everything for the peace mutterings and really don't have the energy to ward off such attacks like today's . . . from me."[20]

Living together became torture. The couple went for a walk every day from ten to twelve. Bertha stayed at her desk, tormented by jealousy. The three of them drove to Vienna together. There were also occasions when Arthur and Marie Louise had things to do in Vienna at the same time, as they said, and Bertha remained in Harmannsdorf—desperate and sleepless. "And besides, the eternal coming and going of dressmakers, hat makers, and porters. The *extravagance* is a ghost," Bertha complained to her diary.[21] Marie Louise was the only one in the Harmannsdorf family who had money of her own from an inheritance, and she spent it lavishly, whereas the others had to count every gulden.

Bertha could not get a hold on her jealousy, and from time to time she forgot her usual generosity. There were quarrels over trivialities, whereas no one spoke a word about the real problem at the center of things, Marie Louise.

Now that Bertha could not rely blindly on Arthur's love anymore, her optimism disappeared, too. "Generally speaking, I am *not* happy," she admitted to her diary in March 1898. "My troubles are too heavy. . . . Our style of life, our hopes are no longer based on bright, courageous truth. So much that is unspoken and unspeakable haunts us."[22]

Then Bertha took up the fight against age. As a very corpulent fifty-year-old woman she applied dogged determination to learning how to ride a bicycle. "One of the servants at the castle was promoted to the position of teacher for me. He helped me up on the thing and I fell down. Up again, down again, some twenty times or so. That was the first lesson." It took weeks, but finally she could stay up on the bicycle, steer it, and even make figure eights. "I felt so good doing it, my blood circulated with renewed energy, speeding along was absolute bliss. Those attacks of feeling dull were gone, I became slenderer and even occasionally had the feeling as though youth, youth was rushing through my veins."[23]

Marie Louise, by then twenty-three years old, busied herself with singing lessons and writing. She wrote a novel for which Bertha supplied a title, based on a summary of the contents but without reading the actual manuscript: *Wie es Licht geworden* (As light dawned).

The book was brought out by Bertha's publishers, Pierson Verlag, in Leipzig. Bertha's entry in her diary on May 28, 1898, was: "Marie Louise's book is selling. It is dedicated to *me*. I thank her for this tribute with a kiss, passing over the fact that actually, one should not dedicate a book without having it read beforehand. I start reading immediately. Become annoyed when the autobiography gets to the attempted conversion that starts to turn into mutual love. [Marie Louise had a strict upbringing as a Catholic and at first tried to convert her unbelieving Onkeles but later took on his liberal weltanschauung]. Now, I know about the raptures of the fourteen-year-old girl. You can get over that.— In the evening I read further. Find that it is worse and spend a sleepless night."

In her book, Marie Louise described, with only very little disguise, her love for Arthur, who was bound in a supposedly unhappy marriage.

According to Bertha's diary, on May 31, 1898, she read Marie Louise's book further "and [found] things that are shocking, that injure me deeply." She wrote about having had a quarrel with Arthur, who, when confronted, insisted on his innocence. She showed him a compromising letter. "He broke out in tears. I burn the correspondence in front of him. 'Does that mean that the suspicion has been burned away for good?' he asked. I say yes—but does the evidence allow one to believe otherwise? In any case, *she* is *boasting* with the very thing he denies, she has published it." But Bertha was happy to be on good terms with him again, "and I also want to spare him any additional cares, he has had enough worry."

She *wanted* to believe him. But doubts nagged: "The fact remains that the relationship between the converting teacher—whose identity we all know, and who was also described with a portrait's likeness, and of whom she herself admits who it is—that this relationship is portrayed not as a fatherly-friendly-educational one, but *bel et bien* as a love affair— that she puts words in *his* mouth that have him express his pain over not being able to establish a home with her and that she reads these parts to him without his crying out loud—*that* cannot be published: if it was true—out of deference to me; if it was not true—then doubly—out of respect for himself." The otherwise so open-minded Bertha now reacted prudishly: "Describing hot scenes of embrace—that is absolutely contrary to any feeling for propriety."

"Since we three were always together, the relationship was protected by my flag, so to speak. One would have had to say that the third one in the "clover leaf" was like an adopted child—and then this book comes along and says, oh, no: we were in love, he wept at my feet, his head in my lap, because we may not possess each other—I was everything to him—and I kiss the ground passionately where he stood."[24]

Bertha filled many, many pages of her diary with the pain she could not admit to even her very best friends.

When Fried wanted to review the book in his peace paper as a favor to Bertha, she protested: "I do not allow any review of *Wie es Licht geworden*. . . . You may recommend the book in other papers, in *mine* you may not. I am not doing that because of family modesty—but because I do not like the book. Marie Louise dedicated it to me, without my having read the manuscript. Such stabs at mother, grandparents, etc., should not have been allowed to appear under *my* patronage, without having asked me first. Mixing up real figures and imaginary things also creates a confusing situation that can lead to many misunderstandings in public—in short, for me the book is a *heavy burden!*"[25]

Bertha never got over this disappointment. "Well, if a valuable vase has been broken (it already had a *crack* for a long time, but I still protected it as a proud possession)—is it possible for me to let myself be convinced it is still whole: the pieces are lying in front of me!"[26] "It's me—not you, says the book in innumerable places." "There is only one situation that could make me happy again: if I could live alone with Arthur in our old satisfied twosomeness."[27]

The czar's peace manifesto tore her out of her grief in the summer of 1898 and offered distraction. But the disillusionment caused by the public's cool reaction threw her into an even greater state of depression in autumn. "I often think it would be such a simple solution if I would get sick and go to sleep. I have done enough for the peace cause; and I have not been necessary for Arthur's happiness for a long time—perhaps the opposite. Have experienced a lot, also beautiful and happy things and have achieved some useful results—what comes now may be bitter, if the end does not come in time?"

She still had three great hopes: "Yes, the Nobel Prize, *Palazzo Dario* [She means a new apartment alone with Arthur], and Marie Louise married. That would really be lovely."[28]

She thought about death a lot. "Told Arthur that I would like to *die* and that he would find an account of my sorrows in my diary."[29] She wrote a goodbye letter to Fried, which she talks about in her diary: "In farewell I give him my blessing. Say how tired I am—that I had already done enough for the peace cause—could disappear without causing damage. He says—no, the friends of peace still need me."[30]

Faced with this situation, Arthur tried to give in. He swore in a letter that the relationship with Marie Louise was platonic: "Was only an adviser . . . friend and refuge, her only refuge. I should be proud that he had such an attachment. My God, I would have been *happy* for him to have this glow of joy in his burdened life—but he has completely forgotten the book, the book!"[31]

She answered him with an understanding and loving letter: "My poor old sorrow-laden thing!" She suggested, that first, he concentrate on the problems of Harmannsdorf and after solving them—in one way or another—on confronting "*l'affaire*." She assures him, "That I love you, love you above everything else—that I can 'forgive' within the limits where I can *understand* everything down to the deepest wrinkle of your heart, that everything I have to give in the way of life, whatever luck I may have, my own strength, all my love (the world has no one else for me), is dedicated to you alone and shall remain dedicated." He should not hide his financial worries from her, "let me be an adviser to you and consoler—Your old desert comrade."[32]

The quarrels with the family continued and finally reached a peak in a raging fight between Marie Louise, her grandmother, and an aunt over an inheritance. Marie Louise insisted on going to court. Bertha was inconsolable: "And I want to ensure peace in Europe and America when my influence does not even go far enough to banish the spirit of war from my own family?"[33]

She was able to confide her sorrow only to her diary. Quarrels with Arthur came up again and again. "The atmosphere here is unbearable. . . . [T]he last shred of the dignity of our house is endangered by the court case, the members of the family are insulted, Arthur is under the fatal suspicion of holding to 'her' against his own [mother and sisters], ruin is being accelerated, any possible rescue made more difficult: none of that affects her."[34] "Oh, I should get away from this *shattered* family life."[35]

Then she gave up her magazine, *Lay Down Your Arms*, which she had run with great effort for seven years without pay. Fried succeeded, however, in getting her to continue her contributions to his own paper, *Die Friedenswarte*.

At the end of the year 1898, Bertha appears to have concerned herself with putting her literary bequest in order and gave Fried directions, with the explanation: "[H]ow disorderly I am with my papers, how the mail seems to disappear in front of me." She told him she had an envelope labeled "Interesting Letters." "They are to be kept and found in my posthumous works."[36]

After the disappointment of the Hague Peace Conference she wrote her will on July 24, 1899. She made her husband sole heir, only so that he could benefit from her manuscripts, since "at the moment I do not own any capital whatsoever." Marie Louise was to inherit the diamond ring Bertha always wore next to her wedding ring. "My widower is to wear my wedding ring on his finger *at all times*—even if he remarries." Then "if possible [to do so] without discontentment," she asked to be cremated, at that time illegal in Austria. (For cremation, bodies had to be taken across the border to Germany, usually to the crematorium in Gotha. Many liberals and anticlericals demonstrated their convictions by having themselves cremated.) The last sentence in the will read: "Undiminished love for the one and only 'Meune.'"[37]

Additional details about the family conflict are not known; Bertha kept destroying parts of her diary. In January 1900, when the diary starts up again, it contains the same problems as before: lack of money, complaints over Arthur and Marie Louise, jealousy. The situation had become more relaxed inasmuch as Bertha became more generous. The generosity resulted because Arthur was apparently ill, or in any case became increasingly more susceptible to illness. Bertha did not want to deprive the sick man of the few happy hours together with Marie Louise. "The poor thing! The sick man! He should have as much happiness as he can. What I cannot *give* him, I should at least not take away from him."[38]

After long battles with herself, she decided to step aside. "I know only too well that I am not everything to him. . . . After a long time, I gathered up the courage today to take a close look in the mirror again. White, old, very old. That is another reason to wind up a lot of things and take a different direction for the few years that are left."[39] Bertha was fifty-seven years old then, Arthur fifty, and Marie Louise twenty-six.

Jealousy remained all the same—despite Bertha's good intentions. "All the joy of traveling is spoiled when she is along," she writes complainingly, and "If I were dead, they would probably marry."[40] "[T]he dream I had . . . of a happy old couple—it's falling apart. The motto of my old age seems to want to be: lonely and poor."[41]

They got on with Harmannsdorf as well as they could, with extensions of deadlines for debts, then seizures, then selling jewelry, and then periods of quiet again.

Arthur had to go to a health spa for a cure. Marie Louise gave him the money for it. Although the spa (Hertenstein, near Krems) was only forty kilometers away, Bertha could visit him only once. She could not get the money together for a ticket more often. She wrote to him every day, grumbled about the middle-sized powers "wanting to silence" the Hague resolutions "to death and not ratify," and about other political adversities. "A reactionary wave is moving across the world now, and it is all one can do to keep from drowning. Oh, to be able to retreat—not to hear about any of it anymore and to live one's old love! Of course, that's egotistical—and since one is *not* an egoist, one cannot do it." She assured him of her love and avoided talking about their marital problems.[42]

Bertha's diary during these years is characterized by a depressing dreariness: quarrels, jealousy, lack of money. From her writings, it is hard to imagine that she also had her successes during this time, gave lectures, wrote books and a large number of newspaper articles. It was without doubt the worst period in her life.

Entries for a whole year, lasting from June 1901 to July 1902, the time during which her silver wedding anniversary occurred, are missing.

The very worst things, therefore, are kept secret. But that which remains is bad enough. Quarrels and money matters continued in 1902. Arthur's illness got worse. At Easter, with a heavy heart, Bertha had to get through a trip to a congress (in Monaco) by herself for the first time. The three warm letters she received from Arthur, his last, she later proudly included in her memoirs—to back up her story of a happy marriage.

In October the couple went to Abbazia, in the hope that Arthur would find relief. Bertha insisted on accompanying him alone—that is, without Marie Louise—and tried to get her husband back on her side again. She read him the new novel by Theodor Herzl, *Alt-Neuland,* "a Zionist novel set in the future. Is something wonderful. Yes, yes, marvelous stalks of a completely revolutionized culture are already sprouting everywhere."[43] She tried to distract him, spoke as little as possible about Marie Louise. But Arthur was restless. He wrote to his niece in secret and wanted to go home.

As a result they went back to Harmannsdorf after about four weeks. Arthur had become so weak in the meanwhile that he had to be carried up the stairs. Marie Louise asked for permission to sleep in the room next to his and to take over caring for him, which Bertha allowed. Marie Louise paid for the doctor. She did everything to improve Arthur's situation. She was also in constant contact with Dr. Nussbaum in Abbazia, who sent her Arthur's hopeless case history. Bertha asked Dr. Nussbaum, "Why all the secrets—I am prepared—It was I who prepared *her.*"[44]

And again there was jealousy. The doctor wrote Marie Louise the phrase, "under your tender care," whereupon Bertha reacted with, "Am I to be excluded from caring for him?"[45]

But she herself finally realized that it was true love that bound Marie Louise and Arthur, and she wrote in her diary, "Marie Louise would sacrifice anything to restore her Onkeles. Even marry Schwarzschild [the wealthy admirer who would save the heavily encumbered estate].—She really loved him."[46]

Marie Louise even had Dr. Nussbaum come from Abbazia to Harmannsdorf because the patient placed such great trust in him.

At the deathbed there was a discussion about whether or not to send for a priest. Bertha was against. "We promised each other we would ward off the intrusion of church ceremonies from our deathbeds." The doctor thought it was necessary to do it "in consideration for his devoutly religious relatives who would never be able to console themselves if . . ." Bertha replied, "I honor the beliefs of others—but it is my responsibility to act in consideration of him, not them. I want to keep the fear of death away from him." Arthur's sister countered, "But think—for his sake, too, his eternal salvation is at stake." Bertha answered, "A righteous God would not hold him responsible for what I do or don't do." A priest did not come.[47]

On December 10, 1902, Baron Arthur von Suttner died at the age of fifty-two. His body was taken across the border to Gotha for cremation. Bertha took the urn with his ashes back to Harmannsdorf with her.

The pacifists had all they could do to console the completly broken widow and point her toward her work, which was all there was that kept her alive.

The greatest consolation was the message Arthur left behind for his "*Löwos.*" Bertha had it printed in her memoirs: "Thank you. You made me happy, you helped me gain the most beautiful side of life, and to enjoy it. There was never a second of dissatisfaction between us, and for that I thank your great intellect, your big heart, your great love!"

Then came the warning that was to become a constant incentive for Bertha to work: "You know that we felt the responsibility within us to do our little bit to improve the world, to work for, to fight for the good, the immortal light of truth. My departure does not release you from this responsibility. The good remembrance you have of your comrade must hold you upright. You must work on as we intended, continue working for the good cause until you, too, come to the end of your short stay on earth. Courage, therefore! Do not lose hope! We are united in what we achieve, and for that reason you must set your mind on achieving a great deal yet!"[48]

It was only a week after Arthur's death that the collapse of Harmannsdorf occurred. The executors had waited because of the landlord's illness. Now there was no mercy left: the castle was auctioned because of overindebtedness. The Suttner family had to leave the house. The animals, mostly dairy cows, were sold, the household articles packed up. Bertha wrote in her diary: "A destroyed, already long destroyed organism, whose hour of dissolution has come. Total ruin. The eighty-six-year-old woman [Arthur's mother] who has to leave the house. The sister with her animals. And me, where to?"[49] Marie Louise was also impoverished by now. She had invested all her financial assets in Harmannsdorf and Arthur's illness.

With this sad disintegration of the household, the four women (Arthur's mother, his sister, Marie Louise, and Bertha), who had been accustomed to being waited on all their lives, were suddenly without servants. Bertha moved temporarily into a small apartment at *Heugasse 20* in Vienna.

Before they left the Suttner castle for good, the women perfomed a last service for Arthur. In a heavy snowstorm, they carried the urn with his ashes up to the *Sonnwendberg* and buried them there. Bertha wrote: "Who—several years ago—could have seen the picture of the future; we three plodding through the snow—the beloved burden in the black cloth in our arms. Then into the earth—everything, everything that is left of him."[50]

To Dr. Nussbaum she wrote, "Now his last wish has been filled: his ashes rest on the highest point of the designated mountain. Yesterday— in snow and storm—we (I carried it next to my heart) took the urn there. That was another hard—and yet so solemn—hour. And another farewell—another farewell. *So* heartsick am I."[51]

Marie Louise was desperate and was thinking of suicide. Bertha, by contrast, was strangely confused and wound up. The writing in her diary is jerky and incoherent, she mixes up dates. Outwardly, there were hardly any signs of her true condition. Every day she wrote dozens of letters in which she lamented Arthur's death but said absolutely nothing about the calamities in Harmannsdorf. Barely a week after the cremation, she asked Fried if he could find a publisher for Arthur's posthumous novel, *Im Zeichen des Trusts* (Under the sign of the trust).[52] Her soul's turmoil during these weeks is noticeable only in her diary.

This turmoil also expressed itself in the fact that during all the despair and sudden loneliness she hung on to life. This life suddenly personified itself in the shape of Arthur's physician, Dr. Albert Nussbaum. Once, in a moment of extreme despair, he had stroked her hand. She took this gesture as a sign of affection and she openly showed her own sympathy toward the doctor, who was a good number of years younger than she. She wrote him many long, somewhat gushy letters and hoped. "He promises to come to Harmannsdorf again. Has, it appears, a longing to do so. A strange, strange feeling on both sides. I do not for a moment forget that I am an—old woman. Don't feel like it, though. He, full of respect and childish tenderness. The experience—I've taken it on as a kind of . . . farewell experience—means a lot to me. Can let my thoughts rest upon it, far away from my horrible grief."

And further, she wrote, "Should think about the peace cause and my work more. Should—should—why shouldn't one want the thing that is most consoling, sip on what intoxicates? A living, good person whom one loves—loves respectfully—isn't that a blessing?"[53]

She issued an invitation—he held back, wrote less than she who constantly waited for mail from him.

Nevertheless, he looked after her on the day when she moved into the temporary apartment in Vienna with her few possessions, and met her at the railway station. Bertha, during her preparation in Harmannsdorf, wrote: "My handwriting trembles, I see—I have been working on old papers and such things, and that always disturbs me so terribly. Good, that the miracle doctor will suggest some rest again in his mild way." And a few days later, she wrote: "Today I am so lonely and wistful I could scream. Blessed are the minutes when one can forget."[54]

When Nussbaum had finally departed after one last dinner together, she wrote: "And so this sunset chapter ended harmoniously. . . . Now evening wants to set in. And it will stay evening."[55]

A welcome distraction was provided by a letter from Prince Albert of Monaco with an invitation to the opening of a peace institute in Monte Carlo. Bertha wrote to Fried: "At the opening of the academy, I am supposed to be present and be a kind of sponsor. Wasn't that a good and kind idea the prince had? I hope to find a bit of distraction from my pain in marvelous nature and with the pacifists there (Albert I at the head), far from the bleeding memories in this place. It is the unexpected that usually happens."[56]

She left the coldness and the dreary surroundings of her house of mourning and entered springtime: "All the fruit trees are in bloom. At the station was expected by the majordomo with a carriage, driven to the castle—here greeted by the prince at the foot of the stairs—led to an apartment. Room for ten. A valet and a maid and a carriage at my disposal," she wrote joyously to Dr. Nussbaum on stationery engraved with *"Palais de Monaco,"* and on the next day: "Got up early and went into my private garden. The most wonderful floral splendor you can imagine! And palms as high as a house and lawns—shorn smooth as light green velvet. Warm sunshine besides. Beauty, beauty in abundance. At 12:30 breakfast (with 7 courses), many guests. This time I sit to the left of Albert I." In the afternoon she drove to Monte Carlo in her carriage: "Everything that wears a uniform greets me (respect for the court carriage). So: *not* disarmament. I can feel a little, thinned out to a thousandth, of what such a great 'warlord' feels at the submissiveness of armies and whole staffs of generals: they don't want to have to do without them."[57]

"Strange the way everything is happening now as though it were taking place behind a gauze curtain."[58] "There is an excess of beauty here. Whether it stills all longing? Oh—you have to be *two* to enjoy beauty, and my second me is—ashes."[59]

She made majestic appearances at the side of the prince. No one who saw her here in all the dignity and elegance she radiated, could have thought it possible for her to have such a wretched material and sad emotional background. She had a weakness for the life of the "grand" world, just as she had had in her youth, which she liked to scoff at so much.

She described for Albert Nussbaum how she, toward evening, was

> led by the majordomo into a drawing room where the prince wanted to chat with me for a half hour before dinner. After this half hour to the great hall where the other members of the household and the guests were already assembled. Among them were Massenet, the French composer, and another composer . . . whose work Albert I is having performed in his theater here; a French count and his wife, a naval officer, a Spanish duchess—and I don't know what all, and he had me sit at his right at table.—Very lively conversation at the round table (in French, of course). Massenet is especially witty and clever. The prince somewhat melancholy, but also very talkative. Science and art are his two passions. In addition to the oceanographic museum (the building cost millions) he is now also building a small anthropological museum for his finds of human skeletons. He found a skull that was shown at the French Academy of Sciences where, as he says, it will create a revolution in the history of the evolution of man.[60]

Suttner wrote with pride about the opening in her diary: "First Moch speaks, then Albert I, then I. Albert said, 'We have the fortune to possess Baroness Suttner, who is the soul of the peace movement and its greatest sponsor.' . . . The viewing of the museum. Splendid building. But tiring to the point of exhaustion . . . Strange how much fascination still lies in royalty even for a democratic-thinking person."[61]

Her feelings became disturbed again, this time because of the prince himself. He had "retained his health and a freshness and elasticity that made him, with his 54 years and his tall, slender build, look like a forty year old," she rhapsodized. "Peculiar person, this prince—does not drink, does not smoke . . . bicycles and it keeps him healthy, young, and elastic. And this intellect!" And alluding to Albert's misfortune in two marriages: "That two geese could leave *such* a man . . . Weird new episode. What will come of it?"[62]

Then she called herself back to her work. "I should, must, and will work. It is only through work that I acquire such opportunities as today's—and it is only through work that I can keep them as long as this 'short life on earth' lasts."

Despite all her social responsibilities in Monaco, she still worked on her articles every day: in the morning from ten to twelve and between activities in the afternoon and evening, frequently up to midnight.

On Arthur's birthday she became fully aware of all her misery: "No one here who loves me, who is capable of loving me . . . and *that* is what happiness is. When people *don't* have it, they always think that luxury is happiness. Now that it surrounds me, I can see so well—no, that isn't it. Only love, love alone."[63]

Nevertheless, the splendor of royal life soon bewitched her again. She observed of a game of billiards in the evening after dinner: "How sleek and young and elegant Albert I looks at billiards!"

She hoped for an opportunity to find a patron for the peace society. "On the 28th, Rothschild is expected, the same man I knew forty years ago in Homburg. That is interesting. Will utilize him."[64] She actually asked Baron Rothschild for a donation for the peace society, expecting a large sum. Full of disappointment and after some rather embarrassing pressure, she was able to accept five hundred gulden. It just about covered her railway expenses to Monaco.

In Monaco at this time, the first proofs of the German translation of Prince Albert's book, *Carrière d'un navigateur* (Career of a navigator), were arriving. Alfred Fried had undertaken the translation; Bertha was horrified at the large number of mistakes and the extremely careless work. In an effort to save Fried's reputation and keep from angering the prince, she did the correcting. It proved to be time consuming and strenuous, but it kept her in close contact with the prince. Again she got her hopes up: "Yesterday, after the translation work, I got the impression for a moment that I had come closer to Albert I, become necessary to him. But in the evening this impression disappeared."[65]

There were so many mistakes that the pages that were already printed had to be pulped again. She consoled the desolate Fried: "Sooner or later the prince would have found out what enormous mistakes had sneaked in; that would have annoyed him terribly and made him ten times angrier at you than if the work . . . were presented to the world in improved form. I would like to prove to you with the enclosed excerpts that we are not talking about trivialities; in some cases the meaning was even changed. I don't want you to think I am simply a nag."

She did everything she could to cheer Fried up; "Strange: the Prince pays a tenor who sings at his opera in Monte Carlo, up to 10,000 for the evening. For translating a piece that would demand six months of intensive work, what did you get? Certainly not enough to be able to give up all your other jobs and devote yourself entirely to it, and perhaps even engage some help besides. You had to do it *on the side,* a certain amount every day despite your other work."[66]

The longer the stay in Monaco lasted, the more melancholy Bertha became. "Oh, this longing I have for a little *love,*" she complained in her diary. And: "the more beautiful the view, the more golden the orange, the bluer the sea, the sadder I am because the Meune [Arthur] cannot see it."[67]

She even missed Marie Louise now: "That would really be the best yet, to live on memories together with Marie Louise." "Marie Louise writes me often and sweetly. It awakens in me a longing to see her because I could weep with her best. Most of all: homesickness. And I don't even have a home!"[68]

Now she had to force herself to face society, she who had always loved grand appearances so much. "Isn't it really very peculiar: *being able* to be in a wonderful opera, court box—interesting people—loving music and preferring instead to be at home. How can that happen? How enviable these opportunities appeared to me when I didn't have them, and now that I have them—that is the compensation here on earth, that the possession does not make the possessor happy, the way envious people think."[69]

For a short time, the appearance of Albert's lovely friend, a sister of Madame Rothschild ("Frau Kohn"), distracted her. "Albert described her to me as the prettiest woman in Paris, intelligent, good—she must be his lover. . . . Will make me jealous." She also found "the little Kohn" very attractive. "Has diamonds and pearls and the most beautiful eyes." But she had "no particular interest" in the translation of the Albert book, which Bertha showed her.[70]

The evening dinners became agonizing: "long sociological, philosophical conversations with the prince . . . [who] tells me that he plans big demonstrations in two years, at which the science and peace movements will be heralded at the same time—with the participation of Wilhelm II.—That's nice. . . . The feeling of mutual boredom is increasing."

Her irritation grew when Albert wanted to convert her "to believing in immortality and ghosts." "For the latter he had especially weak coincidences for proof." After a month she longed for her visit to end.[71]

She was also annoyed over "Nussi." "In any case, he cannot write any letters." "Instead of being a consolation, he does nothing but vex me."[72]

On March 25 she finally left Monaco: "Monaco adieu. It did not produce the miraculous, but some valuable memories at least. . . . Most of all, I am taking with me the lesson that splendor is nothing compared to happiness. Only liking is happiness. . . . Then, farewells to Albert I. He is—or is he—pretending?—sad about it. Kisses my hand, said the salon and this room here will always belong to me."[73]

Her fame, she said, had grown because of this visit to Monaco. She took note of the newspaper reports on it with satisfaction: "*Interesting paper* with impressive picture and article: Baroness Suttner as guest of the Prince of Monaco."[74]

On the journey home she made stopovers in Fiume and Abbazia. After seeing "Nussi," she wrote: "We are picking the last bouquet of life's blossoms—a dear person, who loves me. *Entendons nous:* it is childlike love. When I read this book later, I myself do not want to be confronted with the mistaken impression that I have forgotten the dignity of my age—that I succumbed to the foolish notion that I could have had anything other than childlike feelings. Europe's most famous woman—a grand lady—now, that gives the attraction a special kind of spice, a touch of the novel, a sudden flare of passion."[75]

When talk of another visit to Abbazia came up a year later, she wrote him: "Come to Abbazia? No. Would only stir up the sad memories even more. Right after my loss, I had a period of numbness that resulted from the force of my pain, added to by an attempt at self-anesthetization. That has passed—an all the more intense pain, paired with renunciation of everything, everything, has taken possession of me."[76]

Somewhat later, she was downright ungracious: "Nussi is coming again.—Doesn't he notice that his visits annoy me?"[77]

Now she devoted herself entirely to the memory of Arthur, and even created a cult around him. From then until her own death, his life-size portrait stood next to her desk on a kind of floral altar with the palm frond of peace placed in front of it. "And despite everything: his love for me was faithful to the end. Boulotte, he called out while he was dying—and not Marie Louise. That should be a consolation and a satisfaction to me."[78]

The peace societies launched a donation drive to improve her catastrophic financial situation. The "testimonial" was to be presented to Bertha on her sixtieth birthday in June 1903. The honored recipient was pleased to see that even foreigners were joining the drive, "that French, English and German subcommittees have formed for the testimonial.— Am curious what the results will be."[79]

Just at this time, the *Berliner Tagblatt* published the results of a questionnaire to determine the five most important women of the present. The result:

Bertha von Suttner—156 votes
Carmen Sylva—142 votes
Sarah Bernhard—139 votes
Eleonora Duse—132 votes
Marie von Ebner-Eschenbach—71 votes.[80]

Bertha noted: "That came at just the right time for the project."[81]

She followed the development of the list of donors carefully: "Kinsky and Schwarzenberg as participants made me happy." Adolf Josef Prince Schwarzenberg appears on the list with a modest fifty crowns, the head of the princely Kinsky house with a hundred crowns.[82] But the very fact that they—along with old friends of the Suttners such as Björnson, Henri Dunant, Novikov, Ebner-Eschenbach—did anything at all for the notorious "red Bertha" was something very special that she duly appreciated.

The most generous donations came from the house of the Jewish coal industrialist Gutmann: Max von Gutmann gave two thousand; Bertha's sympathizer, Ida von Gutmann, one thousand crowns. Albert von Monaco was also one of the donors, along with peace societies and women's clubs all over the world, a Berlin Freemasons' lodge, and the writers' association, Concordia.

Bertha's sixtieth birthday was celebrated with due respect on June 9, 1903, by pacifists all over the world.

"Well, it has turned out that my efforts all over the world have commanded respect." The many congratulations cheered her up. "Another decade of work and then perhaps already see victory. Life is lived so fast now that a decade could produce unexpectedly colossal things."[83]

The testimonial made her "secure until the Nobel Prize." Some twenty thousand crowns had been collected, enough to cover her living expenses. Her busy goal for the rest of her life was "Not to be an old pensioner in the village. Have something to say in the world."[84]

She finally found a new apartment near the Ring, at Zedlitzgasse 7, where she was to live to the end of her life. She dismissed short-term scruples about living above her means: "Uncertainty . . . nonsense—have always lived like this, and it was good and elegant. That will also continue for the rest of my short 'life here on earth.' Just have to earn something. That shouldn't be difficult with the reputation my name has."[85]

But when she once again spent too much for furniture, linens, little things, she decided to economize and, for example, bought second-class instead of her usual first-class tickets for the train. But these attempts at thrift did not last long: "You sit so cramped and together with such curious people—I don't like it. How right the Meune was, only to travel first class. A weakness perhaps—but nice, like all his weaknesses."[86]

On her wedding anniversary she started a new book, *Briefe an einen Toten* (Letters to a dead person). "In it, I can write down everything that worries and fulfills me. Perhaps that will free my source of creativity again."[87] It was a book of dialogue with Arthur and a portrait of him. "The picture I conjure up will go down to posterity." "Hope to get things off my chest with this book and provide a worthy tribute to the dead—give myself some joy again. Work is the only thing that can fill, create, and bless my life."[88]

She really worked very hard. For the opening of the IPU conference in Vienna in 1903, she wrote a twenty-five-page article in one day. She gave speeches in Paris on war and arbitration, but was not satisfied with the applause. The compelling power of her personality, which she had earlier called magnetism, was gone. "I don't please them. Cannot speak and cannot charm."[89]

The worries over Harmannsdorf were far from being over. There were disagreements with a number of creditors. Marie Louise's wealthy admirer, Schwarzschild, had bought the castle, but it did not make him happy. In 1905 he shot himself in the castle park. "Another victim has slid silently into the jaws of Harmannsdorf."[90]

She made up with Marie Louise. "He loved her very much and she him: I have to remember that," she wrote in her diary. "She is a legacy. He loved her and would have protected her. Don't I have to do the same? . . . And she loved him. She was the only one who mourned him as much as I did. That, too, should make her worth something to me."[91]

She registered all the appearances of age ruthlessly: "Becoming ugly is taking on serious proportions . . . double chin . . . It would be better for me not to spend too much time falling into ruins." "See a ponderous 60 year old reflected in the shop windows."[92]

"Now a beautiful feature I have always been proud of has left me: my hands. You are judged by your hands. And such red, fat, ordinary hands mine are in the process of becoming would make me be judged falsely." "My getting ugly, my getting weak must not be shown to the world. Yes, it is true. Ministers and statesmen and intellectuals make an impression until they are far beyond 70. We are used to that, while women in public life are still something new—and the term, 'old woman,' which expresses something different altogether than the not really equivalent 'old man' comes on top of it all."[93]

In the summer of 1905 Marie Louise became engaged to a Baron Haebler. Bertha, as her closest relative, negotiated the marriage contract. On the one hand she was very happy about Marie Louise's marriage, on the other, worried: on the wedding day Haebler's former wife and their three children appeared suddenly and threatened to create a scandal. Marie Louise lived abroad after that.

Bertha's life became considerably quieter. The most pressing financial worries were taken care of. She wrote newspaper articles diligently, and they were fairly well paid.

Despite her fame, one thing was withheld from her all her life: recognition by her relatives. The family

> does not show the least interest in my cause. Does not even read the *Friedenswarte* given to it. In this circle, I see what a block of indifference and lack of understanding the reformers are up against. They think we are crazy or at least disturbing. Disturbing to the peace of existing conditions in which they are established. Because they belong to this circle themselves, they recognize the power of resistance the establishment possesses. But they know nothing about the power of the cause of progress—and about that which has already been achieved, they have no idea whatsoever.[94]

As usual, she blamed herself. "Shouldn't I know how to arouse interest in my circle?"[95]

The only thing that she still found enticing was contact with Viennese artists. She went to the premieres of Schnitzler's plays and read his stories. "Filled the evening pleasantly reading *Das weite Land* [The vast domain]. It's a Jewish adultery affair—but very fresh and with intense love scenes. Schnitzler *is* a dramatist."[96]

She also cultivated social contact with the Schnitzler couple. "Interesting afternoon at Schnitzler's. His wife is also highly intelligent.—He is witty.—Says that he reads the *Friedenswarte*. Agrees, but he thinks only in 100,000 years."[97] The corresponding entry in Schnitzler's diary: "Bertha Suttner in the afternoon . . . about the peace question. She thinks in 100 years there will be no more war. I think in 100,000. She was clever and kind."[98]

Bertha also got together with singers and actors. One of these was Johanna Buska, who had initiated the very young Crown Prince Rudolf into the matters of love—that was thirty years before. Suttner wrote about Buska, who was still very beautiful: "Her appearance, her clothes are an aesthetic pleasure, her acting an artistic one."[99]

She admired the actress Stella Hohenfels, but most of all, the operetta tenor Louis Treumann. After attending the "Merry Widow" she wrote in her diary, "This Treumann as Danilo is erotic poison. The mob attendance at this operetta is a kind of mob hysteria *à la* flagellants, table-moving, etc."[100]

She loved opera, as she did when she was young, and was always extremely well informed about all the new productions. She knew Richard Strauss personally, and she was interested in everything of his that appeared. "In the evening, Elektra. Nerve-racking experience. Cannot sleep and acted Elektra myself for Kati [the servant Kathi Buchinger]. The world always has something new to offer." In 1911 the *Rosenkavalier* came out. Suttner wrote: "Magnificent. A great pleasure."[101]

Alfred Hermann Fried, who had meanwhile moved to Vienna, came closer and closer to Suttner's personal environment. As her closest and most active associate, he was in contact with her every day. She saw him as her successor and tried to "educate" him according to her criteria, in order to indoctrinate him with the moral principles of the peace movement: "True, true, always true! No compromises, no secrets or fabrications for the alleged usefulness to a cause. . . . There is only one way to last in the movement without enmity, without strife, with dignity and with success, and that is to remain true to yourself and the truth—not to ever put aside its principles for the sake of opportunism—not to deny the uncompromising ideal in favor of something 'practical'—because to make it 'practical' in the end, it has to have unerring idealists to make it come true.—You forfeit more with unknown followers than you achieve by making compromises with your opponents."[102]

When she had to settle another of Fried's quarrels she wrote: "If I may give you some advice: do not fight for our cause with the weapons that are used in political and other camps. No anger—no substituting other motives for those that are stated—no force and no realpolitik. . . . People like us need passion for the work of reconciliation, not for dissension."[103]

In long letters she begged him to keep peace, to treat others more generously, be more conciliatory, and above all to use better manners, which would help smooth out some of these conflicts. "You do not appear to be shy—rather the opposite. It is almost as though you were what one calls 'arrogant.' You aren't, I know that. But the appearance is there. Force yourself into exquisite worldly politeness. Do not be afraid that it will be interpreted as groveling, as a lack of self-assurance. The higher one stands, the more respect and consideration he puts into his deportment."[104]

Although he respected the "dear *Frau* Baroness" greatly, Fried was often brusque and hurtful to her. Sometimes she generously accepted his criticism as justified, such as the time when he called her peace society a tea party and refused to join the executive committee.[105]

It cost Bertha a great deal of effort to make Fried a "man of the world," and she did not entirely succeed. For all his work, Fried had neglected the job of learning and, most important, never mastered any foreign languages. He spoke French more or less, but translations such as the Albert book and a work by Novikov were too much for him.

Bertha often berated him like a schoolboy because of his failings: "The way you did that was awfully careless," she wrote him after reading the Novikov translation, which she called "steam-work," and insisted, "I *must* teach you French. Belongs to a pacifist career. I mean correct and elegant French."[106]

"As an international peace worker you have to acquire English. Let that be your next entertainment when you have some spare time. As though we poor pack-camels for peace had any spare time."[107]

Five years later she repeated her demands and expanded them to include Italian: "These three languages are necessary for pacifism. Where would I be without this mastery?"[108]

In order not to embarrass himself, Fried wrote drafts of all his important letters in French and English, sometimes even German, to show to Bertha before sending them.

Then Bertha would say he should practice speaking. She sent her friend Hedwig Pötting to Fried's lectures to check on his progress in this respect. "I am afraid you are not a good extemporaneous speaker, but it would be a good thing to practice anyway. You could become one."

Before Fried went to the Inter-Parliamentary Conference in 1906, where both of them expected pacifism to gain a great deal, Bertha sent him a long letter.

I would like to give you a few rules for the table for England—because the English are very fussy about that and the Austrians very lax. Never put your knife to your mouth is something you already observe anyway, but that you should never put your elbows on the table during a meal is a rule I've seen you break a few times.—In general no sideways, nonchalant behavior at the table—straight in front, straight up and down. The handle of the spoon rests on the third finger, exactly like a pen for writing. Also the fork, when it is being used to take up vegetables; for sticking it into meat, however, the three fingers are turned down and the index finger is stretched across the handle. All four fingers must never clasp the handle at once and the little finger must never be closer to the edge of the plate than the index finger. So, that's the whole drill book.[109]

Suttner also placed great value on dressing correctly. In this respect, Fried was never able to comply.

Even though she was constantly plagued by financial want, she was always the born countess and baroness by marriage with the very best deportment. So it is not surprising that she protested twice when a colleague wrote *"Wohlgeboren"* (literally, wellborn) in front of her name on an address. He thought this form of address would be an honor for her, and at first, interpreted Suttner's protest as a kind of modesty. Quite the contrary, as Bertha explained to Fried in no uncertain terms: "And 'Wohlgeboren' is what the wretched Stein calls an *exemplary title*? Does he want to make me furious? Either . . . one is regarded as a whole person and drops all the titles or one is confronted in the conventional manner. Then, a born countess is entitled to '*Hochgeboren*' [high born] at least, as a *Freifrau* '*Hochwohlgeboren*' [baroness, high wellborn] and the devil take the whole business!"[110]

Her perfect mastery of the most complicated questions of protocol made her publisher ask her to write a "catechism on manners in good society." She turned him down: "I am not *indifferent* to the subject since I do have quite passable manners myself, but I did not think it was important."[111]

Fried worked untiringly. His bibliography had grown to well over a thousand articles. In 1908 and 1909 he wrote three books, one right after the other: the *Revolutionärer Pazifismus* (Revolutionary pacifism), *Pan-Amerika* (Pan-America), and finally, *Der Kaiser und der Weltfriede* (The emperor and world peace), an appeal for peace directed toward Wilhelm II. Suttner wrote in her diary: "Fried's emperor book. Am devouring it. The grand prize."[112] And: "The book on the Pan American union was a revelation to me. Oh, what a marvel this world is, the old world had no idea!"[113] "Fried will be of much more use than I can be."[114]

Of course, that did not mean that she always shared his opinions. His view of pacifism was different from hers. Fried's was a much soberer "scientific" pacifism compared with Suttner's "moral" pacifism. "Read Fried's 'Revolutionary Pacifism.' I don't like the lack of ethics in it."[115] She thought he was too austere, too detached. Yet she realized that this pacifism of his appealed to other people more than hers did and thought that was good for the movement: "I was actually glad that emotions are excluded from your book," she wrote to Fried. "It will make a bigger impression that way."[116]

During the last years of Bertha's life, Fried was the most important person for her. He startled her out of depressive phases and forced her to work by imposing rigorous deadlines. Without him, she would have given up her lectures and articles much earlier.

She was noticeably tired. "Being of use, necessary—that is no longer the case with me. The cause is taking its great, certain, historic path toward the goal. The nuisance is that what I can still give to the world with my growing old in public can have a more damaging than supporting effect."[117]

Again and again, Fried gave her a big and urgent job that "only she" could do. Besides, there was the weekly review to write for the *Friedenswarte*—and that by hand! She never was able to get used to the typewriter she bought in 1907 on Fried's advice.

During the last twelve years following Arthur's death, she concentrated entirely on her peace work, driven by Fried. Liberated from the Harmannsdorf calamities and family conflicts, she mourned her beloved Arthur alone, and he became kinder and more of an ideal in her imagination. She was at peace with herself and she had no doubts about her task.

10

The Nobel Prize

The relationship with Alfred Nobel is so important to Bertha von Suttner's biography and to the peace movement that it requires special handling. For that, however, it is necessary to go back to the nineties again.

Both Suttner and Nobel worked for peace and against war. But they had contrary methods for going about it. Nobel counted on deterrence, although not by means of continuous armament. He thought a powerful new instrument of war would generate such great fear of the horrors it could perpetrate that no ruler would ever be prepared to start a war again. Bertha wrote: "In the beginning this was also the only, if rather indirect, way he could imagine that would create a readiness for peace among peoples: on the one hand, frightening away human stupidity and baseness through art and knowledge, rising above suffering through the progress of technology which creates goods, and on the other hand, through waging war to the point of *absurdity* because of its own hellish development."[1]

She tried to convince Nobel that the better system was not to make war impossible through the deterrent effect of fear, but by reaching international agreements, preventing the causes of war, reducing images of hostility, and creating understanding and interaction in the broadest sense through a huge propaganda campaign directed at the people of all countries. ·

She sought and finally found a way to reconcile the two opposing viewpoints. For the present, Nobel's method was still usable; her way of preventing war belonged to the future. She wrote to him in 1896: "Your war machine will still be a means (albeit a somewhat bent one) of preventing war. Because even today strategists believe that attack is the best move."[2]

Suttner, however, did not call a peace that could be maintained only by mutual fear a real peace and answered objections with: it was "a misunderstanding that we friends of peace want to 'keep' *this* immoral, destructive peace, that the current system supposedly 'ensures' from one year to the next. *One* spark is enough to make all the security explode to bits. It has to be *created: para pacem.* That is the meaning and the purpose of the whole movement."[3]

By comparison, Nobel's position was not so clear. At the same time that he avidly developed new explosives, he also supported the peace movement with considerable sums of money and always kept himself informed about its progress. Bertha even adopted Nobel's argument occasionally in later years when she was disappointed by the meager successes of the peace movement: "Inventions may come that will embarrass all the armament efforts so far—liquid air [meaning poison gas] is a material that is already beckoning to us. One wagon load is enough to blow up a whole fleet even if the fleet could be doubled by means of a billion contributed by the working people."[4]

The two friends did not have such different opinions after all, even though they often took a path of confrontation. Both had no greater desire than to help establish peace. Both found out how difficult and complicated the path leading to this goal was. Each was prepared to make concessions to the other, and both clearly realized that there had to be not one, but many ways to reach the same goal.

As enthusiastic as Nobel was about Bertha's book *Lay Down Your Arms,* he was very skeptical at first about her peace organizations. She yielded to his objections: "My God, I know very well that neither the organizations nor their congresses have any real power to make decisions on the abolition of war; the concern here is to create a coordinated demonstration of public opinion in every country."[5]

Despite his reservations, Nobel went to the congress in Bern in 1892, not as an official participant, but as a private observer. He "showed a great deal of skepticism but he also appeared to be eager to have his doubts overpowered."[6]

When the congress was over, he invited the Suttners to spend two days at the Baur au lac hotel in Zurich. (Later, Bertha proudly told about having lived in rooms Empress Elisabeth had just vacated. "A pale, wilted rose" was still lying on the dressing table.)

At dinner Bertha was asked to talk about what happened at the congress. Nobel donated two thousand francs and was made a member of the Austrian Peace Society. Bertha wrote: "What you are presenting to me and what I am thanking you for is more a result of kindness than conviction. Only a few days ago in Bern, you expressed doubts about the cause and its justification."[7]

Nobel replied, "About the cause and its justification—no, I have no doubts about that, only about whether they can be realized—and I also do not know yet how your societies and congresses want to go about tackling the work."

"So, if you knew the work would be tackled well, would you help us?"

Nobel answered, "Yes, I would. Teach me, convince me—and then I will want to do something big for the movement."

She promised to keep him up to date and to "enthuse" him. "Good, try it—I love nothing more than being able to be enthusiastic, an ability the experiences in my life and the people around me have weakened considerably."

According to a different version, also related by Suttner, Nobel is supposed to have said, "If I can really be convinced of the peace cause then I also want to do something for it. Specifically, I would like to give people who can be effective a small fortune, place—say about two hundred thousand francs into their hands so that they would be able to live entirely for this; or I would promise someone who accomplished something in the field this sum as payment."[8]

When Bertha reproached him for his dynamite factories, Nobel answered, "My factories may put an end to war before your congresses: on the day two army corps are able to destroy each other in one second, all civilized countries will recoil and recall their troops."[9] He firmly believed in the positive effects of science and technology.

Nobel invited the Suttners for a motorboat ride across Lake Zurich: "And we talked about war and peace and how lovely this world of God's could be if the divinity that glows in some human hearts and shines in some human brains but is still being suffocated under the force of ignorance and coarseness could break through." Nobel and Bertha decided to write a book together, "a book to fight against everything mean and have already discussed the title," but the project was never carried out.[10]

The main subject was always how Nobel could best use his money for peace. The first concrete plans for a peace prize were discussed on Lake Zurich.

> In his views, Nobel tended strongly toward socialism; and he said
> it was inadmissible for wealthy people to leave their fortune to relatives.
> He thought a big inherited fortune was a misfortune since it had a
> crippling effect. Large collections of possessions ought to be given back

to the general public and be used for general purposes; the children of
the rich [Nobel was childless] ought to get just enough to be well educated and protected from need, but little enough to be encouraged to
work and through this, to enrich the world further."[11]

In his New Year's letter of 1893—with best wishes for Bertha and
"for the great campaign against ignorance and stupidity you are waging
so strongly"—Nobel wrote: "In my will I would like to set aside part of
my fortune for awarding a prize every five years (let's say six times in all,
since if the current system is not reformed by that time there will almost
have to be a return to barbarism). The prize should be for the man or
woman who will have taken the biggest step in the direction of bringing
peace to Europe."[12]

As in other letters he also placed great weight on clarity: "I do not
say disarmament, since that can only be brought about carefully and
slowly, nor even the absolute, obligatory court of arbitration. But the
point can and will soon come when all countries unite in turning against
the one country that is about to attack them first. That will help make
war impossible and force even the mightiest and most unreasonable
power to call upon the court of arbitration or remain quiet. When the
Triple Entente includes all countries instead of only three, peace will be
assured for centuries."[13]

Bertha reacted very doubtfully to the idea of prizes: "Your idea of
making awards to people of goodwill every five years (after twenty
years), does not seem to me to be the most effective method. What people who work for peace need most of all is not prizes, they need the
means to allow them to work." As an example she mentioned the Rome
peace congress again, without which the Austrian Peace Society would
not have come into existence. Moreover, without Nobel's money she
would not have been able to attend and therefore would not have been
able to join the international peace movement. She thought it was more
advisable for wealthy people (she named Rothschild, Hirsch, and Nobel
as examples) to subsidize the work of the friends of peace.[14]

Whenever Nobel talked about disarmament and the court of arbitration as goals that were too far away, Bertha defended herself: "Don't
always call our peace-plans a *dream*. Progress toward justice is surely not
a dream, it is the law of civilization. The amount of savagery and stupidity in the world is certainly still very great, but the amount of kindness and gentleness and reason is growing every day."[15]

In the conviction that she represented a just cause, she hounded her
rich friend with news about the peace movement. Occasionally, however,

she asked to be forgiven, once with a quotation from Goethe: "Everyone 'who feels inside that he can do something good is forced to be a *pest*. He may not pay attention when he is sent away. He has to be what Homer praised in the heroes, he has to be like a fly who, shooed away, always returns and attacks man from another side.'"[16]

And shortly after that, she introduced a request with: "Here she is again, the Goethe-fly!," and asked him for a donation for the Austrian Society of the Friends of Peace. She wanted so badly to see his name on the list of donors that would be published: "[A]n example is such a good thing. What for you is a bagatelle, will be an important, encouraging example to others who are sometimes satisfied with giving *one* franc." And she pointed to her fiftieth birthday as an appropriate occasion for his giving her pleasure by donating.[17]

Nobel did not have to be asked long. He donated far more than the twenty francs she teased him with.[18] But when he was mentioned in the newspaper afterwards, he did not like it at all. "It's unpleasant for you to have your name printed in the newspaper? That cannot be avoided when artists, intellectuals, inventors, politicians, or whatever else join in. *I* am happy about every name that is mentioned in the papers if it is mentioned in connection with *the peace cause,* since that is the most important issue of the present time and everything that can be of use to it surpasses any personal considerations."[19]

She implored Nobel time and again to believe in the peace cause: "The movement's progress is enormous—. Everything is helping us, especially the dynamite-makers; because the great powers will unite internationally against the anarchists and realize that it is not possible to unite against force as long as they show their fists and bare their teeth themselves."[20]

Bertha flattered her friend, invited him to Vienna and, unsuccessfully, to the peace congresses. "Oh, if you would become one of us and bring a little light into our midst—how that would accelerate victory!"[21] "Look, what I need is an associate like you who would put his soul into the cause—and at the same time, would have the *means* to do whatever was necessary. Wouldn't that be a wonderful mission? One would have to be able to travel to set up centers in Paris, in Berlin, in Petersburg, to strengthen the movement—and we also need to make a greater presence in Vienna."

She radiated optimism: "If another two or three years pass without the armament-crazed countries going at each other, the goal can be reached with intensive, accelerated action. A legal framework ought to be established, a tribunal set up."[22]

Yesterday I got a letter from Tolstoy and a short time ago, one from Björnsen. All the great spirits of the century are for us—the young czar [Nikolaus II], the pope [Leo XIII had just emphasized peace as the goal of the Christians], all the Freemasons, the socialists, the *young* people who want to live and love . . . all are prepared to follow our call. Oh, my friend, believe me, there is nothing greater, nothing more important, nothing more sacred in the world than this fight against the yoke of war that our poor humanity wants, more than anything else, to shake off.

Then she got down to principles:

"But the truth is, that what you have done so generously, you did out of friendship to me and not out of irresistible enthusiasm for the cause. And how can I depend on the steadfastness of your friendship? And if I were to disappear?—But no, I do not feel close to death, on the contrary, I feel refreshed vitality since the triumph of Budapest, but how long will that last—at my age?" (She was fifty-three years old at the time.)

She assured her friend that she did not want to introduce a new request with this letter. "I just don't want to have to accuse myself of not having told you everything, not to have opened the door to the possibility that you would become active of your own initiative." "The miraculous, as Ibsen calls it—it can happen."[23]

Nobel understood very well what she meant by "miraculous." He was supposed to provide financial security for the peace movement in his will, and this security was supposed to be independent of his friend and extend beyond the deaths of both of them.

She was persistent: "You once wrote me that you would provide a considerable legacy for the peace work. Yes, do it, I ask you very earnestly. Whether I am here or do not exist anymore: what we have given, you and I, will survive."[24]

The relationship between Alfred Nobel and Bertha von Suttner was by no means limited to a discussion of pacifism and its financial support, as Bertha's later relationship with Andrew Carnegie was. Despite the distance that separated them, their friendship was very strong and very personal. Her twenty-four rather long letters that survive from 1896 alone, the year of Nobel's death, prove this quite sufficiently. She reacted to the problems of this lonely, melancholy man with great sensitivity. She took an interest in his hobbies, cheered him up when he was depressed and pessimistic.

Unfortunately only a few of Nobel's letters still exist, and we can only guess at the contents of the others from Bertha's letters. The otherwise very shy, introverted Nobel told his friend in March of 1896 that he was about to write a play about Beatrice Cenci. (Nobel's literary idol, Shelley, had also written a drama about the Roman woman, who was executed in 1599 for patricide.)

Bertha answered: "Beatrice Cenci? The subject is dramatic. I am very curious. Above all, I am certain that it is well written; I have not forgotten the beauty and strength of the verses you gave me in Paris." She offered to get the piece into a Viennese theater, collaborate with him if he wanted to or translate the piece herself. She even started thinking about a cast and chose the most prominent actresses in Vienna. Then she asked him to send her the manuscript.[25]

She was disappointed when she found out that Nobel had not written it in French but in Swedish, which she could not understand. Besides, the piece had anticlerical features. Bertha wrote: "Well, it's sad: in Vienna, we could hardly risk an anticlerical tendency."[26]

Sometimes it was all she could do to draw him out of his depths of depression, which he could not hide from her, even in letters. "You are incorrigible: I beg you not to squawk, and to write me some cheering, strengthening, brightly happy, affectionately joyous words—and you quote Shakespeare to tell me that everybody who has passed the zenith of his life (you know my age) is in a constant state of fossilization. That is really very nice indeed! If I had turned to the high priest of the ravens, I would not have risked getting a more somber 'Caw! Caw!'"[27]

She offered help and words of comfort. "When I see your handwriting on an envelope, I tear it open with a joyously pounding heart. Because I always expect you to say someday: 'Friend, I want to work with you,' or maybe: 'Friend, I am happy, share this happiness with me' or perhaps even 'Friend, I am sad, share my pain.'" Instead, Nobel sent the "caw-letters," full of melancholy, full of pessimism.[28]

She waited impatiently for mail from Nobel, worried about his health, asked him again and again to send her news—and was disappointed when he did not. This was the case in November 1896. He was very ill. She did not know this and wrote him a somewhat offended letter:

> *Enfin!*: "No one can force love." And I wanted so badly to force your love—not for my unimportant person, but for the great cause I serve and which would be so worthy of being loved by you, you who like the great ideas of social progress so much! The approaching new century could be the opportunity to set up a convention of the peoples of Europe, a confederation, a permanent court of arbitration. The Geneva

Convention—thanks to the efforts of a single man, who dedicated his energy and small fortune to it—brought about the establishment of the Red Cross. With a similarly energetic move, we could erect the banner of the white flag.[29]

Apparently she had not yet received his letter of November 5 from Paris, in which he wrote that he was "sick and bedridden." He decided to "call up a sacred scare of war, that means, to create the best religion, and you have contributed to that nobly and vigilantly. Dear friend, be assured of my deepest affection. Alfred Nobel."[30]

A few days later, she had a success to report: the treaty between the United States and England over the Venezuela question had been concluded. Suttner wrote to Nobel: "What triumphant news. And I know that it was the work of our league. Now the example has been made. The next stage will be to set up a high court of arbitration for the United Nations of Europe. The three years that still separate us from reaching the new century can lead us to our goal if we work energetically." Self-assured, she gave herself a good part of the glory for this success: "They tell me that the half million copies of *Lay Down Your Arms* that were brought out in England and America led to something. Now the motto is, forward."[31]

Nobel wrote his last letter to his friend on November 21: "And I, who have no heart in the symbolic sense, have one that is an organ, and I feel it. But enough about me and my little illness. I am very happy to see that the pacifistic movement is gaining ground, thanks to the civilization of the masses and above all thanks to the fighters against prejudice and darkness, among whom you hold a prominent position. Those are your titles of nobility. Heartily yours, A. Nobel."[32]

Bertha answered him immediately. She was sorry about his heart trouble. "All your philosophy is needed for you to talk about it so blithely. But *no heart*? Perhaps not for me—but even here I have some examples to the contrary. No, I must admit that your heart is closed toward certain people . . . but I do not admit that you are hard and mean."

Once again she urged him to support the peace movement with a large sum of money. She enumerated her own merits:

I have contributed to all that: because of me, the congress in Rome excluded a certain issue [Alsace-Lorraine is meant] which could have destroyed the fragile building; because of me the treasury of the Bern bureau got its *first* support, without which it would never have been founded; because of me the movement took root in Austria and Germany; because of me the society in Budapest was founded . . . but if I continue with this exploration, I have to say that I could have done none, *none* of it without the help *you* gave me and will continue to give me until the day when our work is completed. The power of money is indispensable, . . . give our office a million: that will elevate the world. If in addition to my reputation in literary and political fields at the moment, I also had the means to go to Russia, to Berlin, to Paris—if we could distribute hundreds of thousands of pamphlets, newspaper articles, if we could organize petitions to parliaments, then we could, I am thoroughly convinced, provoke an ultimate institution for the appearance of the 20th century. And for that reason, I implore you: never withdraw your support—*never,* even on the other side of the grave that awaits us all.[33]

These were embarrassingly clear words, in view of the fact that Alfred Nobel was mortally ill and died on December 10, about a week after receiving this letter. He was sixty-three. Bertha had no way of knowing that her urging was unnecessary. Nobel had already made a will on November 27, 1895, that provided for the peace movement very well.

Several weeks of excited expectancy passed before the contents of this will were made known. Bertha wrote to Fried on December 17, 1896: "Nobel, who died on the 10th of this month in San Remo, is a serious loss for me, gave to our society again and again—some 10,000 francs. I still have no news of whether he bequeathed it anything."

On New Year's Day of 1897, she wrote in her diary: "Offended because Nobel forgot the peace cause."

A few days later, the newspapers printed the news that Nobel had left more than thirty-five million crowns and had not bequeathed them to his family. He was unmarried and childless; his nephews and nieces were all very well off. Instead he was said to have provided for prizes, as Bertha joyously wrote in her diary, which "are to be awarded to those who have done the most for the peace cause. I am extremely happy about this striking gratification and support for the cause, also see that a sum should fall to me, which pleases me very much, of course. . . . The whole house is congratulating me. Sleeping badly because of the excitement."[34]

The next day: "Continued excitement over Nobel. Receive a lot of letters. Particularly, Aunt beside herself—should go to Vienna immediately, establish rights, etc. Write to Swedish ambassador."[35]

But in the meanwhile, the news had changed. Universities were to be considered, probably a reference to the later Nobel prizes intended for various scientific disciplines. There was barely talk anymore of promoting peace. Bertha was disappointed: "Still depressed. The joy of the *cause* remains. But I myself am weighed down by work and worries; am so in need of cheering up and real support."[36] During this time, the seizure commissions were coming and going at Harmannsdorf.

Then renewed hope arose: she had to prove her claims, become active, use friends as negotiators. Bertha started to look for Nobel's letters frenziedly. Her correspondence had not been sorted out for years. She did not even file important letters systematically. All the same, she found them and happily wrote in her diary: "Look in the wastepaper basket for the last, doubly precious letter from Nobel and *find* it. That is a joy."[37]

Finally the wording of the will was made known. After subtracting the legacies, the rest of the fortune (thirty-five million crowns) was to form a fund. The interest from it was to be divided annually into five prizes for people who, regardless of their nationality, had done something productive for the good of mankind in the fields of physics, chemistry, medicine, literature, and "for the man or woman who had made the greatest contribution to the brotherhood of mankind, the reduction of armies, and the promotion of peace congresses."[38] These were words that Bertha naturally applied to herself. The term "for him or her" (*à celui ou celle*) was most unusual, since women had virtually no place at all in public and scientific life and were as a rule not even mentioned in connections of this kind.

The first four prize winners were to be chosen by scientific institutions in Stockholm; the peace prize winner, however, by the Norwegian parliament, the Storthing, in Christiania, Oslo. Nobel, who had always supported good relations between the two countries allied in the personal union, apparently did not want Norway to go empty-handed and wanted to acknowledge the peace-loving Norwegians as compared with the politically more aggressive Swedes.

The peace prize also had a special status because the jury was not made up of scientists, but of politicians, namely, the members of the Norwegian parliament. That was to lead to complications very soon.

Suttner wrote to Fried after the contents of the will were published:

The Nobel Foundation? Well, I think it is grand, grand, and am all the more proud because *I* was the one who introduced Nobel to the movement and suggested that he do something important for it. I am also fully aware that I, as the moral author of this 7 million dedication and this so striking support of the peace idea, can lay claim to the first payment—quite apart from the fact that my motto continues to have an effect and that I know that in my hands, such money would bear fruits of peace again. It is also funny that I am getting congratulatory wishes from all sides.[39]

Already on January 12, 1897, a feature by Bertha von Suttner on Nobel and his will appeared in the *Neue Freie Presse*. She quoted Nobel's most important letters in it and underlined her own importance in the peace prize's coming into being.

On January 22 Bertha wrote in her diary: "New phase in the Nobel story. Ducommun drafts a big plan to divide the money wherein personal receipts would be totally renounced. Of course, not everybody will agree to it—I won't, either—and the lovely harmony within the peace camp is endangered."

She sat down for a whole morning and wrote a long letter to Ducommun, the president of the Bern Peace Bureau, "about the respect that was owed to Nobel's last wish." Copies of this letter went to the candidates for the peace prize, first and foremost, to Frédéric Passy.[40] Angered, she wrote to Fried: "In the end, every group would get 350 marks and 75 pfennigs (if things go according to the gentlemen's wishes) and every group could burn one more petroleum lamp in their office. *That* was not what my friend Nobel wanted!—You know, they *begrudge anyone* getting anything really big that would also make it possible to work independently."[41]

She confided her desperation in her diary: "Slept badly because of the three heavy burdens: My work, Arthur's worries and the house problems, *and* the European problems. A bit too much at once. Oh, why didn't Nobel help me out of all that!"[42]

Even Leo Tolstoy got into the discussions about the first Nobel Prize award and made the suggestion in a letter to a Swedish newspaper to honor the Duchoborzes with a peace prize.

This was the Russian sect that had renounced military service and suffered severe penalties because of it. "The Duchoborzes . . . have found the way to make war impossible, because if the population refuses to do military service against its will and to be trained in the skills of handling weapons, it will not be possible to form armies and wage wars." Tolstoy thought it was not suitable to give the prize to pacifists: "If people work for the peace cause, they do it unquestionably because they are motivated by their desire to serve God; therefore they have no need for monetary reward and will probably not even accept one."[43]

All the guessing about the recipient of the Nobel Prize soon proved to be superfluous. Nobel's heirs lodged a protest against the will and went to court. "That's disastrous. I know very well that Nobel who was my friend *wanted* to give me the prize. If he had only made it simpler and clearer."[44]

It was not until August of 1898 that the Nobel Prize made progress again. Suttner wrote in her diary: "Nobel heirs satisfied, now the concern will be how to divide the money. Probably in three parts. Write a protest." "Thinking a lot about Nobel Prize."[45] She was already thinking about what she could do with the money.

Relations between Sweden and Norway grew worse and worse during this time. There was a threat of Norwegian withdrawal from the alliance and a military confrontation between the two countries: not a very good outlook for a peace prize in Norway that was competition of a sort for the prizes to be given in Sweden. All of this delayed making the award.

Reacting in the same way she did to the name of Suttner being mentioned so frequently after the czar's manifesto, she implored Fried to be careful, at least in the peace publication, and not print her name so often: "I feel how it must offend a lot of people, the way my name has been buzzing through the world like a sales slogan recently.—If *I* am suspected of pointing to my own merits, of helping advertise myself, then—in addition to Russia—the *Storthing* will be angry with me, too."[46]

More than ever, she was bent on presenting an impeccable image to the public. When Marie Louise drove to a peace congress in a very elegant four-horse carriage, it did not go unnoticed by the press. Aside from being inappropriate, it also gave the impression that the Suttner family had a lot of money. Bertha's first thought was the Nobel Prize: she complained to her diary that Marie Louise had "perhaps ruined the Nobel Prize with her tactless team of four."[47]

She was very happy about Emanuel Nobel's visit to Harmannsdorf. He had not joined his relatives' protest against the will; in fact, he endorsed his uncle's charity. He himself was the heir to the gigantic oil industries in Baku and lived most of the time in Russia. Bertha reported to her diary:

Nobel. Resembles his uncle. More likable. Tells a lot of interesting things: how the king of Sweden called him for an audience and tried to talk him into contesting the will since the peace cause was dangerous. A Bebel could get the award. The Storthing could even use the money for anti-Swedish purposes. Emanuel Nobel resisted, though. Turned down millions to respect the will of Alfred Nobel . . . King talked about me and my *Lay Down Your Arms.*—Nobel had not worked for "laying down" but for making cannons. Lots of court cases. Big problems.

About Nobel's end. Wanted to get to his desk. Servant didn't let him. The servant turned out not to be sober, by the way.—Nobel read him a letter from me. *He was not married.* Storthing asked Emanuel to find out if Czar Nikolaus would accept the peace prize. . . . It was an interesting, pleasant, gratifying visit.

Afterwards, however, she accused herself of not getting Emanuel Nobel to become a member of the Austrian Peace Society. "There is no worse president and promoter than I!"[48] She would not have been Bertha von Suttner, though, if she had not taken up the issue at the next opportunity. A year later she was able to report to Fried happily "that Emanuel Nobel, in his capacity as the oldest member of the Nobel family, has joined the Austrian society. He donated 600 crowns."[49]

Suttner was in constant fear that Nobel's will could be misrepresented. She was sure that the only thing he wanted to do was help the peace movement. She watched very closely to see what criteria were being used and who would have the right to select the winner of the award. In her opinion, only the Storthing had the right and the responsibility to nominate the prize winner. But the Norwegian parliament gave a very wide selection of people the right to make suggestions, as Bertha found out: "all the governments, ethnic representatives, the Inter-Parliamentarian Union, Bern Peace Bureau, Nobel Laureates, professors of history, philosophy, and international law of all the universities." "When the votes are counted, you can imagine how few will go to real promoters of a movement that is despised or perhaps even unknown by the people being asked. . . . This year's circular also states that 'organizations may also be recipients.' That opens the way of least resistance—all the professors will fall into it."[50]

At the beginning of 1901, Suttner received a letter from the Nobel Committee asking her to nominate a candidate for the Nobel Peace Prize. This finally gave the prize a concrete form. Bertha in her diary: "Naturally" she would suggest Passy. "Now it's getting interesting. I will get it eventually, I think. Am making some plans about it. It will be divided, therefore small. Enough to take care of my old age. That's good."[51]

Alfred H. Fried suggested Suttner for the prize. Bertha praised Passy's merits to Fried:

He is our doyen—and what he has done and will still do—the half-blind man deeply troubled by family problems—it surpasses *your* candidate's claim many hundred times in value, power, devotion. . . . The only advantage your candidate has over the others is the fact that she prompted and actually achieved the whole peace prize foundation. That does not belong to the merits listed in the statutes and in the will, however. I do not want to show false modesty; I am aware of what I have done for the movement; also the fact that Nobel thought of me directly—but Fr. Passy comes first. Also Pratt and Cremer are well deserving campaigners and the person who has done the most for "bringing about the congresses" is certainly Ducommun.[52]

The people and groups scattered all over the world who were empowered to make suggestions got very busy. After a lot of hither and thither, the Austrian group of the IPU decided on an honorary Nobel Prize for Czar Nikolaus ("because we think it is inadmissible to award a prize of money to a sovereign"). Nikolaus, they said, had done the most for "the abolition and reduction of permanent armies" by issuing the peace manifesto and calling the Hague Peace Conference. The monetary prize would be divided among four candidates: Frédéric Passy in Paris and Randal Cremer in London as the initiators of the IPU, Bertha von Suttner ("One of her main accomplishments was getting A. B. Nobel to participate in the peace cause; he supported the propaganda with large sums of money."), and the Belgian professor of international law, Ritter von Descamps.[53]

The pacifists' main candidate, Frédéric Passy, was completely exhausted as a result of the bickering. Suttner comforted him in a very warm, long letter: "No, of course you aren't alone in the world. In addition to your own family, all the pacifists of the world are also your family and love you." She also wrote him that she had suggested him and that she would continue to fight against dividing the prize and against awarding it to an institution: "It would be a real disaster if the first award went to an institution. It would shove all the living candidates aside with one blow, because it would infer that none of them had been found worthy of the prize." She insisted on Nobel's condition that insitutions could be given the prize only if no individual candidate could be found. An award to Passy would be received "with joy and with no jealousy whatsoever by the entire pacifist world."[54]

She was also very happy about the propaganda effect the Nobel Peace Prize created for the movement and wrote Fried: "The best thing of all is the noise about the peace question that will be rustling in the papers again. In Paris everything is full of Passy's candidacy, and maybe that was also one reason why Passy was asked to give a lecture to students at the Sorbonne. The lecture was very successful—it was packed with students. In December, and even earlier, the papers will be full of

Nobel and his prizes. The Nobel institutes will also be very productive."[55] The interest from the capital that accumulated during the years between Nobel's death and the first prize award was used for establishing Nobel Institutes in Christiania, most notably the Central Institute for the Study and Development of International Law. In successive years, a quarter of the interest would also be reserved for use by this institute.

Bertha hoped that the badly needed publicity created by the awards would help the movement. "Just the announcement of the last will and testimony excited public attention, and this sensation will be repeated every year at the time of the awards. An announcement will be made in public—not by an exalted dreamer but by a brilliant inventor—of inventions of war materials besides—that the avowal of the brotherhood of peoples, reduction of armies, promotion of the peace congresses, are among the things that mean the most to the happiness of mankind."[56]

She was more enthusiastic than ever over Nobel's will: "An inspired work of immeasurable consequence." "Not because he is giving away millions, not because it endows prizes for scientific discoveries, but because a completely new idea of charity is being expressed: instead of aid for current and future misery, it demands and supports abolition of future conditions of misery. The ennoblement of human society is envisioned by the noble testator: new findings, new discoveries, ideal works of art should enrich and beautify the world; and the prerequisite for ensuring all these products of all this prosperity: peace."[57]

There were still repeated attempts to award the prize for general humanitarian accomplishments instead of for peace work. Suttner resisted this sharply: "In Nobel's will there is not one syllable about 'humanitarian' things. In the end the peace prize would go to the Brothers of Mercy. . . . The pacifists will have to fight against this welfare tendency forcefully."[58]

The main candidate for a "humanitarian" prize was Henri Dunant, the founder of the Red Cross. Suttner: "I would regard it a misfortune for the cause (even though I would not begrudge the old man) if a Red Cross man, that is a war alleviator, were to be called the most deserving element in the peace cause."[59]

The first Nobel Peace Prize went to Frédéric Passy and Henri Dunant in 1901. Since nothing could be changed now, Suttner tried to claim Dunant for pacifism. "Dunant has been honored chiefly as a friend of peace and not for the Red Cross, and I will give the world proof of this," she wrote to Fried.[60] She also appealed to him "to say something friendly about Dunant, namely, that he was the first who went over to the white flag, something the world at large does not know, but that the Nobel committee may have known. Second, that he paved the way: first of all for international sympathy—second for the possibility for international conventions on war . . . a step along the path toward a possible convention *not* to wage war."[61]

Dunant himself reinforced the opinion that he had been honored as a promoter of the peace idea and wrote: "I feel bound, honored lady, to tell you on the day of my tribute that I have received an official telegram from Christiania saying that I . . . have been awarded the Nobel Peace Prize. This prize, dear lady, is your work, because it was through you that Nobel was initiated into the peace movement and it was you who convinced him to become its patron. For more than fifty years I have also been a dedicated follower of international peace and a fighter under the white flag. The avowal of the brotherhood of man has been my goal for a very long time."[62]

Suttner quoted this letter wherever she could. Of course, Dunant had not written it spontaneously. She had asked him for it specifically: "Give me a few lines, please, in which you prove that you are a bearer of the white flag. Generally speaking, the world knows you only as the founder of an institution that alleviates war; I would so very much like to be able to publish a word from you, addressed to me, dated the day after your nomination for the Nobel award, as proof to the world that you are one of those who (after war has been alleviated) want to abolish war."[63]

Dunant went further and donated a large sum to the Austrian Peace Society, whereupon Bertha immediately sent him a membership card.

In the end, however, all attempts to push the Red Cross into the background and celebrate Dunant as a pacifist failed. Everybody saw in him only the creater of the Red Cross—and hardly anyone knew who Frédéric Passy was, or was interested in the peace movement. A Viennese newspaper even expressed astonishment "that Dunant had to share the prize with a French teacher of languages." Bertha's most revered idol, Frédéric Passy, the founder of the modern peace movement being called a "French teacher of languages!" Suttner praised Passy's accomplishments all the more and was happy when he was properly honored in his own country, France: "[T]he big papers—*Temps* in the lead—full of interviews with Passy," she proudly reported to Fried. "And he, the good man, is holding lectures in all the public libraries, etc.—and is very much in fashion."[64]

She could not help criticizing the Nobel scientific awards in Stockholm: "The celebration must have been lovely. On the one hand, a pity that the peace prize is separate—on the other hand the society of royals and nobles there would not have allowed a peace prize to come into being. At the most, Dunant *alone* and Krupp in the future."[65]

Bertha, plagued with financial worries and property seizures, had to look on helplessly while "her" prize slipped away from her. There were, however, a number of reasons for the prize committee's disregard. For one thing, the current demonstrative opposition to pacifism played a role, but there were also personal reasons: Suttner made powerful enemies in Norway with her all too opinionated and demanding attitude after Nobel's death. A noticeable antipathy against her even continued to echo in Nobel's biographies: she talked all too clearly and loudly about her essential role in the creation of the Nobel Prize. The response was to minimize all these accomplishments. Apparently they did not want Suttner as the protector of the Nobel will, and now they demonstrated the institution's power to deal with this woman who was so bold as to make demands.

But Bertha did not give up. Despite an occasional loss of courage, she awaited with hope and anxiety the anniversary of Nobel's death, which would also become Arthur's: the tenth of December, the day when the recipient of the peace prize was decided.

In 1902 the prize went to the president of the Bern Peace Bureau and close Suttner associate, Élie Ducommun, and to the secretary general of the Inter-Parliamentary office in Bern, C. A. Gobat.

For the Nobel Peace Prize of 1903, the Bern Peace Bureau unanimously nominated Bertha von Suttner. D'Estournelles, a French pacifist highly revered by Bertha, also backed her, a move she commented on in her diary: "D'Estournelles . . . but it makes me happy—because of his brilliantly successful work and his fairness toward me. How different from the German professors. He wrote to the Nobel committee. Would be good, if this balm came to my aid on this terrible anniversary day. Could do a number of useful things."[66] "In the press, the news that four Swedish women's clubs have suggested me for the Nobel Prize. Whether successful or not, it's nice."[67] Then doubts again: "Actually, not getting it would also be an advantage."[68] By that, she refers primarily to the creditors who had given up their claims, and who would immediately go after old debts if there were something to be gained.

December 10, the day of the decision, had come. Suttner entered in her diary: "Passy writes beautifully. Calls it *iniquité* [an iniquity] if I don't get the prize . . . All my friends gather behind me. . . . The name Cremer comes up. . . . Meyer arrives at 10: Cremer, undivided. It's over. . . . Now I have to work hard to keep my head above water."[69]

Bertha's disappointment was kept within bounds this time since her merits were greatly lauded in public. She was regarded as the unjustly treated victim of the Nowegian Storthing, and there were defenders of her claims everywhere.

In the *Berliner Tagblatt,* the freshly honored recipient of the Nobel Prize for literature, Björnstjerne Björnson, made a long declaration against the decision of the Storthing: the honor of the committee should have made it imperative to give Suttner the first peace prize. He mentioned the Nobel nephew, Emanuel, as a witness to the fact that no one else but Suttner "had awakened Nobel's interest in the peace cause. She made him believe, so that the relevant conditions in his will resulted." Emanuel Nobel knew this, not only from the some thirty or so letters from Suttner that were found among Nobel's possessions, but also from a personal statement his uncle made once while reading a Suttner letter: "I will do something for Bertha von Suttner and the cause of peace." In Italy, Björnson also met a witness to Nobel's will who confirmed this and who also said it would have been a disappointment to Nobel to know that Baroness Suttner did not get the first prize—and an even greater disappointment that so far she had received nothing whatsoever. Björnson implored his colleagues in the Storthing: "We cannot go on until we have carried out his [Nobel's] will, which we all know." He was not involved in this year's decision because he was staying in Italy and had no possibility to protest the committee's decision other than a public one.[70]

In the midst of this turbulent atmosphere, Suttner gave generous interviews, in which she paid tribute to Randal Cremer's accomplishments. She also defended him in private letters she wrote to enraged friends: "Randal Cremer, whom I know well, is a deserving man—he has served the peace cause successfully for many more years than I; it was he who went to America and brought about the court of arbitration treaty with England (which failed, however, because it lacked three votes, but laid the foundation for future action on courts of arbitration); he helped Passy found the Inter-Parliamentary Union; he protested bravely in parliament against imperialistic policies during the Boer War; in short: the Storthing has crowned a meritorious man. If my friends remain loyal to me, perhaps I will get my turn, too."[71]

In spite of everything, when she took stock of 1903 her balance was positive: "Not the Nobel Prize; but recognition from the *vox populi* in general, so that I can almost count on it next year."[72]

Indeed, information kept coming in about people who were supporting Suttner's candidacy, including some forty members of the upper house of the Austrian parliament, along with a group from the Swedish legislative body.

During a stay in Paris in March 1904 she heard from d'Estournelles that the Nobel Prize was "absolutely certain."[73] The other pacifists present in Paris also reinforced her confidence: "It seems to be beyond doubt. They wouldn't give me so much positive hope if it were not certain. All the same I have some doubts. Think of all the things that can happen between now and December."[74]

Nobel's nephew, Emanuel, showed his friendship to Suttner demonstratively now. This caused her to have ambitious dreams. Couldn't he finance the big, good newspaper she had always wanted? Besides, as the owner of enormous oil fields near Baku which were important for Russian industry, he had powerful friends in politics, including the finance minister, Witte.

But when she spoke to Nobel at a meeting in Marienbad about supporting such a newspaper, his reaction was negative: "he had . . . reservations. Thought I would work myself to death and wither away."[75]

Since Emanuel Nobel did not take up the newspaper project, Bertha tried a different subject: "Instead of a newspaper I now mention America. He goes for that." That meant that he agreed to pay her travel expenses to the peace congress in Boston. It was also to be her first trip to America, and this startled her somewhat: "My sleep was disturbed a bit by this sudden turn of events: America."[76] But she soon recovered, and four days later she wrote Fried full of anticipation: "The crossing on the most beautiful boat in the world ('*Kaiser Wilhelm der Grosse*') in a cabin on the upper deck will be most magnificent and supply the material for an interesting feature."[77] She was also looking forward to America because she knew how famous she was there because of the newspapers: "Really seem to be better known there than in Vienna."[78]

In America she was highly celebrated and gave a number of lectures, once even in a church ("Makes a good combination: music, hymns, uplifting and edifying feeling," she notes in her diary.[79]). She was received in the White House by President Roosevelt, who told her: "I intend to do three things: first, I will try, through mediation between Japan and Russia, to put an end to the war which is a real throwback of civilization; second, I will propose to all countries, to England, France, Germany, and also to your Austria that they conclude treaties with the United States on a court of arbitration, and I will see to it that these treaties have fewer limitations than those now in force; third, I will call a new Hague conference." Roosevelt expressed confidence in the peace movement: "Believe me, world peace will come because it has to come, but it will come step by step."[80]

Suttner praised America, saying it had an international honor as well as a national one, that Americans worked for the good of all and not only for that of their own country.

She visited the newspaper king, Pulitzer, whose paper, *The World,* supported the peace movement, and Karl Schurz. In reply to her question why this "forty-eighter" (referring to the German Revolution of 1848–49) was so highly respected, she was told that Schurz saw the slavery question from a special angle, namely, "from the point of view of what the problem meant for the country, not the negroes."[81] Bertha was greatly impressed.

Now America became for her the great hope of the peace movement. She thought that Europe did not appreciate the merits of the New World enough. In her novel *High Life* she has an American complain: "Oh, my star-flagged land, my great, vigorous, rational country bursting with freedom—aren't you being misjudged by the Europeans? Aren't you going to be called shallow and unpoetical in your lack of cathedrals, knights' castles, and royal courts? Won't they overlook the fact that your busy 'today' is preparing the glory of 'tomorrow' because that majesty of 'yesterday' is missing?"[82]

The Nobel Peace Prize for 1904 went to the Institute of International Law in Ghent. The pacifists were very angry. Frédéric Passy, furious, wrote his friend Suttner that the institute was in fact useful but its receiving the award was not in keeping with the conditions of Nobel's will by any means: "What war has it prevented? What congresses has it organized? What disarmament has it brought about? There's really no point in going to the trouble to make a will when those who have the responsibility of executing it only follow their own imagination."[83]

Bertha wrote to Albert of Monaco that she had counted on getting the prize this time and was very disappointed, "most of all because of my society, whose budget causes me a great deal of worry. . . . But even beyond that, giving the award to an institute instead of a person violates the intentions of the testator and means that the jury did not find a worthy person. That is insulting to the candidates who were nominated."[84]

The political atmosphere between Sweden and Norway did not improve. On the surface the quarrel was about foreign consulates; in reality it was about Norway's striving for independence. The Nobel Peace Prize was involved in the squabbling to the extent that it was the only Nobel Prize not awarded by Sweden, but by Norway. The money for it, however, was managed solely by Sweden. Cooperation between the two countries was necessary for making the award, but this relationship was soon becoming just as disturbed as the political situation. Suttner wrote to Fried: "The Norwegian-Swedish conflict causes me a lot of headaches. I *cannot* show up as a representative for Norway for a number of reasons."[85]

On June 7, 1905, the Norwegian Storthing declared Norway's separation from Sweden. The Danish prince Karl was elected king as Haakon VII. The political situation was tense, and there was a danger of war. Bertha attributed the fact that a peaceful solution was arrived at without a military conflict to the Swedes. She wrote to Albert of Monaco: "What a beautiful lesson Sweden has just given the world! It respects the decision of its sister-nation and has separated from her without military force."[86]

At the same time she doubts that the Nobel Peace Prize can be awarded in this complicated situation: "I worry about Norway. I am quite certain that no award will be made this year. The Committee has its permanent income of 50,000 crowns—and has now moved into a palace. That's the main thing. Nobel probably did not want more."[87]

In the autumn of 1905 Suttner made an extensive lecture tour through Germany. The trip, organized by a German agent, was supposed to bring in money as well as fame. Her lectures were very well received everywhere.

After her big appearance in Berlin, she reported to Fried: "The main battle is won. Had a lot of applause. . . . What is happening in the world otherwise is a horrible but effective background for my performances. . . . A lot of good is being achieved."[88] Good mostly because many people in her audiences had never heard of the peace movement before. "Terrible, how little the people know about the peace movement, are always astonished about the truth I present to them."[89] She was especially proud when eighty-nine people from the audience in Berlin entered their names as members of the Berlin peace group after her lecture.

Bertha, now sixty-two years old, withstood the exertions of this lecture tour surprisingly well. In her letters to Fried there was even a trace of new vitality after all the resignation of the previous months. In Göttingen, for example, she had to go directly from the railway station to the auditorium after a train ride of six hours—and she did not feel the least tired during the lecture: "The mind does have power over the body after all. I know, for instance, that trying on clothes for five minutes always makes me feel sick; now I stand there and talk, and at the end, I feel no tiredness even if it lasted two hours."[90]

This trip was basically different from earlier ones she had made together with Arthur. Before, she had spent a lot of time socializing with friends. Sightseeing had always been a part of the program, too. Now, without Arthur, she lived only for her work: she went from one lecture to the next, gave one interview after the other, often wrote newspaper articles until well into the night. She concentrated entirely on herself and her work, but she also enjoyed the fame that had come to surround her. At earlier times, she would have shied away from it out of consideration for Arthur.

At this point she was more unsure about the Nobel Peace Prize than ever. In November 1905 she still wrote optimistically to Fried: "They seem to believe in the 10th of December this time. Not me. The Norwegians only have one thing in their heads, and that is their H. Kohn [she means the new Norwegian King Haakon] and will use the prize for some endowment for a memorial to the glorious separation from Sweden. Which is rather tactless since Nobel was a Swede, but they can always be expected to do peculiar things."[91]

She happened to be staying in Wiesbaden when she got the telegram from Christiania—ten days earlier than expected. "Don't want to accept it because of the surcharge. Accept it anyway. Was worth the trouble," she notes in her diary laconically. "Sleepless night.—Strange: instead of joy, it also brings sorrow. But it's still wonderful."[92]

She wanted to surprise her closest friends, Alfred Fried and Hedwig Pötting ("Hex"). She did not mention anything about the good news yet and waited for the official date, December 10: "So, dear Fried—do not miss having coffee on the 10th with Hedwig Pötting, across from the picture of my poor Arthur. I insist." In her absence, they were supposed to wait for the news in Bertha's apartment.[93]

She prepared a letter for the tenth of December that was handed to the two punctually at coffee time: "My dear Hex and my dear Fried. Here's some news to go with the coffee: I've known since the first of the month—wasn't allowed to say so because it was told to me in strictest secrecy—that I have the prize. Commentary superfluous, and now I wish you a hearty appetite!" She added the postscript: "Tell Kati!" Kathi Buchinger was her faithful servant.[94]

The lectures that followed became real triumphs for the Nobel Peace Prize recipient. "Cheers and hurrahs even on the street," she noted in Wiesbaden. And in Cologne: "Lecture the most brilliant of all . . . surpassed all expectations."[95]

Upon her return to Vienna she found a "wonderful festive gift: silver laurel wreath." Aside from her closest friends and associates, however, the Austrian public—as far as it expressed itself in the newspapers—took very little notice of the awarding of the Nobel Peace Prize to the Austrian pacifist.[96]

The check from Norway was greeted with rejoicing. Suttner put part of the money in the bank with the intention of having an annual income of 12,000 crowns—two to three times the salary of a university professor. But in the exhilaration of her new wealth, she spent with a generous hand. For Christmas she gave Arthur's sisters a considerable sum as a present. They were "delighted. I had a good feeling about it, too," she wrote in her diary.

She got letters from relatives and from total strangers alike asking for money, and Bertha gave and gave: "It flies through my fingers. Good that something has been put aside," she sighs.[97]

Her old creditors also announced themselves and made demands: "Am supposed to pay the old Harmannsdorf debts now. And the money is flying away! The Nobel Prize is beginning to . . . revolt me." Finally, a letter came saying "that I still owe 9,000 gulden for my poor mother."[98] Her mother had been dead for thirty years.

An old unpaid bill for bricks for the roof at Harmannsdorf turned up, and Arthur's sisters needed no less than eleven thousand gulden again, which they got.

This begging increased over the next few months. The sisters-in-law built a house near Amstetten with Bertha's permission and money. Called Bogenhof (arched house), it turned out to be a new financial disaster on the model of Harmannsdorf.

Finally, Bertha's brother Arthur also asked for assistance. He was sick and penniless. "Will send money, but will not go there," Bertha wrote in her diary. "Since we have not seen each other for 35 years and never had a tender brother-sister relationship, such a journey would not make sense."[99] Then, after urgent reports, she went to Spalato after all, but learned about Arthur's death while she was still on the way: "I feel remorse for not having been more benevolent and caring toward Arthur during this final period. I wasn't able to understand properly. You can be understanding of everybody if you only put yourself in their position."[100]

After the funeral she had to supervise an inventory. "Servant women quarrel . . . everything needed is missing. Cupboards empty . . . straw sack on the bed. Miserable circumstances . . . doctor . . . talks about poor Arthur's abnormal character. Mind also below normal—no, it would not have been possible to save him."[101]

In the first five months of the year 1906, Bertha spent twenty thousand crowns, five thousand of them for gifts.[102] It became increasingly clear that the Nobel Prize was not the answer to all her financial problems. But after all the decades of money worries, she at least had the marvelous feeling of finally being able to draw from full resources for once. She also bought herself an elegant wardrobe for her trip to Christiania to receive the prize and to deliver her peace speech in April 1906.

She proudly reported on the ceremony for readers of the *Öster-reichische Rundschau:* "With his endowment, Alfred Nobel made the annual award of the prize in the northern countries a governmental matter."[103] During her speech, King Haakon sat in the first row.

"Björnson leads me in. Then I step forward and everybody stands up. Speech succeeds and gets heavy applause. Björnson and Lund are enchanted, I am so dependable . . . banquet . . . Lund speaks for Nobel and for Sweden . . . Swedish minister speaks for Norway—the first friendly word since the separation of the union."[104]

The theme of her speech was, "The Development of the Peace Movement," and of course she acknowledged the role Alfred Nobel played. "The fact that Alfred Nobel gradually convinced himself that the movement had left the cloudy realms of pious theory and progressed to that of accessible and practical objectives, is proved by his will. Next to the other things he recognized as serving culture, namely, science and idealistic literature, he also placed the aims of the peace congresses, namely, the attainment of international justice and the subsequent reduction of armies."[105]

In closing, she emphasized Norway's contribution to the peace movement, its participation at the Inter-Parliamentary conference, its subsidies to the Bern Peace Bureau: "Alfred Nobel knew why he entrusted the administration of the peace legacy to the Storthing."

Her survey of history and the tasks of the peace movement came together in the avowal: "The representatives of pacifism are aware of the insignificance of their personal influence on power. They know how weak they still are in number and reputation. But even though they think of themselves modestly—they do not think modestly of the cause they serve. They see it as the greatest that can ever be served."

The next day was the audience with the king of Norway, who did not show a very peaceful attitude toward Sweden. "Unfortunately the king intends to rebuild fortifications to suit his war minister's ideas," Bertha notes in her diary,[106] but tells her readers in the *Österreichische Rundschau* about her own reaction to this announcement: "Your Majesty, pardon my boldness, but as the recipient of the Nobel Peace Prize, I am entitled to call out: for God's sake—not fortifications again, not this stone and iron gesture of distrust and menace at the edge of a friendly country!" The king's answer to this warning has not been handed down.

An additional high point of the visit in Christiania was the big women's festivity in honor of the first woman to win the prize. There were a women's choir and ladies' orchestra, peace hymns and many long poems in honor of the guest, many congratulatory speeches, bouquets of flowers, and a laurel wreath: "I had to submit to all of that on a kind of throne placed in the center of the platform, and even make a more or less intelligent face."

And then another banquet. "During dessert, everyone was given a page upon which a 'Fairytale in Rhyme' extolled my *curriculum vitae*." A singer sang the song to "his lute attached to a strap." "My neighbor, the foreign minister, and my other neighbor, the Russian ambassador, and the prime minister sitting across from me all sang along bravely. . . . [Y]ou cannot imagine something like that happening in central Europe." The reputation of the peace movement was not as great in the "two big military states" (meaning the German Reich and Austria-Hungary) as it was in other countries.

Then Bertha went to Sweden and gave lectures in Stockholm, Göteborg, and Uppsala. Even the Swedish women's club gave a party in honor of Bertha von Suttner. "Constant triumphal procession with one ovation after the other," she proudly wrote Fried from Stockholm.[107]

She was astonished at public opinion in Sweden that disapproved of the peaceable king and would have preferred a warlike confrontation with Norway to the peaceful solution. She wrote to Fried: "And by the way, what do you say to this: the king is not popular at all here anymore. Because he did not want war. Because Sweden lost prestige that way, especially in the eyes of Wilhelm."[108]

Then she continued to Copenhagen where she had an audience with the Danish royal couple. "King *up to date* on the peace movement. Praised Roosevelt. Mentioned Fr. Bajer [the Danish pacifist]. Says the press is to blame for the war mood. Acknowledges my 'enormous accomplishments.' Thinks I should have spoken in other Danish cities. At the end, while accompanying me to the door: 'I call upon God's richest blessings to descend upon your beautiful activity. Continue to work and achieve!' I say: 'The mighty can help—do it your Majesty!'—'I will do it, as far as it is within my power.'"[109]

In Copenhagen, too, the women's clubs organized a grand tribute. Bertha returned to Vienna, strengthened by all her successes abroad.

She followed the awards of the next few years very closely and never failed to exercise her right to nominate a candidate every year.

In 1906 the American president, Theodore Roosevelt, was awarded the Nobel Peace Prize for his services in connection with the court of arbitration and the upcoming Second Hague Peace Conference. It was an important innovation since this was the first time a politician got the prize. From this time onward, Roosevelt was a constant cause of annoyance to Bertha because he did not in the least back disarmament as the pacifists had hoped—quite the contrary. "So Roosevelt, my colleague, will speak in Christiania in May. Maybe he will find out there what the peace movement is."[110]

Roosevelt continued steadfastly with his armament program. He took no consideration of the fact that he was a winner of the Nobel Peace Prize and held dynamic speeches on which Suttner sadly commented in the *Friedenswarte*. At a Berlin visit in May 1910 he told her in the auditorium of the Berlin University that an "unjust war" was abominable, "but woe to the nation that does not arm against injustice, three times woe to the nation whose men lose the courage to fight, the warring spirit."[111]

During his ensuing trip to Vienna, he also disappointed the pacifists there, even going so far as to say discourteous things about the IPU and the peace societies. Suttner wrote to Fried angrily: "Roosevelt did something disgusting. . . . [T]he mocked, ridiculous fantasts: that was aimed straight at the peace societies and especially at people like Peace Bertha."[112]

But Suttner took no joy from some of her other successors as Nobel Peace Prize winners, either. In 1907 she nominated Bajer, d'Estournelles, Moneta, and Stead as worthy candidates. The prize committee gave Ernesto Teodoro Moneta only half of the prize; the other half went to someone, "who, to my knowledge, has done nothing for pacifism," as Bertha rebuked. Louis Renault had merely been "a reporter on war regulations at The Hague." "Always poisoning the peace cause by mixing in other rites that are diametrically opposed . . . In this domain even . . . war could get the prize."[113]

But when King Victor Emanuel personally congratulated the new Nobel Prize winner, Moneta, she thought it was "simply wonderful." "Made me intensely glad. How the idea trickles *upward!* And how many people that will impress *below*. A good idea after all, the Nobel Prize." Of course, she compared Victor Emanuel with Emperor Franz Joseph and wrote with resignation: "Prohaska [her nickname for the emperor] would not have congratulated me."[114]

11

Hope in the Mighty

For Bertha the peace issue was not a matter of "high" and "low," of the rulers and the ruled, the mighty and the people. She wanted both: to enlighten the people and to win over the rulers. *"The Great League of Culture*—it must permeate upwardly and downwardly all of mankind and radiate from the educated, thinking, refined people.—In truth, power today rests with the heads of governments and ministers; if they are in favor of establishing a condition of peace and justice, then we have what we want—as *friends of peace;* our other goals are still untouched, however."[1]

For these "refined people" to be able to work for peace successfully, however, they needed two things: one, the money of the financially mighty for peace propaganda and two, social or other connections to the politically mighty, with whom the decision on war or peace lay.

Suttner was so successful because she used both directions equally— propaganda "downward" and personal influence "upward," and she even created competition between them: "What is going to fulfill our ideals quicker? The rulers, once they've been shown reason, or the masses declaring with one voice: we won't shoot?"[2]

Again and again she complained, "the fact that we do not have the influence and achieve the success that is desirable is due to our poverty."[3] The death of Alfred Nobel was a great loss for Bertha, especially in this respect. This close personal friendship that resulted in big donations and constant assistance, was a stroke of luck that would never repeat itself in Bertha's lifetime. But she had recognized the power and the necessity of money and after Nobel's death did everything she could to find another financier and patron.

In 1901 the Russian railway industrialist and pacifist Johann von Bloch also died. He had spent a great deal of money for peace propaganda and was personally active in giving lectures and writing newspaper articles. He paid travel expenses for pacifist colleagues who were less well off and paved the way for a peace museum in Lucerne. Suttner lamented Bloch's death very much: "If only the family continues what he started—at least the museum; somebody else can do the rest: the lectures, the articles. Whether he bequeathed something for that purpose? I don't think so. He had too great a consciousness of being the sole bearer of salvation."

But a few days later she was able to report favorably to Fried: Bloch had "left 50,000 rubles at the disposition of the Bern office, with specific instructions . . . furthermore . . . [he] entrusted his son with complete authority to carry on with the Lucerne museum."[4]

The museum was formally opened in June 1902 in the presence of prominent pacifists. Suttner wrote to Theodor Herzl: "This museum means as much to the peace movement as ten congresses."[5]

Suttner did not tire of trying her luck with Austrian industrialists, but her attempts to get money proved extremely unpleasant and embarrassing. For a socially ambitious woman it was humiliating to have to "sponge on" wealthy people whom she regarded as her social equals.

She reacted with a very bad temper and envy when the wealthy made luxurious donations for other purposes, and she usually gave vent to her indignation in letters to Fried; for example, in 1905 she wrote: "So. Now Rothschild alotted another twenty million for charitable purposes. Mentally ill (some hundred or so) are to be cared for. None of the wise philanthropic gentlemen give anything to save hundreds of thousands from disaster, ruin, misery, and premature death."[6]

Then at the turn of the century a new, great hope surfaced: Andrew Carnegie. A Scotsman by birth, he emigrated to the United States with his parents at the age of twelve and worked his way up in the railway industry. His sleeping car business earned him an enormous fortune very quickly, and he used it to buy into oil companies and the steel industry. Finally he was even named the "Steel King" of the United States. In old age, he found meaning in life by using his fortune for charity. In a pamphlet called "The Gospel of Wealth," which also appeared in German in 1892, he said "the responsibility of a wealthy person" was "to live modestly and without grandeur, free from bragging and foolishness." He was "simply an agent acting on behalf of his less well-to-do brothers; he places his enlightened judgment, his experience, his administrative abilities at their service and thus achieves results for them which are better than those they would have attempted and would have been able to achieve by themselves."[7]

Carnegie spent his money first of all for education and science, in a firm belief in the progress of humanity. Some thousand libraries and the buildings that housed them were erected with his money. Then he, the confirmed free-thinker, endowed no less than four thousand church organs because he thought the "solemnity of music, especially organ music, elevates the soul." With fifteen million dollars, he endowed a "heroes' foundation," not for war heroes, but for rescuers of life. "*They* are the heroes of civilization, as opposed to the heroes of barbarism who have slain their fellow men."[8] This foundation soon showed how close he was to the peace movement—and that the pacifists were right in placing their hopes in him.

Already at the turn of the century, he had had contacts with pacifists. The American delegate to The Hague, Andrew White, had interested him in the international court of arbitration and suggested that instead of building just one library for international law for The Hague, as Carnegie had planned, he should build a "Peace Palace" for this court.

When Suttner learned that Carnegie wanted to take part in the peace congress in Glasgow in 1901, she put Fried on to him since she herself could not go to the congress: "Carnegie will be in Glasgow at the same time. He could be our millionaire—but he has already refused Moscheles. Who knows, maybe he will weaken this time; if *he* were to embrace the cause, think how propaganda could be carried out then."[9]

Ten days later she wrote to Fried: "On the day of the opening of the peace congress, Carnegie was made an honorary citizen of Glasgow. . . . [A]mong other things, Carnegie talked about the cultural aims of the Anglo-Saxon race and said the things I have enclosed, which would be suitable for the *Friedenswarte*."[10] It is interesting to note that Suttner, who was not in Glasgow, informed Fried about this speech of Carnegie's, which she learned of from the *Herald Tribune*.

She pulled her strings circumspectly and was better informed in isolated Harmannsdorf than the very active Fried, who frequently missed the important things at the very place where they were happening because his knowledge of languages was not good enough.

She commented on Carnegie's pacifist speech: "Why is it then, that Carnegie does not back up his convictions with donations . . . millions for publications on peace information, would that not be better than for libraries that are full of old literature glorifying war?"

From then on, she beleaguered Carnegie, sent him articles she thought he would like and kept reminding him of her. "I wrote Carnegie again. . . . In the end I will get this billionaire—this newest potentate of the earth—on our side."[11]

In 1903 the news of success finally came: "Wonderful that Carnegie gave 1½ million [dollars] for the Hague peace temple." "[T]hat he invited d'Estournelles is something we can only be happy about. And it is also lovely that he will pay for the St. Louis trip [for the Inter-Parliamentarian Conference in 1903]. I hope he is generous—not just that the crossing is covered."[12]

Suttner looked for Carnegie at the peace congress in Boston in vain and wrote to Fried with disappointment: "Carnegie not present. Not a single billionaire in sight."[13]

In her new novel, *Der Menschheit Hochgedanken* (Elevated thoughts of mankind), she made a rich American her hero. He uses his money to finance a big international peace festival and calls on humanity to fight evil and war—her idealized portrait of Carnegie.

And Carnegie, whose contact with international pacifism grew closer and closer, and who was enthusiastic about his new calling, donated in truly grand style. He not only had the Hague Peace Palace built, with its big international law library, he also appeared at the Second Hague Peace Conference personally and spent one million (probably dollars) just on the hospitality of the guests, as Bertha reported to Fried with astonishment: "But it is still insulting that Carnegie did not think of us. He remembers the *cause* magnificently, at least, and I hope he will let his founding of the library lead to a new use of his millions. But it is not *America* that needs the patronage, it is Germany and the people who . . . create the mood for endless armament."[14]

Carnegie, approached for money from all sides, examined every request thoroughly, which disappointed Bertha at first: "Carnegie does not enter into anything vague. He does not say, 'Here is a million, do something you think is useful with it,' but wants to know something definite beforehand."[15]

First of all, Suttner wanted to get the billionaire to pay a fixed annual sum to the penniless Fried, so that he could finally devote himself to pacifist work without worrying about money. In 1908 she visited Carnegie in his Scottish Skibo Castle while she was attending the London Peace Conference. She reported to Fried: "Dubious success in the matter in question. . . . It was doubly embarrassing for me as a *guest*. Did it anyway because it was the reason for making the trip north.—Result: put off with promise of foundations." To Carnegie's question of how much Fried needed: "Said two hundred marks a year. Only scoundrels are modest—and I am a scoundrel.—Please tear up this letter!"[16]

In her diary, too, she deeply regretted the fact that she approached Carnegie for money: "Was terribly dumb in Skibo. Absolutely ruined this chance to make friends!"[17]

Then again she was very happy when a short time later, Fried actually got some money: "Fried is relieved of some of his worries for this year, after all." The news filled her "whole day with joy (instead of work)."[18]

Bertha's repeated statement that Fried had received two hundred marks is false, however: according to a letter from a Carnegie secretary, the sum was two hundred pounds sterling, a far greater amount.[19]

She kept Carnegie informed of Fried's work. "I tell you about it because I think you will be happy to hear that the man whose work you are so kindly supporting is proving to be worth your support and really works very hard and seriously." She assured Carnegie that the pacifists were placing their hopes on America: "The restoration of Europe's health will come from America."[20] Of course she wrote newspaper articles about the new patron, mentioned him in her lectures, and compiled polite thank-you letters in English for Fried to send Carnegie.

Andrew Carnegie, "the most active and most powerful of the living pacifists in respect to accomplishments,"[21] even succeeded in having a conversation with Emperor Wilhelm. Carnegie asked him to support peace. Wilhelm answered "that he was already a protector of peace, within his powers,—only according to a different method." Whereupon Carnegie replied: "But everything depends upon the method, Your Majesty," and gave several examples, including: "There is a very great difference whether I hold my hand like this (praying gesture) or like this (nose-thumbing gesture)." The emperor laughed.[22]

In 1910 Bertha noted with satisfaction: "Carnegie is thoroughly into pacifism—that will be very useful. His standpoint of approaching war as a barbarism deserving disgust is agreeable to me. He must not be the only one, but he must not be missing. The fact that he took Taft's word literally is very clever. He has appointed him the leader."[23]

In 1910 Carnegie made the American president, William Howard Taft, the honorary president of the board of trustees of his new peace fund, which he endowed with ten million dollars. This was a triumph for the pacifist movement.

Excited with joy, Suttner wrote Fried in April 1910: "What do you say to that? Taft at the general meeting of the peace society! And what he said! . . . The way our avalanche is getting its push from America. It's marvelous, marvelous!" In contrast she criticized the German delegation once again. "But these people must be learning amazing things now in America. Head of State at the peace society . . . Something has happened again, with consequences people cannot imagine. It's in all the papers."[24]

Now Carnegie and Taft gave their combined support to the court of arbitration, an international agreement on disarmament, and most of all to a "peace league of enlightened powers." This league was supposed to ensure peace between nations, but it was also supposed to be able to take action against possible violators of the peace, if necessary with a combined army.

To create a forerunner for the peace league, Carnegie supplied ten million dollars for the "Pan American Office" to promote trade and friendship between the republics of South and Central America and the United States. President Taft opened the office in April 1910 and explained his idea of using intervention to maintain peace, giving the example of Pan America: "We twenty-one republics cannot tolerate having two or three quarreling with one another. We must put an end to it, and Mr. Carnegie and I will not rest until nineteen of us can intervene with the proper measures to suppress the quarrel between two of the others." Suttner quoted these words in the *Friedenswarte* and commented: "Couldn't something like this—aside from Europe—also be aimed at for the Balkans?"[25]

Bertha could not praise the work of Carnegie and President Taft for the peace effort enough: "Certainly, the impetus given to the cause by yourself and Mr. Taft is very strong—and I, too, feel sure that great things will be attained. The biggest obstacles will be found only in the military spirit of the men in power in central Europe, backed by the ignorance and apathy of the people. Much and intense propaganda work is needed here."[26] Carnegie financed this propaganda in a grand style. He gave a yearly subsidy of 125,000 francs to the Bern Peace Bureau alone, as Suttner proudly wrote to Albert of Monaco in 1911.[27]

The personal contacts between Suttner and the terribly wealthy American, Carnegie, became a well-known fact in Vienna—and the requests for intervention came immediately. One day even Archduchess Maria Theresia, the stepmother of Crown Prince Franz Ferdinand, asked Bertha to come to her, a situation she found "weird." Up to now, no member of this royal house had bothered themselves with her. "What does she want from me? Actually, funny: letter of recommendation to Carnegie. Partly hospital—partly Portugal. [Maria Theresia was born a Braganza princess.] She has read my memoirs . . . says that my work has been useful in influencing the world."[28]

Suttner complied with the wealthy archduchess's rather unusual request to help get a donation for a charitable purpose from an even wealthier American. Maria Theresia actually went to Scotland to see Andrew Carnegie—armed with a letter of recommendation from Suttner ("one of the most charming and high-souled princesses of Europe"),[29] but she was not successful.

Carnegie continued to give to the peace movement generously. To Bertha's distress, however, he concentrated on the United States and was not particularly interested in the Austrian or German peace societies. (It was not until 1912, on her big lecture tour through the United States, that Carnegie approved a lifetime pension for Bertha. By then she was almost seventy and was only able to enjoy it for a very short time.)

Determined, Bertha was constantly on the lookout for additional patrons. A newspaper article about Bertha Krupp and her charitable work gave her the idea in 1910 of writing the wife of the German cannon king in Essen and asking her to join the peace movement: "Alfred Nobel, the dynamite king, did great things for the peace idea, and the cannon queen could also make exceptional contributions in this same field." Unfortunately, nothing is known about a reaction to this letter.[30]

Bertha von Suttner did not give up hope. She knew a rich man who was a pacifist *and* an aristocrat, even a sovereign ruler, albeit of a small country: Prince Albert of Monaco. When she was his guest in 1903, she hoped to use Albert to influence his friend, Emperor Wilhelm II, who was the decisive ruler in Europe as far as the question of war or peace was concerned. Alfred nourished her hopes when he told Bertha "that Wilhelm II had drawn him a sketch for the peace flag on the menu at dinner."[31] The prince also said once that "Wilhelm II" had written "him today about the peace cause again."[32]

Suttner kept up her contact with Albert through friendly letters and newspaper articles. She boasted about him to other journalists and here to Theodor Herzl:

> Prince Albert I (probably one of the most unappreciated men in the world) is a strange person. A nobleman in the highest sense. The press *had* to print a feature on his *Carrière d'un navigateur* [the book Fried translated into German so poorly that Bertha had had to work it over in Monaco] and *you* were called upon to write it—the gentle melancholy that wafts through the book suited your recent moods perfectly. Your latest features have a touch of wistfulness, and a glance directed toward distant horizons and oceanic depths, like that of Albert I. *I* (as a guest and particularly as one decorated by the prince) may not write such reviews because it would look as though I were fawning.[33]

She welcomed and, when possible, reinforced all of Albert's pacifistic statements. About the preface she wrote in German for his autobiography, she said, "By the way, the whole preface is a protest against military politics, an anti-Machiavelli. With a few strokes of the pen, it gives the

world a picture of a prince who will be so badly needed in future times—
if future times will still need princes at all."[34]

She, who despised Wilhelm II as a militarist, tried to influence the
German emperor through Albert and to "modernize" him, as she called
it. For her, that meant bringing him closer to pacifistic ideas. To this
end, she suggested that the prince dedicate his book to Wilhelm II, and
she even formulated the wording for Albert: "I dedicate the German
translation of this book to His Majesty the Emperor Wilhelm II, the
monarch who fosters science and thus prepares the way for the accom-
plishment of the most noble desire the conscience of man harbors: the
union of all the powers of culture to bring about the reign of inviolate
peace."[35]

When Bertha found out that the German emperor wanted to go to
the Kiel Regatta in 1904 at the same time as his uncle, King Edward
VII, she made a request of the prince: "I hope very much that you will
be there, *Monseigneur*. This meeting between uncle and nephew appears
to contain a promise of pacifistic action, and your presence, *Monseigneur*,
could be very useful. In any case, it would add prestige to the role you
have so courageously accepted in our movement."[36]

Albert was active in Kiel: he invited the French pacifist, Baron d'Estournelles to a *déjeuner* on board his yacht together with the German
emperor and the king of England. D'Estournelles took the opportunity
"to give the emperor information about the objectives toward which he
has been working for years already." Suttner wrote to Fried: "Of course,
a German-French treaty is not to be expected with the first collision, but
it has certainly had an effect on the German-English one."[37]

When Prince Albert made a visit in 1907 to Berlin, she implored
him to support the movement. She drew his attention to the initiatives of
Sir Henry Campbell Bannerman, who had championed international disarmament. She wrote to Albert about it: "That is an idea that certainly
does not appeal to your imperial host. But I tell myself that your influence may be able to change his mind. Oh, if he wanted to—he would
have the power to save humanity from the worst misfortunes and the
heaviest burdens."[38]

She hoped that Albert would be able to influence Wilhelm to do
something for the reconciliation between France and Germany, and she
could not thank him enough for his efforts in this direction.

Meanwhile, Albert had read *Lay Down Your Arms*—somewhat belat-
edly—and he complimented the author on it. He became more and more
a part of the international peace movement. Both he and, of course,
Bertha were among the speakers at the peace congress in Rouen in 1903.

In keeping with his style, he gave a dinner for the friends of peace on his yacht.

Suttner was happy about this congress because the French finance minister was the chairman of the big meeting attended by some twenty-eight hundred people. The peace idea was making progress, and it seemed appropriate for her and Passy to be brought back to the hotel in an automobile after the meeting as guests of honor. "True modern closing for this modern congress," she wrote with satisfaction in her diary.[39]

By now her contact with Monaco had become so important that she accepted Albert's invitation in 1904 again, despite "wardrobe problems": "I think it is good for my cause and my *prestige* to accept such friendship."[40] This time she made an arrangement with the *Neue Freie Presse* to send four reports from Monaco—for a whopping fee that totaled 480 crowns. Her travel expenses were covered.

At the royal court Bertha met Crown Prince Rudolf's widow, who had meanwhile married Count Lónyay. Bertha wrote of Stephanie, who was not particularly popular in Austria: "So different from her reputation. Full of vitality and spirit . . . against war, against duelling, and against pigeon-shooting. Lónyay against militarism." Of course Stephanie was also used for the peace movement: "Wants to give me a letter to the czarina of Russia."[41]

In Monaco she also made the acquaintance of the Prince von Hohenzollern, the former candidate for the Spanish throne in 1870, who, she said, manifested "respect for the peace movement."

Court gossip told of an Austrian who was supposed to have said that Suttner "stood at the peak of the big international spy network. Amusing," says Bertha in her diary.[42]

She talked to Prince Albert "about America, the Nobel Prize, Andrew White." She also wrote that in Albert's garden, she was able to "surprise him with an idyll about little Kohn."[43] Her personal relations with Albert proved to be cooler than she had imagined: "In him I have *no* friend that can be called a friend. Like Bloch has been, for example. Well now, all his affection belongs to the little Kohn."[44]

And the sign of friendship she had hoped to get from Prince Albert regarding the America trip in 1904 did not materialize either: "Could have asked me to come with him."[45] He preferred instead, to attend the peace congress in Boston independently of "Peace Bertha."

In 1905 Bertha von Suttner once again took the opportunity in Monaco to get to know prominent politicians. She met Prince Ferdinand of Bulgaria, upon whom she placed fresh hopes. To Fried: "Do you know who Prince Ferdinand of Bulgaria has the greatest respect for? For

Jaurès and Pressensé. 'They are men who are on the path to truth.' . . .
Pacifism as an *idea* is pervading the whole world now."[46]

Of course she told her readers in the *Neue Freie Presse* all the details
about Ferdinand's trousers, his tie pin, and pale yellow boutonniere, but
she also told them about the conversations they had. "In a serious, moving tone" he had explained to her, "I am working with the same intentions as you, Baroness—all my efforts are directed toward preventing a
conflagration in the Balkans. Not everybody believes that. I am seen as a
troublemaker, an intriguer, ambitious for myself." He said he only
wanted the best for his country: education, good morals, well-being:

> [T]hat's the point of it all, not whether a certain scrap of land belongs
> to this side or that. If they had only come to understand that the goal of
> political action should be seen as service to the community as a whole
> and not as a means for profit for one's own person and the suppression
> of the others! And the greater the influence a prince has, the more
> careful he has to be about thinking not only of the good of his own
> country, but also of that of his neighbors.
>
> So Your Highness is of the opinion that the Christian command-
> ment, "Love thy neighbor as thyself," should also be applied to state
> affairs?
>
> I am of the opinion that the social law of solidarity is a law of
> nature, and violating it is just as unwise as it is immoral.[47]

Ferdinand's predecessor in Bulgaria, Alexander von Battenberg, was
also in Monaco at this time and claimed to be a pacifist. Bertha wrote of
the *"très beau garçon:"* "Knows me and my book. And talks about peace
as though he were a d'Estournelles. This war should be the last. One
does not have the right to wage war anymore; it is a crime. The Princess
Battenberg says her husband has been an admirer of mine for many
years.—They live in Darmstadt, I must remember that. Might result in a
lecture." Battenberg had good connections with the Italian royal house—
reason enough to give rise to the Suttner plan to negotiate with the king
of Italy on peace, with the help of Battenberg intervention.[48]

Conversations with other high-ranking guests of Prince Albert's
made Bertha realize again, "how unjust people are in regard to the great,
by thinking they are stupid. We will achieve the Federation of Europe
with them, not against them."[49]

This opinion was also held by other pacifists who enjoyed the atmosphere surrounding the Prince of Monaco. One of these was the Hungarian, General Türr. According to Bertha, he wanted to get the King of

Italy to create a union of all sovereigns. "Prince Albert is also working in that direction."[50]

Even before the Hague Peace Conference, Türr had used his contacts with the king of Italy and "talked about the necessity of combining the Double and Triple Ententes to form a European confederation."[51] The results of this conversation were meager, however. "Türr . . . sees a black future, because Europe has no direction now, no prince, no statesman— everything is progressing *à la dérive* toward its ruin. . . . He spoke with the king of Italy about the necessity of doing something for peace. But he does not have the energy it takes, either."[52]

Türr was not the only person to experience disappointment. Bertha's enthusiasm for the former and the ruling Bulgarian princes soon gave way to disillusionment. What could they really do for Europe, anyway? The cliché-ridden character of their avowals of peace became clearer to Bertha the longer she stayed in Monaco: "The royal personages are rather interesting; but now I know them," was her reserved entry in her diary.[53]

Once again she had taken polite after-dinner conversation for a pre-paredness to work with her.

In her features for the *Neue Freie Presse,* she reported proudly from Monaco, told about Albert's hobbies—everything from motor boat re-gattas to deep sea exploration—and repeated the chats she had with royal guests in front of the fireplace.

Karl Kraus had an easy time making fun of her in the *Fackel.* He simply quoted the shallow utterings of the royalty the way Suttner re-ported them—and made them appear ridiculous. "At some point one really has to show what a very important writer the lady is who has made Europe rebellious for years by placing herself on peaceful footing with all the ruling powers."[54]

But Bertha's stay in Monaco was not as untroubled as she presented it in her newspaper articles. Her hope in Albert I was dashed: "[W]ork together with Albert for the peace cause? Out of the question. Every whale is on a higher level than he. The electric sparks are missing be-tween us," she wrote in her diary, complaining that her "awkwardness, lack of proper clothes and jewelry" made her "less ornamental from year to year" and showing faint hints of jealousy of "little Kohn."[55]

Her attempt to get Albert's support for a peace mission to Rome to settle the differences between Austria and Italy failed: "[T]alked about it to Albert I. He thought it very nice of me—broke off, though, just as he did before the Petersburg trip. An active friendship in the cause of peace like the ones with Bloch and Nobel are not to be found here."[56]

Bertha was forced into the realization that Albert's main interest was not the peace idea, it was oceanography. She felt neglected, even offended: "Cinderella next to Princess Oceanography," she wrote Fried. "Will appeal to Albert's conscience."[57]

The Peace Institute in Monaco did not fulfill her high expectations, either: "Deep sea museum will flourish, institute will crumble into dust."[58]

Albert did not react to her careful requests for financial support; perhaps he did not understand how desperately she needed money. She wrote to Fried in disappointment: "Got a letter today from Albert I. Three pages describing a motorcycle tour he made, enjoyable projects for his next oceanic voyage—complaints about the blindness of the great powers who wage war, assurances of fondness, and thinking about me often. But not a word about the . . . problems hinted at in my letter. Signing *'ami'* is not enough by itself." "Well, you can't expect the grand gesture from Albert."[59]

When Fried began to get excited about Albert, she warned him: "Albert's speech is nice. He always talked that way—from the very beginning it was *'science et paix'*—but no money for the latter."[60] "So far, I have not gotten as much as a box of chocolates from my devoted friend."[61]

When the Peace Institute cut Fried's fee for translation work in half, she had to ask for the Prince's help, as unpleasant as that was. Her objections were carefully clothed in jest: "Three institutes are your daughters, *Monseigneur*, the oceanographic, paleological, and pacific. The two older ones have all the luxuries one could desire, splendid wardrobes so that they can attend the court ball. The youngest, however, is something of a Cinderella." Certain of victory, she added that the Prince married Cinderella in the end, not one of the magnificent sisters.[62]

Before the Second Hague Conference, of 1907, she asked Albert for money again. Together with Fried, she organized a press service for information on conference events. At the First Hague Conference, she had seen "that the reports in Austrian and German papers were inexact, incomplete, and, most of all, hostile." This time, "Our press correspondence will confront this danger." The whole project, including printing and mailing expenses, would amount to twelve thousand francs. She could raise half of that, and she had asked several Austrian pacifists to come up with the rest, "but whether they do not feel wealthy enough or do not think it is interesting, I have only had refusals." She urged him "to give his friendly support to this unique and important opportunity."[63]

To Fried she wrote that this was the "most unpleasant, embarrassing letter" she had written in a long time.[64] But she was successful. Albert consented by telegram. Not only would he provide for the press service, he would pay for the trip to The Hague, too.

The long journeys to Monaco in the springtime gradually became too strenuous for Bertha, because of overwork and the realization that Albert was not such an enthusiastic pacifist and patron after all. Yet she reproached herself for not going: "I've cut myself off from lovely possibilities. But I don't fit into that kind of *milieu* anymore."[65] She felt she was no longer attractive enough, thought she was ugly, boring, inelegant, unimpressive.

She read the newspaper reports from Monaco with a bit of envy. Fried was sometimes invited in her place now. "How lovely that would have been . . . four days of festivities. In all the papers. Would have made my name stand out, created buyers for my book. Feel regret. Why have I taken leave of life while I'm still alive? When will the real death take place?"[66]

She actually went to Monaco again in 1911, accompanied by her servant, Kathi Buchinger, who "never abandoned her state of astonishment" at all the unaccustomed splendor. Her beloved *"Frau Bertha,"* however, was bored at the polite conversation of the court: "[E]venings especially deadly. I feel that I am boring to the same degree that I am being bored. Lots of talk about bull fighting."[67]

After three weeks in the Grimaldi castle, she left. "Dissatisfied with my visit, that is, with myself. With unused opportunities."[68] One more time, she had not dared to ask the prince for various kinds of support, but she caught up in letters. First she asked for travel expenses for Austrian pacifists going to the peace congress in Rome in 1911. He sent fifteen hundred francs.[69]

Then she wrote about her hopes for a generous "Monaco Foundation," a European counterpart to the Carnegie Foundation, which of course concentrated on American peace activities. "Here, especially, in this atmosphere of warlike tradition and militaristic spirit, is where a society supporting our cause ought to be operated with determination."[70]

She wrote to Fried impatiently:

> I think Albert should give three million as a core for a European fund for the movement. Then others would help, too—his friends, Henry Rothschild, etc., for a start.—It ought to be a counterpart to the American Carnegie and then grow, grow to a hundred million and *to that end*, no palace with libraries, no reviews, just propaganda—pilgrimages, advertisements, posters, lectures by top intellectuals, the greatest artists. And as *managers* of the whole thing, a few highly paid experts in pacifism *à la* Moch, Fried, Stead, etc. . . . We are living in the age of the advertisement. If the main ideas in slogans: what war costs—what needs to happen to establish international justice—and the sayings of Taft, Grey, etc., etc., appear in a big and often repeated advertisement

for a big Viennese department store or a mouth rinse [actually appears],
that would have to make people notice the cause.[71]

Nothing came of the lovely plans, and Bertha had to keep on waiting: "Oh, where is the young Napoleon of Pacifism we need? In America's Taft. He has not put in an appearance in Europe yet. But he's sure
to be alive already."[72]

And even if the millions did not pour in for the peace advertisements, she still nourished her hopes in the day's great politicians. "Who
knows, maybe a powerful person will turn up in the auditorium, who,
when he takes hold of the white flag, will be in a position to mount it on
the highest parapet. For even the great of this earth, even though their
greatness has come down from ancient times and has grown from the
ideals of an old spirit, are powerfully gripped by the spirit of the new
times; they, too, are searching for brighter goals—the desire to turn
away from the world of menacing misery that fills their hearts, too—they
do not lie when they admit it."[73]

"I want to approach the bearers of crowns. In order to check the
Satan: war. *They have the power to do it.* At this moment. And when you
are in a hurry to perform an act of rescue, you turn immediately to those
who possess the means of rescue." With her intentions of working together with the people in power at the time, she placed herself in opposition to social democracy. They wanted first of all to break the power of
capitalism. According to their claims, this would necessarily secure peace.
Bertha countered: "Time is crucial. Let us turn—at a running pace—
toward the place where the fire extinguisher can actually be found."

"Currently, as a result of the overall historical and political development, the unlimited power over war and peace rests with the heads of
state, and only with them. The people everywhere put up with a situation (it is incomprehensible, but true) in which a few persons, princes,
presidents, and diplomats—the latter indirectly—are able to condemn
millions of people to death and ruin at will, by the power of one word of
command, the power of one stroke of the pen."[74]

Another of Bertha von Suttner's tactics was to reach the powerful
through their wives. Henri Dunant had bet on the charity of the "highest
placed" women in founding the Red Cross and was successful. Suttner
wrote him: "The women of the aristocracy, the queens. Oh, dear God, if
we could put them to work, that is, if they would only think and feel as
we do, there would be no more war."[75]

She also appealed to them in her lecture, "Women and International Peace:"

> A great deal of power over the fate of the people lies today in the hands of the mighty of this earth. Later democracy will assume this power everywhere, at the moment it is still exercised by the potentates. And therefore, it would be suitable now, during the transitional period this moment offers, for queens and princesses to get together in a league for the support of pacifism. It only needs one to make a start, and almost all would follow. Alleviating war: no one turns away from this charitable task anymore. But the noble task of preventing it would fill the knowing, the understanding women among you with joyful satisfaction.[76]

In the first approach she attempted, Bertha wrote Empress Elisabeth of Austria in 1894:

> Your Majesty! They say the world belongs to the bold—I am quite aware that what I am doing is not only overly bold, it is perhaps even tactless. But where the issue surpasses personal matters, etiquette stops. Your Majesty knows that there is a movement that is aimed at establishing a system of international law that would eliminate the institution of war. The fact that I have joined this movement with my whole heart and soul, and place everything I possess in the way of devotion and of modest literary powers at its service, I do not expect you to know, but that is what gives me the courage to write this letter.
>
> What I implore would be a sign of approval from the hand of my Empress. Not for me, but for the great cause! It may take many generations to achieve what the present time is striving for; but it can only be achieved at all if the desire and the will of the greatest and noblest are with it.
>
> Such a statement—signed Elisabeth of Austria—going down in history; it is impossible to think what blessings might spring from it to the benefit of the fight for all cultural ideals.
>
> In profound respect, Your Majesty's humble servant, Bertha von Suttner-Kinsky.[77]

There was no response to this letter.

A year later Bertha started a renewed attack and sent the empress a copy of the second edition of her book *Lay Down Your Arms*. Whereupon the chief mistress of ceremonies sent her thanks, and wrote "that Her Majesty the Empress and Queen has . . . deigned to . . . accept the twelfth edition of your work, *Lay Down Your Arms,* for Her Highness's private library."[78]

The disappointment over this apparent failure was especially great because Suttner thought she had found a person of like mind in Empress Elisabeth—and in fact, she had. But it was not until 1984, when the empress's private diaries became known, that her great aversion to militarism came to light.[79] At the imperial court in Vienna, so strongly influenced by military tradition, and next to an emperor who felt himself to be the leading soldier of his empire, there lived in Elisabeth a woman who thought in a cosmopolitan way, was very well read, held on to republican ideas, and wrote rebellious poems against war and royalty:

> Who knows! If there were no princes
> There would be no hostility;
> It would be over, the costly thirsting
> For battles and for victory.[80]

But this was the wrong time. Elisabeth's only son, Crown Prince Rudolf, had committed suicide at Mayerling, and she herself was already very ill and very shy. She had lost her ability to make contact with other people, even when she felt an interest, as she may very well have felt in Bertha von Suttner's case. Elisabeth lived in her fantasies far away from the Viennese court. No one, not even the emperor, was able to get close to her anymore. Bertha had to bury her hope in her empress, a hope that would have been justified twenty years before.

In 1897 Bertha had an audience with Emperor Franz Joseph. The occasion was the call for peace made by the "Arbitration Alliance" in London. All heads of state were presented with a proposal for an international court of arbitration with 170 signatures of prominent members of the English clergy. The most prominent pacifist in each country was selected to present its sovereign with this list of signatures. Suttner, accompanied by Prince Wrede, was very excited. She wrote in her diary: "Mrs. Moser [her hairdresser] very touchingly blesses my task. At 9:45 I drive to the castle. . . . The whole hall full of generals. The walls covered with battle scenes and here we come—the peace delegation. After a short wait, admission."[81]

In her memoirs, Bertha explained why she did not have to wait long, as most audience visitors did. "This favor was not due to the fact that the executive board of the peace society handed over an 'arbitration petition,' but was simply because my escort was a prince—at court everything goes by rank and title."[82]

"The Emperor took a few steps forward. 'It is very kind of you—I thank you very much for taking the trouble to come to me.' Whereupon

I say my little speech—he takes the roll and the book and places them on the table: 'Will look at it in detail. But will it be successful?'—'The success lies in attracting the attention of Your Majesty to the cause.' The emperor thanks us again—curtsy. And we leave."[83]

One can hardly call such results a success. Bertha, however, had not expected more: "The words that were sown were mere seeds, or a better illustration—blows of a hammer. New ideas are like nails—the old conditions and institutions like thick walls. It is not enough to hold a pointed nail against them and deliver only one blow—the nail has to be hit hundreds and hundreds of times—on the head—for it to sit fast."[84]

Later she changed her mind about Franz Joseph's "peaceful attitude." Referring to him as "Prohaska," in the same way she called Wilhelm II "Lehmann," she wrote: "Oh, I have sized Prohaska up correctly, as protector of all the clergy—enemy of the Hague conference, impassioned militarist."[85]

What do all the efforts for peace amount to when "the father of the country goes to a shooting competition and says of good marksmanship: 'That's the main thing.' Oh, what a horizon."[86]

She got angry when the same worn-out phrases were repeated at official visits while the real conflicts were carefully avoided. This was the case in 1903 when Edward VII visited Vienna. She had hoped for a reconciliation between Austria and England. But alas, "The toasts at the imperial table yesterday vacuous—the same old song. Franz Joseph emphasizes that there is no conflict of interests—and therefore, he hoped, no disturbance in relations. Just think of private people talking like that as hosts to their neighbors. For an answer, Edward VII makes Franz Joseph a general in his army. You know how much Franz Joseph likes to play soldier. A clown's show.—And the menu, of all things—and that's something the whole newspaper world should read about: *soufflé au Schmankerl* [tidbit souffle]."[87]

When Wilhelm II came for a visit a few days later, she criticized: "Wilhelm arrived. Ringstrasse closed to traffic. The masses put up with it and even cheer!"[88] And: "Great, great joy in view, rejoice ye people," she scoffs in her diary. "When Prohaska visits Lehmann, the former will be shown the new field artillery weapons!"[89]

And in reference to Austria's problems with Italy: "What is Prohaska thinking about at a time when a reconciliation with Italy is sorely needed? About new Hungarian and Austrian *landwehr* [militia] cannons! . . . I assure you, what's standing in the way of the movement at the moment is first and foremost those two, Prohaska and Lehmann."[90]

Both emperors, however, liked to call themselves "peace emperor."

"Can one have this title simultaneously with Supreme Military Commander? We have two emperors of peace in Europe and they have prevented the Hague conference from being a peace conference."[91]

After she let her fictitious princes of peace have their say in her novel *Schach der Qual,* she wrote with resignation:

> How far away does fulfillment lie? How long will it take the views and convictions I placed in the mouths of crowned leaders to become habitual thinking in those spheres, to become the desired direction? Brought up with a soldier's spirit, surrounded by a wall of defense against modern ideas, occupied with government business to the point of exhaustion, with the compilation of firing lists that show 33,000 pieces of wild game were shot. How are they supposed to find out what is fomenting in the souls of the people, in the spirit of the century?[92]

Of course, Bertha eagerly took in all the information she could about Emperor Franz Joseph's private life, especially when she was the guest of the former Crown Princess Stephanie and her new husband, Count Lónyay, in Oroszvár. Here they "did not speak well of Prohaska," as she confided to her diary: "Emperor has no heart. He can't help the fact that he is stupid, but he is also without feelings."[93]

Since she met with practically no interest in pacifism in Oroszvár, she focused on the gossip, most of all, of course, on talk about Crown Prince Rudolf and Mayerling. Count Lónyay, for instance, said "that the crown prince had a murderous nature, often threatened the life of his wife."[94] Then Baroness Gagern did her best with her opinion on the crown prince tragedy: "Fifty years after the death of the emperor she will present her story. A banquet: Prince Coburg, Baltazzi, Wolkenstein, Vetsera. That night crown prince tells Vetsera that emperor does not permit divorce. She took revenge with a knife during the night. When he woke up, he shot her first, then himself." These revelations were followed by entertainment appropriate to the Lónyay house: "In the evening, table tipping. The little table really runs."[95] (Meanwhile, the "secret of Mayerling" has been solved: Rudolf shot his seventeen-year-old lover, Mary Vetsera, and then himself.)

The reason for the invitation was not Stephanie's interest in the peace cause, as Bertha had hoped, but something else. The lady in waiting "ordered . . . a feature story. It is desired that the world learns of the domestic happiness and the domestic splendor."[96]

As soon as she got back to Vienna, Suttner got down to work. The feature appeared at the beginning of January 1907 in the *Neue Freie*

Presse. She was not proud of the article at all and wrote in her diary: "I'm a little ashamed. It's an advertisement . . . not worthy of Bertha von Suttner."[97]

She was quite right to criticize herself. Karl Kraus responded immediately, and under the title, "Chamber Maid," in the *Fackel,* he called the article, the "most lamentable gossip from aristocratic servants' rooms." "Twenty-three lines about Countess Lónyay's spitz! That's too much! The greatest poets have done worse in the *Neue Freie Presse,*" and "Praise God in the highest, if he protects us from strong-willed women" (Bertha von Suttner was occasionally referred to this way). The scorn went far beyond this particular incident, however, and also attacked Suttner's peace work. Kraus ridiculed the "ambition . . . to put an end to the Russian-Japanese war with a telegram to the President of the United States."[98]

The next year, Bertha did not accept Stephanie's invitation and wrote in her diary: "I'm not going to Oroszvár. No, I do not have the energy for royal visits anymore. And while it's so cold. Would have to buy a fur first."[99] Two years later she went again after all, but did not enjoy the visit very much: "The couple of the house pretends to be socialistic and republican. . . . But the socialism is limited to founding poor houses and tolerance 'without distinctions of religion, except for Jews'— 'Incidentally, Jews are also human beings.'"[100]

Bertha was undoubtedly partial to titles and positions, especially when they were coupled with political power. At the same time she was very critical of this power and was horrified at the way it was often used to make basic political decisions for an entire people. She had one of her characters in a novel say, "I was . . . filled with a great disgust over the kitchen of gossip and intrigues where the fateful soup is brewed for the unsuspecting masses. Well, people have no idea what petty means the great men who make world history employ, what petty aims they pursue: issues of personal envy, conglomerations of lies and mistakes and coincidences from which the mighty events proceed that are interpreted as an expression of God's will or as a world event caused by nature. It's the other way around: the great men up there know nothing about the masses; they lack the ability to comprehend their sufferings and hopes."[101]

Regarding the "Highnesses'" pleasures and interests, she complained with resignation: "Oh, if only the interest the various sovereigns had in the things that are critical now were greater! . . . They watch target practice and they honor marksmen's celebrations with their presence; and the instructions for the coming autumn maneuvers are already being carefully worked out."[102] "If you think that such people have it in their power to raise the white flag and don't do it—don't even try it—it makes you shudder."[103]

The biggest problems for the pacifists were created by the German emperor. From the very day of his coronation, they were afraid that he constituted a serious threat to European peace. His conduct and his speeches were very militaristic. "Whenever the man opens his mouth, I go into a mild rage,"[104] Bertha wrote of the young Wilhelm.

She got especially angry over the connection of militarism and Christianity, which she thought was particularly blasphemous. He used the combination often in his speeches. Bertha wrote: "Meanwhile, Wilhelm has to my mind, given the people whose 'earthly master' he is, another good lesson, . . . one cannot be a good soldier without being a good Christian at the same time."[105]

In 1890, she still thought she could not give such a person a copy of her antiwar book: "[T]he mystical-megalomanic, bellicose-adventurous spirit that drives this restless Hohenzollern will not shy away at my words. He thinks he is a demi-god: 'One must not manipulate the meaning of imperial words,' is his most recent peculiar saying. We will not be kept from doing it—we will not, for any ruler, lie down in the dust so that the dust keeps us from seeing anymore."[106]

The acute antiliberal policy in Berlin resulted in trials, arrests and prison sentences for people who had shared Bertha's views for many years. Among them were the professors Ludwig Quidde and Friedrich Wilhelm Förster. "Now the liberal papers are griping that so much darkness is coming out of the *marvelous* German unity. As though light and liberty could grow from a regime built upon blood and iron. No, you cannot bring cannons and the arts to blossom at the same time."[107]

When Wilhelm and the king of Italy sent Queen Victoria their congratulations in 1900 at the end of the Transvaal war, Bertha raged: "Congratulations on the slaughtered blood of the land. Oh, these throned monsters! Their 'historical' education has suffocated every bit of noble morality in them."[108]

But it was not in Bertha's nature to lament for a long time. She wanted to do something, or at least try to do something, in this case have some kind of influence on the emperor. She was too thoroughly convinced of the power of the "mighty." She wrote to Fried: "Wilhelm II wanted ships and demanded them and *has* them. If he had wanted the peace congress just as badly—he would have it. Since the economic situation would truly favor the latter over the former."[109]

In addition to Carnegie and Albert of Monaco, the fourth son of Emperor Wilhelm, August Wilhelm, seemed to her to be a suitable mediator. She had been told that he "could be won over to [her] ideas—only loves art, science, hates war and the military, attends workers' meetings."[110]

Suttner also tried to establish contact through other relatives of the emperor, but failed.

During her Berlin trip in 1905 she tried to get an audience with the German emperor after all and wrote to Fried: "Wilhelm II hates the idea of the court of arbitration. He wanted to prevent the tribunal, and he succeeded in preventing the armament stop. The restrictions that make the treaties almost worthless are *his* text. He will only endorse the future conference if the agenda contains only articles of war. He hates ententes, and that's why he is mixing into the English-French agreement—and even at the cost of war. Well, making him modern will be hard. I hardly think he will receive me and if he does, all that will happen is a pat on the shoulder."[111]

The audience was not granted, and Suttner fumed on: "Wilhelm gave a terrifying speech," she wrote in her diary somewhere around 1910. "Arming is the only guaranty of peace. The grace of God. Against women. Military virtues."[112] "Yes, the kings are beginning to realize—but not the essential one"—by whom she meant Wilhelm II, of course.[113]

The German Reich under Wilhelm II continued to arm heavily. Bertha wrote in 1905: "How these Germans always think it is dangerous and damaging when work for conciliation and harmony is supposed to be carried out somewhere."[114] "It's a disgrace how obstinate the former land of poets and thinkers now is in regard to the new spirit. It's become a land of noblemen and knaves."[115]

Fried admitted once in anger: "Sometimes you catch yourself wishing that the German arrogance would be smashed flat by war."[116] "Germany is the black and weak spot in the peace movement."[117]

Every time powerful leaders got together, the pacifists placed their hopes on the outcome. They thought personal attachments among the mighty might be able to improve relations between nations and raise the threshold to war. For this reason royal visits to relatives, hunting meets, weddings, and funerals were eagerly and expectantly observed, and the importance of the bond of royal blood highly overestimated.

The expectations placed in the new English king, Edward VII, were already dampened by his first speech to parliament. Bertha wrote to Frédéric Passy in 1901: "We've never heard a noble speech from such a high place (with the exception of Nikolaus II). That's sad. People ought to have philosphers and poets as their regents. They content themselves, however, with soldiers and indolents."[118] And to Fried she wrote: "Well, how did you like the English king's speech? All our hope that something will happen to retard the Mars that has been released among those crazed with the fever of war and the idolators of militarism is in vain. No dying queen [Victoria], marrying queen [Wilhelmina], no royal succession can help—not even the plague can help."[119]

Later, however, this underestimated Edward VII turned into a pacifist hopeful. The pacifists watched Edward's visit to Emperor Wilhelm and Emperor Franz Joseph in 1907 with great sympathy and hope, in view of the escalating differences in the European system of alliances. Bertha wrote in the *Friedenswarte:* "Edward VII made friends with Japan, France, Spain, Italy and is now also offering his hand to Germany and Austria. These trips are not attempts at surrounding or reconciliation." These meetings were intended "to disperse the repulsive clouds that had spread over England and Germany from the inkwells of the chauvinists and weapons-interests on both sides."[120] But Edward lacked the right partners in his efforts at making friends—both Wilhelm and Franz Joseph were standoffish.

At the peace congress in London in 1908, Suttner finally got together with the English royal couple. She was received at Buckingham Palace as a member of a congress delegation. In a paper read at the reception, Edward VII was addressed as a "peacemaker." "Edward's answer and the tone of voice he used to deliver it, would be reason enough to call the conference a total success. We don't need to negotiate anymore—the King has chosen the congress as a platform for accepting the title 'peacemaker' before the whole world and to declare that his goal assists our goal, and our work, his work."[121]

Bertha's confrontations with the monarchs of Belgium, Holland, and the three Scandinavian countries produced barely more than noncommittal, hackneyed phrases about peace. The invitation from the Rumanian queen, Elisabeth, who wrote poetry under the name Carmen Sylva, also led to disappointment even though Carmen Sylva was one of the signatories of the peace declaration for women at the first Hague conference.

In 1911 Bertha was received at Peles Castle in Sinaia. The Rumanian queen, Elisabeth, was "dressed in white, more like draped, wound with scarves, rosy, radiating face." The table conversation centered around wars, including the Russian-Japanese. "I told [them] about Carnegie. . . . Then I'm taken through the castle by the royal couple—paintings, artifacts, Murillo, Renaissance—study magnificent. Queen shows me her needlework. Tells me something would have been missing in her life if she had not gotten to know me."[122]

Her impression of the visit was contradictory: on the one hand Bertha was flattered, on the other, her hopes in the mighty were diminishing. "[P]eace will not come from *such as these*. Workers' demonstrations offer . . . more hope!"[123]

12

Her Confederates

The late nineteenth century was a time of collapse for the old order and of attempts to create new orders: socialism, the Christian Social movement, the women's movement, the peace movement, Zionism; and in smaller dimensions, innumerable new kinds of societies worked out principles that were supposed to lead to a better future.

Bertha von Suttner concerned herself with many of these new movements. She fought against discrimination directed at women, against an all too prudish upbringing of young people; against the class society, trade barriers, racial hatred, and nationalism; against religious intolerance, the death penalty, and duelling; against animal experiments, and a great deal more; and she always supported greater freedom, tolerance, "truth," "justice," and "reconciliation." She showed openly—also in her novels—her joy in the variety of the "modern" movements and welcomed the spirit of the awakening. "So, everywhere, on all sides, this addiction to muster the power to make propaganda for ideas that are supposed to steer the course of culture in special tracks—and despite the sameness of the means, what a difference there is in the goals!"[1]

She was firmly convinced that a "noble person" had to work openly for these goals since this was the only way to fight evil and elevate man to a higher, more noble plane. "1/1000th of the world consists of a screaming pack that spreads terror and 1/10,000,000,000,000th of good people who openly avow their goodness. The others are all silent cowards, none of them dare *say* anything," she complained to Theodor Herzl.[2]

Inter-Parliamentary Union

The Inter-Parliamentary Union (IPU) was closely connected with the peace movement, was even a part of it for a time. During its early history, Bertha von Suttner played a not insignificant role. The IPU was supposed to be something of a seed for a future European parliament, even a world parliament, a place where international solidarity ranked above national egoism. Its members were parliamentarians from most of the European countries. Around the turn of the century they numbered some fifteen hundred. They were people who made it their responsibility to back the international court of arbitration and disarmament in their own parliaments. (The socialists always boycotted the IPU.)

In the first phase, the union leaned heavily on the international peace movement. They held their congresses at the same time and in the same city as the peace movement, but as a separate event. Suttner even spoke out for holding a common congress: "The two bodies are basically only two forms of the same movement, belonging close together, one having emerged from the other: upper and lower house of the same parliament, so to speak."[3] When possible she pointed out the importance of the IPU: "These events actually represent the more important branch of the peace movement."[4]

She tried in many newspaper articles and lectures to explain the principles of the union, especially on the occasion of the IPU conference in Vienna in 1903. Full of pride, she wrote to Fried: "How this institution has developed in the short twelve years. It's marvelous.—The fact that it was *I* who brought about the founding of the Austrian group in 1891, is something I don't talk about, of course. You should not remind such great, distinguished gentlemen of their modest origins—that's not good." "630 participants have registered for the conference. How it all grows—and our opponents still do not notice it!"[5]

She was, by contrast not at all pleased with the efficiency of the IPU in the national parliaments. In her opinion, the IPU members did not do enough to back disarmament and the court of arbitration and viewed the conferences "more as pleasure trips; the union will gradually have to limit itself to members who really work and act according to the intentions of the union—who do not vote enthusiastically for all the cannon purchases without even mentioning the idea of a court of arbitration."[6]

Even as an international organization, the union frequently excited Suttner's displeasure: "Inter-Parliamentary Union. They say: the German group—oh, my God, are the others better? What have the Interparliamentarians done about the Boer War? Didn't open their mouths."[7] And another time she wrote: "If they weren't all so mealy-mouthed!"[8] And again two years later she wrote: "Very annoyed about . . . the delegates. Irresponsible, cowardly pack—belong to the Inter-Parliamentary Union and not a syllable that it has to be different and cannot go on like this."[9]

In the course of the years, the IPU intentionally made a clear distinction between itself and the peace movement, emphasized its independence, and felt superior to the peace societies. After the death of her friend, Pirquet, the chairman of the Austrian IPU, Bertha felt a strong reservation on the side of the parliamentarians, especially the new president, Ernst von Plener. She thought he was "politically arrogant" and believed that he "looked down" on her.[10] She found that he showed far too little interest in pacifism and was negligent and careless in his work for the IPU. She complained to Fried: "I was livid with rage over Plener. Austria is the Hottentot region of pacifism."[11] And: "*He* is the president of our interparliamentary group. . . . [T]here may very well be armaments animators among statesmen loyal to the government, but as members of the union—that's pure betrayal."[12]

In the purely masculine society of the IPU, Suttner felt she was not taken seriously. In her novel, *Der Menschheit Hochgedanken,* she has an IPU member who is an opponent of the peace movement say, "I am a friend of peace, belong to the Inter-Parliamentarian Union, but it is not compatible with the dignity of a politician to join a society in which— you know, though—a woman—an old bluestocking—excuse me, spinster, I have high regard for women, you know, but they have to know their place."[13]

Bertha was treated with noticeable arrogance by the Austrian and the German parliamentarians, even when she appeared at the IPU congresses. She had a particularly unpleasant time of it in 1908 at the Inter-Parliamentarian Conference in Berlin. She was not given a place of honor at the opening. No one took notice of the Nobel Prize winner, who had done so much for the IPU. Fried wrote on the subject: "The fact that an Inter-Parliamentary Conference could take place in Berlin and was even welcomed with goodwill by the government was her gratification. She herself knew that it was she who had made it possible for this change in the situation to come about in the first place, through decades of hard work. And the pioneers in Berlin are very often seated in the balcony."[14]

When the IPU did not invite her in 1910 to an official banquet in honor of the expert of international law, Lammasch, under the pretext that this was an occasion for "gentlemen without ladies," Suttner complained about the "undeserved discrimination." "Saying 'lady' because there were no other ladies present, is not a sound argument. It was my place, as laureate of the peace prize, to be there. Would a banquet of intellectuals in Paris—even if the wives of the delegates were not present—exclude Madame Curie because she is a woman?"[15]

Bertha had to defend herself in a number of newspaper articles against the defamation of the peace movement by IPU members. But she also pointed to their common meeting points, to their common origins, to the necessity of cooperation so as to be more effective in working for their common goals. She was very pleased when Count Albert Apponyi, the chairman of the Hungarian IPU group and a judge on the Hague Court of Arbitration, celebrated Peace Day in 1911 together with the Budapest Peace Society. She placed this incident before the arrogant Berlin parliament as a good example and warned them not to deny the relationship between the two organizations: "Wanting to establish a contradiction between the general peace movement and the Inter-Parliamentary Union is just as unjustified as wanting to call this or that limb of a tree the independent and far superior opposite of the tree."[16]

She celebrated the successes of the IPU as she did her own. When the English cabinet invited representatives of the IPU groups meeting in London for talks in 1906, Suttner was enthralled and wrote Fried: "Great, great news . . . With one move, this organization has now stepped into the foreground of the political activity of the whole world." She wanted to go to London, hoping that the issue of disarmament would finally be discussed by the English government and the IPU: "I have to be there. . . . I have to report to the stupid Austrians what is going on there. That's going to be one of the greatest stages in the triumphal march of pacifism: the conference *invited* by the cabinet! Not having to ask the minister first with a few gracious words, but called by the premier himself. Of course a reception by the king."[17]

She openly admitted the advantages of the IPU over the peace movement: "The union, an unofficial, so to speak statesmanly organization comprised mostly of experienced practical politicians and working under the eyes and auspices of the governments, does not work as casually as the peace movement, on the one hand, and with much more certainty of success on the other, because it wisely limits itself to working toward the next achievable concession step by step and eliminates everything from its negotiations that could be interpreted as interference in the internal politics of its own or a foreign country."

The peace movement should not be underestimated because of this. It had a different purpose: "The congresses of the societies have more freedom—perhaps even more naïveté. They can aim at more distant goals, do not have to dwell on the next phase and can dare to include more distant issues—like abolishing customs barriers, religious tolerance, etc. in its platform." The peace congresses had developed into a "voice for the awakening 'cultural conscience'" and did not shy away from "protesting with fiery indignation against atrocities perpetrated under the sign of brutality." They were in any case, "so much bolder because they are more impotent." Step by step the IPU, as a "practitioner of peace," would reach the great goal of the peace movement in the course of time.[18]

Socialism

"The deplorable state of affairs in society is not a product of inescapable natural laws, but the product of awkward social institutions. We simply have to create other institutions," Suttner demanded already in *The Machine Age*.[19]

The "noble people," a phrase she used sometimes as a synonym for "intellectuals" or "learned persons," had a special task, particularly in the social battle. They did not work for themselves, they strove for improvements for those with fewer rights—in the service of humanity. "Surely no one can deny that the social issue fills our present day with immense importance and presses for a solution? The working class is tired of suffering, and there are some among us who are tired of *watching* it suffer. I, for my part, can no longer look on idly, with all the unnecessary pain, burdens, and dangers under which my fellow men are suffering."[20]

With this standpoint, both of the Suttners placed themselves in opposition to their family and their social surroundings, whose position in social matters Bertha described this way: "What they were afraid of was that someone would tear their property from them by force to distribute it among the poor, and then goodbye riches—goodbye, too, to all the comforts, because, if there are no more poor devils around, who would see to the comforts?"[21]

She also talked about how the "reactionaries" intended to conquer social problems: "Oh, bah, we'll soon take care of that rabble: all we need is some good, strict discipline, tough laws, exile, military intervention. If workers strike, soldiers have to help out in the mines and factories—shoot at the workers if necessary; some state aid in the way of accident insurance and old age pensions—along with diligent emphasis on moderation, religious obedience, strong faith, and submissive allegiance. All of this should make the thing work."[22]

According to Bertha, the people affected, especially the workers, did not have the might to fight for their rights by themselves, if only because they could be accused of selfishness. They needed the help of people with property and education. For that reason she proposed "cooperation between workers and intellectuals." She demanded new "people's universities" that would have two objectives: first, to educate the masses (for liberals and for Suttner, that was the same as "ennobling"), and second, to educate the upper classes to "social awareness, to an understanding of human solidarity."[23]

Both were necessary to arrive at a better future: the social understanding of what had so far been the advantaged classes and the education and training of the lower classes. All of them had to make an equal effort for progress. Suttner in her novel, *Before the Storm,* wrote: "Political rights of the masses? Absolutely. But before that, the masses have to be educated to morality. They have to rise above their coarseness." And "since in the first, second and third estates, meanness and blindness are still rampant, you socialists think it is enough to give the power to the fourth estate, for justice and wisdom to move in?"[24]

She argued energetically against the position that social democracy was directed exclusively toward the working class. She has one of her middle-class protagonists in the novel clearly say: "I am a social democrat. And they exist in all the estates. We do not stand for class rights, but for human rights."

She could never make friends with narrow-minded party spirit. As a true liberal, she defended the achievements of the individual. Social democracy, according to the novel, "threatens the rights of the individual. It is a kind of tyranny: the unlimited dictatorship of the majority. . . . Now it is a minority that terrorizes and rapes the masses—but what will happen when the masses rape the minority? . . . Personal freedom, personal freedom! Don't you see how this precious good is being endangered by your socialistic 'doctrine?'"[25]

The Suttner hero of the novel protests against the accusation that he is fighting socialism and answers that he even looks on "approvingly at the way socialism tries to fight other tyrannies. But if it should come into power—and that is possible in the not too distant future considering the way its membership is growing—when the socialization of all means of production has taken place and the scheduled regulation of production is to be put into effect, then the spirit of personal freedom will revolt against this regulation. The individual does not want to let itself be brutalized, either."[26]

She despised class war as much as she did wars about nationalities and religion, and she continually confronted socialists with her own ideal of "brotherhood," which would not allow a class war.

A big impression was made on her in 1903 by the words of the

American socialist and millionaire, Gylord Wilshire, whom she quoted with obvious delight: "You know what the foundation of socialism is called?—Brotherhood." It is "the same magic word" that also lies at the bottom of the peace movement.[27]

Bertha wrote: "You have to watch out for class prejudices—from above and below—also watch out for racial prejudices. In general cultural matters, people cannot be grouped according to the country and class they belong to, but according to their convictions, and according to the degree of their ethical soul-thermometer."[28]

Bertha's criticism of the socialists did not weaken the great sympathy she always professed to feel for the ideals of this movement. The internationalism that lay at the bottom of pacifism and social democracy alike, seemed to her to be a guaranty of productive cooperation. She closely observed what prominent European socialists had to say about the peace issue and was thrilled at the unmistakable positions taken by Liebknecht and Bebel, for example. In 1892 she wrote Carneri, to whom she usually complained about German nationalism: "The only reasonable people in the hall were [Karl] Liebknecht and [August] Bebel. The former called from the tribune, 'Lay Down Your Arms,' the second said an agreement with France would be in order."[29] And she wrote: "The social democrats and the fear of them will bring the world forward after all. . . . They take a resolute position on the peace issue."[30]

When Liebknecht printed one of her antiwar stories in the socialist party organ, *Vorwärts,* and what was more, during the election campaign, she wrote to Carneri, not without pride: "The *Deutsche Volksblatt* calls me 'The Red Bertha' because of this."[31]

Like most of the pacifists, she was entirely on the side of the socialists in the 1895 conflict with Wilhelm II. The emperor had made the celebrations commemorating the Battle of Sedan a "Victory Jubilee," as Bertha called it, with a lot of sword rattling in the direction of France. Angry over such a big demonstration of militarism, the German social democrats sent their French comrades a telegram with their "protest against war and chauvinism." "Long live the people's sovereignty." The irritated Wilhelm then said in public that there was "a bunch of people without a fatherland," "who did not deserve to be called German and whom the other people should keep at bay, and if this did not succeed, then he would call upon his guard to destroy such elements."[32]

A storm of indignation followed these words. Karl Liebknecht was arrested, and soon afterward the pacifist and publisher of the magazine, *Ethische Kultur,* Friedrich Wilhelm Förster, in Berlin. He had accused Wilhelm II of "taking it out on a great political party of his country in words such as those that have only been heard before in world history immediately prior to the outbreak of civil war." In the speech for his defense in court, Förster said he regarded it his duty to raise his voice in protest against the incitement of the working class. He worked "independently of all parties and all religious faiths" and did not belong to the social democratic party. It was, however, a question of morals to stand up for those who are treated unjustly. He wanted to tell the misinformed emperor "that the social democratic comrades were not the dangerous and despicable people they must have been shown to be to the bearer of state authority."[33] Förster was sentenced to three months in prison. Bertha commented to Fried: "But I foresee an era of great oppression in the united Germany. Confiscate everything and lock it up." "I could run up the wall! When will it be our turn?"[34]

A quarter of a year later, she had new reason for being excited, this time because of the Munich pacifist, moralist, and historian, Professor Ludwig Quidde, who was sentenced for offense against the sovereign. The reason was his little book about Caligula, in which he all too clearly drew parallels between the brutal ruler of antiquity and Wilhelm II. A harsh wind was blowing against the German pacifists and social democrats.

Professor Wilhelm Förster, the father of the sentenced Friedrich Wilhelm Förster, also a pacifist and moralist, answered Suttner's sympathetic letter: "You are right, it is a sad time, especially for the Germans who live in such disgraceful servitude, under a regime of such a dangerous mixture of good and evil that a large part of the German people already find themselves in a true frenzy beyond good and evil."[35]

Suttner openly professed her sympathy for Bebel and Liebknecht in her newspaper when they were insulted at a socialist meeting in Lille in 1896 by German and French nationalists alike for being "without a fatherland": "It is strange how internationally unanimous the nationalists are in the fight against the international idea."[36]

At that time she still hoped that she would fight the fight for peace together with the socialists. In fact she even thought it was certain and self-evident that she would do it. Her hopes were not only reinforced by Liebknecht's attitude toward her books, but also by the Austrian socialist, Engelbert Pernerstorfer, who was active from time to time in the Viennese peace society as well. "Pernerstorfer is absolutely wonderful.— He was one of the most enthusiastic speakers at the founding meeting of my peace society."[37]

The fact that cooperation between bourgeois and socialist pacifist movements was possible is seen in the Swiss example. There, the social democrats as a body joined the International Peace Bureau, which was founded by bourgeois conservatives. The second president of this bureau, the Belgian Henri Lafontaine, was one of the leaders in the Belgian workers' movement.[38]

But the hopes for international cooperation between conservative and socialist pacifists did not hold up against political reality. At both of the international congresses of the social democrats in Brussels in 1891 and 1893, a guideline was laid out stipulating "that only the creation of the socialistic social order can bring about peace among peoples, that the energetic protest by the proletariat against the lust for war is the only means to avert the terrible catastrophe of a world war, and that world peace can only be established by the collapse of capitalism."[39]

Suttner and Fried thought this attitude was "untenable." There was not such a thing as an "only" way to peace. There were a number of ways. And all initiatives that worked for peace were to be welcomed without exception. Everyone who wanted peace should work together and not place party interests above the interests of peace. But for the socialists, the basic principle of the class war stood above the peace ideal, much to the sorrow of the "bourgeois" pacifists.

A unanimous resolution passed by the international congress of socialist organizations in 1896 in London made "economic conflicts, not religious or national" conflicts responsible for the "primary cause of war." First of all, the working classes of all countries had to "gain political power in order to eliminate the capitalistic method of production and at the same time to deny governments, which are the tools of the capitalistic class, the means to maintain the current circumstances." The call "Lay down your arms" echoed in the workers' movement "just like every other appeal to a feeling of humanity in the capitalist class. Only the working class can seriously have the will to take power and create world peace."[40]

These statements called forth indignation in the international peace movement. Friedrich Wilhelm Förster criticized the "condescending phrases" directed at nonproletarians: "They are none other than a repetition of the ancient talk of a chosen people and have nothing to do with the idea of world peace, which demands honest modesty of each participant in favor of the equally recognized cooperation of the other." As long as the working class turned "to warring instincts" to such a high degree, it had no right "to eulogize itself as the protector of world peace."[41]

For the rest of her life, Suttner argued against what she thought was a much too one-sided materialistic interpretation of history. She held fast to the idea that individual people, not only social classes, were very important to the question of war and peace:

> I do not believe that the American war *only* took place for humane motives or the Russian *only* to free Christians. But I have just as little belief in the force of *economic interests alone.* The whole system consists of thousands of wheels and smaller wheels. And the people who turn the wheels are politicians, diplomats, kings, military leaders. When a Skobelev says, "I want my war so that I can be famous" or when Bismarck forges the Emser Dispatch and Eugénie plans *"une petite guerre"* beforehand—then the outbreak of war has little or nothing to do with the profits of capitalism.[42]

Bertha continued the discussion about the value of the personality in politics and argued against the socialist doctrine of class war.

When the socialist *Vorwärts* called the Spanish-American War about Cuba in 1898 a "sugar war," Suttner wrote Fried that the newspaper might "be right that the war resulted in profits for the sugar factories, but there is no proof whatsoever that the war was undertaken solely for this profit. The social democrats (the class-party ones) are also getting to be so one-sided. As the clerics attribute everything evil to waning faith, those party people want to blame everything on the economic interests of the bourgeois. Chauvinism, and in the American war, human indignation over Cuban suffering, etc., etc., certainly played a role in the outbreak of war—quite apart from the sugar interests."[43]

The peace movement does not need a "red ribbon around the white flag," but: "*At the same time,* the ethical, the ideal, the religious (that means enthusiastic) element has to work with the *economic* element in the transition of the world. With the current economic order, no peace—but also, with the current militarism and code of force, no just economic order either. If one waits for the other, neither will succeed. *Together!*"[44]

This cooperation did not mean that the one movement would lose itself in the other. Quite the contrary, each would have to retain its own characteristics. Suttner called the social democrats the "only openly avowed friends of peace. We should not amalgamate with them because of that, however. We don't help them that way. We can also have social democrats among us. We have to show our raison d'être in this: other 'elements' than those of the 'pack' also protest against war, out of real disgust, not as a point on a party platform or out of fear of the protectors of 'order.'"[45]

She thought one important difference in socialist peace work was their attitude toward soldiers: "I do not concur with the proposal for a soldiers' strike made at our congress. That belongs to socialists' congresses. What we want is new *laws,* not rebellion against the law. We want militarism to be abolished and made superfluous from *above.* Nikolaus already wanted that, and maybe he will eventually get his colleagues to want it, too."

The socialists could do what they wanted. "Her" pacifism, however, had to toe the line: "Friends of peace and soldiers do not need to be enemies to strive to annihilate each other. They should be united in a higher union: in the army of guaranteed international law."[46]

When Fried blamed the murder of Empress Elisabeth in 1898 on the military education of the assassin, the Italian anarchist Lucheni, Suttner shortened the article drastically and explained to Fried:

> I do not think it is a just method of fighting to attribute Lucheni's crime to his upbringing in the barracks. That is like the conservatives who always scream: "modern school"—or "socialist depravity"—or "Jewish influence" whenever anybody does something bad. We have to remember that our paper must never say anything illogical just because of the opportunity. Soldiers read us, too, noble soldiers. They would think us unjust if we insinuate that Lucheni murdered the Empress *because* he was a cavalryman. It is true that the barracks did not make him more refined—and that stayed in the article.[47]

Suttner's confrontation with military tradition in the Kinsky family certainly played a role when she insisted: "The future will stop braiding wreaths of glory altogether. But the heroes' glory of the past does not need to be denigrated because of it."[48]

She did not turn against all soldiers as such, if only for the reason that she believed they were being cheated themselves:

> And it is genuine patriotic enthusiasm, true sacrificial courage which drives the electrified masses and the individual to fight with the rest and to persist. If war were only to use unleashed vices, wild instincts of hate and the desire to kill, of the sport of the manhunt and of greed to operate it, today's mankind, with its highly developed moral and religious ideals, would have shaken it off fairly quickly; but unfortunately, it also exacts human virtues as its due: devotion, loyalty, boldness, bravery, yes, and even piety—for all military deeds are accompanied by the blessing of a priest. . . . War is in fact such a conglomeration of injustices, that not only do those who wage it commit wrong, they are also wronged against.[49]

Suttner resolutely defended herself against socialist accusations that the "bourgeois" peace movement wanted to leave the world with all its injustices as it was and was averse to any change because it meant a danger of war: "It is true that the social democrats accuse us of wanting to maintain the status quo," she wrote Fried. "The misunderstanding, however, lies in our wanting to have the status quo assured only in respect to changes made in the use of force—not in respect to legal and organizational changes."[50]

She was still not understood. The socialist parties closed themselves off from the peace movement, boycotted the IPU, and in doing so, condemned it to failure. They ridiculed and scorned the czar's peace manifesto and the Hague peace conference.

Bertha bemoaned the damage that took place because of this lack of cooperation in an increasingly tense international situation. She took the rejection of the Hague conference especially badly: "The Hague is a farce and the czar a dangerous warmonger—this dogma will be repeated in all the German camps. How the social democrats have fallen into the *trap* laid by the chauvinists!"[51]

The attacks made by the socialists always hit her very hard. "It is repulsive how the German socialists always fall upon the bourgeois who assist their ideals. . . . [H]ow different the English are!" And on another occasion she sighed: "As though only workers were human beings!"[52]

But the attractiveness of the socialist ideal of international solidarity was undiminished—and just as steady was the disappointment over the fact that after the turn of the century, the socialists drifted more and more into national channels. In cases of conflict they did not automatically think along international lines, but national ones.

The socialists achieved special importance in parliament during the debates on the war budget. Bertha placed all her hopes on them, but she was disappointed once more: "These cannon-exalting social democrats are outrageous. I hope a storm will rise in their own camp over this. Such a stupid idea, that you can use cannons to protect yourself from being shot dead—whatever it is that's being suggested from above— these people take it up now—unbelievable! Where are the 'proletarians of the world,' etc.? In the end, our party of the friends of peace is the only consistent one."[53]

But she was always quickly reconciled and never gave up hope in social democracy. At a meeting of the International Socialist Office in Brussels in 1906, the German and French socialists, under Bebel and Jaurès, agreed to do everything in their power to maintain peace. Suttner called this "a highly important, promising sign of the new spirit that is dawning." Of course this battle for peace was not supposed to be fueled by "party slogans" because: "If a fire threatens to spread, everyone whose property and precious livelihood would be swallowed up by the flames ought to hurry to douse the blaze without others having to call: help, help!"[54]

Bertha's enthusiasm for the writer Upton Sinclair was also partly due to his activity in the socialist movement. In 1911 she wrote in her diary: "Still reading Upton Sinclair at night. He is right about socialism."[55] "In the evening I read 'Jungle.' It opens up a new world. A world of sorrow!—Upton Sinclair—who sent me the book himself—is a great writer. . . . At night my dreams are completely be-jungled." "Marvelous work of art and a great social masterpiece."[56]

In 1909 she recommended to Fried: "But read Upton Sinclair's appeal.—Splendid.—And that's what will happen. We reformistic and revolutionary and integral pacifists plod on like gravitational snails, while behind us the greyhounds will storm ahead, and they will simply say: 'We don't want to anymore.'"[57]

Bertha von Suttner advocated social reforms and broader suffrage. And the more the socialists continued to ridicule the "Baroness," the more she was denounced in "her" circles, the middle class and the aristocracy, as "Red Bertha."

Leo Tolstoy

There were many points on which Bertha von Suttner and Leo Tolstoy agreed. His dislike for worldly power and the dogmas of the church can also be seen in Suttner: his call for human goodness, his declared fight against nationalism, anti-Semitism and above all, false patriotism. Suttner quotes one of Tolstoy's writings, *Patriotism and Christianity*, in her memoirs in full agreement: "But how can patriotism be a virtue today, when it demands of people an ideal that diametrically opposes our religion and our moral code, not equality and brotherhood, but supremacy of one nation over all the others?"[58]

According to Tolstoy, peace could only be achieved through an unconditional observance of a ban on killing. That meant refusing to do military service.

Tolstoy thought the work of the pacifists was not very effective. In an interview in the *Neue Freie Presse* in 1896 he also talked about Bertha von Suttner. He praised *Lay Down Your Arms* and wished the book an "increasingly wider distribution." But then he said that he could not agree with the conclusion drawn by the book: "A peace court in Europe that is supposed to keep the peace; the plan is reminiscent of the children who wanted to catch birds by sprinkling salt on their tails. A peace court will only increase the danger for the peaceful, since there will always be a Napoleon or a Bismarck, and there will always be patriots who will willingly serve in their armies. No, the war against war must be waged in a different way." And he repeated his demand for an unconditional refusal to do military service.[59]

In 1901 he explained his position to her in detail:

> Even if I should bore you by repeating what I have already said in my books many times and have probably also written to you, I cannot get around telling you again that the older I get and the more I think about the problem of war, the more convinced I become that this problem can only be solved if people refuse to be soldiers. As long as every man between twenty and a hundred years of age renounces his religion—not only Christianity, but also the law of Moses, *Thou shalt not kill*—and declares himself prepared to kill all those people his leader commands him to, even his brothers and sisters and his parents, like this verbose and inhuman idiot who is referred to as the German emperor requires at every opportunity—there will be war, and it will be even more horrible than it is today.
>
> Annihilating war requires neither conferences nor peace societies. All it needs is the rebirth of the only true religion and its result, the rebirth of human dignity.
>
> If only a little of the enthusiasm which is presently being used for articles and nice speeches at peace conferences and in peace societies were employed to rot out the false religion and spread the true one in schools and among the people—war would soon be impossible. Your excellent book is so very effective because it depicts the misery of war in easily understood terms. Now people have to be shown that it is they themselves who cause all this misery of war by being more obedient to people than to God. Permit me to give you the advice to take up this mission as the only means for achieving the goal that you are pursuing.[60]

Whereupon Bertha reported to Fried: "Got an interesting four-page letter from Tolstoy yesterday. He's sticking to it: the only way is refusing military service.—I don't believe in *only* ways—there always have to be a lot of ways being tried, and we must not abandon ours, which the czar has already adopted. If the social democrats want to strike against war— so much the better. We will not hinder them."[61]

The penalties for conscientious objectors in Austria-Hungary were drastic. For instance, in 1895 the physician Dr. Bela Skarva, citing the teachings of Tolstoy, refused to perform his military service. The military court handed down a sentence that not only stripped him of his military rank and made him serve as a common soldier, it also called for three months of severe imprisonment and deprivation of his doctoral title.[62]

Suttner thought such enormous sacrifices could and should not be demanded of average people and that it drove them into senseless martyrdom. She felt it was better to help change the law. She readily admitted that in this conflict, "the more consistent logic lay on the side of Yasnaya-Polyana." "The path he proposed was straighter, but it cannot be trod upon yet. It leads—even today—to a dangerous pitfall: disrespect for the law."

In the course of time she became more tolerant of the mass conscientious objection Tolstoy and some socialists propagated. She thought this form had a better chance since the state could not very well pass sentence on thousands of people.

But the most important thing to her was, as always: "Hundreds of motives—this is the point where the peace societies and the most rational of all the pacifists in the world, Tolstoy, separate. He wants to base his teachings on a single principle—we on a hundred. A hundredfold are also the motives from which the institution of war has grown."[63]

Suttner could not make friends with the relentlessness of the Tolstoy teachings. More than anything, she reacted strongly, even angrily to Tolstoy's condemnation of physical love and his demands that married couples should live together as brothers and sisters. After Tolstoy's "The Kreutzer Sonata" she scolded: "Tolstoy, it's a pity! has really become rather foolish.—Do away with love!"[64] Even six years later, she had not calmed down and wrote Fried that a newspaper had called Tolstoy "reactionary and hostile to culture." The only reason she could imagine was: "Well, because he wanted to eliminate love; that was his mistake. Humanity needs the three sacred elements: peace, freedom, and joy, that's all that is certain."[65]

Although he did not think much of peace congresses, Tolstoy defended the czar's manifesto against attackers, and Bertha reprinted his article proudly in her magazine: "To regard our czar's proposal as an impossible dream that cannot bring any practical results is just as undignified and ignoble as it was to regard the plans of Alexander II to abolish serfdom in Russia as premature and unfeasible. . . . That is the way of the future. There are three historical steps of development for humanity: those of war, of progress, and of Christian love. At present we are entering a time of transition from the first step to the second, and the third step is already in sight."[66]

Tolstoy used a different tone of voice in talking about the Hague conference. He registered doubt and persisted in his opinion that conscientious objection was the one and only way to peace. People had to stop "voluntarily depriving themselves of their rights by making themselves slaves to others and subjecting themselves to being trained like animals in what they call military discipline." An end to the war will not be achieved "by the power of the will of the government, but in the contradiction of this will."[67]

When Russia waged war against Japan in 1904, he called to the Russians in his famous "peace manifesto" to refuse to kill. He also demanded that all opponents of war remember the Christian commandment not to kill. "Whatever my situation may be, whether the war has begun or not, whether thousands of Russians or Japanese will be killed, whether Port Arthur alone will be taken or not, or Petersburg and Moscow, too—I cannot act in any other way than as God demands of me."[68]

Bertha commented to Fried: "Tolstoy Manifesto—despite the Christian element—but again splendid and useful. Shakes up a few consciences."[69] And in a newspaper article, she wrote that Tolstoy expressed the pacifists' thoughts exactly when he condemned the Russo-Japanese War "since there is not one among them who would not agree with the view that the war is both a mass crime and a mass misfortune." Then she objected: "But we hesitate to call its supporters criminals." There were certainly criminals among the warring parties and in the yellow press; "but for the millions of others who serve the institution of war out of a feeling of duty, of sacrifice, or simply because they have not given it any thought and have a sickly feeling of having to, we would like to hold out a word from the gospel to Tolstoy: 'Lord, forgive them for they know not what they do.'"[70]

In times of disheartenment, when Suttner faltered in her belief in the success of the movement, she placed her hope in a general workers' strike by the socialists and on conscientious objection after Tolstoy. "Tolstoy, in my opinion, would not have been a calamity," she wrote Fried in 1909 when she was annoyed over the new air force. "He is the most consistent of all the war-haters. He says 'One doesn't do that.' And the workers' syndicate announces a strike again when war is declared. They will beat us to it. All the better."[71]

She implored Alfred Fried to recognize such attitudes as those of Tolstoy as important: "Whatever you do, please do not fall into the one-sided opinion that the peace cause has only *one* aspect. It has as many of them as people have hearts and souls. As does militarism, too. It also appeals to the emotions with all its pathetic heroes' poses.—And what

Tolstoy wants: tell that to everybody at last: 'I do not want to, cannot and will not commit the crime,' that is sure to come eventually. If I were a man, I would already have said it."[72]

After Tolstoy's death on November 21, 1910, Suttner wrote an obituary in the *Friedenswarte* about the "High priest of the peace idea" and pointed to the characteristic reactions of parliament: "In the Duma, in the German Reichstag and in the Austrian Reichsrat the liberals and the socialists were *for* honoring the dead poet and apostle, with a reference to his love of peace and mankind, while the 'true Russian men,' the clerics, the reactionaries, either resisted or kept silent." In Austria there was no official tribute to Tolstoy: "Presumably because he had been excommunicated. And so a piously minded government may not pay homage, may not admit—what is after all, the truth: Tolstoy was Europe's most consistent—perhaps only—Christian."[73]

United Europe

The idea of a united Europe was also discussed at the peace conferences and was viewed as one of the objectives of the movement. At the peace congress in Bern in 1892, Suttner put forward a motion, together with the Italian Moneta and the Englishman Capper, entitled, "A European Confederation of States." Suttner later wrote: "At that time still an idea no one understood; generally mixed up with 'United States' after the North American model, and disapproved of for Europe. Disapproved of so much that a Swiss paper with the title, *Les Etats Unis d'Europe,* was not allowed to enter Austria."[74]

The motion stated that the dangers of war "have their foundation in the lack of legal definition in the dealings between the various countries of Europe." A European confederation, "which would also be desirable in respect to the interests of trade relations between all the countries," would "create a lasting legal framework in Europe" without "infringing on the independence of individual countries in respect to their own internal affairs, and therefore also their forms of government." The European peace societies were called on "to strive toward a confederation of states based on their common interests as the highest priority of their propaganda."

Peace between the peoples of Europe was to be the first great step on the way to peace all over the world. It was also to be a complement to Carnegie's efforts to establish a "Pan America" with the United States, South, and Central America. Suttner wrote in 1913: "We need a gathering of the reasonable people. We have to be united beneath *one* party flag, and we have to shout just as loud as the Camelots, the Pan-Slavs, the Pan-Germans that we want a Pan-Europe."[75] The very young Count Coudenhove-Kalergi, who was later to found the Pan-European movement, took his first inspiration from "Peace Bertha."

Of course, a reduction of customs and trade barriers also belonged to a united Europe as she envisaged it. Suttner repeatedly argued against nationalistic economic policy: "These customs debates! You see again how little sense is being used to rule the world. Not a common point of view (except for national egoism) among the important and determining personalities. Only the social democrats speak well, but not radically enough by far.—Instead of making a European customs union and allied states of Europe, new fortresses are being built, customs wars inaugurated, new cannons imported, Polish children beaten, Catholic professors employed. . . . How long will this reaction last?"[76]

In 1908 Bertha appeared at the opening of a free-trade congress in London: "Is just like the peace congress," she wrote in her diary. "'Peace and Good Will' also stands above the podium. Winston Churchill speaks."[77]

In May of 1913 Suttner wrote in the *Friedenswarte* hopefully: "The European federation—this old demand of the peace movement—is ripening." She gave a summary of the activities to date: "Pandolfi raised the issue at the peace congress of 1891 in Rome and published a series of articles on it in the review 'Lay Down Your Arms.' Emil Armaud christened his publication, '*Les Etats Unis d'Europe*'; Novikov published his classic book, 'La Féderation de l'Europe.'" The English pacifist Sir Max Wächter had started a new project by this time and intended to found a "European Federation League." The address to which sympathizers could write was printed in the *Friedenswarte*. Suttner saw this move as a "sign of—still embryonic but already pulsating life—a process of becoming for the European Union."[78]

The greater the danger of war became in Europe, the more urgently Suttner pressed her ideal: "'A united, confederated Europe,' this must be the codeword of an enlighted pacifism from now on. That cannot be repeated often enough."[79]

13

The Question of Women

Bertha von Suttner did not see the question of *woman* as an isolated issue, but always in connection with the general progress of the "Machine Age": "Yes, the human being has come of age. This sentence offers the key to *all* the battles that motivate our time. Governments want to treat us like *children;* priests, too. 'Be good, now'; 'Behave well': a person who has come of age is not satisfied with *this* kind of moral standard anymore. And the question of women, what is it but the awakening of a woman who is treated like a child by society and the law?"[1]

Men and women ought to be educated in like manner toward this goal: to be a "noble human being" in a free, self-assured partnership, each living according to his or her abilities, with the same preconditions of education and political and personal rights, without separate morals and without prudery. It is not only women who ought to change their opinions of themselves, but men, too. "Through the falling of the bonds which the one sex has worn so long, not only they, but also the other sex would" soar "to higher levels of human dignity," the woman would not take on "rough, masculine defects," the man would not sink into "effeminate femaleness." "Instead both would be united—the best, strongest, most talented, and the brightest among them" should develop "themselves into examples of a higher order."[2]

According to the Suttner peace ideology, there would also be no war between the sexes. She was never prepared to assume an aggressive tone against men.

When a magazine asked her about the "moral destiny of the woman," she answered hesitatingly:

For one, I do not believe in destiny—that is, in predetermined purposes; second, it would appear to me that in matters of ethical culture
the tasks of humanity should not be separated according to sex. Physiological differences do not give rise to ethical differences. Please excuse
the somewhat prosaic comparison: which tasks fall to the mare on the
raceway and the bitch on the hunt? Exactly the same as the other racers
and the rest of the pack. In humanity's ethical tasks: ennoblement and
refinement of the spirit, the heart and the customs, require the same
accomplishments from both sexes.

Of course, "given the cultural and social conditions of today this is
not really possible; today there are virtues that are placed in the care of
the female sex alone: purity, moderation, gentleness; and characteristics
that a man regards as his exclusive domain: courage, intelligence, readiness for action."

That would have "to change now," she wrote and demanded "the
annihilation of *all* the defects and vices that seem to be allowed today,
half of them to one, half to the other sex: aggressiveness, dissipation,
toughness—in short: the coarseness of men; vanity, ignorance, depen-
dence—in short: the shallowness of women."

"Women have to adapt themselves to virtues that are considered specifically masculine while holding fast to the virtues considered specifically
feminine. With this they would achieve such a high ethical ideal that men
would have no other choice but to shed their privileged vices (which
would include the institutions that support them)." In this way, the great
goal could be reached: "the higher type of complete human being—in
view of whose cultural accomplishments the question whether man or
woman does not even come into consideration."[3]

She wrote on her favorite theme in many variations:

Up to now only masculine emotions have been decisive in shaping
society. Not until feminine emotions get the same scope as the masculine, not until the one extreme can keep the balance with the other,
when his severity can balance out her extreme softness and the latter his
too great severity, not until then will society be able to do justice to the
needs of all its children through fatherliness and motherliness. But if
feminine feelings of tenderness wither—then we stay at the same point
as before woman entered the game.[4]

The ideal was: "Man and woman side by side, born equal, with equal
rights—woman strengthened, man made milder, both ennobled to the
evolving genre of complete humanity."[5]

She was thoroughly convinced that she had achieved this ideal in her marriage with Arthur.

Bertha von Suttner gave practically no reports of her unfortunate experiences as a woman. She did not enter the fight for women's rights because of a hopeless personal situation, like so many other champions of women's rights. Much like her involvement in the peace movement, her interest grew from reading and through critical confrontation with the reality of her aristocratic surroundings. Suttner portrayed the life of "young ladies from better families" and married aristocratic women so clearly and with so many typical details in several of her novels that for us, they are an important source of everyday life of the better-situated woman in Vienna during the nineteenth century.

In the dialogue between a count and her modern heroine, Daniela Dormes, Suttner portrayed the traditional picture of the woman of society. The count insists that women "have to be curious and a little vain and—"

Daniela responds: "'Go on! Name the whole litany of sins that make up your female ideal!' 'And flirtatious—illogical—fickle—moody—irritable.' 'Wait a moment. I see the whole picture before me: a little doll with vibrating nerves and a bird brain—sweet-toothed and shy, addicted to flippery and weak—a mixture of the show-off and the simple-minded.' 'And isn't that a charming picture? Especially when the endearing characteristics are mentioned along with the charming defects: dignified, gentle, sympathetic, graceful, cheerful, sensitive.'"[6]

At another time this prototype of the conservative says excitedly: "What fools, these women are who strive for equal rights! The first thing they lose is our adoration. They want us not to look down on them and begin by getting used to not looking up to us; they are sorry not to be on the same level with us and climb down from their own pedestal; they demand that we wrestle with them, and then we can no longer kneel before them. They will cut off their hair, put on spectacles, wear triple-soled boots, smell like the dust from old documents, and make us forget that there is a beauty."

But no matter what, a woman would never be able to achieve true heights regardless of all she managed to learn: "She can only be a mediocre doctor, a listless merchant, an inferior intellectual. . . . Women have never produced a Newton, a Descartes."

Bertha's heroine responds: "You are making a simple mistake in arithmetic if you want to make your point with these facts. Just think about the fact that for hundreds of millions of educated and intellectually creative men, there's only one Newton. . . . The number of intellectually active women has been so minimal up to now that the same percentage has not yet been proved, a corresponding proportion cannot be set up."

Daniela Dormes finally calls off her engagement to the arrogant and intolerant count and, to the horror of her surroundings, marries a Jewish tutor who accepts her as an equal. She makes the change into a world "where sport, high-life-marriages, and colza harvests were not the most important things, but where lively interest was brought to the accomplishments of literature and science and the events of the day."[7]

The novel's heroine violates a taboo: self-assurance, independence, and intellectual work were terms that were not compatible with the female ideal of the nineteenth century. These were "masculine" virtues. "But then, some character weaknesses were considered contemptuous in men and excusable, if not desirable, in women: faint-heartedness, lack of willpower, thoughtlessness. Wherever a woman wanted to shed these adorable defects, where she showed vigor and self-confidence, a few would praise her for her masculine character, but others would express their apprehension that in discarding feminine vices, the feminine virtues would necessarily break up as well."[8]

Suttner thought that bringing about a change in this point of view would be hard because so many women did not want it. "Who oppresses and guards young girls most severely? Women who are oppressed themselves. Only those who are free disperse freedom generously."[9]

Girls did not count for much in themselves, but only in terms of the kind of future husband they could catch, and he should be as rich and distinguished as possible. The only way for girls to achieve something in life was to make a "good match." As a result they presented themselves, with the eager help of their mothers, the way such a dream man wanted a wife to be: beautiful, stupid, chaste. Chastity was seen to by the traditional convent education and the strictest supervision possible. Used in connection with women, the word *immoral* meant, "not the idea of violations against truth, against honesty, against charity," but only expressed the fact that "the person concerned had a love affair. 'Immoral reading material' did not mean writings that stirred up hatred of other ethnic groups or those that wanted to suppress reason, but those that spoke of the joys of love without condemning them."[10]

The second condition for a "good match" was beauty. It became an expensive and extremely time-consuming cult, which, as Suttner lamented, left no time for education (except for playing the piano and learning languages). Worrying about her hairdo and clothes and a hundred or so accessories filled a girl's day completely. Bertha wrote: "If you think that the path of civilization and the development of human behavior and welfare it entails depends upon the intellectual progress that is made, and if you also reckon how much thought, how much intellectual effort, how much talent half of humanity has expended on the problem of clothing, you can estimate the degree to which the happiness of our sex has been retarded by the so-called beautiful sex's desire to be beautiful."[11]

This kind of lifestyle was not compatible with a serious education and a strenuous profession: "How could . . . a profession that requires endurance and intellectual faculty get along with this superficial thinking, with the jealousies between female rivals, with the eternal worries about their own charms—with the eternal desire to please?"[12]

The topics of conversation among young girls in "top society" were strictly limited to traditional female themes, as one of the Suttner figures in a novel complains:

> How much I would have liked, many times after dinner, to go off to a corner and exchange opinions with some of our well-traveled diplomats, eloquent parliamentarians, or other important men—but that was not advisable; I had to stay with the other young women and discuss the wardrobes we were planning for the next big ball. And if I had intruded myself into that group, the conversations about the national economy, Byron's poetry, about the theories of Strauss and Renan would have grown silent immediately and somebody would have said, "Oh, Countess Dotzky! . . . you looked enchanting at the ladies' picnic yesterday . . . and you're going to the reception at the Russian embassy tomorrow, aren't you?"[13]

Suttner thought the ignorance of women, held in place by social pressure, was the main problem: "Everywhere, lack of freedom is so closely connected with a lack of education that the best means of holding on to those bound in this manner has always been to keep them in ignorance as much as possible. That's where a man's instinctive resistance to female knowledge comes from; against education of the lower classes by those in higher ranks; against enlightenment of any kind by priests—the prison guards of reason."[14]

She loved to argue against the prejudice that women are stupid by nature: "There are just as many female dumbheads as male dumbheads; probably more, not because of the . . . supposedly 'physiological mental weakness of the woman,' but as a result of the way women are traditionally educated, even today."[15]

The so-called female activities of embroidery, crocheting, and knitting were, as far as Bertha was concerned, a waste of time. On her trip to America, she saw with great satisfaction that the daughter of the Pittsburgh industrial king Kennedy did not "restrict her interests to imaginative needlework, but studied prison systems, visited prisons under guidance so that she could participate in reforming the penal system. To *contribute* something to the elevation of human society: in the American world that is a requirement of decency, so to speak, for both high and low, young and old, man and woman."[16]

As in the matter of peace, Suttner also saw America as a forerunner in the matter of women: the educated American girl was far ahead of the European in her development. The hindrances disguised as moral precepts that worked against European girls were only one of many backward features of Europe. In America there was more partnership than flirtatiousness.

In her novel *High Life* she has an American realize with astonishment that the species, "young girl," did not exist in Europe: "There are grown-up female children who are taken straight from the nursery to the registry office without their lifting a finger, and turned into women; as such they decorate the world and—play the coquette."[17]

If a woman achieved her life's goal, she became what people liked to call her "husband's crown," a decorative accessory. When Carneri also used this phrase once, Bertha wrote to him, eager for the fight, saying he must surely believe he was giving her pleasure with this description. Quite the contrary, she wrote: "That about the woman is polite and nicely said, but I don't like it because it presents woman as a creation that has been perfected by man. Crown-Bearer! Does our life have a crown? Maybe you think it's a husband? Certainly not!"[18]

Even in the life of a married woman, education had no place. In *High Life* Suttner described a genteel lady's typical day between riding school, shopping, pleasure drives, five o'clock tea, dinners, balls, theater and asked: "With such a full existence, where is there time for interests of the mind, for the worries and joys of the family? . . . [I]t is a hectic succession of activities, a strenuous effort at pleasure that exceeds the measure of time and the ability to enjoy. There is no place here for contemplation, for looking into your own heart, for peace of mind and for calm." "From the overburdening with pleasure" there grew "the so-called illnesses of the century: indifference, neurosis, anemia. In the weaker forms, their symptoms are called: gentility, sensitivity, delicateness—and the condition is called: modernity."[19]

The ladies in top circles had very little to do with their children, because they were raised either in military academies or convent schools.

With the strenuous social life and constant traveling, it would also have been difficult to be actively concerned with children. All the same: parental love was demonstrated, as Suttner criticized:

> Parental love is a very highly favored feeling in genteel circles. The children themselves are kept at a distance as much as possible, but it is thought to be quite clear that they are their parents' greatest and dearest joy. Just as you have your family diamonds, you also have certain virtues that you keep put away in a locked cupboard: piety, a sense of charity, parental tenderness, etc. For special occasions, these virtues are taken out and polished up, that means you loudly proclaim that you possess them.[20]

Childlessness was a catastrophe for a woman in these circles. Her only task was "to give children" to her husband. Suttner violated a taboo by proudly declaring that a woman could lead a full life without children: "Some people have felt sorry for us because we have remained childless; since having children is thought to be the greatest fortune." But she and Arthur had "never raised a complaint in this respect. Perhaps if we had known this happiness, we would not have been able to understand that doing without does not cause pain,—but the fact is—being childless has not cost us *one* sigh." In retrospect she explained this position, which was unusual for her day, with the fact that both of them "found complete satisfaction in each other" and besides, "that need to live on in the future" was satisfied by their common work, work "that aimed toward the future, that looked forward to something that was still small but growing, blossoming." Moreover: "literary creation" was also a "kind of parenthood."[21]

The real tragedy for a woman began when making a "good match" did not work out. By her mid-twenties she was considered an "old maid." Since she had no professional training, she could not provide her own livelihood. As a result she was dependent on her parents, and after their death, on her brothers and sisters. She lived with them but was not always treated well.

Bertha was well acquainted with this problem. In her own neighborhood of landed gentry around Harmannsdorf, it made her shudder to see what an uneventful and pitiable life unmarried ladies led: "The beauties gradually fade and experience nothing. Appear to come apart in silken shreds."[22]

In a future, more just social order, "every woman should enter the world either with her own income or her own earning power; that would make her free to choose the man her heart desires and also to take up the battle of life anew if it turns out she has made the wrong choice."[23]

In Roman Catholic Austria of that time, which did not even allow divorce by law, she demanded a monstrous thing: legal possibility for divorce, which she saw as combined with the financial independence of the woman. She thought this would not only help women: "No, the liberation of the man would go hand in hand with it; he would also be able to separate himself from the wife who had become contemptuous or despicable, without having the terrible responsibility of throwing a person who had once been dear to him onto the street, or into the arms of starvation—or even worse."[24]

Suttner always saw education as the royal path toward a freer and more self-assured life that would make it possible for women to practice a profession, think independently, and take part in public life. Women should not, for lack of education, "voluntarily keep away from the places where matters of the greatest public interest are being dealt with."

Active and passive suffrage and other important rights had not been fought through yet, "but women and even girls can already exert an influence. But how are they supposed to make full use of their views in a helping and ennobling manner if, because of their intentional ignorance, they are too far away from the things that regulate the mechanisms of social, political and economic life? If she is not allowed to have a voice in the most important issues upon which well-being or misery, war or peace depend, because she is always being told and even has to say to herself: 'You don't understand that'?"[25]

Here again, her plea was not directed primarily to the state, but to the individual, who would have to rethink matters first of all, then mobilize one's own capabilities and free oneself of social pressures, true to the liberal slogan of the nineteenth century, "The world belongs to the competent." The blatant difference between men's and women's education also had an effect on literature: "Women's literature" was considered, especially by men, to be second-class literature. Literature for girls and women was naturally gauged to their lower level of education and also had to take the strict moral requirements for "innocent" young girls into account—a matter every publisher gave special attention to. Suttner wrote, with irony: "We need harmless, purposeless, unreflective, unstimulating stories with exciting plots and satisfying endings." "Justice has been done to this need, so much justice that the entire German literary output has come into disrepute."[26]

Even in her own circle of colleagues, the woman as a writer was not given much serious attention. Bertha was particularly annoyed when Max

Nordau said "that women are only able to write about one thing, namely, about children. This tone surprised me greatly from Nordau, who is a thinking person otherwise. So free and unprejudiced about everything—and in this matter so narrow-minded. How does that come about?"[27]

Despite the huge successes of such women writers of this time as Marie von Ebner-Eschenbach, Maria della Grazie, and she herself, Suttner was convinced that if the author's name was a woman's, a book was automatically qualified as inferior "women's literature." When she wrote her intellectually ambitious book *The Machine Age,* she was afraid she would not reach "serious" readers because of her name (which had the added handicap of being attached to shallow magazine stories of the very kind women were accused of writing). Thus, she took the way out by publishing the book under the pseudonym "Someone." Besides all this, the book contained a biting anticlerical chapter ("Religion") and two sections ("Women" and "Love") that violated the moral code by treating the sexual morality of the nineteenth century intensively—chapters that were addressed primarily to men.

Deeply concerned, Bertha criticized the fact that love was "divided into two parts: either . . . elevated to metaphysical spheres or lowered into mud. Visionary platonism on the one hand, common depravity on the other: these were the divided halves, the one profaned, the other— lifeless."[28]

> Oh, the lack of reason in your wretched dualism, your ridiculous disregard for nature from which nothing but self-torment can grow, which makes you into hypocrites and assassins! . . . You deny noble, "pure" love the right to strive for physical union; and the higher, the more refined the feeling, the more you want to see it torn away from the earthly substantiality in which it is rooted. For such a love, only such women are deemed worthy who would rather die than give themselves or who . . . have to be so "innocent" that they could not even *know* what awaits them in marriage. You do not admit that by maiming spiritual love, you have actually placed the vice of fornication into the world, since this vice is none other than the satisfaction of the ineradicable sexual drive *without love.*[29]

The consequence of this double moral standard for the woman was disastrous: "Love and marriage were namely the very things in which the apparent idolization and actual oppression of the woman were most clearly expressed. Love gave men rights and pleasures, women responsibilities and—crime. In general a serious curse of sin, a deep ban lay on this most blessed of all drives; but the whole curse lay upon the heads of women, the whole state of being outlawed had to be borne by the weaker sex."

Love in the nineteenth century was not a queen; it was a "slave, trampled in the dust, bound, tightly enshrouded, slandered and disowned, tormented and reviled, deprived of rights!"[30]

Don Juan's list of 1003 conquests excited admiration, wrote Bertha angrily. "The condemnation attached to the act of satisfying the love drive fell to the female participants alone. In order to create this nimbus of glory, a thousand and three victims had to lapse into sin and grief; in the same way that a certain number of skulls from defeated foes were necessary to make a wild chieftan's headpiece."[31]

"It was not the seducer in the crime, it was the woman seduced into it who was considered the criminal. She alone had to pay the price—she was the fallen one. He, the strong one, who brought about her downfall, could go his own way with a smile and was usually the first and the bitterest of her contemnors."[32]

The consequence of such a "fall from grace" for a woman was merciless. A "good match" was closed to her forever. Contempt and a loss of social status were a certainty for her. The transitions leading to prostitution (think of the famous "sweet young girl" in Schnitzler) flowed from one to the next. "A whole class of women—a despicably contemptuous expression called them 'the lost ones'—plunged into this situation because of need, misfortune, or recklessness, went to their ruin in this disgrace. It was an army of slaves, to do the lowly work of lust. Cast away from society, from womanhood, these unfortunates did not really belong to humanity; since all the terms applying to the dignity of humanity, to its rights and ideals, lay outside their sphere; their existence was the negation of everything the law of morality promoted."[33]

"Voluptuous pleasure (the mere words may not pass pure lips), is what you renounce as common, animal sensuality in the profoundest contempt, even though you idolize it in private to the point of ruining your health. You think all the pains of love are noble and they may be bewailed in prose and verse, only love's desire is scandalous. This desire adheres to the physical, you say scornfully; every animal feels it; it belongs to the realm of dirt, base nature as opposed to the Godly, in whose image man was created."[34]

She also called for naturalness and truthfulness in this connection: love and sexuality must not be separated, they belong together. A woman must be able to live out this energy just like a man, without prudishness, but in respect for the other.

The real sin was not the violation of a moral code based on error, it was the crime against life itself, war. It experienced absolutely no discrimination: "While you worship death and even killing so much that you know of nothing higher and proclaim nothing louder than the glory of battle, you think there is nothing more disgraceful, nothing that has to be kept so secret as begetting life."[35]

It was not until the third edition of the book, nine years after the first, that Suttner proudly revealed her secret. The reason for her hiding behind a pseudonym was fulfilled: the book had found "serious" readers and no one had suspected the author to be a woman. This also supplied her with the proof "that there is no specific female way of writing and thinking."[36]

Woman and Peace

Bertha von Suttner was profoundly convinced of the equality of men and women. She defended herself vehemently against any defamation against women, and also against the overeagerness of some of the women's rights enthusiasts to attribute special qualities to the female sex. This conflict arose most in connection with the subject "woman and peace." Not a few of the proponents of women's rights were—and still are today—of the opinion that woman, in contrast to "warlike" man, is peace loving and gentle by nature, that is, the innate pacifist. Lida Gustava Heymann, the German women's rights advocate, created a slogan during this time: "For female character, female instincts are identical to pacifism."[37]

Bertha von Suttner always opposed this idea vigorously and did not by any means limit her denunciations to warlike attitudes among men. "As far as my personal experience goes," she wrote in a fundamental article in her magazine, *Lay Down Your Arms,* in 1895, "there is no difference between the male and the female sex in regard to their position on the peace issue. Enthusiasm for the deeds of war and war heroes is to be found among women as well as men, while enthusiasm and energy for the peace movement is just as intense among women as among men, and finally, the great indifference, the adhering to routine, the lack of understanding for a new idea also belongs to everybody, without exception."

She resolutely resisted all temptation to present the peace movement as a typically feminine movement against the masculine principle of war:

"It is futile to expect women *as such* to make the peace movement their thing; they would also not be able to achieve anything if they placed themselves in opposition to men. The tasks of the advancing ennoblement of humanity are such that they can only be fulfilled in like-minded and equal cooperation of both sexes."[38]

Just as in her confrontation with social democracy, she also held to a consistent, individualistic position in the matter of women.

It was "one of the common misunderstandings" that the peace movement was a thing for women (and therefore not for men!), she wrote to Fried. This misunderstanding came from one simple fact: "because women also support the peace movement, namely, *Frau* Bertha."[39]

In her opinion the prejudice of "feminine" pacifism and "masculine" war also included the accusation of cowardice and of egoism: "Women who wail: 'The war should stop because *we* suffer under it, because *we* could lose what we love most!' ranked . . . considerably lower than those who said: 'What difference does our misery make, the general good comes first!' or those who called to their sons: 'Either come home a victor or dead!' Each for special reasons—whether it be the interests of a group, a class or a sex—the development of opposition does not need ethical explanations and therefore has no ethical influence."

She saw more value in the motives of the woman "who rises up against war, not because *her* house is threatened, but because she has realized that it is a disaster for the whole of humanity. Not because they are daughters, wives, and mothers do modern women want to shake off the institution, 'war'; they do it because they have become the sensible half of a humanity that has become sensible, and they see that war is an obstacle to cultural development and that it is damaging and reprehensible from every standpoint—the moral and the economic, the religious, and the philosophical."[40] The fight for peace was a general human concern, which had to be supported by men and women alike.

She reminded those of her "sisters" who talked far too much about female superiority in matters of peace "that there are also women's groups who start collections for torpedo boats and within a short time bring 800,000 crowns together for this cause; that princesses consider it one of the highest honors to be the head of a regiment, that *none* of the present ruling queens has uttered one *word*, let alone performed an act, against war, that mothers are the best customers of factories that make tin soldiers, that Bismarck could say in all confidence to the delegation of women paying tribute to him, that *women* will educate the coming generation to have patriotic, military convictions."[41]

To show that women in politics were no less military in their actions than men, she gave the example of Queen Marie Christine of Spain. In 1895, she beat down an uprising in Cuba against Spanish rule and showed "that women know how to wave just as energetic a scepter as men; since there is no knowledge that the Queen hesitated the slightest instant to send the children of her country into battle, or that she had been overcome by the foolish utopian and inane idea that there could be other means than cannons to get rid of the dissatisfaction of the rebellious population."[42]

To Bertha's disappointment, very few mothers joined the peace movement: "Mothers? Well, great numbers of them are either indifferent or proud that their boys are cadets."[43] She accused women who had been brought up according to tradition of provoking war in two ways: "Silently, through admiration they harbor for war and through their liking for uniforms; out loud, by direct encouragement to lay into the fight."[44]

How much effort was needed for peace work among women is demonstrated by the following example. In 1895 a certain Countess Kielmannsegg had formed a ladies' committee that wanted an honorary flag for a warship and asked for donations for it. Suttner took this as a welcome opportunity for a counteraction: "All right, I thought, the 'old custom' gets its due through this call, but may the *new* idea that is now filling the air also find its expression." Then she issued a call to women to donate toward a white flag of the peace society. "And if someday—perhaps already at the turn of the century—all the various flags will be raised to celebrate the officially instituted European Peace Federation (that would certainly be a more desirable moment than the 'serious battle,' whose coming we want to prevent!), then the flag belonging to the Austrian women should also wave among them and give witness to their participation in the beautiful, blessed work."[45]

She asked women who wanted to accelerate "the reaching of the cultural goal: the legal alliance of nations" for a donation of at least one crown. After a week there was enough for a flag of war; but only five crowns, donated by three women, had come in for a peace flag. Of course, the caricaturists took hold of this new defeat for "Peace Bertha" and heaped public ridicule on top of her disappointment.

She took up every women's project for peace all the more joyfully and did everything she could to publicize each of them. She quoted a letter from the "women of England to their sisters in France" dated April 28, 1895, which called for a common fight for solidarity and against military spirit. It got a very friendly answer from a French women's committee.

The call for peace issued by English and French women was soon joined by women from Germany, with Lina Morgenstern at the lead. Bertha also signed the call, but remarked in her magazine that "the expression '*the* women of France' or '*the* women of Germany' sounds too all-inclusive when it is referring to a declaration made by five or six women."

Untiringly, she argued against the cult of the uniform that women all too frequently succumbed to. Feminine favor ought to be bestowed according to different criteria than those applied before: "When a greater reward of love beckons to men for the heroic deeds of peace than for those of war, when men know that they can gain the admiration of the best of the women only by standing up for the new ideals of justice and, on the contrary, awaken the disgust of noble-minded women when they support the system of horror, then one of the strongest motives that now drive young men into war will be eliminated."[46]

She denounced the many attempts made by politicians to indoctrinate women with national conceit and to assign them the job of raising battle-worthy, patriotic soldiers as their main mission in life. She criticized one "Bismarck Women's Calendar" that listed the five primary talents of the German woman: "Stimulate enjoyment, prepare food, make clothing, keep order, teach." That it also demanded "healthy national egoism" and avoidance of "international raptures," annoyed Suttner especially.[47]

Of course Bertha worked together with the women's movement and had personal contacts with the important pioneers in improving the position of the woman. Among the first expressions of approval for the founding of the Austrian Peace Society in 1891, was an enthusiastic letter from the Austrian feminist, Auguste Fickert. She wrote that Bertha's efforts had been greeted "with rejoicing" in her circle, and she was happy "that in our fatherland, a woman, following the deepest urges of her genuinely feminine character, has stepped to the head of a movement that will free humanity from the last remnants of a barbaric age."[48] She offered the cooperation of women in the peace league and asked Suttner warmly for her participation in the fight for women's suffrage.

Bertha turned down this request. In 1892 she wrote to the "very honorable comrade" Auguste Fickert: "In principle, I *must* stick to the one sphere of activity I have taken upon myself and which makes demands upon me to an exceptional degree. You cannot imagine the burden of work that has fallen to me in dealing with the peace societies, publishing my paper, composing specialized articles, etc.—As it is, I already know how to cope with it all."

For this reason she could not become active in the women's movement. "However, I will send in a declaration of sympathy, . . . which will fill the purpose of showing that I approve of your goals."

She sincerely asked for understanding: "In addition, I still have to be literarily active and that I do this in a way that also works for equality of our sex is something all my sisters will admit."[49]

She even had to turn down Marianne Hainisch ("Dear honored, courageous lady"), whom she admired: "So, I am not declining to join the fight against venereal disease out of prudishness—but because it is just as important . . . as a dozen other things: protection of mothers. Protection of children. Marriage reform. Anti-alcohol. Tuberculosis. Peoples' housing, etc., etc. No, I can't manage all of that."[50]

In her refusals to the feminists, she never forgot to promise them her moral support. She encouraged the Polish feminist, Milena Wlodzimirska, to create a women's peace league: "But the kind of league that aims for the high ideals of the three little *F*s: *Friede, Freiheit,* and *Freude* [peace, freedom, and joy]—and a fourth *F* for *Frauenrecht* [women's rights] to go with it—can be assured of my fullest approval."[51] Of course, she repeatedly gave lectures in women's clubs.

There were times when feminists and pacifists poured out their troubles to one another. Unlike their American brothers and sisters, they had very little success in Austria-Hungary and in the German Empire. But they persisted bravely, and Auguste Fickert assured Suttner during one of their common projects: "What we are not able to accomplish in Vienna in terms of quantity—the Baroness knows how poor interest in public matters is here—we have to make up for in representing the cause well."[52]

They looked upon the size of the women's movement in Anglo-Saxon countries with envy and admiration. Bertha ranked the American feminists higher than the European. When she was offered the presidency of the World Federation of Women in 1904, she refused—very flattered—and backed the American whom she greatly admired, Mary Eliza W. Sewall, completely. "A great woman. In my eyes, anyway, much greater than the Peace Bertha." "Well, am I glad that I did not accept the presidency of the World Federation of Women. Such things are still impossible in our country. You need America or England for that. Mrs. Sewall told me that 300,000 men had also joined her organization."[53]

She wrote about the political activities of the American feminists with admiration in her novels and newspapers, praised them in her lectures as models for the central European peace movement. During her trip to America, she observed the extremely successful public relations work of those women very closely and learned a great deal that would help her in organizing her peace societies.

In America she wrote in her diary: "World situation would be so suitable for big pacifist activity. I see though, *how* (found out through the women's groups) a cause has to be managed. The idea does not work through its own strength, but as a result of agitation and through 'funds.'"[54] And these were exactly the things that did not succeed in Europe.

Despite all her sympathy, Suttner occasionally felt that the women's movement was competition as well as an incentive.

When the new *Brockhaus-Lexikon* (the leading German encyclopedia) came out in 1902, it listed the women's movement but, to Bertha's consternation, not the peace movement. She wrote Fried: "Oh well—the women's movement is about ten years older than the peace movement. Ten years ago there weren't even ten lines in the lexicon about the women's cause. We ought to write Brockhaus from various sides to complain and enlighten them."[55] And a similar situation is referred to in another letter to Fried: "The *Woche* prints half a column of '*Frauenchronik*' [Women's chronicle] regularly now. The peace chronicle will also have to make its entry into the papers soon, too. The increasing numbers of inter-parliamentary conferences, arbitration treaties, etc., would supply enough material for them."[56]

She kept track of the progress of the women's cause in her diary, as shown by this entry from November of 1907: "In Australia, women have the vote and can be elected."[57] Happy and proud, she noted in 1911 that for the first time in Norway, a woman became a member of parliament. Already, in her maiden speech, parliamentarian Rogstad showed herself to be a friend of peace and a supporter of the international court of arbitration. Full of hope, Suttner remarked in the *Friedenswarte:* "It is interesting and deserves to be mentioned that the first woman to function as a parliamentarian spoke out for the future international legal system with her first words."[58]

At the big demonstration for women's suffrage in 1911 in Vienna, a famous feminist, the socialist Adelheid Popp, also declared her belief in the goals of the peace movement and said: "We also want to fight against the waste of millions for the purpose of murder and fratricide. We want the murderous arming to come to an end, and these millions to be used for the needs of the people." Bertha quoted these lines with obvious satisfaction in the *Friedenswarte* and commented optimistically: "Feminine politics? No: humane politics. And the budding assistance of the half of humanity that has been without rights up to now is only one symptom of the fact that the time is approaching when the welfare and the rights of humanity will rank as the highest guiding principle in politics."[59]

In June 1904 Suttner was one of the prominent personalities at the International Women's Conference in Berlin. However, on the very first day an Australian spoke in favor of armament. "Overly loyal. Would melt the bullets herself, etc.," was Bertha's disapproving entry in her diary. One high point of the conference was the women's big peace demonstration, with a Suttner lecture. "Quite simply *a triumph* . . . Lady Aberdeen given an award . . . I highly celebrated. Even still out on the street."[60]

The Berlin newspapers confirmed the big success and printed a summary of the contents of her speech. It was about the role of the woman in the peace movement. Again Suttner warned women of "listening with emotion and enthusiasm" to calls for peace and then "buying their children toy soldiers" and trying their best to get "a place in the military training school for their sons." The modern woman must "leave her former sphere defined by sex." "We want to raise a sensible sex, endowed with logical thought processes, with education and goodness."

Men would have to change, too: "The 'dashing' man who is given a great deal of credit for his vices, drunkenness, fighting spirit, etc., will no longer be most desirable; it will be the man who unites peaceableness and mildness with courage and intellect."[61]

These vigorous declarations were a challenge to opposition. The *Posener Tagblatt,* for instance, rejected Suttner's picture of a woman: "More than ever, our age needs men capable of thinking and handling weapons, women who are gentle, thoughtful and mild. God preserve us from manly women and the crazy cranks this international congress has brought together in all too large a number."[62]

And the *Leipziger Neueste Nachrichten* argued against the pacifist ideal: "Without a fight, there's no life—this primary principle of the very essence of masculinity, this phrase that makes a man a man, is something Bertha von Suttner will never grasp." Success in her efforts would "make eunuchs of humanity" and "rob it of everything . . . of value it has ever possessed."[63]

Despite all the scorn the *Leipziger Tagblatt* heaped upon Suttner, it had to admit: "One has to admire the courage of this woman who holds her ideal of world peace erect and defends it in a time that seems to be a true insult to peace; who, in a country like Germany, where the army plays such a great role, says: The day will come when women will no longer admire the heroes of war, but the heroes of peace who are the greater of the two!"

Suttner, spoiling for her own fight, responded to the famous poem of Felix Dahn: "The sword belongs to man,—where men fight, the woman is bound to silence" with: "She won't keep silent, Professor!" And the *Leipziger Tagblatt* wrote in resignation: "No, the woman won't keep silent anymore when it comes to the peace question."[64]

The Nobel Peace Prize, which she was the first woman to receive, was really what made Suttner the great pride and example of the international women's movement. And it was mostly women who celebrated and cheered Suttner on her second American trip in 1912. More than ever, she implored women to take an active stance against war: "We have to look misery in the eye, not to complain about it as a misfortune, but to accuse it as an evil. Because it is not a natural catastrophe—it is the result of human error and human callousness. Let us not be deterred by accusations of 'sentimentality.' We have the right, we women, to show our feelings." Women especially, must not forget "that the work of pacifism does not consist of studies of international law, socio-economic considerations, and political actions alone; it is work that is filled with the glow of a painfully burning soul, with the deepest devotion."[65]

One of the last manuscripts she wrote before her death was devoted to the "Women's Union of the German Peace Society." She called for "perseverance, perseverance, and again perseverance" from her "honored warriors" in the movement. Women should fight in all areas where possible for them, "because today no social study is denied us any longer, and every day more public offices are open to us." Reason would have to rise up against war, "but let us not suppress the indignation of our hearts because of this."[66]

14

Before the Great War

The most famous woman in the world, Nobel Peace Prize winner, internationally courted speaker: Bertha von Suttner could not complain of a lack of esteem from her surroundings, at least not from abroad. In her own country, Austria, fame did not fare as well. Followers and admirers were a much smaller circle, while the public at large enjoyed ridiculing "fat Bertha" and making fun of her "fuddled peace ideas."

This discrepancy between international fame and national contempt is described by the widely read pan-German writer Countess Edith Salburg, who had witnessed "Peace Bertha" at a congress in Geneva: "Geneva . . . Inebriated with the idea of world peace, the peace-intoxicated kings and benefactors of mankind, preoccupied with Bertha von Suttner, whose talents have borne an idea worth exploiting to new heights, until she became vain and somewhat ridiculous . . . And this Geneva . . . this seat of revolutionary ideas, frustrated lives, this city, a Frenchling of the most unhealthy kind, the center of Freemasonry, of world demagoguery, paid homage to the fat, attractive Austrian woman in whom the countess and the adventuress are so strongly united. . . . Skeptical Austria has never courted Kinsky-Suttner, she was boycotted by the army, a comical figure. Now, we saw her here as a saint, and crowned heads . . . sang psalms in her praise."[1]

This quotation makes some of the reasons for Bertha's unpopularity in Austria clear. There were the ideological reasons, her anticlericalism, her free spiritedness, her fight against anti-Semitism. Then, there was also her internationalism, which was frowned upon in Vienna, by pan-Germans especially. It should be noted that she was never criticized for being "un-Austrian," but for being "un-German" and occasionally—because of the city of her birth, Prague—for being a "Czech, which was

275

not used in the sense of nationality or homeland," to which she added the remark in her diary, "which happens to be true."[2]

It is probably no coincidence that the two most prominent German-speaking pacifists of this time, Suttner and Fried, were Austrians. If their homeland had an influence on their development as pacifists, then it was certainly not as a harmoniously functioning multiethnic state. Quite the contrary: there was no place where the catastrophic power of nationalism was more painfully evident than in this state whose people confronted one another with hatred and enmity, fought one another and, as a result, ruined the state.

Suttner's supranational convictions, which she also applied to domestic politics, were an exception in Austria-Hungary when they should have been the rule. She always thought of herself as an "Austrian" and in doing so she recognized a supranational principle of the state. With the growing aggression against this idea, she refused to be counted among the "Germans," both in Vienna and on her visits to Prague. (In keeping with the Kinsky family tradition, she always placed the common "Bohemian" idea in the foreground.)

She withdrew from any kind of nationalism: "Oh, there is nothing that perverts thinking so much as this nationalistic feeling that is praised as the 'highest.'" "It is time for people to group themselves in some other way than according to nations."[3]

While the pacifists in national states like France or the German Reich were accused of not being nationalistic enough and thus not patriotic enough, the situation in Austria-Hungary was different: it was a conglomerate of many nations. In Austria-Hungary, especially, pacifistic convictions could have been a political factor that would have helped hold the multiethnic state together. In this case, the supranational idea did not threaten national patriotism, but it would have been very well suited as a reinforcement in trying to overcome the nationalistic tendencies that did threaten the state. Not a single politician recognized these advantages of pacifism for Austria-Hungary, and most of its citizens did not feel like supranational "Austrians" anyway. They were national Germans, Czechs, Italians, Hungarians, Rumanians, Poles and so on.

Bertha von Suttner thought pacifism offered a big chance for reconciliation for her country, "since its basic principle is the respect and full recognition of the rights of every nationality to act freely, but in friendship and cooperation with the others and to work in the best interest of all, which consists of ethnic progress and 'peace.'" "Pacifism is the vanquisher of national chauvinism."[4]

"The friends of peace know very well what nationality means—namely, that groups and individuals should have the same right: the right of self-determination. But with hitting out, oppression, arrogant overestimation of its own capabilities, and looking down on the others, a nation will achieve just as little recognition as it allows the well-behaved individual."[5]

In September 1909 the Day of Catholicism even had to be called off in Vienna, "because it showed that Slavs and Germans did not find enough unifying power in their religion to silence their national contradictions," as Suttner lamented.

Of course the pacifists could not take sides in this matter, but they could take a stand: "Their principles, which rest on justice and freedom, would, if they were followed, bring about national and international peace by themselves. Away with all the inhibitions and tyrannies—and also, away with all the acts of violence and baseness. The peace societies will offer their hand so that in their midst, the elements of the various nations that are united in a higher ideal can devote themselves to working together for national peace."[6]

The German-nationalist newspapers derided the pacifists in the crudest manner. In the agitated nationalistic climate in Vienna, it was only a matter of time before this feeling of hatred would vent itself in action against "Peace Bertha." In November of 1903 this point was reached. Suttner reports in her diary: "I am preparing to speak before the students' Union. . . . Pan-Germans have occupied the auditorium. Meeting is closed. Moment of panic—great bewilderment among the convenors. I find it all very interesting."[7] Attempts at intimidation like this merely strengthened her conviction for her cause.

After the turn of the century, she thought the conflict with the Italian Austrians was the most dangerous problem since it was bound to a great hatred for the kindgom of Italy, officially a partner in the Triple Alliance. "Our war parties are now working systematically on this conflict with Italy," she wrote Fried in 1906.[8] In 1908, he got the idea for Suttner, together with the Italian pacifist and friend Moneta, to found an Italian-Austrian friendship committee to work against the hate-filled mood between the two countries. The news of this new committee was presented to both of the foreign ministers. The Austrian-Hungarian foreign minister Ährenthal told the two signatories that he "would support . . . any undertaking . . . that made the promotion of friendly relations between the two peoples its mission." The Italian foreign minister Tittoni wrote in a similar vein.

Suttner gave these texts to the press. One of the goals of the project, namely, to promote the peaceful coexistence between her fellow countrymen and their Italian neighbors was thus accomplished, and Suttner was happy about it: "What would the ministers have done with our dispatches several years ago? Wastepaper basket."[9]

But what could a few friendly phrases from the minister do to oppose the nationalism that was mainly being fought in nasty battles at Austria's universities? Suttner wrote Fried in September 1908, when the Austrian-Italian friendship project was in full swing: "This nationality-madness is the poison that will ruin Austria. These 'Teutons' at the university who have been allowed to sing the *Wacht am Rhein* [Watch on the Rhine], are treating their Italian fellow students and countrymen like total strangers and are calling for them to be chased away—because they sing an Italian nationalistic song. The demand for an Italian university is completely justified. Their German comrades should help with this—not shout 'ugh.' We're living among barbarians."[10]

In the *Neue Freie Presse* she answered a skeptical article by Hermann Bahr very clearly and named the objectives of the peace committee:

> to bring those groups closer together on both sides, who are determined to avert the terrible misfortune of a break with all their strength, and to place them in the foreground; second to work toward both nations getting to know each other better, so as to overcome prejudice and antipathy which stems from the times when in Italy, Austrians were held to be the prototype of the oppressive police power and here the Italian was seen as the prototype of the sly 'dago.' In addition, organizing mass excursions, exchanges for professors and children, a trip by the Austrian men's choral society to Rome, a visit by Italian intellectuals to Vienna, and much more of the same. Finally, in the event of a really threatening situation, energetic steps would have to be taken in the direction of conciliatory mass meetings.[11]

Faced with the increasing numbers of new fights between nationalities, her hopes sank: "It is hard to stage events for international brotherhood during the *national* war that has actually broken out in Austria now."[12]

The pacifists' well-meaning attempt at conciliation was not only a blatant fiasco in the universities. It also failed miserably with the Austrian and Italian public. Already by November 1908 Suttner had to report to Fried: "Moneta is now being hounded by the Italian papers because of Austrian friendship."[13]

Meanwhile the battle of the nationalities was taking on more and more severe forms in the Bohemian lands as well. There were brutal street fights. Suttner remarked in her diary in September 1908: "The newspapers full of nationality battles throughout Slovenia and Bohemia. Oh, madness of nations!"[14]

Even the celebrations in 1908 for the sixtieth anniversary of Emperor Franz Joseph's reign were overshadowed by fierce fighting. "The fights at the university and in Bohemia provide a nice prelude for the parade. Of course, it too is honoring various kinds of fighting. As long as confessional and national stupidity is not disapproved of, you can count the civilized people on your fingers."[15] She was referring, of course, to the "festive parade of allegiance to the Emperor" in which all the war heroes, especially, were held up as a national ideal: from Rudolf von Hapsburg to Radetzky, the victor of the Italian revolution. "I get very angry about this parade. A to-arms ballyhoo. Totally blind to the modern spirit. Glorifying all forms of wildness."[16]

She no longer had hopes in Emperor Franz Joseph: "Ten years ago, at the fiftieth jubilee of his reign, I wrote that the emperor should use the celebration to create a general European alliance and thereby a reduced need for arms. At the time I still thought he would be receptive to such an idea. Today I don't think so anymore."[17] In this situation, she wrote to Fried angrily: "We are socialists. Or even worse. I, at least, tend strongly toward Hervé." (The Frenchman Gustave Hervé worked for a general strike and conscientious objection.) But Bertha added a postscript: "The only thing I disapprove of is the use of force in this."[18]

The magnificent parade was only a part of the jubilee celebration. In August the "Emperor's Birthday" was observed especially magnificently, and Bertha's excitement took off on a fresh start. "The reports are disgusting, for ten days, all about the emperor's birthday celebrations in every corner of the monarchy—today from Seeboden and Schluderbach. The spirit of Byzantium is poison for us—and that other one: the Radetzky spirit. The latter will make the Italo-Austro project harder for us."[19]

It turned out to be much worse. The empire was to be enlarged to mark the extraordinary jubilee. On October 5, 1908, Austria-Hungary declared the annexation of the Turkish province of Bosnia, which had already been occupied since 1878, and Herzegovina. This step was supposed to unite the southern Slavs under the rule of the Danube monarchy and in doing so, forestall similar plans of Serbia. But what was thought would be a nonviolent takeover of a land that was already occupied anyway turned out to be much more difficult. A serious foreign policy crisis resulted that took Europe to the brink of war.

Russia felt cheated; the western powers had not been sufficiently informed. Serbia and Montenegro saw themselves threatened. Weak Turkey's only defense was to boycott Austrian goods. The Balkan conflict that had been smoldering for years burst into flame.

On October 5 Bertha wrote worriedly in her diary: "If only it all passes without war: great test of strength for pacifism." On October 8 she wrote: "Things in the orient are working up to a Serb war." And on October 11 she wrote: "Serbs decide not to declare war. Who knows for how long. Danger has courted violence. Was that a deed for a 78-year-old 'Peace Emperor' in his jubilee year?—The press says: yes. Energetic, great . . . I'm absolutely furious."

In the highly lauded "Augmentation of the Empire" Suttner saw "the breach of international treaties and an immediate danger of war . . . which would be the result. Also, the many millions which it costs to prepare for war and the new cause for further increase in armament—not only in Austria-Hungary but in all the countries of Europe—can be viewed as a consequence of this same action."[20]

She answered the most recent insults about pacifist impotence with: "For example, are we supposed to prevent the Serb hotheads from arming their mobs by holding protest meetings in Vienna or Bern? The way our Europe is still organized and even more so, disorganized, a conflagration could break out at any moment." The civilized world needed a "fireproof building. As long as it stays under a straw roof and pours gasoline into its hallways besides, it can be prepared for the conflagration; when the flames start licking, then it's too late . . . to call in . . . the safety technicians who are supposed to help; and then no one is justified in deriding them because their methods are of no use—no one has employed these methods."[21]

Faced with the danger of war, the national centers of unrest flamed up again. At Trieste University there were fights between German nationalists and Italians; in Ljubljana, Celje, and Maribor there were Slovene attacks against Germans; in Prague there were even street riots that climaxed in Czechs calling, "Long live Serbia!" Suttner wrote in her diary that at these Prague riots the "Austrian flag was torn and thrown into the Moldau."[22] The German nationalist students calling, "You should be starved," succeeded in having the university dining hall closed to Czechs. On the day of the jubilee, December 2, 1908, there were also big riots in Prague. Martial law had to be imposed. All the same, Suttner still hoped for a peaceful end to the crisis.

Austria-Hungary got backup from Berlin: the German chancellor approved full support. During these critical weeks there was a lot in the papers about the beneficial effect of the German-Austrian alliance that prevented war. Suttner commented: "Nonsense, the very idea that you can count on peace because Germany sticks up for Austria."[23]

Russia disappointed Serbia's hope for help. In Berlin this was attributed to fear of "German bayonettes" and the strong German armament— an argument that Suttner did not accept: "If he [the czar] was really not peace-loving but only trembling, then it's because he felt weaker, because he was not prepared for war due to the exterior and interior calamities that he had to withstand, in other words, was not armed well enough. What does that do to the claim that only strong armaments can protect peace? In this case . . . a lack of a country's arms was the reason for avoiding war."[24]

For her, averting war was a pacifist success: "A war would have broken out long ago under the existing conditions, if the seed sown by the peace movement had not made strong growth, if the people's need for peace had not caught on all around, if one Europe were not about to create a union. This Europe did after all achieve a postponement of the outbreak of war and created a possibility for legally binding understanding, at a time when the clouds gathered darkest over the Balkans."[25]

She took the opportunity and issued a call in the *Neue Wiener Tagblatt* for money to strengthen peace propaganda in this enormous international crisis. The lack of success was shameful: three donors sent in twenty crowns each. A second appeal brought in a single crown. The caricaturists had their target again. "The result of the sixty crowns with the first and the *one* crown for the second article shows just how little effect my voice has."[26]

But even when the matter at hand was not money, there were hardly any sympathizers to be seen. "Yesterday's event clearly showed the impotence again, the 'shrinkage' of the Austrian peace society—was supposed to have been a demonstration rally of the people, a sensation of voices raised high and mighty: instead of that, empty evening lecture and a friendly gathering of four Eumenides. Five including me."[27]

The crisis was finally put aside with an agreement between Austria-Hungary and Turkey in February 1909 and a high settlement paid to Turkey. She admitted to the Prince of Monaco: "I trembled because I was a witness to how much the military really wanted this war."[28] The trouble spot smoldered on, and the agitation for war continued on this side and that, in increasingly aggressive forms.

The English proposals for solving the problem of Bosnia and Herzegovina with the right to self-determination of peoples did not get Suttner's approval because of the complicated connections. "The Herzegovinians and Bosnians cannot suddenly declare where they want to go now. They consist of Serbs, Turks, and of Austrians who have been settled there for thirty years. Austria would really look good if it were to call all its nationalities to a plebiscite!"[29] And: "I still think that there will be war. . . . A top that is so wound up, eventually takes off with a whirr!"[30]

She was also skeptical when a "peace tribute" for Emperor Franz Joseph took place in April 1909: "Peace tribute yesterday did not produce one pacifistic thought, but glorified the 'just and inevitable war and the well prepared army.'"[31]

Her reply to this "peace tribute" came in April 1909 in an accusatory pamphlet on "Armament and Overarmament," an appeal to rulers to stop arming and to conclude international treaties: "Blindly, head over heels, always from day to day without counting the consequences, without regard for current financial resources, without guarantees for the future, from one year to the next, from one session of parliament to the next, from one chance discovery to the next, always expanding, expanding— without plan, without form, without limits. It is a race to disaster."[32]

She denounced the immense costs of arming, which resulted in a population reduced to misery:

> But there is not only the matter of cost. Armament also has to be judged by the moral atmosphere it creates. An atmosphere in which the joining of the people, the establishment of international law (let alone the feelings of brotherhood) cannot prosper. It is not possible to smile with bared teeth and shake hands with balled fists. Actually, it is incomprehensible that it is possible to live and be active at all in the midst of all these threats of destruction, to stroll calmly on the laid mines and in front of the jaws of the cannons that are stretching up everywhere. That it is possible to maintain polite and even well-intentioned manners while preparing to . . . tear . . . each other to shreds as thoroughly as possible.[33]

But the ruling class was not alone; the public at large also thought constant armament was a guarantee for the future. Bertha's report to Fried on the results of a newspaper poll on whether it was better to arm or not, bears this out: "All those questioned were unanimously in favor; all for a more secure peace, the way it was just borne out so brilliantly, so that 'the population has come to realize more and more,' that arming, arming is the most beneficial solution. Pattai [a Hungarian politician] says: 'You cannot avert war with Bertha Suttner.'"[34]

When Andrew Carnegie sent an appeal for peace to the *Times* of London in June 1909, Suttner thanked him, but did not hide her doubts:

> I suppose the English government and especially the King would be quite willing to act up to your suggestions. But central Europe?—Do

you know that last year your noble King [Edward VII] proposed to Francis Josef (at Ischl) to use his influence on the German emperor in favor of an arrest of the navy-armaments—and that our emperor refused; and what is worse, that all our papers openly *boasted* of that refusal?

Austria is a stronghold of militarism. All our archdukes are soldiers, and the press seems a branch of the war department. The education of public opinion in Germany and Austria is one of the most pressing tasks of our movement.[35]

She sharply denounced the claim that there were no more cabinet wars, that is, those waged without democratic sanction, and that the political greats had little power ("now it is the people who want the war, who . . . their most sacred interests, etc., etc."): "That's just not true; the conditions and preconditions that make cabinet wars possible have not been done away with, and the ethnic hatred is only being incited and held awake so it can be used at the right moment for taking the responsibility for the war as well as making it possible to wage it."[36]

Her pessimism was nourished most of all by the constant talk of the necessity of a preventive war against Serbia: "Therefore, start it immediately so that it won't threaten in the *future*. So that the patient won't have a relapse in some future year, kill him now. And the stupid people accept it all. . . . Army newspaper recommends evacuating the Serb population (women, children, etc.) as fast as possible and placing it in concentration camps on our soil (lessons from the Transvaal war)."[37]

Preventive war, as suggested in the press and elsewhere, was also the right way to deal with (the ally!) Italy. The Army newspaper even went so far as to use the terrible Messina earthquake in 1909 as an occasion to demand war against Italy immediately, since it thought the war was unavoidable anyway and Italy at that point was weakened by the catastrophe. This provoked Suttner to make a new public appeal. It did not take her long to find like-minded supporters, including the writers Arthur Schnitzler and Hermann Bahr. They complained of the

unbearable relationship with the Italian neighbors. Won't our eyes finally open now to the fact that this war between Austria and Italy, painted on the wall by agitators and representatives of the war industry, is not only avoidable, no, that friendship between these two countries is possible, necessary and the prerequisite of a happy future for both? I recently suggested to an Italian friend in Trieste that we should work toward presenting all the current issues concerning ourselves and Italy to a common senate, elected by the parliaments of both countries, for a decision. Do we not have a statesman who possesses ambition in a grand style?[38]

Parallel to the Austrian-Italian committee, several Czech and German-Austrian intellectuals, led by Hermann Bahr, founded a "Czech-German Cultural Committee which is supposed to take a position in public against every excess committed by the people of both nations and use every opportunity to repeat in public that we belong together, do not want to fight but want to understand each other and see in every oppression of the other nation the damage to our own," as Hermann Bahr wrote to Suttner.[39] She answered: "I am happy to join the Czech-German Cultural Committee in planning. The latest procedures in parliament make it absolutely necessary to find a common ground where cultivated people—the gentlemen—of both nations can unite against nationalistic excesses and false teachings. I shall write several friends in Prague today so that I may be able to name a few personalities prepared to work with us."[40] This move proved to be just as fruitless as the other well-meaning efforts on behalf of ethnic reconciliation within the Danube monarchy.

Several natural scientists attempted an attack against constant armament in 1911. One of them was the Suttner associate Professor Wilhelm Exner, who said that from a technological and scientific standpoint, a continuation of the construction of the great battleship "Dreadnought" should be rejected. This project was carried out so listlessly that Suttner let out a great sigh to Fried: "These Austrians are obviously not wearing seven-league boots. Theirs are more like ½ centimeter!"[41]

The press did not support peace initiatives. Bertha wrote: "The workers are demonstrating marvelously against the Moloch, and the middle-class press is silencing the fact to death. Isn't this a sin against the *responsibility* the press has to inform the public?"[42] And much to Suttner's intense anger, the common German-French congress of the socialist party was not mentioned in the *Neue Freie Presse*.[43]

The growing nationalism in Europe took on warlike characteristics: "This whole European war party is doing a good job of driving us toward a catastrophe, and perhaps the only way for this low civilization to make place for a higher is to be swept away. It's not possible to have so much explosives collect without them finally going off. Wretched madhouse."[44]

She took advantage of every opportunity to appeal to journalists' consciences and to ask for their help with the peace work. At the international press conference in Vienna in 1904 she gave a speech that was reprinted as the lead article in the *Neue Wiener Tagblatt* in both the English and French versions: "The press is one of the powers—perhaps even the mightiest today—which can have a decisive effect on war and peace. When a war is avoided or when one breaks out, it happens with the influence of the press. . . . Journalists, my brothers, you who are imbued with the responsibility of your office and who feel the awareness of your power, use it to take mankind forward on its path to happiness."[45] Her appeal went unheeded.

As the crises piled up after 1908, the tenor of the international press became more and more aggressive. Suttner wrote in a worried letter to Fried in 1911: "If only this blustering, repulsive German-Austrian newspaper mob wouldn't drive us into a world conflagration."[46] In Bertha's opinion, the nationalistic press also played a considerable part in the worsening relations between Germany and England: "That certain word has already been uttered: 'A war between Germany and England is unavoidable.' A criminal word . . . It is time, high time, for just and thinking people to declare just as loudly: such a war does not have to come, and not only that—it must not come. Such an insane double suicide of two highly developed nations, related by blood and culture, must be prevented."

Again she did everything she could to counteract the agitation. However, she had meanwhile given up trust in the power of the peace societies: "Societies are usually poor in numbers and poor in external influence." Other, greater movements were needed, a "peace army," by which she meant a protest of all who wanted peace, beyond all societies.

Her English pacifist associate, Sir Thomas Barclay, suggested having a sign of recognition for all the followers of a brotherhood of nations: against a blue field, the three golden letters, F.I.G., for *"Fraternitas inter gentes"* (Brotherhood between peoples). Of course, the word formed by the initials, *fig,* was unfortunate, since it stood for something worthless, trivial. Kalauer left no time in saying, "I don't care a fig for Sir Thomas' league."[47]

In 1911, three years after the annexation crisis, the Italians exploited Turkey's weakness to perpetrate a robbery and annex the last Turkish possessions in North Africa, including Tripoli. Suttner wrote to Hermann Bahr:

> The move made by the Italian government was marked by a brutality that has not appeared in such an undisguised form in a long time. Turkey could not defend itself.
>
> And that offers the only ray of hope for a possible end to the war.

A strange war, fought by only one party. We don't see two opponents here, just robber and victim and passive onlookers. The other powers are accomplices, they've all robbed before (only with a bit more form). For that reason we 'have to turn over a new leaf.' Medieval robber baronage has to give way to the era of international law. Otherwise everything will end in ruin.[48]

Once again, no other power tried to mediate. Suttner, disappointed, wrote: "The Tripoli move was not only an attack against Turkey. It was also an attack against The Hague. And the behavior of all the European cabinets is passive participation in this attack." The war showed: "For one thing, that the eternal assurances by governments that armament was only intended for defense and order, are intentional untruths, for we see now that the armies and fleets are—just as in Alexander's time—used for conquest." Moreover, it had become clear "that the assurances of statesmen and diplomats are intentionally false, as they were in Machiavelli's time . . . because only a few weeks before the Tripoli campaign, the Turkish heir to the throne was received in Rome with all due honors, and while he was being kissed on both cheeks and the campaign was being prepared secretly with wonderful precision, assurances were made to him that Italy did not have the slightest intention of taking over the North African provinces."[49]

The Austrian Peace Society sponsored a public protest demonstration against the "brutal act by the Italian government." "Italy fills me with disgust now," Bertha wrote to Fried. "The war the country is waging is bad enough—but the enthusiasm it incites is a thousand times worse."[50]

This patriotic enthusiasm was something even the Italian pacifists could not resist. Bertha watched with great dismay as her old associate, the Nobel Peace Prize winner Moneta, sanctioned the war, and Theodore Roosevelt, also a recipient of the Nobel Peace Prize, backed new armament: "They ought to take the prize away from Roosevelt and unfortunately, Moneta, too," she wrote to Fried with disappointment. "That comes from the disastrous 'patriotism.' If you try to bring it safely into the peace movement (and Moneta constantly does that) you slither into the abyss of war."[51]

Moneta, torn this way and that between patriotism and pacifism, is reported to have said: "War is an evil—but there are greater evils—therefore preferably: war." The Suttner commentary was: "Yes, a secession will form in Italy, too. The terribly sad thing will still be that the head of Italian pacifism . . . whinnies enthusiastically like an old war horse at the first sound of the trumpet. And we all loved him so!"[52]

Then, Moneta even believed in an international conspiracy against Italy, originating from the Freemasons. "Only the version that this comes from indignant legality and humanity is one that does not occur to those intoxicated minds."[53]

The subject of Moneta occupied Suttner for a long time, because it showed so glaringly how greatly pacifism was threatened, not only by external enemies, but even by famous leaders within the movement who thought pacifism was unrealistic in concrete situations. Bertha complained about the Italian pacifists: "We've lost them completely." "Anybody in Italy who says one word against the war today is lynched."[54]

The English pacifist Stead fought hardest against the Tripoli war. He wrote burning newspaper appeals and demanded, among other things, a boycott against Italian pasta: "There's blood on macaroni!" Suttner's commentary to Fried: "What energy and what true military genius this Stead has: unbelievable! . . . Only he's much too fierce."[55]

Stead's death in the *Titanic* catastrophe in April 1912 hit the international pacifists very hard. Bertha wrote: "Poor Stead . . . How blind nature is! It takes away the best, most useful."[56]

The Tripoli war reinforced the opinion of the imperial military leaders that a preventive war against Italy looked more promising than ever. One exponent of this opinion was the chief of staff, Franz Graf Conrad von Hötzendorf, whose sudden resignation in December 1911 gave rise to speculation. "Conrad von Hötzendorf had to go. Emperor does not want war. Crown prince does.—What will happen? Will all Europe burn?" "Papers awful regarding Hötzendorf. It shows that the people are in the hands of the militarists."[57] The press and the military leaders tried to defend Conrad's plans. Barely a year later he was back in office.

The pacifists had practically nothing to set against the massive war propaganda. They did not even have enough money for fliers or pamphlets.

The Tripoli war, along with the annexation of Bosnia, fanned the flames of greed in the Balkan states. The Russian envoy in Belgrade brought about an alliance of the four Balkan states, Serbia, Bulgaria, Greece, and Montenegro in February of 1912, while the Tripoli War was still going on. The declared goal of the members of the alliance: the partitioning of European Turkey among the Balkan states. This laid the foundation for the next war. Armament went ahead at a feverish pace everywhere. Bertha wrote: "Oh, we are in a military morass here."[58]

In Austria-Hungary there was only slightly more of a morass than in the rest of the European states, however: "In the Sorbonne under chairman Clemenceau (he was always a chauvinist) there's agitation for collections to pay for building a fleet of airships. And an industrialist pledged 100,000 francs immediately. . . . [T]he stubbornness of people is abysmal!"[59]

The sudden eagerness shared by all the European powers to build up a strong air force as quickly as possible was also the result of the Tripoli War. Here, for the first time in history, bombs were thrown from airplanes. The outcome of this "experiment" encouraged military leaders in their conviction that this new weapons technology would be decisive in future wars.

For centuries war had been waged in two ways, by army and by navy—and now a third had joined them with breathtaking speed, one that had been beyond imagination only a short while before: the air force. Suttner wrote to Fried: "By creating a third armed force in all countries, this rabid armament has gone into such a paroxysm that either it or the people will break down under it."[60]

When the first invention for air travel was made, a balloon that could be steered, Suttner hoped and dreamed that this new achievement would make war impossible: "The separating borderlines would be blurred, since neither blockades nor customs barriers, nor border defenses can be erected in the air; the easier and ten times faster traffic would bring the people even closer than they are already with railway and steamship travel, and coming closer would also make enmities disappear; and the mere joy that would be awakened in the hearts by such a wonderful achievement would take people out of their trivial feelings of hatred and envy."[61]

The French newspaper *Journal* planned a tour from capital to capital (Paris, Berlin, London, Brussels, Paris) under the motto: "The aeroplane, instrument of peace." The pacifists applauded, but the French nationalists made a successful protest against this "unpatriotic" idea.[62]

Ever since the Tripoli war, at the latest, the importance of "air machines" had become quite clear. The pacifists all over the world did everything in their power to describe the horrors of this new weapon in the most drastic terms to try to bring about a ban on them. In England three hundred prominent personalities from science and the arts protested against using armed airships and recommended an international agreement.

Suttner wrote a paper, "The Barbarization of the Air." She said the new weapons had the same effect as if two chess players were to sit at a board and declare: "We want to keep all the old rules of the game: the pawn can only take one step at a time, the knight can jump as before; the queen has the most power, the king can retreat into his castling, but we want to add a new rule: every one of us may let something fall on the board from above and knock all the players over. A charming twist—the chess champions would certainly be grateful."[63]

She was concerned about the indolence of her contemporaries in view of the terrible prospects for the future: "Without a care in the world, they looked at this fuse lying in front of the magazine of war arms, just waiting for a single spark."

She quoted in detail the like-minded English writer, H. G. Wells, who described the deceptive security: "Up to the eve of the air-war, nothing but a single picture of progress, safety the world over, incredible showplaces of marvelously organized industry and orderly populations, gigantic cities which stretched themselves to infinity. Seas and oceans strewn with ships, the land covered with networks of railways and highways. And then all of a sudden, the air fleets sweep across the scene unexpectedly, and we are standing at the beginning of the end."[64]

And "[a] general social collapse was the logical consequence of the world war. Wherever there were big populations, there were also masses of people without work, without money, unable to earn a livelihood." What followed was starvation and sickness. "The big countries and the wealthy have become mere names on the lips of the people. Everywhere there are ruins, unburied dead, weathered pale-faced survivors in a deadly apathy." *"But war knows no halting.* The flags are still waving. New air fleets are coming into being, new shapes of airships. And beneath their gliding battles, the world is getting darker and darker. . . . All the lovely order and welfare of the world have shrunk together like a burst bubble."[65]

"Those, then, are the visions of things that may not happen but which are being wished for and dreamed of by some spirits and in any case are being made possible through diligent work."[66]

The increasingly desperate efforts to prevent the "great war" gave Fried the idea of holding the international peace congress for the year 1914 in Vienna. Bertha von Suttner moaned when she found out about his plans. She pointed to her age, the poor condition of the peace society, which could hardly be of any help in organizing, and listed another hundred or so reasons against the idea. But she began to write letters begging for money for the project all the same. After all, she had "friends like Carnegie, Butler, Ginn [all wealthy American pacifists], Monaco—and nothing can be accomplished here in the name of friendship?"[67]

She often wrote until late into the night. "Of course, I am not doing these things without misgivings that my dignity could suffer and that I might do more damage than good. But on the other hand, if I don't do anything, what then? We'll see. I *have to* get somewhere even if my powerful friends who swear their friendship don't stand by me."[68] Fourteen days later one thousand dollars came from Butler in the United States.

Support from the Austrian government was not to be expected. She complained to Fried about "the unsuitability of Vienna" for such a congress: "Not *one* personality from the political, intellectual, industrial, or literary world. And all this hostility from the court, aristocracy, and church (while in London, for example, all three participate). And this attitude in the press—and this general pathological militarism! A pond frozen a meter high to swim through—that's what Vienna looks like to me in respect to a peace conference."[69]

She found the Austrian Peace Society more isolated and ridiculed than ever, certainly not a good situation for an international congress. "It will be absolutely impossible to find any official people of ours willing to place themselves in the service of a society that is run by a woman (she, however, is issuing the invitation to the congress); and," she wrote Fried reproachfully, "among the anti-Semitic Christian Socialist leaders—with whom you always want to make an arrangement, there will be no one who will have anything to do with a Jew. We will stand there alone, we two—without money, without the help of the press, without a prominent committee: it would do a lot of damage to the peace cause, embarrass us in front of the English and the Americans . . . Austria, the bulwark of militarism and clericalism. This truth can be imparted to the world to explain how impossible it is to summon the pacificists here just to expose them to official contempt."[70]

As usual, it was the "higher circles" she expected the most of and was the most disappointed in. They were simply not interested in such things as the peace movement. "Sports, the hunt, business deals, card games, and a narrow horizon of interests: that characterizes our upper classes. In politics, the greatest responsibility is the dogged defense of the privileges of class."[71]

It was embarrassing to have to admit to the foreign pacifists that there were so many failures connected with the preparations for the Vienna congress. All the same, Suttner encouraged Fried to be completely frank in disclosing the full misery of the situation when he went to the Bern Peace Bureau: "Please tell the office plainly that the Austrian ministers have said they do *not* want to support the congress."[72]

Every day she became more aware that her strength was leaving her:

her eyesight was worse, walking was difficult, after doing strenuous work she needed more rest than before. Her seventieth birthday was approaching and, faced with the failures in the peace movement, she came close to retiring from active life.

It was Alfred Fried who repeatedly heaped new jobs upon her and who, as she put it, "whipped [her] like an old horse." He knew how much she needed work, despite her occasional complaints. She was grateful for this pressure and scoffed at him with great kindliness: the almost ninety-year-old Frédéric Passy "is holding a lecture at the Sorbonne right about now—on Tolstoy. You are going to hold this miraculous dotard up to me as an encouraging example, aren't you?"[73]

The aged Suttner greatly admired Fried's capacity for work and his devotion to the common cause: "You are de facto the only one we have in central Europe to represent pacifism here and who can make it come alive in publication," she wrote him, full of praise.[74] Although Fried did not find much recognition in Germany or Austria-Hungary, he was well known in other countries. In 1911 he was discussed as the candidate for the Nobel Prize. Bertha had already suggested him in previous years but had not thought he stood a chance. In December she wrote in her diary: "Fried comes—throws himself, weeping, on my breast—I think his wife is dead—no, the misfortune is as follows: 'I have the Nobel prize.' . . . Fried and wife are rid of their worst worries. . . . My prophecy that he would have a career one day has proved good."[75]

The reaction of Austria-Hungary to Fried's Nobel Prize was less than reserved. The newspapers hardly took notice of this honor.

All of Bertha von Suttner's lectures, newspaper articles, and books from this time are full of the deep sorrow due to the "great misfortune threatening or oppressing all fellow men." "It is impossible to do anything but shudder when you take a new look at the tragedy of the present and coming situations, and you are tortured by the intense longing to see the approaching calamity averted at least—for God's sake averted *in time*. There is no such thing as simply shaking off worries like these."[76]

In the restless, increasingly hectic work of averting the foreseen and feared world war, Suttner became more and more anxious and pessimistic. During this time she went through difficult crises, doubted the sense of her work, and then told her friends she wanted to withdraw from public life. Fried wrote: "When she says that, she does not tolerate any contradiction." But her friends only needed to wait a while. "They know that she will be there at the next peace alarm, like a battle horse when he hears the bugle blow. In her innermost being, she does not seem like a person who could bring herself to sit in retirement and wait for her exit. She is far more likely to die in harness."[77]

When the worries over the Balkan conflict, air force, and the enthusiasm for war became unbearable, Fried suggested a lecture tour through America. D'Estournelles and Stefan Türr had made similar promotional trips for pacifism before with great success. Suttner was famous and highly revered in the United States, and she herself saw a better, more advanced world in America and admired the American pacifists.

In 1911 the Anglo-American arbitration treaty had just been concluded and was being celebrated by pacifists all over the world as a triumph. In the treaty England and the United States rejected the use of war in the case of differences and obligated themselves to observing the arbiters' decision. Andrew Carnegie's opinion was: "That is the most benevolent proclamation that has ever been made in the history of mankind, because it rang in the death knell for war."[78] He thought that other countries would follow this example soon. Carnegie's speech reinforced Suttner's hopes in America as the guarantor of a better future.

She was, after all, sixty-nine years old, not entirely healthy anymore and physically very awkward when she decided to make the trip. Organization was taken over by Andrea Hofer-Proudfoot (she was a descendant of a relative of the hero of Tyrolean freedom, Andreas Hofer), a friend of the American publisher and pacifist Edwin Ginn. Mrs. Proudfoot arranged lectures in big cities and universities in the United States for the seven-month tour.

"Isn't the whole America trip a little bizarre?" Bertha asked her friend Alfred Fried, rather anxiously.[79] Then later, it was Fried who was worried: "The choice of a freight steamer for the crossing, embarking second-class on Whit Saturday are not the signs of a grand and comfortable tour. More like an impoverished undertaking, interlarded with privations, which you really don't have to put up with. . . . That's being reckless, Baroness. . . . The tour . . . has to be *first-class*. Or you shouldn't dare undertake it. . . . If you arrive in New York on a freighter, you'll be discredited."[80]

Suttner answered him bravely: "Nonsense.—Well, without a little of that there won't be enough courage to carry it out. I'm not going on a joy ride; I'm making a last crusade for the cause."[81] After docking in New York, she continued with the Pacific Railway to San Francisco, where a marvelous reception awaited her. "Papers celebrating my arrival like that of a queen. Evening, speech in a church. On the door in illuminated writing 'Lay down your arms.' The pastor who introduced me told me he had preached on the book. Ovation."[82]

She was hailed most of all by the American women's clubs. She took part in an education congress in Chicago and a suffragist congress in Philadelphia. She called "on the organized and federated women of America" to support the European peace activities and told them her own country, Austria-Hungary, was threatened with "being drawn into the horror of the slaughter and the hostility," and that the same danger existed for the other countries of Europe.

"We, the peace society, are powerless because the states do not take us seriously even though the Hague tribunal is our recognized defender." She needed moral, spiritual, and financial support: "We need funds in order to come to the foreground, to make them listen to us, to publicize the true facts that censored Europe is hiding. We have to be capable of announcing the truth to the press which at present generally supports militarism, even war."[83]

She spoke in schools and churches and in the big lecture halls of America to packed audiences.

Fried describes the appearance of the aging Suttner like this:

She steps up to the podium slowly and with difficulty, supported by friends who rush to help her. Then she stands there, a tall figure, whose *embonpoint* is effectively retouched by the widow's veil billowing down from the gray curls on her head, so that she looks almost slender. Her head is thrown back proudly; her glance appears to look beyond the crowd with disdain. Of course that is a deception produced by the Baroness's extreme short-sightedness. She looks "beyond" because her eyes cannot focus on anything. A long time passes before she starts to speak. She appears to be searching for words. And then she speaks softly, very softly and slowly, separating the individual words with little pauses. She never moves a hand; never makes a gesture. When she wants to emphasize something in her speech, she does it with the tone of her voice, by throwing her head back sharply. All of it together creates an impression of royalty. If there were a throne behind her, no one would doubt for a moment that they had a queen in front of them.

Because of this impression, the audience forgot that Suttner was actually "a bad speaker," which she frankly admitted herself. Fried said she spoke "too softly . . . too slowly . . . too wearily—much too wearily and too full of pain." Her style of speaking was "second Empire," that is, old-fashioned and too high and mighty. It was "the power of this personality" that fascinated the audience.[84]

Sometimes she held her speeches during the day, and then they were followed by receptions, interviews, and long train rides at night to the next lecture site. Her health was remarkably stable despite all these exertions; she even seemed to be stimulated and was much livelier than in Vienna. She found very little time to write to Fried: "*This* enthusiasm! If only we weren't so far away from each other—I feel as though we were on a different star. And I'll confide in you alone: in spite of all the greatness and glory—I long to be back on the small, narrow ground of home. There *are* roots and very old trees like me. . . . I'm being torn apart here."[85]

While in America, she continued to write her political reviews for the *Friedenswarte*. The mail took a long time arriving, though. Bertha became restless because her normal rhythm was disturbed, and she received her usual publications either with huge delays or not at all. Barely four weeks after her arrival she wrote to Fried: "The *distance* from Europe gets on my nerves. American newspapers say practically nothing about Europe. I don't know how the things that interest me are getting along—and letters are so slow. . . . Exiled soul. I only hope I get home alive and see the people again whom I love, who love me."[86]

She found that American enthusiasm for peace was not nearly as far advanced as she had imagined from her impression of the competent American pacifists she knew: "The syndicate for armament appears to be at it all over the world . . . and here 70% of the federal income is spent for military purposes." And another time she enlightened Fried: "America is not *all that* pacifistically advanced, as we thought. The great masses are just as dull and unknowing as they are at home regarding the issue, and politicians (Roosevelt at the head) don't want to hear anything about *real* pacifism."[87]

In Philadelphia she witnessed the election campaign. She was a party supporter for the later victor, Woodrow Wilson, and placed great hope in him. She did not think much of his opponent, her fellow recipient of the Nobel Prize, Theodore Roosevelt, and was "not only disappointed" in his oppositional speeches, she was "indignant. . . . Calling the Taft treaties criminal and stupid—praising battleship construction as the best way to peace!—That is a scandal for a Nobel Peace Prize winner."[88]

In Beverly, she talked to the revered President William H. Taft on a golf course. She wrote Fried: "Taft, according to his secretary, held 1,500 pacifist speeches all over the country. That is something Franz Ferdinand would never do. . . . Yes, Hapsburg should sit on its throne, supported by bayonettes and stupidity! *That* is the whole meaning of history in the eyes of these gentlemen." Then, however, she added: "You say we will have to emigrate? And yet I am drawn back. I am 'at home' there, after all."[89]

She had herself informed at length about social problems and even held what she called a "socialist speech" at a "labor federation meeting." "Spirit moves me. Am really living up to my mission. This is a phenomenon worth looking into." A worker who spoke before her "held an inflammatory speech" and then she called "for cooperation between all classes. You can't just wait and let one of them win. Got applause.—rising votes."[90]

When, a short time later in Baltimore, she saw herself forced into "diplomatic" behavior, she did not like it at all: "But really, under socialism it was nicer—more directly to the point."[91]

She saw the first football game in her life and noted in her diary: "Columbia, football game, Missouri loses 29 to 0. I, as a guest of honor, sit in the bleachers with a white-rimmed flag on the ballustrade."[92]

She reported approvingly in her diary on such details as: "Berkeley . . . Mayor of the city . . . shows us the cannon that was hidden under roses on May 18 in front of City Hall."[93]

The "Peace Bertha" (she was called "the angel of peace" in the newspapers) accepted an invitation to the hacienda of the newspaper king, William Randolph Hearst, and in Pittsburgh she visited the "magnificent home" of the Kennedys. Very soon, being a celebrity got to be too much: "Have had enough of being famous and not deserving it."[94]

When she got the news that war had been waged again since October 1912 in her native Europe, she scolded in a letter to Fried: "Oh, this old mountain swineherd they made king!"[95] She meant Nikita I of Montenegro, who took the title of king in 1910. He was the driving force in the Balkan War of the four allies (Serbia, Bulgaria, Greece, and Montenegro) against Turkey. "All the Greeks and Bulgarians and Serbs in America are donating money and rushing off to the "Fatherland" to take part in the battle festival; people are such a pack of fools that it makes one sick sometimes to take trouble with them. And I have to make a speech every day on peace. . . . D'Estournelles wrote a harsh letter to Nikolaus of Montenegro. Bravo."[96]

In her lectures now, she mostly dealt with the current political situation. "I oppose the point of view that a large part of the American public has seized the opinion that this war was necessary for the liberation of the Christians in the Balkans and that, by pushing the Turks out of Europe, it might have favorable consequences. *No war* is necessary today, I maintain, and none can bring about favorable consequences. Combining slaughter with religious issues is an anachronism, hypocrisy and blasphemy."[97]

She was very worried that Austria-Hungary would be drawn into this war and wrote in her diary: "News from Austria shocking: all the powers full of good intentions for making agreements, even Russia peaceful, also Serbia says it will bow to decree from the powers, only Austria's posture is one of 'I won't give up anything.'"[98]

She complained about all of them, "except for the pacifists and socialists," during these critical weeks in America. "If only Serbia does not get a harbor; for us, that is of the greatest interest to mankind. Cholera, bankruptcy, anarchy, starvation, destruction: all of that is secondary." She turned to Carnegie: "Central Europe needs help. If European war breaks out, the whole business will be brought to ruin. . . . What will I find in Vienna? Serbs and Russians?"[99]

But, she wrote, "The socialists are upright everywhere. Bravo Jaurès—also bravo Viennese. The rest of the Viennese papers beneath all contempt."[100] The peace demonstration by the women of Vienna also reaped praise: "Good of the women. Of course, I should have been there."[101]

Even in America all her thoughts were directed to Austria, despite all the distractions. When the organizers talked about whether to invite President Taft to the big farewell banquet for Suttner, she wrote bitterly: "In Vienna it would hardly occur to anybody to consider the head of state as a speaker." All the same, she was homesick: "Where is that land where our ideas blossom and one can still be at home?—Oh, the feeling of home. How I miss that here! I couldn't feel the difference much more on Saturn than here."[102]

Fried was so disturbed by these complaints that he wanted to send Bertha's housekeeper, Kathi Buchinger, to America. Suttner protested: "*The* idea! to send Kathi to me! From such a distance you can't know what is possible and what is impossible. . . . You ask if I can hold out four months?—My God, there are people who are imprisoned for four months."[103] "On the whole, I will have had experiences and gained impressions that will enrich the end of my life more than a visit to Stockern [the castle owned by the Suttner relatives]."[104]

At the end of her seven-month stay in America, she gave lectures for a week in New York, including one at Columbia University. Andrew Carnegie presided at a banquet in her honor and a bit later wrote her a letter promising her a pension for the rest of her life. "And will a carefree old age really await me because of Carnegie?" Bertha asks hopefully in her diary.[105]

On December 14, 1912, she said, "Goodbye America."

> The America trip showed me a wonderful horizon, brought me a great deal of honor and perhaps even a pleasant old age. In any case, there's a surplus of some 20,000 crowns. [By way of comparison: a grade school teacher then earned 120 crowns a month.] And being able to avoid the terribly unpleasant events at home . . . What kind of conditions will I find in that scandalously medieval country?—Here everything was quite different: this wealth, this splendor, these opportunities—and these masses of people who live for the highest ideal—young people are being steered in this direction. Of course, a lot of bad examples are being brought over from Europe.[106]

The Suttner journey found an echo in the Viennese papers. In an interview printed by the *Neue Freie Presse,* the capable Mrs. Hofer-Proudfoot outlined the advantages this lecture trip held for Austria: "At all the public meetings the Austrian flag could be seen next to the American one in honor of the Austrian guest. It is to be hoped that this great natural advertisement for Austria-Hungary will be expressed in the tourist travel statistics."[107]

On the day before Christmas in 1912 Bertha arrived in Vienna and took renewed hope, "That the horizon has brightened—and that in Basel the socialists have reached an antiwar decision . . . street procession: four men carrying a big book with 'Lay Down Your Arms' inspires hope."[108]

But the situation remained tense. The skies of the future did not look bright. They were "full of Damocles' swords. And that's what people call 'peace,' which they try to maintain by threats, bluffs, balancing the power and other similar methods."[109]

Meanwhile, the Balkan states had beat Turkey. In Austria, the public was angry with the "Balkan mob." A preventive war against Serbia was being pushed. "Turkey (poor worm) appears to be giving in. The war-wishers aren't getting their money's worth.—Who knows, maybe the current 'crisis' will really bring about recuperation! If I could only live another fifty years! . . . and the world is *so* interesting!"[110]

As always, she tended all too quickly to give pacifist activities the credit for peace and wrote to Fried proudly: "Today I met someone in a salon who told me Conrad von Hötzendorf had complained that the military leaders could not decide by themselves, that so many others had to have their say—otherwise we would have had the desirable war much sooner."[111]

But as ever, she also advised extreme caution: "Yes, yes, we're advancing, certainly, and at a pedestrian pace—the others, though, are going at express or even storm tempo. It can let loose at any minute." And on another occasion she wrote: "By the way, we're all dancing and writing and planning on a volcano."[112]

Austrian politics were very often the target of her criticism: "Russia says it doesn't want to create danger of European conflagration. All the others say it, too. But you never hear a word of this in Austria. The danger of Europe burning is never taken into account in the Serb, Rumanian conflicts."[113]

Just as annoying to Suttner, however, were the politics of the German ally: "The fact that the German papers (the conservative ones) turn down Churchill's proposal for an armament *pause*, is so genuinely German-conservative. They don't want to *dis*arm, they don't want to *restrict*—and now they don't even want to make a pause."[114]

In the spring of 1913 the Balkan crisis came to a head again. The four victors could not agree on the distribution of the booty.

Her diary entry for March 25, 1913, noted: "World situation and world gossip point to war and to the hopeless stupidity of our proclaimers of truth. I accuse myself for not letting my voice be heard."

On April 1, 1913, she wrote: "The European situation getting worse and worse. And I cannot find the right word I would like so much to scream into this fearful Niagara-force alarm. . . . On the whole it appears to me that the great European blowup is preparing itself. How can so much sowing of weeds not sprout, so much piled up gunpowder not explode. Lethargy, indifference, numb passivity, letting things happen, are accomplices of the zeal the evil and the dumb unfold."

She experienced the mood felt by "good society" among her relatives: "Here in Stockern they argue like this: Austria has proved its great love of peace in the way it dealt with the provocations of the swine Serbs."[115] And a few months later: "Here they only think that the Russians are to blame for everything and that war with them is unavoidable!"[116]

The small group of pacifists fought on for disarmament, at least for a limitation to armament. In 1913 German and French pacifists made a simultaneous appeal to their governments to stop the arms race: "A single government, a single parliament, a single people cannot be the first.

But with goodwill, there are ways to bring about an understanding for a simultaneous and common course of action. Neutral powers can take over mediation if that makes it easier for an agreement to take place."[117]

The pacifists had to defend themselves repeatedly against the accusation that they lacked success. Bertha explained to one of the skeptics that the Balkan War was "the result of the still existing supranational lawlessness that we are fighting. If the forceful oppression of the Turks had not come before, there would be no need for a forceful shaking off of the yoke. With a secure international legal system, it would be possible to liberate a people from disagreeable rule, without war." The Balkan War showed:

> 1. what infinite devastation and loss modern war brings down upon the vanquished *and* the victor—losses that no longer have any relationship to possible gains;
> 2. what dangers are attached to new conflicts and new wars;
> 3. that the world of today has such closely connected economic and other interests that the losses suffered in one country, be it ever so far away and ever so small, cause losses and suffering in every other country;
> 4. that because of modern weaponry and modern armies, wars bring about such immense horror, sickness, and ruin that they have already exceeded the measure of human tolerance;
> 5. that such a strong will for peace and such an intensive need for peace have permeated the world, that despite these Balkan disturbances, the great European war that should have started long ago according to prophecy, has not broken out and, in fact, efforts are being made to prevent it with all sorts of surprising, diplomatic, and other means; that finally, therefore: it is *high* time to implement the world organization already taking form through various institutions (Hague Court of Arbitration, treaties, etc.) and place it on a secure legal foundation.[118]

In this politically dangerous situation, Suttner was supposed to hold a "peace address" at the Seventh General Meeting of the Austrian Women's Clubs in Graz in April 1913. A copy of the speech she was asked to submit ahead of time became an object of contention. The president of the Austrian women's clubs, Marianne Hainisch, received a telegram with the following message: The Graz local committee must unequivocally reject Suttner's speech as highly political, therefore against the statutes, under the present circumstances, any peace address at all entirely impossible, would do unpredictable damage to the women's movement."

Protest letters came in. One of the ladies wrote: "Certainly, peace propaganda, as long as it is treated and claimed as an academic issue, is unpolitical by nature, but *today,* when Austria is standing with its hand on the hilt of the sword . . . we cannot possibly treat this subject in a meeting open to the general public." Another letter spoke of the address being "out of place . . . in view of the blood flowing in rivers and the general mood of war." "Military circles and other official circles will probably withdraw entirely. The name of Suttner is a matter of policy and at the moment, a highly political one."

"The mayor, a woman who had put a great deal of effort into making an evening reception possible, would get into a great deal of trouble through Suttner's presence in Graz. She is in a true state of desperation," since the event was supposed to take place in the military casino.

And yet another of the women stressed the fact that Suttner was "by her name alone like a red cape in front of a bull, and where Austria's disgrace in regard to the Balkan states is felt deeply on all sides, it is understandable that the army will not lend its casino for an evening, if the despised peace is being spoken for in the morning."[119]

In her diary, Bertha treated this event—which was only one of many—tersely: "My name like a red cape. Of course I'll withdraw. I'll get hold of the letters. Are interesting letters. Later Hainisch will come herself. Is totally worn down."[120] Marianne Hainisch, who agreed with Bertha absolutely, did at least get the women's meeting in Graz to write the disinvited speaker a friendly letter, which was printed in the *Neue Freie Presse.* Thus, the unfortunate affair was resolved.

In May 1913 the head of the information service of the imperial army, Colonel Alfred Redl, was discovered to be a spy for Russia and committed suicide. Although a great deal about this case was hushed up, the affair could not be concealed entirely. Stefan Zweig, who was thirty-two years old at the time, wrote of Redl: "A shudder of horror went through the army. Everybody knew that in war, this man would have cost the lives of hundreds of thousands and that the monarchy would have been taken to the brink of disaster; in this moment we Austrians realized for the first time how very close we had been during the past year to a world war."

By chance, the writer ran into Bertha von Suttner during this time and reported: "She approached me very excitedly. 'People don't understand what is happening,' she screamed very loudly on the street, although she normally spoke so gently, so kindly and calmly. 'That was the war already and they have hidden everything from us again and kept it secret. Why don't you do something, you young people? It concerns you most of all! Fight back, get together! Don't always leave everything to a few old women nobody listens to.'" Zweig told her he was going to Paris and perhaps he would "try a really joint manifestation." "Why only perhaps?" she pushed. "Things are worse than ever, the machine is already running." Zweig: "I had difficulty calming her down; I was disturbed myself."[121]

During this hectic time, Bertha's seventieth birthday came up in June 1913. Countess Pötting organized a collection for an "honorary gift" on the occasion. One of the donors this time was an archduke: Ludwig Salvator gave a thousand crowns and wrote a very friendly letter to Fried besides. Bertha wrote: "I was terribly happy about Ludwig Salvator. It's wonderful the way he places himself openly in the pacifist camp and recognizes one's accomplishments so respectfully," and added with resignation: "I understand why they think he is insane in our court circles!"[122] (Archduke Ludwig, from the Tuscan branch of the Hapsburg family, did not live in Vienna; he lived on the Balearic Islands, together with a local woman who, of course, was not acceptable at court. He wrote travel books and loved to shock the court toadies with his uncourtly behavior on his occasional visits to Vienna. He was definitely one of the most intelligent Hapsburgs from around 1900 but was very much an outsider because of his provocative behavior. His support of the pacifist movement was quite in line with his peculiar, uncourtly manner and does not, by any means, indicate that the peace movement had taken hold in the imperial house—a fact that even the otherwise optimistic Bertha did not misinterpret.)

"For My Seventieth Birthday," she wrote an article to herself in the *Neue Freie Presse* in which she appealed for confidence and optimism: "Once upon a time there was a last *auto-da-fé*, a last slave market, a last witch trial, so the Balkan War can also be the last European war." What was needed was not "sentimentality and fanaticism," of which she was often accused, but "energetic intervention" and "tenacious strength of will . . . borne on enthusiasm," to prevent "the general war of the future."[123]

As warmly as the pacifists all over the world honored "their" Suttner, the conduct of the Austrian public was and remained all the more disappointing: there was no official gesture in her honor.

In contrast to Vienna, Prague, the city where Bertha was born, honored her as a "great daughter of the city . . . even though she is a German woman," as the *Friedenswarte* reported.[124]

Suttner took this birthday as an occasion to write a new will. She made her sister-in-law, Baroness Luise von Suttner, her universal heir and gave her servants, chiefly Kathi Buchinger, generous legacies. Alfred Hermann Fried, however, was the true heir: he was to get the literary estate, the diaries, letters, and books: "As a pacifist and journalist he will know best how to make use of them." Like Arthur, she wanted to be cremated in Gotha: "Religious ceremonies at a funeral are something I neither avoid nor desire. I die as I have lived—without belief in dogma."[125]

The peace of London that ended the Balkan War in May 1913 did not last long. Already in June, Bulgaria attacked Serbia: The second Balkan War followed the first. This time Serbia, Greece, Rumania, and Turkey joined in fighting Bulgaria. Suttner wrote on July 9, 1913: "War fever has broken out all over Europe. Enthusiasm for German defense. Acceptance of a three-year period of service in France. Incitement against Russia here. It is as though the undisputed 'war of the future' is bound to come. The triumph of suggestion."

"This whole witches' sabbath in the Balkans," as she wrote Fried, did not bring about a change of thought: "The *lessons* of the war there are already so noisily and bloodily and hellishly clear, according to *our* principle that the numbness of the world around us and the press makes you want to cry out that they do not understand these lessons, on the contrary, they sink all the more deeply into worse militarism." She complained of the "mutual accusations of massacre and horror" among the warring parties. "They argue whether Bulgarians, Greeks, Serbs, or Turks are the worst, wildest beasts and do not notice that the beast is war itself." "And the next Hague conference (*if* it takes place) will once again place various methods for polishing the claws of war on its agenda."[126]

The Bulgarians suffered a crushing defeat, and the dispute over new boundaries began. "And the way the public is being molested with these various borderlines—as though the happiness of mankind depended on whether a strip of land belongs here or there. And this new fetish: balance!"[127]

Fried and Suttner worked all the more doggedly on preparing the peace congress. The lottery that was staged to finance it was a blunt, even disgraceful failure. Bertha had the feeling she was not up to the demands of the fight anymore: "I stay in my easy chair for hours on end, like a stupid turtle.—'Physical and mental sluggishness in old age is a physiological law,' I read today. Absolutely right."[128]

There were never such hateful caricatures of the unshapely, old Suttner as now. In his anger, Fried wanted at one time to have a paper with an especially mean caricature banned. But Suttner declined with resignation: what good would it do? She had not been worried about personal vanity for a long time. Her only concern was the cause of peace—and it was in worse shape than ever.

The German-nationalist writer Edith Countess Salburg wrote agitating articles and derided the fact "that we, if we survive, will also be old women eventually—the fact that such people are afraid of war and want their peace and quiet, is natural—but when you stand in the midst of life, you know that it means unrest and fighting." Suttner's response: "Oh, wisdom: as though it satisfied an old woman's need for quiet to take up a fight against thousands of institutions and travel across half the world. . . . It would be interesting to have a little disputation with the lady."[129]

She suffered greatly under pacifism's inability to counteract the excessive war propaganda. In spring of 1914 a pamphlet by Sven Hedin ("Second Warning") was distributed. It argued against Sweden's neutrality and demanded affiliation with the policies of the Triple Alliance, especially the German *Reich*. Suttner wrote: "It would be interesting to find out who bore the cost of printing and distributing a million copies. We pacifists know how hard it is to have a pamphlet that pleads *for* neutrality and taking care of the eventualities of war printed and a few hundred copies sent out—but everything that works in favor of war has sums in the millions at its disposal."[130]

All the same, Bertha did not give up. She placed her hopes in the effects of propaganda from the peace congress and urged Fried to do "something for the public at large." Perhaps President Taft would even come from the United States along with other famous speakers: "Israel Zangwill for the Jewish, Rudyard Kipling for the English colony—Or names of equal rank . . . mass meetings for women." The prominent American pacifist, William J. Bryan, should make a peace tour: "He would capture all the big cities along the way and end up in Vienna with a kind of triumphal procession. He is the greatest living pacifist at the moment. . . . The congress in Vienna should be a big affair. . . . The public would have to be overwhelmed."[131]

She kept surprising the already overworked Fried with new plans: "They have to be sensational people from abroad, famous people outside the societies, but world famous: Anatole France, Bernard Shaw—Gerhart Hauptmann and such. I would take over the job of wearing down their resistance with letters. They would have to speak for pacifism—

nothing literary. And for the papers, masses of material prepared and ready."[132]

Bertha's vigor was overpowering; so was her compelling optimism, despite all the current adversities. The writer Moritz Necker confessed after visiting Bertha in Vienna: "One comes and goes from this seventy-year-old with feelings only young people nurture: the feeling of joy for the world, belief in the future of mankind even though many an event at the present time seems bent on shattering it."[133]

Alfred Fried worked far beyond his actual strength to create an ear for pacifism and damaged his health doing it. "Fried . . . feels neuropathic. Nicotine poisoning. Claustrophobia," she wrote in her diary, along with: "Now the whole Balkan is breaking apart. Austria will probably have to endure the next collapse."[134]

In August 1913 the international pacifists met at the opening of the new peace palace in The Hague and at the IPU conference. Suttner gave a few lectures.

In Austria, however, the hundred-year anniversary of the Battle of the Nations near Leipzig was commemorated. "The emperor lays a wreath at the Schwarzenberg monument. The highest office, the highest service, the highest rank: still the warrior.—Baroness Bienerth forms a committee for the patriotic work of the air force. Will be promoted with tango teas."[135]

On October 18, 1913: "Austria issues an ultimatum to Serbia. Fried says there won't be anything left to do but go to war to clear up this Austrian militarism," an astounding opinion for a pacifist.

On October 21 "Serbia gives in. Thus, this danger is averted. The necessity for a European gendarmerie is getting to be more and more obvious."

The organizers of the peace congress thought the prevention of imminent war was a good omen. Fried wrote: "Since the feared European war resulting from the Balkan disturbances was prevented by the powerful word of our monarch," it created an opportunity "to promote this Vienna world peace conference as an international homage to the elderly prince of peace."[136] Emperor Franz Joseph could even take over the patronage of the congress.

In November of 1913 the German socialists held their party convention. Bertha von Suttner followed the reports on it with the greatest interest and went into raptures to Fried: "Yes, the socialist convention was wonderful. I read all about it. Leuthner's speech is a splendid pacifist pamphlet."[137] She also mentioned Rosa Luxemburg's antiwar speech: "What do you say to Rosa Luxemburg. There ought to be hundreds of thousands saying that in every country—then I'd like to see what they'd do about locking them all up."[138]

In December 1913 the Zabern affair set off a serious crisis between France and Germany. The conflict was soon put aside but it, like all the other international crises at this time, showed how close Europe was to war. Suttner wrote: "The military boots, the Prussian character, weighs heavily on Central Europe." "A lot of Zabern in the press. Flagrant militarism. And the only ones in parliament who speak out against it are the socialists. The chancellor is carried away with 'true soldierly spirit.' Confusing fatherland and army."[139]

The Balkan conflicts proceeded undiminished during all this time. Public opinion tended toward "laying into them" and "creating order." Suttner's diary from February 12, 1914, reads: "The press's warmongering between Austria and Russia is in full swing. Perhaps war will break out and it will make it impossible to hold the congress." On February 14, 1914, it reads: "Papers full of armament and war."

In view of new agitation, she wrote in April 1914: "The ever present *suggesting* 'the' (not 'a') *approaching world war* will not stop." Again and again "a welcome fuse is found for the European powder keg yearning for war."[140]

She placed her last hopes in the czar's love for peace, evoked it childishly. "It seems, by the way, that something is going on in secret: peace intrigues by the czar," she wrote conspiratorially to Fried: "I would not be surprised at him. He corresponds with Emperor Wilhelm, with Queen Wilhelmine, he wants to call the third [Hague conference] himself—I wonder what will happen."[141]

Bertha did not feel well, especially when she was alone. Because of her corpulence, her legs gave out. She was frequently tired and accused herself of not working enough, although she still worked half the night writing sometimes, and even still made lecture trips.

There were also financial problems connected with the family, which always needed money, and then problems with the tax authorities: "The tax office has piled up my newspaper articles," she wrote in her diary.[142] On a sudden impulse, she bought a house in southern Styria as a place of retirement, without looking at it. This gave her additional trouble with taxes, she who had been extremely inexperienced in money matters all her life. "Tax officer Rohitsch sniffing around and pestering."[143]

Her strength was visibly leaving her. In March 1914 she noted: "I . . . have already begun to withdraw: not to Hague for Stead unveiling, not to Bern for general meeting—actually all evasions of responsibility. But I have to stop sometime. And physically; I can no longer cope. And know that I no longer have magnetic power, that the cause will not lose much through my withdrawal."[144]

Now she longed for rest; "Oh, to be able to enjoy nature blossoming somewhere where it is quiet and green! Without general assemblies, without congresses! And it seems to be working, but the whole movement is not against the next outbreak that is being worked toward so energetically. It will be useful for the *future,* it will contribute to becoming different, but for the moment it's still too mighty *this way* and not another. Robbers, murderers, fanatics—all in the name of nationality."[145]

But she continued to hope, despite impending war: "I am still waiting for the miraculous. For the great apostle.—It could not have been more wonderful than it was 16 years ago with Nikolaus II.—And then this relapse after all."

On the same day, an official came to her on the "highest mission" with Emperor Franz Joseph's answer to the invitation to take over the peace congress. Bertha noted: "Flat refusal—does not accept honorary chairmanship. Too old—withdrawing from everything. Oh, patrons, peace patrons, enthusiasts, where are you?—After me, they will come— probably by the dozens. In the meanwhile we, Fried and I, have to battle against overpowering millions."[146]

A Norwegian cinema company planned to film the novel *Lay Down Your Arms* to coincide with the approaching world peace congress in Vienna and also to present a warning against the threat of war. Bertha, very taken by this plan, was afraid of only one thing: "*Lay Down Your Arms* would probably not pass the censorship for Austrian cinema. Agitating for peace is treason."[147]

On April 20, 1914, a camera team came to her apartment to shoot a film on the famous author at her desk. The script itself, written by Carl Theodor Dreyer, was not unremarkable. The film really was created for the peace congress and was supposed to be the high point of the meeting. It would be shown in Suttner's honor. The outbreak of war prevented this premiere. It was finally shown in the twenties but had become antiquated by that time and was not a success. Today it is stored in the film archives[148] and provides us with documentary scenes of the seventy-year-old Suttner two months before her death: with somewhat disheveled hair, sitting at her desk in front of a pile of papers, taking up first one and then another piece of paper, visibly nervous about being in front of the camera, but overall, a very self-assured, important woman, by no means the stereotype of an old woman.

In her diary she spoke of nausea and violent stomach disorders, in addition to the now longer periods of tiredness. She needed a lot of sleep and reproached herself for it. "Is such laziness admissable? Illness or vice?"[149] It became ever clearer that this was really illness.

She had to decline taking part in the big women's congress at the end of May in 1914: "The good Hainisch! No, I am not so good. My strength has left me," she wrote remorsefully in her diary.[150] She sent an official letter excusing herself, and after the "warmest greetings to my dear sisters," she added a confidential remark to Marianne Hainisch: "And personally I want to tell you that I am truly and honestly *miserable*. . . .—I cannot eat; cannot stand for five minutes—am filled with pain and nausea. Oh, I no longer have the power of resistance you have. I am full of admiration and respect."[151]

On May 13, 1914, she wrote: "So much sorrow and discomfort as I now have, I have not had for a long time. The worries about the congress and the lottery! And it is impossible to fight against the excessive militarism that is now filling the atmosphere. The only ones—because they are also a power—you can place any hope in for averting mass war, are the social democrats. The 'bourgeois' peace movement here is really so listless, there's nothing to compare it with. Oh well—it's led by an old woman! Where are the young, strong, enthusiastic fighters?"

On May 22 she still took part in a meeting. "And I even speak and not badly. . . . At home back to bed." As a distraction, she took a trip on May 23 with Kathi Buchinger to southern Styria to see her new house. The effort was as great as the disappointment: "Splendid situation, but far from any culture." She would not be able to live there. "Farewell forever to my estate. Villa tantrums cured," she noted in her diary in a very shaky handwriting. Thoughts of death intruded more and more: "Oh, anyway—it's probably the end—if only I don't have to suffer much more!"[152]

On May 26 she wrote to Fried from Styria, saying she did not feel better. "Lose strength from hour to hour." This, of course, did not prevent her from giving new instructions: "If someone comes from America, asks to participate in congress in name of Carnegie—please receive him nicely and explain that we need money for publicity, publicity, and more publicity!"

She wrote the last of her some five thousand letters to Fried on May 29 from Graz. It was a cheerful, extremely warm farewell letter to her spiritual heir and successor, the faithful cofighter for decades, who had just informed her of the composition of the honorary committee for the peace congress: he had won over the imperial foreign minister, Leopold

Count Berchtold, as president, and the prime minister, Count Stürgkh, and the imperial finance minister, Leon von Bilinski, also gave their names for the peace congress—it was therefore a great success, contrary to all expectations, about which Bertha was extremely happy: "My dear"—it was the first time she ever addressed Fried without using his name. "That is a magic program. I offer my expression of great respect for this success. Whether a word to the ministers from the emperor is not behind it. The thing was presented on a silver platter! But without your energy and your faith it would not have come about. I congratulate us and pacifism—it will be a brilliant congress."

On May 30 she arrived back in Vienna and had to go to bed immediately. "Think a lot about dying. Kati, too, since she's bawling."[153] "A lot of mail and newspapers—but can't read."[154] On June 2 she noted the news that Carnegie had actually wanted to donate one thousand dollars for the congress but did not after all because of the American-Mexican conflict. Then there were some remarks about all the things she had to do—the last entry in her diary.

Resolutely, she refused to have any additional doctors, as Fried suggested. "With almost sickening energy," he wrote later, she insisted that the illness—the diagnosis was stomach cancer—take its course. "Why then?" Fried asked her. "I've lived long enough, I've done something with my life; when my time has run out, that should be it. I do not hang onto life."[155]

Up to the twentieth of June she was completely conscious and kept herself informed of daily events. In delirium she called out: "Lay down your arms, tell everybody!" The last words that could be understood: "I'm going to Durazzo." There were new Balkan conflicts over the possession of Durazzo, which belonged to Albania. According to her physician, Dr. Gustav Gärtner, the disturbances in Albania shook Bertha more than the illness. Shortly afterward, she lost consciousness and "fell asleep like a tired person in the evening."[156] The date was June 21, 1914.

Seven days later, on June 28, 1914, the fatal shots were fired in Sarajevo that killed the Austrian-Hungarian crown prince, Franz Ferdinand, and his wife.

On July 28 Austria-Hungary declared war against Serbia. On July 31 in Paris, the French socialist, pacifist, and champion of a German-French agreement, Jean Jaurès, was murdered. On August 1 the German *Reich* declared war on Russia, on August 3 on France and Belgium, too. At the same time, efforts at mediation by President Wilson failed; he had called upon the Hague Convention. Many declarations of war followed—until almost the whole earth was drawn into this great war, which would last four years and cause almost ten million deaths.

The big international peace congress in September of 1914 and the socialist congress planned for almost the same time did not take place. Even the socialists, the aged Bertha von Suttner's last hope, acted in national rather than international interests now.

Any activity by the Austrian Peace Society was officially prohibited. The *Friedenswarte* had to quit publication. Fried emigrated to Switzerland. The two-volume collection of Bertha von Suttner's political articles, published in 1917 under the title *The Battle for the Prevention of World War* was, of course, banned immediately in Austria and Germany.

Later, after the collapse of the Old World, people remembered the pioneer work of the two Hague Peace Conferences: the League of Nations was founded, which required its members to provide mutual protection against violations of the peace and to recognize the arbitral award of the permanent International Court of Justice in The Hague.

World peace, for which Bertha von Suttner fought until her death, failed to come.

Notes
Index

Notes

313

StBM	Stadtbibliothek München (Munich City Library). Manuscript Collection.
StBW	Stadtbibliothek Wien (City Library of Vienna). Manuscript Collection.
StLM	Steiermärkisches Landesmuseum Joanneum Graz.
StUB	Stadt- und Universitätsbibliothek.
ThS	Theatersammlung (Theater Collection), ÖNB Wien.
To Carneri	Letters from Bertha von Suttner to Bartolomeus von Carneri, at the UN, Geneva, Suttner-Fried Collection.
To Fried	Letters from Bertha von Suttner to Alfred H. Fried, at the UN, Geneva, Suttner-Fried Collection.
UB	Universitätsbibliothek.
ÜLuM	*Über Land und Meer* (magazine).
UN	United Nations, Geneva, Suttner-Fried Collection.

1. Countess Kinsky

1. Diary, Oct. 23, 1907.
2. *Memoirs,* 15 f.
3. BvS, *High Life,* vol. 1 of *Collected Works* (Dresden, n.d.), 209.
4. Ibid., 214.
5. This and the following quotations are from *Memoirs,* 18–24.
6. Ibid., 25.
7. Ibid., 39.
8. Ibid., 57.
9. BvS, *High Life,* 50.
10. *Memoirs,* 58.
11. *NIZ,* Sept. 7, 1884.
12. *MZA,* 114.
13. Ibid., 140.
14. *Memoirs,* 63.
15. This and the following quotations are from BvS, *Trente et Quarante* (Dresden, 1893), 17–21.
16. *Memoirs,* 62.
17. Diary, Jan. 30, 1898.
18. This and the following quotations are from *Memoirs,* 64–68.
19. Ibid., 72.
20. *MZA,* 132.
21. *Memoirs,* 76.
22. UN, Man. Erinnerungen, 10.
23. *Memoirs,* 85.
24. Ibid., 89.
25. Ibid., 92.
26. *ÜLuM,* 1887, 274.
27. UN, Man. Erinnerungen, 10.
28. *Memoirs,* 105.
29. UN, Man. Erinnerungen, 13 f.
30. Fürstl. Archive Sayn-Wittgenstein-Hohenstein, Laasphe. File on Adolf SWH, letter of July 27, 1872.
31. Laasphe, Aug. 9, 1872.
32. Ibid., Sept. 26, 1872.

33. UB, Münster, Oct. 9, 1872.
34. To Fried, Sept. 10, 1908.

2. Governess and Secretary

1. *Memoirs,* 137.
2. Diary, July 14, 1906.
3. *Memoirs,* 132.
4. H. Schück and R. Sohlman, *Nobel* (Leipzig, 1928), 228.
5. *Memoirs,* 132.
6. Ibid., 133.
7. Ibid., 133.
8. Ibid., 133 f.
9. BvS, reminiscences of Alfred Nobel, *NFP,* Jan. 12, 1897.
10. *Memoirs,* 134.
11. Schück and Sohlmann, *Nobel,* 177.
12. RASt, Oct. 29, 1895, Fr.
13. This quotation and the following ones recounting her reunion with Arthur are from *Memoirs,* 134.
14. ÖNB, Mss, AvS, letter from Stourzh's lawyer, Dec. 21, 1876.
15. *Memoirs,* 137.
16. To Carneri, July 27, 1892.
17. Beatrix Kempf, *Bertha von Suttner* (Vienna, 1964). 16, Fr.

3. In the Caucasus

1. *Memoirs,* 137.
2. *ÜLuM,* 1887, 274.
3. Ibid., 303.
4. This and the following account of Kutais are in *Memoirs,* 139 ff.
5. Further in *NIZ,* 1887, vol. 1, 123.
6. *ÜLuM,* 1887, 303.
7. *Memoirs,* 142.
8. *ÜLuM,* 1887, 303.
9. UN, BvS, Man. Erinnerungen, 23.
10. *Memoirs,* 14.
11. Ibid., 146.
12. Ibid., 147.
13. Ibid., 148.
14. *NIZ,* Sept. 7, 1884.
15. The manuscript is in the UN library in Geneva.
16. BvS, *Es Löwos,* vol. 1 of *Collected Works* (Dresden, n.d.), 287.
17. Ibid., 290.
18. *Memoirs,* 156.
19. BvS, *Inventarium einer Seele. Collected Works,* vol. 6 (Dresden, n.d.), 95 f.
20. BvS, *Inventarium,* 138 f.
21. *Memoirs,* 155.
22. Ibid.
23. BvS, *Es Löwos,* 324.

24. *NIZ*, 1881, No. 41 ff.
25. BvS, *Es Löwos*, 317 f.
26. Ibid., 294.
27. To Irma Troll-Borostyáni, Feb. 20, 1888.
28. *Memoirs*, 151.
29. HAJ to Th. Herzl, Oct. 17, 1902.
30. BvS, *Es Löwos*, 323.
31. Membership in Freemasonry is clearly proven in Arthur's correspondence, chiefly with the Freemasons Groller and Conrad.
32. To Carneri, Jan. 24, 1890.
33. *Memoirs*, 149.
34. Ibid., 150.
35. BvS, *Es Löwos*, 338.
36. *NIZ*, Sept. 7, 1884.
37. *Die Gesellschaft*, vol. 1, 1885.
38. BvS, *Inventarium*, 371.
39. Ibid., 69, 71.
40. Ibid., 101 f.
41. Ibid., 119 f.
42. Ibid., 118.
43. Ibid., 107.
44. Ibid., 108.
45. UN, Apr. 28, 1883, Fr.
46. *Droeba*, 1884, Nov. 30, Dec. 1, 4, 5, 8, 9, 1885, Mar. 14; *Iveria*, 1884, No. 11 and 12: 68–102. This information was made available through the kind offices of the Shota Rustaveli Institute in Tbilisi. The assessment of the quality of the series was made by the Deputy Director of the Institute, Prof. Zaischwili.
47. *Memoirs*, 158.
48. BvS, "A Manuscript," Collected Works, 3:7 and 9.
49. ÖNB, Mss. N. AvS, Cat. 732, Aug. 19, 1895, dun from Leo Koscheles.
50. Information kindly given by the Neunargia Museum in Zaishi near Zugdidi in Georgia.
51. Museum in Zaishi, newspaper clipping.
52. State Historical-Ethnographical Museum in Zugdidi, letter from Batum, Mar. 23, 1885.
53. *NIZ* (1885), Vol. 2, 555 f.
54. *MZA*, 297.
55. UN, BvS, Man. Erinnerungen, 23.
56. *DWN* (1893), 71.

4. The Writer's Life

1. *Memoirs*, 163 f.
2. A. H. Fried, "*Bei Suttners*," *Der Friede*, Nov. 9, 1894.
3. *Memoirs*, 233.
4. To Carneri, Jan. 5, 1890.
5. To Carneri, Apr. 8, 1890.
6. Diary, Feb. 3, 1897.
7. Diary, Jan. 19, 1897.

8. UN, Letter from Löwenthal to AvS, Oct. 26, 1886.
9. StBM, to Conrad, May 8, 1885.
10. *MZA*, 298.
11. BvS, *Schriftsteller-Roman* (Dresden, 1888), 272 ff.
12. BvS, *High Life*, 210 f.
13. Ibid., 212.
14. And the following: Ibid., 121 f.
15. Ibid., 122.
16. BvS, "Dienstboten Roman" (Servants' Novel), *Illustrirter österreichischer Volkskalender*, 1893, 3.
17. BvS, *Schriftsteller-Roman*, 253 f.
18. *Memoirs*, 391.
19. BvS, *Schriftsteller-Roman*, 196.
20. UN, BvS to Troll-B., Oct. 14, 1886.
21. BvS, *Schriftsteller-Roman*, 111 f.
22. Ibid., 295 f; *Memoirs*, 166.
23. BvS, *Schriftsteller-Roman*, 302 f; *Memoirs*, 167.
24. BvS, *Schriftsteller-Roman*, 308.
25. Ibid., 312.
26. Ibid., 313.
27. Ibid., 314.
28. ÖNB, Mss. N. AvS, Jan. 29, 1895.
29. *Memoirs*, 335.
30. Ibid.
31. *MZA*, 35.
32. Ibid., 9.
33. Ibid., 40.
34. Ibid., 49.
35. Ibid., 54 f.
36. *Memoirs*, 236.
37. Ibid., 171.
38. BvS, "Erinnerungen an Alfred Nobel," *NFP*, Jan. 12, 1897.
39. BvS, *Schriftsteller-Roman*, 123 f.
40. *Memoirs*, 172.
41. Ibid., 171 ff.
42. Ibid., 173 f.
43. BvS, *Die Waffen nieder, Collected Works*, Vol. 11, (Dresden, n.d.), 64.
44. *Memoirs*, 173.
45. Ibid., 175.
46. Ibid., 175.
47. BvS, *High Life*, 140 f.

5. *Lay Down Your Arms*

1. UN, Ms memoirs, 3 f.
2. Ibid., 10.
3. *MZA*, 277 f.
4. *Memoirs*, 176.
5. *MZA*, 316 ff.

6. *Memoirs,* 177.
7. Ibid.
8. *MZA,* 309 ff.
9. Ibid., 311.
10. See Brigitte Hamann, *Rudolf—Kronprinz und Rebell* (Vienna, 1978).
11 *MZA,* 322.
12. Ibid., 323.
13. A. H. Fried, "BvS for her 70th Birthday," *NFP,* June 9, 1913.
14. To Carneri, Nov. 11, 1889.
15. StBW, Mar. 25, 1890.
16. *NFP,* Apr. 17, 1890.
17. StBW, May 10, 1890.
18. *Memoirs,* 180.
19. Ibid.
20. BvS, *Die Waffen nieder, Collected Works,* vol. 11 (Dresden, n.d.), 262.
21. Ibid., 308.
22. Ibid., 309.
23. Ibid., 269.
24. Ibid., 345.
25. Ibid., 176.
26. BvS, *Inventarium,* 122.
27. BvS, *Die Waffen,* 176.
28. Ibid., 248.
29. Ibid., 392.
30. *Memoirs,* 181.
31. UN, Nov. 24, n.d. (1889), Fr.
32. *Memoirs,* 183, Paris, Apr. 1, 1890, Fr.
33. *NFP,* Mar. 15, 1890, 1.
34. Stenographic minutes of the Austrian Reichsrat. Apr. 18, 1890 (not 1891, as stated in the *Memoirs,* 183), 14277.
35. StBM, Feb. 27, 1890, to M. G. Conrad.
36. RASt, Dec. 24, 1892, Engl.
37. BvS, *Krieg und Frieden,* special printing of a lecture in Munich on Feb. 5, 1900, 17.
38. To Carneri, Apr. 15, 1892.
39. To Carneri, Apr. 25, 1890.
40. To Carneri, Apr. 25, 1890.
41. To Carneri, Mar. 27, 1891.
42. To Carneri, Sept. 11, 1890.
43. To Carneri, Oct. 22, 1890.
44. To Carneri, Nov. 18, 1893.
45. To Carneri, June 10, 1891.
46. Tolstoy Museum, Moscow (copy, UN), Oct. 16, 1891, Fr.
47. *Memoirs,* 210 f.
48. L. N. Tolstoy, *Polnoe sobranie socinenij,* jubilee edition of the collected works, Vol. 52 (Moskva, 1952), Oct. 24, 1891, 56. With thanks to Ms. Jana Starek.
49. To Fried, Aug. 23, 1902.
50. UN, BvS, Ms memoirs, 3.
51. To Carneri, Jan. 6, 1892.

52. To Carneri, June 20, 1890.
53. StUB, Geneva, to Dunant, July 18, 1896, Fr.
54. *Memoirs,* 192.
55. StBW to Necker, Dec. 9, 1889.
56. *Memoirs,* 193.
57. BvS, *Stimmen und Gestalten* (Leipzig, n.d.), 110.
58. *Memoirs,* 195.
59. Ibid., 197.
60. UN, Jan. 16, 1896.
61. Felix Salten, "Die Suttner (zum 70. Geburtstag)," newspaper clipping, UN.
62. StBW, Aug. 20, 1890.

6. Founding the Peace Societies

1. A. H. Fried, "BvS, for Her 70th Birthday," *NFP,* June 9, 1913.
2. *Memoirs,* 313.
3. RASt, Feb. 6, 1891, Fr.
4. RASt, Feb. 6, 1891.
5. RASt, Sept. 17, 1892, Fr.
6. *Memoirs,* 200.
7. To Carneri, June 28, 1891.
8. To Carneri, Sept. 19, 1891.
9. *Memoirs,* 238 f., Sept. 14, 1891.
10. To Carneri, Sept. 6, 1891.
11. To Carneri, Sept. 11, 1891.
12. StLM, Sept. 8, 1891.
13. UN, Sept. 10, 1891.
14. UN, Sept. 19, 1891.
15. UN, June 25, 1892.
16. UN, Oct. 9, 1891.
17. To Carneri, Oct. 6, 1891.
18. To Carneri, Oct. 2, 1891.
19. To Carneri, Oct. 6, 1891.
20. Ibid.
21. To Carneri, n.d., 1892.
22. *Memoirs,* 257, Oct. 31, 1891.
23. UN, Nov. 22, 1891.
24. To Carneri, Oct. 2, 1891.
25. Ibid.
26. *Memoirs,* 221.
27. Ibid., 222, Oct. 9, 1891.
28. To Carneri, Oct. 13, 1891.
29. To Carneri, Oct. 17, 1891.
30. To Carneri, Oct. 6, 1891.
31. RASt, Oct. 24, 1891.
32. *Memoirs,* 239 f., Oct. 31, 1891, Fr.
33. RASt, Nov. 4, 1891.
34. *Mittheilungen der österreichischen Gesellschaft der Friedensfreunde* (1892), 12.
35. *Memoirs,* 168.

36. Ibid., 225.
37. *Mittheilungen der österreichischen Gesellschaft der Friedensfreude* (1892), 14.
38. Ibid., 17.
39. *DWN,* Feb. 1, 1892.
40. RASt, Nov. 26, 1891, Fr.
41. RASt, Sept. 27, 1892, Fr.
42. To Carneri, Dec. 24, 1891.
43. To Carneri, Jan. 6, 1892.
44. To Fried, Nov. 22, 1891.
45. To Fried, Dec. 7, 1891.
46. To Fried, Dec. 27, 1891.
47. To Fried, n.d. (Jan. 1892).
48. To Fried, Jan. 2, 1892.
49. To Fried, June 12, 1892.
50. Carneri to Suttner, Feb. 11, 1892.
51. Carneri to Suttner, Mar. 3, 1892.
52. To Carneri, Mar. 1, 1892.
53. To Fried, Mar. 1, 1892.
54. Carneri to Suttner, June 14, 1892.
55. To Carneri, June 17, 1892.
56. Carneri to Suttner, June 19, 1892.
57. To Carneri, June 20, 1892.
58. To Carneri, Mar. 5, 1892.
59. StBW, Apr. 5, 1894.
60. UN, Apr. 26, 1894.
61. To Fried, July 21, 1892.
62. To Carneri, May 22, 1892.
63. *Memoirs,* 394.
64. Carl Dolmetsch, *"Our Famous Guest": Mark Twain in Vienna* (Athens, Ga.: University of Georgia Press, 1992), 185.
65. *Memoirs,* 417.
66. UStB, Geneva, Oct. 7, 1895, Fr.
67. StBW, n.d.
68. Steiermärkisches Landesmuseum Joanneum, Graz, N. Rossegger, May 2, 1892.
69. *Mittheilungen der österreichischen Gesellschaft der Friedensfreunde* (1892), 52 f.
70. RASt, Dec. 24, 1892.
71. To Fried, Aug. 4, 1892.
72. To Fried, Sept. 19, 1892.
73. To Fried, Feb. 24, 1893.
74. To Fried, Mar. 9, 1893.
75. To Fried, Feb. 1, 1892.
76. To Carneri, Feb. 1, 1892.
77. To Carneri, Feb. 20, 1892.
78. To Fried, Mar. 1, 1892.
79. To Fried, Mar. 4, 1892.
80. To Fried, Apr. 9, 1892.
81. To Fried, n.d. (Oct.-Nov., 1892).
82. *Memoirs,* 268.
83. To Fried, Nov. 14, 1892.

84. To Fried, Nov. 5, 1892.
85. To Fried, Nov. 18, 1897.
86. To Fried, Oct. 21, 1894.
87. To Carneri, July 27, 1892.
88. To Fried, Sept. 11, 1894.
89. RASt, Apr. 11, 1894, Fr.
90. BvS, *Schach der Qual* (Dresden, 1898), 191.
91. BvS, "Mein Aufenthalt in Prag," *DWN,* Dec. 1905.
92. To Carneri, Dec. 17 and 21, 1895.
93. RASt, Jan. 12, 1896, Fr.
94. To Fried, July 27, 1904.
95. BvS, *Wohin? Die Etappen des Jahres 1895* (Berlin, 1896), 131.
96. To Fried, Jan. 23, 1896.
97. Feb. 20, 1904, printed in *NWT,* Feb. 22, 1904.
98. To Fried, Oct. 28, 1902.
99. *DWN,* May 1898.
100. To Fried, Apr. 24, 1898.

7. The Fight Against Anti-Semitism

1. *Freies Blatt,* Apr. 15, 1894. Brigitte Hamann, "Der Verein zur Abwehr des Antisemitismus," in *Die Macht der Bilder: Antisemitische Vorurteile und Mythen* (Vienna, 1995), 253–63.
2. *Memoirs,* 214.
3. Ms. at the UN.
4. BvS, "Wehrt Euch!" *Freies Blatt,* No. 45.
5. *Memoirs,* 214 f.
6. To Carneri, Apr. 2, 1891.
7. To Carneri, May 15, 1891.
8. BvS, *Vor dem Gewitter* (Vienna, 1894), 332 f.
9. StBW, Feb. 14, 1889.
10. StBW, Jan. 16, 1890.
11. UN, Jan. 17, 1890.
12. And the following: *Freies Blatt,* 1894, No. 112, 3.
13. To Carneri, Mar. 12, 1891.
14. *Memoirs,* 215.
15. To Carneri, May 15, 1891.
16. To Carneri, May 21, 1891.
17. Amos Elon, *Theodor Herzl* (Vienna 1979), 114.
18. To Carneri, June 2, 1891.
19. To Carneri, June 5, 1891.
20. To Carneri, June 28, 1891.
21. *Memoirs,* 216.
22. To Carneri, May 25, 1891.
23. BvS, *Schach der Qual* (Dresden, 1898), 100, 97.
24. Ibid., 100.
25. And the following: Tulo Nussenblatt, *Ein Volk unterwegs zum Frieden* (Vienna, 1933), 56 ff.
26. To Carneri, Aug. 7, 1891.

27. To Carneri, Nov. 12, 1892.
28. UN, Dec. 11, 1892.
29. *Freies Blatt,* Oct. 9, 1892.
30. *Freies Blatt,* Oct. 23, 1892.
31. BvS, *Schach der Qual,* 111 f.
32. *Unverfälschte Deutsche Worte,* Aug. 16, 1891.
33. To Carneri, Aug. 22, 1891.
34. *Freies Blatt,* 1891, No. 7, insert.
35. To Carneri, Oct. 17, 1892.
36. UN, Jan. 30, 1892.
37. *Memoirs,* 326.
38. To Carneri, Dec. 14, 1891.
39. BvS, *Marthas Kinder* (Dresden, 1903), 326 f.
40. Ibid., 329.
41. To Fried, Jan. 22, 1893.
42. *Freies Blatt,* 1893, No. 45, 4.
43. *Freies Blatt,* 1894, No. 112, 2 f.
44. *Freies Blatt,* June 2, 1895.
45. RASt, Report from the *NWT Abendbl.,* Apr. 14, 1896.
46. Herzl Diaries, Vol. 1, 7.
47. *Memoirs,* 323, after diary entry, Jan. 22, 1905.
48. *Memoirs,* 326.
49. RASt, Apr. 30, 1896, Fr.
50. Diary, Aug. 21 and 28, 1897.
51. *Das freie Blatt,* Sept. 1, 1896.
52. Diary, June 3, 1897.
53. Nussenblatt, Mar. 7, 1896, 101.
54. Theodor Herzl, *Der Judenstaat* (1896), 11.
55. Printed in *Die Welt,* 1897, No. 3, 6.
56. *Die Welt,* 1897, No. 2, 4 f.
57. BvS, "Gesprache über den Zionismus aus dem Hague," *Die Welt,* July 14, 1899.
58. HAJ, Sept. 5, 1897.
59. *NFP,* June 7, 1903.
60. To Carneri, Dec. 30, 1897.
61. BvS, "Friedenscommunion," *Ethische Kultur,* Vol. 7, 1898, 140.
62. To Carneri, Feb. 26, 1898.
63. Ibid.
64. *Memoirs,* 500.
65. Diary, Nov. 6, 1900.
66. UN, Apr. 2, 1898.
67. BvS, *Briefe an einen Toten,* 3rd ed. (Dresden, 1904), 138.
68. Diary, Nov. 14, 1905.
69. Theodor Herzl, Diaries, Jan. 16, 1899.
70. HAJ, Jan. 17, 1899.
71. UN, May 22, 1903.
72. Diary, May 22, 1903.
73. UN, concept, n.d.
74. To Fried, July 6, 1904.

75. HAJ.
76. To Fried, July 7, 1904.
77. To Fried, Aug. 6, 1904.
78. To Fried, Nov. 1905.
79. Diary, Sept. 19, 1902.
80. Diary, Mar. 30, 1907. *NWT,* Apr. 6, 1907, BvS, "Es ist stark übertrieben."
81. BvS, *Wohin? Die Etappen des Jahres 1895* (Berlin, 1896), 80.
82. To Fried, Sept. 10, 1892.
83. To Fried, Jan. 1, 1893.
84. UN, May 21, 1909.
85. UN, May 24, 1909.
86. To Fried, Feb. 19, 1906.

8. The Hague Peace Conference

1. RASt, Oct. 28, 1894, Fr.
2. RASt, Nov. 28, 1894, Fr.
3. RASt, Jan. 12, 1896, Fr.
4. BvS, "Friedenscommunion," *Ethische Kultur,* Vol. 7, 1898, 140.
5. *NWT,* Apr. 21, 1899, BvS, open letter to Steinbach.
6. And the following: BvS, "Was wir wollen," *DWN,* 1893, s.
7. BvS, *Briefe an einen Toten,* 3rd ed. (Dresden, 1904), 25 f.
8. *DWN,* Feb. 1896.
9. *DWN,* 1896, 291.
10. BvS, *Schach der Qual,* quoted in memoirs, 364 f.
11. *DWN,* Vol. 3, 458.
12. BvS, "Das Friedensmanifest des Zaren," *Die Zeit* Sept. 3, 1898.
13. *MZA,* addendum, 341.
14. Diary, Aug. 29, 1898.
15. To Fried, Aug. 29, 1898.
16. Summary in Johann von Bloch, *Die wahrscheinlichen politischen und wirtschaftlichen Folgen eines Krieges* (Berlin, 1901), 25.
17. BvS, "Die Zwischenfälle im Roten Meere im Lichte der Friedensbewegung," *Die Zeit* Aug. 20, 1904.
18. BvS, "Zur Vorgeschichte der Haager Konferenz," *Deutsche Revue,* Vol. 4, 1901, 346.
19. Copy, UN, Sept. 4, 1898, Fr.
20. *Memoirs,* 402–5.
21. To Fried, Aug. 30, 1898.
22. *DWN,* Oct.-Nov. 1898, 377.
23. BvS, "Krieg und Frieden," Lecture in Munich, 1909, 32.
24. UN, Sept. 5, 1898.
25. *Deutsche Rundschau,* Vol. 97, 1898, 201 ff.
26. UN, Sept. 8, 1898, quoted in *DWN,* 1898, 441.
27. Diary, Sept. 7 and 9, 1898.
28. To Fried, Sept. 4, 1898.
29. *Memoirs,* 429 f.
30. BvS, *Die Haager Friedenskonferenz* (Dresden, 1900), 70.
31. Ibid., 21 f.

32. Ibid., 47.
33. To Fried, Dec. 13, 1898.
34. To Fried, Feb. 10, 1899.
35. Beatrix Kempf, *Bertha von Suttner* (Vienna, 1964), 52.
36. BvS, "Graf Mourawiew in Wien." *NFP,* Oct. 25, 1898.
37. BvS, *Haager Friedenskonferenz,* ix f.
38. Ibid, xiv.
39. Diary, Oct. 24, 1898.
40. To Fried, Nov. 26, 1898.
41. *Deutsche Revue,* 1898, 352.
42. StUB, Geneva, May 9, 1899, Fr.
43. *Memoirs,* 269.
44. To Fried, Mar. 25, 1899.
45. BvS (publ.), *Herrn Dr. Carl Freiherr von Stengels und Anderer Argumente für und wider den Krieg, Vienna 1899.*
46. To Fried, Dec. 28, 1898.
46. Diary, Mar. 7, 1899.
48. BvS, *Haager Friedenskonferenz,* 306.
49. To Fried, Feb. 21, 1900.
50. *DWN,* Mar. 1899.
51. StUB, Geneva, N. Dunant.
52. To Fried, Nov. 15, 1898.
53. To Fried, Mar. 23, 1898.
54. To Fried, Nov. 7, 1899.
55. BvS, *Haager Friedenskonferenz,* 2 f.
56. HAJ, Mar. 27, 1899.
57. HAJ, Apr. 5, 1899.
58. HAJ, Apr. 13, 1899.
59. HAJ, Apr. 28 and May 9, 1899.
60. And the following: BvS, *Haager Friedenskonferenz,* 14 f.
61. And the following: Herzl article in *NFP,* June 13, 1900.
62. HAJ, to Herzl, June 13, 1900.
63. BvS, *Haager Friedenskonferenz,* 300.
64. BvS, *Zur nächsten Intergouvenementalen Konferenz in Haag* (Berlin, 1907).
65. Andrew D. White, *Aus meinem Diplomatenleben* (Leipzig, 1906), 379 f.
66. To Fried, Sept. 4, 1899.
67. To Fried, Aug. 23, 1901.
68. To Fried, Aug. 29, 1901.
69. To Fried, Aug. 19, 1902.
70. To Fried, Oct. 26, 1899.
71. Carl Dolmetsch, *"Our Famous Guest": Mark Twain in Vienna* (Athens, Ga.: University of Georgia Press: 1992), 195.
72. To Fried, Aug. 29 and Sept. 5, 1901.
73. To Fried, Aug. 5, 1903.
74. To Fried, Feb. 13, 1902.
75. *Die Fackel,* beginning of Aug. 1899, 8.
76. BvS, *Krieg und Frieden* (Munich, n.d.), 33 f.
77. To Fried, Sept. 1, 1899.
78. To Fried, Apr. 5, 1900.

79. BvS, "Der Transvaalkrieg und die Friedensbewegung," *Die Wage,* Nov. 12, 1899.

80. BvS, *Krieg und Frieden,* 36.

81. BvS, "Offener Brief an Meister Adolph Wilbrandt," *NFP,* Aug. 23, 1901.

82. To Fried, Aug. 7, 1900.

83. To Fried, Sept. 26, 1902.

84. Diary, Aug. 21, 1900.

85. *Memoirs,* 511.

86. UN, Apr. 23, 1901.

87. To Fried, Aug. 21, 1900.

88. To Fried, Nov. 10, 1901.

89. *NFP,* June 13, 1900.

90. StBW, to Nussbaum, Feb. 17, 1903.

91. Diary, Feb. 9, 1903.

92. StBW, to Nussbaum, Feb. 17, 1903.

93. *Memoirs,* 535.

94. Diary, Aug. 21 and Oct. 3, 1903.

95. BvS, *Briefe an einen Toten,* 184 f.

96. *Die Wage,* Jan. 23, 1904.

97. BvS, "Was haben die Friedensfreunde für einen möglichst raschen Abschluß des russisch-japanischen Kreiges getan?" *Deutsche Revue,* Vol. 3, 1904, 324.

98. UN, newspaper clippings, n.d.

99. UN, newspaper clippings, n.d.

100. Diary, May 29, 1904.

101. Diary, Feb. 23, 1905.

102. Diary, July 12, 1905.

103. To Fried, July 30, 1905.

104. To Fried, July 23, 1907.

105. UN, concept.

106. Apr. 6, 1907.

107. Diary, June 15, 1907.

108. Diary, July 7, 1907.

109. Diary, Aug. 10, 1907.

110. HHStA, N. Mérey, Box 3, Aug. 27, 1907.

111. BvS, *Stimmen und Gestalten* (Leipzig, 1908), 96.

112. To Fried, Sept. 29, 1907.

113. BvS, editorial, *NWT,* Oct. 21, 1907.

9. Human, All Too Human

1. Diary, Dec. 6, 1897.

2. To Fried, Nov. 23, 1898.

3. To Carneri, Aug. 7, 1891.

4. To Fried, June 13, 1895.

5. HAJ, Nov. 5, 1901.

6. Diary, Apr. 9, 1900.

7. Diary, Nov. 4, 1900.

8. RASt, Aug. 12, 1894, Fr.

9. Diary, Dec. 9, 1900.

10. Diary, July 22, 1897.
11. Diary, Feb. 26, 1898.
12. RASt, Aug. 24, 1893.
13. Diary, Oct. 20, 1897.
14. Diary, Mar. 3, 1897.
15. Diary, Apr. 3, 1897.
16. Diary, May 22, 1897.
17. UN, to Arthur, May 17, 1900.
18. To Carneri, Mar. 31, 1892.
19. A. H. Fried, *Persönlichkeiten: Bertha von Suttner* (Berlin, n.d.), 7.
20. UN, family letters, n.d.
21. Diary, Oct. 20, 1898.
22. Diary, Mar. 26, 1898.
23. *Memoirs,* 499.
24. Diary, June 1, 1898.
25. To Fried, July 11, 1898.
26. Diary, June 23, 1898.
27. Diary, July 1 and June 26, 1898.
28. Diary, Oct. 1–14, 1898.
29. Diary, Oct. 20, 1898.
30. Diary, Oct. 20, 1898.
31. Diary, Oct. 21, 1898.
32. UN, family letters, Oct. 21, 1898.
33. Diary, Nov. 17, 1898.
34. Diary, Nov. 30, 1898.
35. Diary, Dec. 1, 1898.
36. To Fried, Nov. 6, 1898.
37. UN, personalia.
38. Diary, Mar. 3, 1900.
39. Diary, May 9–16, 1900.
40. Diary, July 14 and Aug. 15, 1900.
41. Diary, Oct. 14, 1900.
42. UN, family letters, May 16, 1900.
43. To Fried, Oct. 28, 1902.
44. StBW, Dec. 5, 1902.
45. Diary, Nov. 25, 1902.
46. Diary, Nov. 28, 1902.
47. BvS, *Briefe an einen Toten,* 3rd ed. (Dresden, 1904), 76.
48. *Memoirs,* 539.
49. Diary, Dec. 22, 1902.
50. Diary, Jan. 13, 1903.
51. Diary, Jan. 14, 1903.
52. To Fried, Dec. 23, 1902.
53. Diary, Jan. 6, 1903.
54. StBW, Jan. 15 and 19, 1903.
55. Diary, Feb. 4 and 8, 1903.
56. To Fried, Feb. 2, 1903.
57. StBW, Feb. 20 and 21, 1903.
58. Diary, Feb. 21, 1903.

59. StBW, Feb. 21, 1903.
60. StBW, Feb. 20, 1903.
61. Diary, Mar. 25, 1903.
62. Diary, Feb. 20, 1902.
63. Diary, Feb. 21, 1903.
64. Diary, Feb. 22, 1903.
65. Diary, Feb. 24, 1903.
66. To Fried, Mar. 10, 1903.
67. Diary, Feb. 26 and 27, 1903.
68. Diary, Mar. 3, 12, and 13, 1903.
69. Diary, Mar. 3, 1903.
70. Diary, Mar. 3, 14, and 21, 1903.
71. Diary, Mar. 20, 1903.
72. Diary, Mar. 9 and 18, 1903.
73. Diary, Mar. 25, 1903.
74. Diary, Apr. 23, 1903.
75. Diary, Mar. 28, 1903.
76. StBW, May 29, 1905.
77. Diary, Mar. 10, 1906.
78. Diary, Apr. 11, 1903.
79. Diary, May 14, 1903.
80. *Berliner Tagblatt,* May 7, 1903.
81. Diary, May 8, 1903.
82. UN, list of donations.
83. Diary, June 10, 1903.
84. Diary, July 5, 1903.
85. Diary, June 27, 1903.
86. Diary, Aug. 21, 1903.
87. Diary, May 3, 1903.
88. Diary, June 12 and July 1, 1903.
89. Diary, Mar. 29, 1904.
90. Diary, May 19, 1905.
91. Diary, July 26 and 30, 1903.
92. Diary, Apr. 2 and May 1, 1905.
93. Diary, Apr. 2 and Oct. 18, 1906.
94. Diary, Aug. 17, 1906.
95. Diary, Aug. 20, 1906.
96 Diary, Oct. 20, 1911.
97. Diary, Oct. 29, 1913.
98. Arthur Schnitzler, *Diary 1913–1916* (Vienna: Österreichische Akademie der Wissenschaften, 1983), 71.
99. Diary, Jan. 30, 1906.
100. Diary, Oct. 29, 1906.
101. Diary, May 24, 1909 and June 9, 1911.
102. To Fried, Mar. 7, 1899.
103. To Fried, May 9, 1899.
104. To Fried, Sept. 5, 1901.
105. Diary, Apr. 13, 1909.
106. To Fried, May 18, 1901 and June 13, 1905.

107. To Fried, Aug. 21, 1900.
108. To Fried, Oct. 3, 1905.
109. June 13, 1906.
110. To Fried, Oct. 23, 1894.
111. To Fried, June 17, 1904.
112. Diary, July 9, 1910.
113. To Fried, July 3, 1911.
114. Diary, Jan. 19, 1908.
115. Diary, Sept. 5, 1908.
116. To Fried, Sept. 9, 1908.
117. To Fried, Aug. 29, 1907.

10. The Nobel Prize

1. BvS, *Stimmen und Gestalten* (Leipzig, n.d.), 136.
2. RASt, June 3, 1896, Fr.: wording of the correspondence by Irwin Abrams, "Bertha von Suttner and the Nobel Peace Prize," *Journal of Central European Affairs* 22 (1962): 286–307.
3. To Carneri, June 27, 1894.
4. BvS, *Krieg und Frieden,* lecture in Munich, 1909, 43.
5. RASt, Apr. 16, 1892, Fr.
6. *Memoirs,* 267.
7. And the following: *Memoirs,* 270.
8. UN, corr., etc., 137, concept.
9. *Memoirs,* 271.
10. *NFP,* Jan. 12, 1897.
11. *Memoirs,* 271.
12. *NFP,* Jan. 12, 1897.
13. UN, Jan. 7, 1893, Fr.
14. RASt, Feb. 8, 1893, Fr.
15. RASt, Feb. 15, 1893, Engl.
16. RASt, June 7, 1893.
17. RASt, June 21, 1893, Fr.
18. RASt, July 17, 1893, Fr.
19. RASt, Dec. 1, 1893.
20. Ibid.
21. RASt, Apr. 11, 1894, Fr.
22. RASt, Jan. 11, n.d.
23. RASt, Jan. 12, 1896, Fr.
24. RASt, Mar. 28, 1896, Fr.
25. RASt, Mar. 23, 1896, Fr.
26. RASt, Apr. 6, 1896, Fr.
27. RASt, May 26, 1894, Fr.
28. RASt, Oct. 28, 1894, Fr.
29. RASt, Nov. 12, 1896, Fr.
30. ÖNB, Mss, papers, AvS, cat. 733.
31. RASt, Nov. 15, 1896, Fr.
32. *Memoirs,* 369, Fr.
33. RASt, Nov. 28, 1896, Fr.

34. Diary, Jan. 4, 1897.
35. Diary, Jan. 8, 1897.
36. Ibid.
37. Diary, Jan. 9, 1897.
38. *Memoirs,* 369 f.
39. To Fried, Jan. 9, 1897.
40. PPA, Jan. 23, 1897, Fr.
41. To Fried, Mar. 27, 1897.
42. Diary, Feb. 13, 1897.
43. *Ethische Kultur,* Vol. 5, 1897, 360.
44. To Carneri, Dec. 12, 1897.
45. Diary, Aug. 6 and 7, 1898.
46. To Fried, Nov. 15, 1898.
47. Diary, July 14, 1900.
48. Diary, Oct. 26, 1900.
49. To Fried, Sept. 1, 1901.
50. To Fried, Dec. 20, 1901.
51. Diary, Jan. 31, 1901.
52. To Fried, Feb. 3, 1901.
53. UN, Pirquet to the Nobel Committee, Mar. 26, 1901.
54. PPA to Passy, Feb. 16, 1901.
55. To Fried, Feb. 10, 1901.
56. *Memoirs,* 370 f.
57. BvS, *Stimmen und Gestalten,* 140.
58. To Fried, Nov. 20, 1901.
59. To Fried, Sept. 24, 1901.
60. To Fried, Jan. 5, 1902.
61. To Fried, Dec. 14, 1901.
62. *Memoirs,* 521 f.
63. StUB, Geneva, Dec. 11, 1901, Fr.
64. To Fried, Dec. 29, 1901.
65. To Fried, Dec. 12, 1901.
66. Diary, Aug. 11, 1903.
67. Diary, Oct. 25, 1903.
68. Diary, Nov. 17, 1903.
69. Diary, Dec. 10, 1903.
70. UN, newspaper clippings, n.d.
71. Brno Státni oblastní archiv, N. Chlumecky, Dec. 11, 1903.
72. Diary, Dec. 31, 1904.
73. Diary, Mar. 26, 1904.
74. Diary, Mar. 28, 1904.
75. To Fried, Aug. 26, 1904.
76. Diary, Aug. 24, 1904.
77. To Fried, Aug. 28, 1904.
78. Diary, Apr. 14, 1903.
79. Diary, Oct. 9, 1904.
80. *Neue Badische Landeszeitung,* Dec. 2, 1904, Lecture report.
81. BvS, *Stimmen und Gestalten,* 166.
82. BvS, *High Life,* Vol. 1 of *Collected Works* (Dresden, n.d.), 215 f.

83. UN, Dec. 11, 1904.

84. Monaco, Dec. 12, 1904, Fr.

85. To Fried, May 3, 1905.

86. Monaco, June 22, 1905, Fr.

87. To Fried, July 27, 1905.

88. To Fried, Nov. 13, 1905.

89. To Fried, Nov. 8, 1905.

90. Diary, Nov. 19, 1905.

91. To Fried, Nov. 27, 1905.

92. Diary, Dec. 1, 1905.

93. To Fried, Dec. 6, 1905.

94. To Fried, Dec. 8, 1905.

95. Diary, Dec. 13 and 15, 1905.

96. Brigitte Hamann, BvS and Alfred Hermann Fried, in *The Nobel Peace Prize and the Laureates: The Meaning and Acceptance of the Nobel Peace Prize in the Prize Winners' Countries,* ed. Karl Holl and Anne Kjelling (Frankfurt and New York, 1994), 83, 93; and Salomon Wank, "The Austrian Peace Movement and the Hapsburg Ruling Elite, 1906–1914," in *Peace Movements and Political Cultures,* ed. Charles Chatfield and Peter van den Dungen (Knoxville: University of Tennessee Press, 1988).

97. Diary, Mar. 1, 1906.

98. Diary, Jan. 14 and 28, 1906.

99. Diary, May 17, 1906.

100. Diary, May 21, 1906.

101. Diary, May 23, 1906.

102. Diary, July 6, 1906.

103. BvS, "Erinnerungen an meine skandinavische Reise," *Österr. Rundschau,* 1907, 451.

104. Diary, Apr. 18, 1906.

105. BvS, *Stimmen und Gestalten,* 87 ff.

106. Diary, Apr. 19, 1906.

107. To Fried, Apr. 26, 1906.

108. Ibid.

109. Diary, May 1, 1906.

110. To Fried, Mar. 21, 1910.

111. *Kampf,* 2:254.

112. To Fried, n.d. (June 1910).

113. To Fried, Dec. 11, 1907.

114. To Fried, Dec. 18, 1907.

11. Hope in the Mighty

1. To Fried, Oct. 22, 1896.

2. To Fried, n.d. (Apr. 1910).

3. *NWT,* Dec. 23, 1908.

4. To Fried, Jan. 13 and 17, 1902.

5. HAJ, June 12, 1902.

6. To Fried, June 13, 1905.

7. Andrew Carnegie, *Das Evangelium des Reichtums* (Graz, 1892), 27.

8. UN, BvS, Carnegie Peace Endowment, Ms.

9. To Fried, Sept. 5, 1901.
10. To Fried, Sept. 16, 1901.
11. To Fried, Oct. 25, 1902.
12. To Fried, Apr. 29 and Aug. 5, 1903.
13. To Fried, Oct. 6, 1904.
14. To Fried, Mar. 24, 1907.
15. Diary, Aug. 23, 1906.
16. To Fried, Aug. 16, 1908.
17. Diary, Aug. 25, 1908.
18. Diary, Aug. 29, 1908.
19. Carnegie Endowment for International Peace, Lowenthal Library, Washington, BvS to Carnegie, Aug. 7, 1909, Engl., courtesy of Mrs. Marion Powell.
20. Ibid., June 26, 1910, Engl.
21. *Kampf,* 2:186.
22. See footnote 8.
23. To Fried, June 9, 1910.
24. To Fried, Apr. 1910.
25. *Kampf,* 2:270.
26. See footnote 19, Jan. 14, 1911, Engl.
27. Monaco, May 25, 1911, Fr.
28. Diary, Apr. 23, 1913.
29. See footnote 19, May 1913, Engl.
30. UN, Nov. 9, 1910, concept.
31. Diary, Feb. 25, 1903.
32. Diary, Feb. 6, 1903.
33. HAJ, Feb. 23, 1903.
34. Monaco, Apr. 30, 1903, Fr.
35. Monaco, June 1, 1903, Fr.
36. Diary, Dec. 27, 1904, Fr.
37. *NFP,* May 15, 1905.
38. Monaco, Apr. 6, 1907, Fr.
39. Diary, Sept. 27, 1903.
40. Diary, Dec. 27, 1903.
41. Diary, Mar. 6 and 17, 1904.
42. Diary, Mar. 8, 1904.
43. Diary, Mar. 15, 1904.
44. Diary, Mar. 25, 1904.
45. To Fried, Sept. 1, 1904.
46. To Fried, Mar. 24, 1905.
47. *NFP,* May 15, 1905, BvS, letter from Monaco.
48. Diary, Mar. 17, 1905.
49. Diary, Mar. 11, 1905.
50. To Fried, Mar. 24, 1904.
51. *DWN,* 1899, 6.
52. To Fried, June 18, 1904.
53. Diary, Apr. 5, 1905.
54. *Die Fackel,* Apr. 30, 1906, 25–28.
55. Diary, Apr. 5, 1905.
56. Diary, Mar. 30, 1905.

57. To Fried, Mar. 27, 1905.
58. To Fried, May 30, 1905.
59. To Fried, June 21 and Aug. 5, 1905.
60. To Fried, Apr. 26, 1906.
61. To Fried, May 24, 1905.
62. Monaco, June 12, 1906, Fr.
63. Monaco, Apr. 13, 1907, Fr.
64. To Fried, Apr. 13, 1907.
65. Diary, Jan. 19, 1909.
66. Diary, Mar. 26, 1910.
67. Diary, Feb. 28 and 27, 1911.
68. Diary, Mar. 14, 1911.
69. Monaco, May 28 and Aug. 19, 1911, Fr.
70. Monaco, June 16, 1911, Fr.
71. To Fried, June 18, 1911.
72. To Fried, Dec. 8, 1911.
73. *DWN,* 1893, 2:3.
74. BvS, *Schach der Qual* (Dresden, 1898), 138 f.
75. StUB, Geneva, July 18, 1896, Fr.
76. UN, lecture ms.
77. UN, concept, Aug. 16, 1894.
78. UN, Mar. 24, 1896.
79. Kaiserin Elisabeth, *Das poetische Tagebuch,* ed. Brigitte Hamann (Vienna: Österreichische Akademie der Wissenschaften, 1984).
80. Ibid., 479.
81. Diary, June 3, 1897.
82. *Memoirs,* 380.
83. Diary, Mar. 6, 1897.
84. *Memoirs,* 382.
85. To Fried, Nov. 27, 1903.
86. Diary, June 10, 1903.
87. Diary, Sept. 1, 1903.
88. Diary, Sept. 18, 1903.
89. Diary, Apr. 18, 1903.
90. To Fried, Nov. 14, 1904.
91. Diary, Oct. 13, 1907.
92. BvS, *Schach der Qual,* 214.
93. Diary, Nov. 5, 1906.
94. Diary, Dec. 24, 1906.
95. Diary, Dec. 26, 1906.
96. Diary, Dec. 25, 1906.
97. Diary, Jan. 9, 1907.
98. *Die Fackel,* Jan. 23, 1907, 14–17.
99. Diary, Mar. 1, 1908.
100. Diary, Dec. 22, 1910.
101. BvS, *Der Menschheit Hochgedanken* (Berlin, n.d.), 36 f.
102. BvS, *Die Haager Friedenskonferenz* (Dresden, 1900), 174.
103. To Carneri, June 17, 1892.
104. To Carneri, Oct. 19, 1889.

105. To Carneri, Nov. 23, 1890.
106. To Carneri, Sept. 25, 1890.
107. To Fried, Mar. 30, 1898.
108. Diary, Mar. 1, 1900.
109. To Fried, Mar. 10, 1898.
110. Diary, Aug. 20, 1907.
111. To Fried, Nov. 9, 1905.
112. Diary, Aug. 27, 1910.
113. To Fried, May 3, 1906.
114. To Fried, May 25, 1905.
115. To Fried, Aug. 13, 1905.
116. To Fried, May 15, 1906.
117. Diary, Mar. 23, 1905.
118. *Palais de la Paix,* The Hague, BvS to Passy, Feb. 16, 1901, Fr.
119. To Fried, Feb. 18, 1901.
120. *Kampf,* 2:43 (Aug. 1907).
121. Diary, Aug. 25, 1911.
122. Diary, Nov. 14, 1911.
123. ÖNB, ThSanBahr, Nov. 19, 1911.

12. Her Confederates

1. BvS, *Vor dem Gewitter* (Vienna, 1894), 107.
2. HAJ, Dec. 23, 1897.
3. *DWN,* Feb. 1, 1892.
4. To Egidy, Aug. 8, 1897. Heinz Herz, *Alleingang wider die Mächtigen* (Leipzig, n.d.), 297.
5. To Fried, Aug. 18 and 19, 1902.
6. To Fried, Aug. 26, 1902.
7. To Fried, Dec. 19, 1901.
8. To Fried, Aug. 2, 1905.
9. Diary, Jan. 17, 1908.
10. Diary, Oct. 2, 1906.
11. To Fried, Mar. 5, 1910.
12. To Fried, June 25, 1910.
13. BvS, *Der Menschheit Hochgedanken* (Berlin, 1911).
14. A. H. Fried in *Frankfurter Zeitung,* June 28, 1914.
15. To Fried, Nov. 24, 1910.
16. BvS, "IPU und Pazifismus," *Friedenswarte,* 1911, 227.
17. To Fried, June 5, 1906.
18. BvS, "Die Interparlamentarier in Wien," *NFP,* Sept. 6, 1903.
19. *MZA,* 302 f.
20. BvS, *Marthas Kinder* (Dresden, 1903), 210.
21. *MZA,* 298 f.
22. Ibid., 301.
23. BvS, *Stimmen und Gestalten* (Leipzig, 1908), 83.
24. BvS, *Vor dem Gewitter,* 141.
25. Ibid., 144.
26. Ibid., 148.

27. BvS, *Briefe an einen Toten,* 3rd. ed. (Dresden, 1904), 158 ff.

28. *NFP,* Aug. 28, 1908.

29. To Carneri, Dec. 14, 1892.

30. To Carneri, July 18, 1893.

31. To Carneri, June 19, 1893.

32. Bvs, *Wohin? Die Etappen des Jahres 1895* (Berlin, 1896), 84.

33. *Ethische Kultur,* Vol. 3, 1895, 388 ff.

34. To Fried, Sept. 13 and Dec. 1, 1895.

35. UN, Feb. 15, 1900.

36. *DWN,* 1896, 339 f.

37. To Fried, Nov. 15, 1895.

38. Werner Simon, BvS, unpublished lecture, 17.

39. A. H. Fried, "Sozialdemokratie und Friedensbewegung," *Die Zeit,* Mar. 8, 1902.

40. *Ethische Kultur,* Vol. 4, 1896, 262 f.

41. Ibid.

42. To Fried, Mar. 24, 1898.

43. To Fried, Aug. 16, 1898.

44. To Fried, Apr. 24, 1898.

45. To Fried, Sept. 7, 1895.

46. To Fried, Aug. 29, 1901.

47. To Fried, Nov. 29, 1898.

48. To Fried, Oct. 28, 1898.

49. BvS, *Krieg und Frieden,* lecture in Munich, 1909, 39 f.

50. To Fried, Nov. 8, 1909.

51. To Fried, Aug. 4, 1904.

52. To Fried, June 9, 1911 and June 18, 1904.

53. To Fried, Oct. 12, 1897.

54. BvS, *Randglossen zur Zeitgeschichte. Das Jahr 1906* (Leipzig, 1907), 29.

55. Diary, Apr. 29, 1911.

56. Diary, Dec. 23 and 26, 1908.

57. To Fried, Oct. 19, 1909.

58. Leo Tolstoy, *Patriotismus und Christentum* (Berlin, 1894), 78 f.

59. *NFP,* May 29, 1896.

60. To Fried, Sept. 5, 1901.

61. Ibid.

62. *DWN,* 1897, 6.

63. BvS, "Gleiches Ziel, andere Wege," *NWT,* Aug. 9, 1904.

64. To Carneri, Aug. 6 and Sept. 20, 1890.

65. To Fried, Apr. 28, 1896.

66. *DWN,* 1898, 395 f.

67. *Ethische Kultur,* Vol. 7, 1899, 158.

68. *NWT,* June 29, 1904.

69. To Fried, July 4, 1904.

70. *NWT,* June 29, 1904.

71. To Fried, Sept. 4, 1909.

72. To Fried, Jan. 6, 1910.

73. *Kampf,* 2:481.

74. *Memoirs,* 265.

75. StBM, Apr. 12, 1913.
76. To Fried, Dec. 9, 1901.
77. Diary, Aug. 25, 1908, addendum.
78. *Kampf,* 2:418 f.
79. *Kampf,* 2:518, Oct. 1913.

13. The Question of Women

1. To Carneri, Nov. 11, 1889.
2. *MZA,* 137.
3. *Ethische Kultur,* Vol. 2, 1894, 93.
4. BvS, "Eine erwachte Frau," *Pester Lloyd,* June 29, 1907.
5. BvS, "Offener Brief an Meister Adolph Wilbrandt," *NFP,* Aug. 23, 1909.
6. BvS, *Daniela Dormes,* Vol. 7 of *Collected Works* (Dresden, n.d.), 47 f.
7. Ibid., 191, 193, and 247.
8. *MZA,* 136.
9. BvS, *Eva Siebeck,* Vol. 2 of *Collected Works* (Dresden, n.d.), 244.
10. *MZA,* 143.
11. Ibid., 115.
12. Ibid., 116.
13. BvS, *Die Waffen nieder,* 65.
14. *MZA,* 123.
15. BvS, "Offener Brief," 47 f.
16. *Friedenswarte,* 1913, 18.
17. BvS, *High Life,* 152 f.
18. To Carneri, June 12–14, 1891.
19. BvS, *High Life,* 73 f.
20. Ibid., 183.
21. *Memoirs,* 280 f.
22. Diary, Feb. 8, 1904.
23. BvS, *Schriftsteller-Roman* (Dresden, 1888), 280.
24. Ibid.
25. BvS, *Der Menschheit Hochgedanken* (Berlin, 1911), 130 f.
26. *MZA,* 256.
27. UN, to Irma Troll-B., Oct. 14, 1886.
28. *MZA,* 152 f.
29. Ibid., 163 f.
30. Ibid., 138, 139.
31. Ibid., 144.
32. Ibid., 157.
33. Ibid., 145.
34. Ibid., 164.
35. Ibid.
36. *MZA,* Preface to the 3rd ed.
37. Gisela Brinker-Gabler, *Frauen gegen den Krieg* (Hamburg, 1980), 66.
38. *DWN,* 1895, 254 ff.
39. To Fried, Jan. 27, 1903.
40. BvS, *Haager Friedenskonferenz* (Dresden, 1900), 106 f.
41. DWN, 1894, 254 ff.

42. BvS, *Wohin? Die Etappen des Jahres 1895* (Berlin, 1896), 75.
43. To Fried, Jan. 28, 1893.
44. BvS, *Haager Friedenskonferenz,* 107 f.
45. *Freies Blatt,* June 1895.
46. BvS, *Haager Friedenskonferenz,* 109.
47. *DWN,* Apr. 1896, 179.
48. UN, Fickert to BvS, Oct. 20, 1891.
49. StBW, BvS to Fickert, Apr. 13, 1892.
50. StBW, BvS to Hainisch, Mar. 14, 1907.
51. ÖNB, Mss 124/4, Nov. 5, 1901.
52. UN, Fickert to BvS, Dec. 24, 1901.
53. To Fried, Apr. 8 and June 18, 1904.
54. Diary, Nov. 28, 1912.
55. To Fried, n.d. (June 1902).
56. To Fried, July 9, 1902.
57. Diary, Nov. 26, 1907.
58. *Kampf,* 2:318 f.
59. *Kampf,* 2:319.
60. Diary, June 6, 1904.
61. *Berliner Morgenpost,* June 11, 1904.
62. UN, *Tägl Rundschau Berlin,* June 15, 1904.
63. UN, *Deutsche Volkszeitung Reichenberg,* June 15, 1904.
64. UN, *Leipziger Tagblatt,* June 13, 1904.
65. BvS, "Die Friedensfrage und die Frauen," *Neues Wiener Journal,* June 8, 1913.
66. Gisela Brinker-Gabler, *Frauen gegen den Krieg* 51, 54.

14. Before the Great War

1. Edith Countess Salburg, *Erinnerungen einer Respektlosen.* vol. 3 (Leipzig, 1928), 81 f.
2. Diary, Dec. 30, 1908.
3. To Fried, June 28, 1909 and Apr. 15, 1911.
4. BvS, "Ein Sammelruf," *NWT,* Dec. 7, 1908.
5. *Kampf,* 1:428.
6. *Kampf,* 2:197 f.
7. Diary, Nov. 27, 1903.
8. To Fried, Dec. 7, 1906.
9. To Fried, Aug. 5, 1908.
10. To Fried, Sept. 24, 1908.
11. *NFP,* i.28.1908, 5.
12. To Fried, Oct. 30, 1908.
13. To Fried, Nov. 24, 1908.
14. Diary, Sept. 27, 1908.
15. To Fried, May 20, 1908.
16. To Fried, June 9, 1908.
17. To Fried, n.d. (1908).
18. To Fried, Oct. 22, 1908.
19. To Fried, Aug. 27, 1908.
20. *Kampf,* 2:399.

21. Ibid., 133.
22. Diary, Nov. 30, 1908.
23. Diary, Dec. 22, 1908.
24. BvS, *Rüstung und Überrüstung* (Vienna, 1909), 69 f.
25. *NWT,* Dec. 7, 1908.
26. Diary, Dec. 10, 1908.
27. To Fried, n.d. (Mar. 1909).
28. Monaco, Apr. 7, 1909, Fr.
29. To Fried, Mar. 1, 1909.
30. To Fried, Mar. 20, 1909.
31. Diary, Apr. 19, 1909.
32. BvS, *Rüstung und Überrüstung,* 17.
33. Ibid., 38.
34. To Fried, May 31, 1909.
35. BvS to Carnegie, June 30, 1909, Engl. Carnegie Endowment, Washington, D.C.
36. BvS, *Wohin? Die Etappen des Jahres 1895* (Berlin, 1896), 104.
37. To Fried, Mar. 23, 1909.
38. UN, Bahr to BvS, n.d.
39. UN, Bahr to BvS, Feb. 7, 1909.
40. ÖNB, ThS to Bahr, Feb. 8, 1909.
41. To Fried, Jan. 15, 1911.
42. To Fried, Nov. 9, 1911.
43. To Fried, Apr. 3, 1911.
44. To Fried, Jan. 24, 1911.
45. *NWT,* Sept. 13, 1904.
46. To Fried, Aug. 29, 1911.
47. BvS, "Friedensheer," *Deutsche Revue,* Vol. 1, 1906, 43.
48. ÖNB, ThS, Oct. 5, 1910.
49. BvS, "Der Tripoliskrieg und die Friedensbewegung," *Friedenswarte,* 1911, 316.
50. To Fried, Aug. 27, 1912.
51. To Fried, Oct. 24, 1911.
52. To Fried, Oct. 28, 1911.
53. To Fried, Nov. 17, 1911.
54. To Fried, Nov. 8, 1911.
55. To Fried, Nov. 30, 1911.
56. To Fried, Apr. 19, 1912.
57. Diary, Dec. 1 and 2, 1911.
58. Diary, Mar. 22, 1912.
59. To Fried, Feb. 13, 1912.
60. To Fried, Sept. 3, 1908.
61. BvS, *Die Barbarisierung der Luft* (Berlin, 1912), 1.
62. Ibid., 22 f.
63. Ibid., 7.
64. Ibid., 10.
65. Ibid., 12 f.
66. Ibid., 18.
67. Diary, May 25, 1911.
68. Diary, May 29, 1911.

69. To Fried, May 22, 1909.
70. To Fried, July 12, 1909.
71. To Fried, July 16, 1909.
72. To Fried, Aug. 31, 1911.
73. To Fried, Mar. 5, 1911.
74. To Fried, Sept. 10, 1912.
75. Diary, Dec. 6, 1911.
76. UN, Ms. *Erinnerungen,* 1909, 9.
77. A. H. Fried, *Persönlichkeiten: Bertha von Suttner* (Berlin, n.d.), 20 f.
78. *Friedenswarte,* 1911, 257.
79. To Fried, Apr. 12, 1912.
80. UN, May 19, 1912.
81. To Fried, May 20, 1912.
82. Diary, June 27, 1912.
83. UN, Ms.
84. Fried, *Personlichkeiten: Bertha von Suttner,* 14.
85. To Fried, July 13, 1912.
86. To Fried, July 16, 1912.
87. To Fried, Aug. 20, 1912.
88. To Fried, Aug. 9, 1912.
89. To Fried, Oct. 2, 1912.
90. Diary, Nov. 3, 1912.
91. Diary, May 12, 1912.
92. Diary, Oct. 19, 1912.
93. Diary, July 1, 1912.
94. Diary, July 11, 1912.
95. Diary, Aug. 16, 1912.
96. To Fried, Oct. 11, 1912.
97. *Friedenswarte,* 1913, 17 f.
98. Diary, Dec. 12, 1912.
99. To Fried, Nov. 23, 1912.
100. Diary, Nov. 26, 1912.
101. To Fried, Nov. 29, 1912.
102. To Fried, July 24, 1912.
103. To Fried, Aug. 20, 1912.
104. To Fried, Aug. 27, 1912.
105. Diary, Nov. 11, 1912.
106. Diary, Dec. 14, 1912.
107. *NFP,* Dec. 29, 1912.
108. Diary, Dec. 25, 1912.
109. *Friedenswarte,* 1913, 19.
110. To Fried, Jan. 22, 1913.
111. To Fried, Jan. 26, 1913.
112. To Fried, Jan. 28 and 29, 1913.
113. To Fried, Jan. 29, 1913.
114. To Fried, Mar. 28, 1913.
115. Diary, July 9, 1913.
116. To Fried, July 10, 1913.
117. *Friedenswarte,* 1913, 190 f.

118. StBW, Mar. 1, 1913.
119. These letters are at the UN.
120. Diary, Apr. 14, 1913.
121. Stefan Zweig, *Die Welt von gestern* (Hamburg, 1965), 194 f.
122. To Fried, Jan. 5, 1913.
123. *NFP,* June 9, 1913.
124. *Friedenswarte,* 1913, 269 f.
125. Stadtarchiv Wien, BvS estate files, will dated June 4, 1913.
126. To Fried, July 26, 1913.
127. To Fried, Aug. 4, 1913.
128. Diary, Jan. 20, 1914.
129. To Fried, Aug. 4, 1913.
130. *Kampf,* 2:564.
131. To Fried, Sept. 9, 1913.
132. To Fried, Sept. 21, 1913.
133. *NWT,* June 7, 1913.
134. Diary, July 4, 1913.
135. Diary, Oct. 16, 1913.
136. Alfred H. Fried, "Das Lebenswerk Bertha von Suttners," *NWT,* June 23, 1914.
137. To Fried, Nov. 8, 1913.
138. To Fried, Feb. 22, 1914.
139. Diary, Jan. 15 and 24, 1914.
140. *Kampf,* 2:160.
141. To Fried, Mar. 8, 1914.
142. Diary, Feb. 1, 1914.
143. Diary, Mar. 1, 1914.
144. Diary, Mar. 5, 1914.
145. Diary, Apr. 4, 1914.
146. Diary, Feb. 23, 1914.
147. To Fried, Jan. 21, 1913.
148. Copy in the Österr. Filmarchiv, Vienna.
149. Diary, Apr. 28, 1914.
150. Ibid.
151. StBW, to Hainisch, May 21, 1914.
152. Diary, May 27, 1914.
153. Diary, May 31, 1914.
154. Diary, June 1, 1914.
155. *NFP,* June 23, 1914.
156. *NFP,* June 22, 1914.

Index

341